PLATE I

JEWISH SYNAGOGUE AND COLLEGE
From an Italian Prayerbook written in Ferrara (?) in the latter half of the fifteenth century
[Me. E. Bicart-Sée's collection]

JEWISH
TRAVELLERS
in the
MIDDLE AGES

19 Firsthand Accounts

Edited and with an Introduction by
ELKAN NATHAN ADLER

DOVER PUBLICATIONS, INC.
New York

This Dover edition, first published in 1987, is an
unabridged republication of the work originally published in the series "The Broadway Travellers" by
George Routledge & Sons, Ltd., London, in 1930 under
the title *Jewish Travellers*. The illustrations appear in
different locations in the present edition.

Manufactured in the United States of America
Dover Publications, Inc., 31 East 2nd Street, Mineola,
N.Y. 11501

Library of Congress Cataloging-in-Publication Data

Otsar masaᶜot. English. Selections.
Jewish travellers in the Middle Ages.

Translation of selections from: Otsar masaᶜot.
Reprint. Originally pub.: Jewish travellers. London :
G. Routledge, 1930. (Broadway travellers)
Includes index.
1. Voyages and travels—Collected works. 2.
Travel, Medieval—Collected works. 3. Travelers,
Jewish—Collected works. 4. Palestine—Description
and travel—Collected works. I. Adler, Elkan Nathan,
1861–1946. II. Title.
G277.088213 1987   910'.89924   87-13434
ISBN 0-486-25397-X (pbk.)

PREFACE

IN 1926 Mr. J. D. Eisenstein, of New York, published a collection of twenty-four Hebrew texts of Jewish travellers between 1165 and 1839. His *Ozar Massaoth* ("Treasure of Travel") is an admirable quarto volume of 352 pages with maps, notes, and index. He was welcomed by the *Times* Reviewer as a Jewish Hakluyt, and the hope was expressed that he should issue a companion volume in English.[1] The Publishers of the Broadway Travellers asked permission to use his book, and this he fully accorded in a most generous and appreciative spirit. The result is the present volume, in which his texts and notes have been largely adopted, but which differs in scope, for it contains both less and more.

It begins with the ninth and ends in the middle of the eighteenth century. Some of the Palestine itineraries have been omitted ; the texts are frequently abridged, and the translations are not always original. The main object of the work has been to give a conspectus of Jewish travel during the Middle Ages, and no attempt has been made to provide a critical edition of the various texts.

I wish to express my gratitude to Mr. I. Wartski, the learned lecturer in Modern Hebrew at the School of Oriental Studies, who has been so good as to go through the whole of these translations with me.

ELKAN N. ADLER.

---

[1] *The Times Literary Supplement*, 6th October, 1927.

CONTENTS

LIST OF ILLUSTRATIONS

LIST OF ILLUSTRATIONS

PLATE II

GOLIATH AS A CRUSADER BARKED AT BY DAVID'S DOG

From a Manuscript Pentateuch and Prayer Book written in France and illustrated by Benjamin ha
Cohen ca. 1278.

(British Museum Add. 11639)

INTRODUCTION

THE wandering Jew is a very real character in the great drama of history. From Ur of the Chaldees to Palestine and Egypt and then back again to the Holy Land and then to Assyria [1] and Babylon and Egypt and the farthermost cities of the far-flung Roman Empire, he has travelled as nomad and settler, as fugitive and conqueror, as exile and colonist, as merchant and scholar, as mendicant and pilgrim, as collector and as ambassador. His interest in foreign countries both near and far was fostered by Scripture and the famous chapters of Isaiah and Jeremiah and others [2] are a very mine of ancient geography. He was of necessity bilingual and therefore master of many languages and able to make himself understood, wherever other Jews were to be found. He was the ideal commercial traveller and interpreter.

The Diaspora extended far beyond Palestine, even before the destruction of the First Temple. After the Babylonian captivity, there were always more Jews outside Palestine than within. In the second century B.C. the Jewish Sibyl says of the Diaspora : " Every land is full of thee and every sea." Philo, Seneca, and the author of the Acts of the Apostles testify to its dissemination over the whole of the world.

After the rise of Islam in the beginning of the seventh century, the civilized world was partitioned between Moslems and Christians, the three caliphates of Kairouan, Damascus, and Cordova and the two

[1] 2 Kings xvii, 6, in Habor by the River of Gozan and in the cities of the Medes.

[2] E.g. Isaiah xiii–xxiii; Jeremiah xliv–li; Numbers xxiv; Psalm lxxxiii.

Empires—the Eastern at Byzantium, and the Frankish. The story of Jewish travel, as shown by the literary material still extant, which the present volume seeks in part to reproduce, begins appropriately enough with Isaac the interpreter to the two ambassadors sent by Charlemagne to Harun-ar-Rashid at the very beginning of the ninth century. As Sir Mathew Nathan aptly puts it : " The Jews of this time did not only travel in merchandise, Jacob ibn Tarik or Aben Scheara, as he is called in Hebrew, is said about the year 820, to have carried astronomical books from Ceylon to Baghdad, and Joseph of Spain to have introduced to the Western World, from India, the so-called Arabic numerals. While Baghdad was the centre of the West Asiatic learning, Moslem Spain became the home of civilization in Europe." [1]

Next we have Ibn Khordâdhbeh's account of Jewish merchants from Persia, travelling with goods from China to Aix la Chapelle. About the middle of the ninth century the famous Eldad the Danite, coming from the African coast of the Gulf of Aden, appeared in Cairo, Kairouan, and Spain, and declared that he was of the tribe of Dan, which with other neighbouring tribes of Naphtali, Gad, and Asher, were each autonomous. His story roused the utmost enthusiasm among his co-religionists, who lived round the Mediterranean Sea. He gave them, as they believed, an account of all the lost Ten Tribes. His letter and the inquiry about the customs he described and the response of the Gaon Zemach of Sura in Mesopotamia, have been reproduced in very many manuscripts and printed in Italy before 1480 and twice in Constantinople before 1520 and frequently afterwards. It has been the custom among many hypercritical scholars to regard him as an impostor and his story

[1] See his Presidential Address on Jewish Travellers, delivered in 1912, to the Union of Jewish Literary Societies.

as an invention. But such scepticism is unjuſtifiable in the face of the corroboration of contemporaries and the internal evidence in his favour. Some of the details in his own account may be rejeſted as travellers' tales, and there are undoubtedly additions and corruptions in the various texts. The chapters here given are translations of Epſtein's critical edition. To this very day, the Persian Jews recite in Synagogue Eldad's story in the vernacular.

Eldad's ſtory receives ſtrong support, in the next century, from Rabbi Chisdai ibn Shaprut (915–70), the vizier of the Caliph of Cordova. Chisdai is notable, because he introduces a new faſtor into the charaſter of the Jewish traveller, the missionary sent by Jews to inquire about other Jews. Chisdai had heard of the Khozars of the Crimea, a converted Tartar people governed by a Jewish King. We give here translations of Chisdai's letter and the King's reply. The fashion of dismissing the tale about the Khozars as also incredible and therefore untrue is no longer in vogue. Inasmuch as the famous poet philosopher Judah Halevi (1085–1140) founded his *Cuzari* on the Khozars, the tale was thought to be merely the poetical offspring of his imagination. But hiſtory has now accepted the account as undoubtedly true and attributes some of the charaſteriſtics of the Russian Jew as due to their descent from Tartars, converted to Judaism, rather than from Jews even of the loſt Ten Tribes. The Caliphs of Cordova were great patrons of learning and, says Major Martin Hume : " One bookish Caliph after the other sent Jewish bibliophiles throughout the Eaſt searching for books for the splendid libraries that grew up in Cordova, Toledo, and elsewhere." Judah Halevi himself spent his life in Granada in happy surroundings, but, like so many of his co-religioniſts, felt an irresiſtible impulse to end his days in Paleſtine.

He left home and, tradition has it, met his death near
Jerusalem at the hands of a Crusader. A translation
of his beautiful poem on his pilgrimage is given here
as a picture of the Jewish pilgrim. The famous
Saadya Gaon (882–942) is known to have visited the
Holy Land. Schechter published a fragment of two
leaves at the Cambridge University Library describing
part of what was perhaps his itinerary there from
Bagdad by way of Arbela, Mosul, Nisibis and Aleppo.
(See J.Q.R. xiv, 503.)

Another pilgrim was Rabbi Jacob ben Nathaniel
ha Cohen, who journeyed in Egypt and Palestine
during the Crusades and may have been a German by
origin. His story is only extant in the unique
manuscript at Cambridge. His avowed object was to
visit the tombs of his fathers and to return again and
die in the Holy Land. The narrative is jejune and
mostly a record of tombs and places. But, as we have
omitted several of such accounts, which figure in
Eisenstein's volume, Jacob's is given here.

A much more interesting traveller was Abraham Ibn
Ezra (1088–1165), poet, Bible commentator, and
grammarian, a native of Toledo, who visited Egypt,
Palestine, and Mesopotamia, Rhodes, Italy, France,
and England. He was in London in 1157, where he
wrote his *Iggereth ha Sabbath* and his *Yesod Mora*.
Unfortunately, although we come across interesting
allusions in his works, such as to fogs and the length
of the crossing from France to England, we have no
autobiography or journal of his wanderings. This
is a pity, as there is some ground for holding that
his travels extended to India (see Steinschneider,
"Ist Ibn Esra in Indien gewesen?" Z.D.M.G.
xx, 427).

Benjamin of Tudela, who wandered over the greater
part of the civilized world of his day, in the second part
of the twelfth century, is described by Purchas, who

published an English translation of his Itinerary in
1625, as " reckoned one of the greatest travellers that
ever lived ". There are many manuscripts and countless editions and translations of his work. The best
manuscripts are in the British Museum and the
Casanatense at Rome. The Hebrew was first published
at Constantinople, Ferrara, and Freiburg early in
the sixteenth century, and the best edition, with text,
English translation, notes, and the map here reproduced is that of Marcus N. Adler in 1907. Benjamin
spent a considerable time in Rome, Constantinople,
Alexandria, Jerusalem, and Baghdad between 1166 and
1171. He went through Catalonia, Southern France,
Italy, Constantinople, the Greek Archipelago, Rhodes,
Cyprus, Antioch, Palestine, Damascus, Baghdad,
through Persia to Basra and the Island of Kish in
the Persian Gulf, and thence home by way of Aden and
Assouan. What he says of India and China is probably
only hearsay, but he is the first European writer
who so much as mentions China. His travels were too
extensive to be those of a mere merchant and, inasmuch
as the hitherto prosperous Jewish communities, along
the Rhine and the route to Palestine, had been dispersed
by the fanaticism aroused by the Crusaders, and as,
even in the Caliphate of Cordova, his brethren were
being bitterly persecuted, it is probable that Benjamin's
object was to discover where his expatriated co-
religionists might find asylum. Everywhere he notes
the size and importance of the Jewish community.
A considerable part of the itinerary is here given, with
Mr. H. M. Adler's permission, from his father's
edition.

Another such traveller was the German, Petachia
of Ratisbon, who less than twenty years after Benjamin
also visited Palestine and Mesopotamia, but by quite
a different route.

Petachia journeyed from Prague through Poland,

Kief, Tartary, and Persia to Damascus and Jerusalem. His story is told in the third person, and is less accurate and less attractive. He was evidently a man of substance, perhaps a merchant. His liberal back-sheesh enabled him to enter tombs which were closed even to non-Jews who could not afford so much. The object of the journey may have been the same as Benjamin's, but the narrator gives us extraordinary rather than useful details of the places visited. Manuscript sources are scanty and the text, the basis of Benisch's translation here reproduced, is late and not too accurate. Petachia is important for what he tells us of Russia, more than seven hundred years ago, and for the earliest account of Karaïte Jews in that country.

The thirteenth century is mainly notable in Jewish annals for Maimonides, who died in 1206. With his father, he fled from Cordova, when the Moslems had begun to persecute the Jews, and he eventually settled in Cairo as physician to the Caliph. An interesting account of his day's work is extant, and his " Letter to Yemen " (*Iggereth Teman*) marks the approach to conformity with the rest of Jewry of the Arabian Jews, of whose autonomy Jewish travellers have so much to tell. A contemporary letter from the Cairo *Geniza*—that now famous hoard of lost Hebrew MSS—is here translated, as giving an indication of the routes of the Jewish merchant.

Judah-al-Ḥarizi was the greatest Jewish traveller of this century. His masterpiece, the *Tachkemoni*, is full of clever but bitter gibes at the meanness of the notables of the various cities he traversed. As a satirical poet he rivalled in Hebrew the Arabic *Makamat* (literary gatherings) of his model Hariri. He was himself something like Hariri's hero, " a witty, clever, amiable rogue, well read in sacred and profane lore, who turns up—in all possible places." We give here a translation of three Arabic poems of his, which also come to us from the Cairo *Geniza*.

INTRODUCTION

In 1210 Rabbi Samuel ben Samson of Sens travelled from France to Palestine, as secretary perhaps to his companion, the eminent Rabbi Jonathan ha Cohen, to whose patronage we owe the Hebrew translation of two of the most important Arabic works of Maimonides. Jonathan is always described as *Resh Gola* (Head of the Captivity) and must have been the most influential and wealthy French Jew of his time. Samuel's Itinerary, as will be seen, is hardly more than a pilgrim's guide to the graves of Jewish saints and Rabbis. It is important, however, for the reference to a letter handed to him by the King of Jerusalem, which invited Jews to visit Palestine, and seems to have resulted in the famous pilgrimage of three hundred French and English Rabbis in 1211. He may have been the advance courier of their party. The pilgrimage has been dated as late as 1257, but the earlier date is probably correct. In 1210 there had been what has been called a sort of Zionist conference in England and several of the English members of the party have now been identified.[1] The famous Bodleian Bowl found in a Norfolk marsh, with a long Hebrew inscription, was probably the gift of R. Jose b. Yechiel, who had intended to emigrate to Palestine, but, on his appointment in 1209 as Archpresbyter of the English Jews, had to abandon his intention. The purpose of the bowl was probably for the collection of subscriptions for the pilgrims. The pilgrimage may have been inspired by the messianic hopes of the Jews of the time, who, by a calculation based on Daniel, had been led to expect the advent of the Messiah in 1211 or 1216. Of the three hundred pilgrims, many settled in Palestine, and we meet with their descendants for generations later. Maimonides refers to the pilgrimage

---

[1] See *REJ*. 82³³⁵ and 85⁷⁰.

and Harizi and others call them "the men of Frangiſtan".

About a quarter of a century later, we come across the travels of one Rabbi Jacob, described as the "messenger" of R. Jechiel, Chief Rabbi of Paris, sent to Paleſtine and Iraq to colleɛt funds for his Paris Rabbinic college, which then had three hundred ſtudents. As will be seen, his account is also a rather dry liſt of places, diſtances, and graves. The persecution of French and English Jews had waxed with the Crusades and culminated in their expulsion, 16,000 from England in 1290 and 100,000 from France in 1306. But for the syſtematic extortions to which they were being subjeɛted, pride would have prevented them from begging from their Eaſtern brethren. These were themselves poor enough and, indeed, when Nachmanides visited Jerusalem in 1268 he, like Petachia before him, found there only a single Jewish resident.

Prominent among the French exiles was Eſtori Farchi (1282–1357), a Provençal, who, after spending some time at Barcelona, went to Egypt and Paleſtine. He ultimately settled at Bethsean (Scythopolis), near Jerusalem, and compiled there the firſt scientific description of the Holy Land. This he entitled "Kaftor u Ferach" (Knop and Flower) alluding both to the enlightenment derived from the golden candleſtick, symbolizing Paleſtine, and to his own flowery name. The book was published at Venice in 1545, at Berlin in 1852, and at Jerusalem in 1897. This book was used by Isaac b. Joseph ibn Chelo, a Spanish Kabbaliſt of Aragon, who in 1333 went to Jerusalem with his family and settled there. At that time, the Holy Land was deemed to be the seat of the myſterious doɛtrines of the Kabbalah, and many Spanish Kabbaliſts were there already. He describes Jerusalem in a letter to his father and friends and

gives seven routes to the various notable sites con-
verging at that centre. The whole work is called
Shebile Jerusalem (i.e. Jerusalem Roads), and is extant
in a manuscript miscellany at the Bibliothèque
Nationale in Paris, published by Carmoly at Brussels
in 1847 and by Luncz at Jerusalem in 1903. The
original has disappeared, and was evidently abstracted
from the miscellany. Luncz's and Eisenstein's
Hebrew text is a retranslation from Carmoly. The
translation into English here given is from the latter's
French translation. It is characteristic of the
author and his school that his narrative inclines
to the extraordinary and the prodigious. He cites
ancient legends, but quotes extensively without acknow-
ledgment from Benjamin of Tudela and Farchi.

The fourteenth century, with its discovery of the
mariner's compass and the preparation of charts or
" portulani " as they were called, revolutionized,
because it simplified, navigation. To this the Jews,
and notably the " Map Jew ", Jafuda Crescas,
materially contributed. His Catalan portulano (1375)
embodied not only the maritime knowledge of his
time, but also the land routes of Benjamin and Marco
Polo to the Far East. The century which followed saw
the great discoveries of Vasco da Gama and Columbus,
in which Jews also took part, for no navigator sailing
to unexplored regions, thought himself safe without his
Jewish interpreter. The unknown world was held to
be assuredly inhabited by descendants of the Ten
Tribes, and who so able to converse with them as their
brethren ? Abraham Zacuto's nautical almanac was
used by Columbus and, on his second voyage, saved
his life by enabling him to predict an eclipse and
thereby intimidate the natives of Hispaniola.
Eisenstein gives five representative Hebrew travels
of the fifteenth century, of which the 1411 letter, of
R. Isaac ibn Alfara of Malaga to R. Simeon Duran,

describes the chief Jewish tombs in Palestine (with
two similar lists) and the journey, in 1495, of a
Venetian to Corfu, Rhodes, Beirut, Damascus, Safed,
and Jerusalem are not reproduced here. We give,
however, translations of the 1438 letter of R. Elijah
of Ferrara, and of the travels of R. Meshullam of
Volterra in 1481 and of the famous R. Obadiah of
Bertinoro in 1487. The first refers to the plague in
Egypt and Palestine, describes life in Jerusalem and
repeats what he was told about the Ten Tribes in
" India " [1] and Ethiopia. Obadiah and Meshullam
came across each other at Palermo and travelled
together in the Archipelago. In 1492, the Jews were
expelled from Spain and migrated, some to Bayonne,
Antwerp, and Amsterdam, but most to Turkey and
the North African coast. The exiles were the most
cultured men of their time, and it is therefore not
surprising that they established printing presses at
Fez, Salonica, and Constantinople in the first quarter
of the fifteenth century. Their publications varied
from the sacred to the profane, from Talmud to Amadis
of Gaul, from Bible to nautical tables and chanties.
They included travels such as Eldad's and Benjamin's
and contemporary accounts of visitors to Turkey
and Egypt and the homes of the independent Jews
along the Persian and Arabian Gulfs. A physician,
Moses b. Joseph Hamon, who was on the staff of
Solyman the Magnificent, went with the forces to
Syria and " recorded useful information with regard
to the Kurds, the Druses, and others ". Eisenstein
reprints, from a Leghorn edition of 1785, the story
of an anonymous Venetian Rabbi's journey in 1522–3
through Corfu, Tripoli, Beirut, and the whole of
Palestine and back again by ship direct from Beirut
to Venice.

[1] In the Middle Ages Abyssinia and Arabia are spoken of as
" Middle India ".

INTRODUCTION

Most important, however, of modern Jewish travellers was his contemporary, David Reubeni, who declared himself to be the brother and emissary of the King of Khaibar in " Middle India " and commander of his army. Between 1522 and 1525 he journeyed from Arabia by way of Abyssinia, the Soudan, Alexandria, and Pesaro to Rome, Lisbon, and Spain. He travelled in some state and was received on terms almost of equality by the Pope, King John of Portugal, and Charles V. The object of his mission was to offer the Christians help against the Turks, especially in India, and in return to recover Palestine for the Jews. His brother was at the time an independent Jewish King, and on the Indian mainland there was also the independent Jewish Kingdom of Cranganore, a considerable part of what is now the State of Cochin. No Europeans were better acquainted with Asiatic conditions than the monarchs with whom he negotiated, and, but for the victory of the Turks over the Jews of Cranganore, which unluckily coincided with David's visit, he might have been successful. Neubauer and others treat him with scorn as an arrant impostor—and a German impostor at that. They base their scepticism on the diction of his Diary, the bulk of which is here translated. Occasionally the writer, who may have been David's secretary, uses the expression " after eight days ", the German idiom for a week, and so he must have been a German ! But the Diary speaks for itself, and gives internal evidence of its accuracy. The Hebrew, like Eldad's, is not Rabbinic but Biblical. There is much interesting information, for instance, as to the Jews in the Arabian Gulf and the Marranos in Portugal. Moreover, his story is corroborated by contemporary diplomatists. Thus, in the Calendar of Venetian State Papers,[1] we read that Marco Foscari, in a letter

[1] Calendar of State Papers (Venetian), 1520–6, p. 810.

addressed on the 14th March, 1524, from Rome to the "Signory", writes that "An Ambassador has come to the Pope from the Jews in India offering him 300,000 combatants against the Turk and asking for artillery". This is in strict accord with David's own account. Khaibar, just north of Medina, was undoubtedly a great Jewish centre and Burton, in his "Pilgrimage to Al-Medina and Meccah", has a curious note upon it, in which he, with some hesitancy, accepts the Moslem view that there are no Jews left there now. David's object was to secure a national home for his co-religionists in Palestine. He refers to the independent Jews of Cranganore and the Indian mainland as neighbours and friends, but, unfortunately, during this stay in Europe, the Jews were driven out of Cranganore by Turks [1] and the Turks in turn by the Portuguese. Jewish help was no longer necessary, and David was made to leave Portugal, after being treated with distinction at Court for nearly a twelvemonth. His boat was shipwrecked and he himself imprisoned by the Inquisition but released by Charles the Fifth. His disciple, Diego Pires, who after his conversion to Judaism, was known as Solomon Molcho, was a famous character in Jewish history ; he was martyred at Mantua in 1532. David was ultimately thrown into prison, where he died in 1537.

In 1537 a German settler in Hebron compiled a list of "Tombs of the Patriarchs," edited by the Italian R. Uri b. Simeon, and printed at Safed in 1564, at Heidelberg with Hottinger's Latin translation in 1569 and 1662, and in French and Hebrew by Carmoly and Luncz. About a generation later,

[1] Rae's *Syrian Church in India* (Blackwood, 1892), p. 147, quoted by the writer in a paper on "Indian Jews and European Potentates in the Sixteenth Century" in a paper submitted to the 13th International Congress of Orientalists at Hamburg in 1902 (see *Transactions*, viii, 5).

INTRODUCTION

Gershon of Scarmela, on his return from a pilgrimage to Palestine, wrote another list called "Tombs of the Righteous", printed at Mantua in 1561 and translated by Carmoly in his *Itinéraire*. Neither list is reproduced here or by Eisenstein, who does, however, give a copy of a long letter written in 1563 to his family in Pesaro from Famagusta, by a merchant Elijah of Pesaro. Elijah had intended to settle in Palestine, but was delayed in Cyprus by the plague which had broken out in the East. His description of the island is vivid, and its interest enhanced by the fact that six or seven years later the Turks, under Don Joseph Nasi, the Jewish Duke of Naxos, captured it from the Venetians and continued to hold it until its peaceable occupation by Great Britain fifty years ago.

Great Jewish travellers of the sixteenth century were Joseph del Medigo (1591–1657) and Pedro Texeira. The former was a native of Crete, who had studied medicine in Padua and travelled in Egypt, Constantinople, Poland, Russia, and Lithuania. His *Maase Tobia*, printed at Amsterdam in 1628, with a fine portrait, contains many interesting facts. Texeira was a Marrano of Lisbon, who went to India and in 1587 took part in the Portuguese expedition from Goa to Mombasa, Muscat, and Ormuz, and went afterwards to Persia and Malacca, returning home by way of Borneo, the Philippines, Mexico, Cuba, Florida, Bermuda, and Spain. Probably the first Jew to go round the world, he published in 1604, his "Narrative of my Journey (overland) from India to Italy". He died in Amsterdam, a conforming Jew, about 1650.

Although the *Ozar Massaoth* contains some ten other texts of subsequent travellers out of a much larger number, who, as its Editor explains, could have been included, we are constrained to give extracts from only two more—Samuel Jemsel, the Karaïte, and Haïm

David Azulai, known as the "Hida". Jemsel was a native of Troki in Lithuania. In 1641 he travelled to Palestine, with a group of a hundred Jewish pilgrims, by way of Eupatoria, Constantinople, Gallipoli, Rhodes, Alexandria, and Cairo. After his return home, he probably fell a victim in 1648 at one of the Chmielnitski massacres. The account of his voyage, here translated, is from a unique MS. in Leningrad, published by Gurland at Lyck in 1866. A fragment of eight leaves had been previously printed at Upsala with a Latin translation about 1690. The Leningrad Manuscript contains also two other Karaïte travels, printed by Eisenstein, but not here translated.

Azulai, a great Kabbalist, born at Jerusalem in 1727, made three journeys to Europe to collect funds for the Hebron Rabbinical Seminary. The first (1753–8) was to Italy, Germany, Holland, England, France, Sicily, Smyrna, Constantinople, Chios, Rhodes, Cyprus, Beirut, Jaffa, and back to Jerusalem. The second was in 1764 to Italy, France, Germany, Holland, and England. His last journey was again to Italy in 1781, where he stayed at Leghorn till his death in 1806. His chief interest was in manuscripts and books, of which he himself published many. The extracts here given are translated from Professor Freimann's edition in the *Mekize Nirdamim* of the original autograph manuscript now at the Jewish Theological Seminary, New York.

After the sixteenth century, geographical discoveries had made the whole world familiar to most people, and the traveller only journeyed afield, with a specific object, which could hardly be of general interest or importance. The wandering Jew becomes less the diplomatist or scientist and more of the bagman and beggar. But he still remains a loyal link between the scattered members of the Diaspora, pious and alert and generous both in what he expects and what he gives.

PLATE III

THE EXODUS FROM EGYPT

From a Provençal Hagadah on vellum of the fourteenth century
(No. 514 of Mr. David S. Sassoon's collection)

PLATE IV

CONTEMPORARY JEWISH COSTUMES

From a High German Bible Manuscript on vellum, written in South Germany between 1190 and 1202
[Now in the Pierpoint Morgan Library, New York. Dörling, Hamburg, 1928. Auction Catalogue,
XXVI, No. 932]

EGINHARD OF FRANCONIA (A.D. 801)

Eginhard of Franconia, secretary and biographer of Charlemagne, wrote the *Annales Francorum*, describing in Latin the principal events between 741 and 829. He was the hero of one of Longfellow's *Tales of a Wayside Inn*. The following extracts from his Annals refer to Isaac the Jew, whom the Emperor had sent in 787 to Harun-ar-Rashid as interpreter to the Embassy. (From Teulet's edition, Paris, 1840.)

THE Emperor went from Spoleto to Ravenna, stayed there a few days, and reached Fara. He was there informed that Ambassadors from Harun, King of the Persians, had entered the Port of Pisa : he sent to meet them and had them presented to him near Vercelli. One of them—there were two—was a Persian of the East and the envoy of the King of the Persians, the other was a Saracen from Africa. They announced to the Emperor that the Jew Isaac, whom he had sent four years previously to the King of the Persians with Sigismond and Lanfred, was returning with great presents, but, as to Lanfred and Sigismond, they were both dead. The Emperor then sent the Notary Erchinbald to Liguria to prepare a fleet to carry the elephant and the other things which Isaac was bringing with him. . . .

In the month of October of this year (801), the Jew Isaac returned from Africa with the elephant, entered the Port of Vendres and passed the winter at Vercelli, because he could not cross the Alps, which were covered with snow.

On the 20th July, Isaac came and brought to the Emperor the elephant and other presents which the King of the Persians had sent him. The elephant's name was Abulabaz.

THE BOOK OF WAYS AND KINGDOMS
(*ca.* 817)

This book, written by Abu'l Kasim Obaidallah ibn Khordâdhbeh (see De Goeje's *Bibliotheca Geographorum Arabicorum*, Leyden, 1889, xol. vi, p. 114), whose father was Governor of Tabaristan, contains the following reference to Jewish merchants, called ar-Rhâdaniya (Radanites).

THESE merchants speak Arabic, Persian, Roman (i.e. Greek and Latin), the Frank, Spanish, and Slav languages. They journey from West to East, from East to West, partly on land, partly by sea. They transport from the West eunuchs, female slaves, boys, brocade, castor, marten, and other furs, and swords. They take ship from Firanja (France), on the Western Sea, and make for Faramâ (Pelusium). There they load their goods on camel-back and go by land to al-Kolzom (Suez), a distance of 25 farsakhs (parasangs). They embark in the East Sea (Red Sea) and sail from al-Kolzom to al-Jar (port of Medina) and Jeddah (port of Mecca), then they go to Sind, India, and China. On their return from China they carry back musk, aloes, camphor, cinnamon, and other products of the Eastern countries to al-Kolzom and bring them back to Faramâ, where they again embark on the Western Sea. Some make sail for Constantinople to sell their goods to the Romans ; others go to the palace of the King of the Franks to place their goods. Sometimes these Jew merchants, when embarking in the land of the Franks, on the Western Sea, make for for Antioch (at the mouth of the Orontes) ; thence by land to al-Jâbia (? al-Hanâya on the bank of the Euphrates), where they arrive after three days' march. There they embark on the Euphrates and reach

Baghdad, whence they sail down the Tigris, to al-Obolla. From al-Obolla they sail for Oman, Sind, Hind, and China. . . .

These different journeys can also be made by land. The merchants that ſtart from Spain or France go to Sus al-Aksa (Morocco) and then to Tangier, whence they walk to Afrikia (Kairouan) and the capital of Egypt. Thence they go to ar-Ramla, visit Damascus, Al-Kufa, Baghdad, and al-Basra (Bassora), cross Ahwaz, Fars, Kirman, Sind, Hind, and arrive at China. Sometimes, also, they take the route behind Rome and, passing through the country of the Slavs, arrive at Khamlij, the capital of the Khozars. They embark on the Jorjan Sea, arrive at Balkh, betake themselves from there across the Oxus, and continue their journey toward Yurt, Toghuzghuz, and from there to China.

ELDAD THE DANITE (*ca.* 880)

Eldad of the tribe of Dan lived in the latter part of the ninth century and, according to his own story, came from the East of Africa, near the Gulf of Aden, perhaps Somaliland. According to a Karaïte author, R. Judah Hadassi, he made two voyages, first to Egypt, whence he returned home, and secondly the journey of which contemporary accounts, including his own, survive and are here in part reproduced.

In this second journey, he suffered shipwreck and fell into the hands of cannibals called Romrom or Domrom. These were vanquished by other natives, who sold him to a Jew of the tribe of Issachar. This appears from his own story, contained in the letter he wrote to the Jews of Spain in 883. From contemporary accounts, he appears to have been in Baghdad and afterwards in Kairouan. The Jews of Kairouan consulted the Gaon R. Zemach about him and the practices with regard to slaughtering and other matters which he reported as being observed by his own tribe and the tribes of Naphtali, Gad and Asher, which, he stated, lived in the vicinity of the tribe of Dan.

The material parts of the Case and the Gaon's Response are given here, though the details as to slaughtering have been omitted as not being of general interest.

In Kairouan, Eldad conversed with R. Judah ben Korash. From the letter of R. Chisdai ibn Shaprut it appears that he also visited Spain. It is probable that he voyaged from Azania in Yemen, by way of the Indian Ocean, to the north-east of the Persian Gulf and thence overland across the mountain of Paron (Parvata) to Bagdad and thence to North Africa and Spain. The Hebrew language of his letter differs from the Rabbinic and approached the Biblical diction, though clumsier than the similar diction of his contemporary, the author of the Josippon or pseudo-Josephus.

The closest parallel to this diction is that of the diary of David Reubeni, the traveller from Arabia to Europe, in the sixteenth century. Eldad pretended not to understand Ethiopic or Arabic, but there are many words of his which are clearly derived from the latter language. It has been the fashion among scholars, such as Ibn Ezra, R. Meïr of Rothenburg, and many modern scholars, to regard him as an impostor. Pinsker and Graetz

4

called him a Karaïte missionary, but the practices he describes
are quite different from those of the Karaïtes. P. F. Frankl in
1873 called him a faithless swindler and Reifmann regarded
his story as a late fabrication, but Chisdai in the eleventh
century and Maimonides at the end of the twelfth quote him
with confidence and the weight of modern Hebraic scholarship
is in his favour. Of critical works on the texts, which undoubtedly "have undergone alterations and suffered from
interpolations," the most important are Epstein (1891), D. H.
Müller (1892), and particularly Max Schloessinger in "The
Ritual of Eldad Ha-Dani reconstructed and edited from
manuscripts and a Genizah Fragment with notes and introduction and an Appendix on the Eldad Legends" (Haupt,
Leipzig-New York, 1908).

THE LETTER OF ELDAD THE DANITE

Being his Letter to the Jews of Spain according to the
text printed in Italy about 1480.

In the name of the Lord God of Israel ! May the
name of our Lord the King of Kings be praised who
chose Israel from all the nations and gave us the law
of truth and planted eternal life in our midst, the law
of the upright to live thereby. Our brethren, sons
of the captivity, be of good courage and strengthen
your hearts to perform the law of our God in due
season, for whensoever Israel doeth the law of the
omnipresent, no nation and no tongue can rule over
them. Peace be with you our brethren, sons of the
captivity, and peace to Jerusalem, the city of our
glory, the place of the Temple of our God which has
been destroyed and the place of the kingdom of the
house of David and Judah, who wrought justice and
righteousness, and the place of the Holy of Holies.
Peace to all the elders of Israel, and to the faithful in
the law of God and to its interpreters, its priests and
Levites and all the tribes of Israel and Judah great
and small. May the Lord strengthen your hearts
in the Law and in the true prophet Moses, our teacher,
the servant of the Lord !

And now we shall tell our brethren, the tribes of Jeshurun, of Eldad the Danite, who relates all this, how he went forth in all the countries after being separated from the tribe of Dan and the Lord miraculously saved him in many places and from many troubles, which passed over him, till he came to this land, so that he might go and tell all the children of Israel, who are scattered in Israel, matters concerning him, that he might bring you good tidings of comfort and speak good words to your heart.

I

And this was my going forth from the other side of the rivers of Ethiopia.

I and a Jew of the tribe of Asher entered a small ship to trade with the shipmen and behold, at midnight, the Lord caused a great and strong wind to arise and the ship was wrecked. Now the Lord had prepared a box and I took hold of it and my companion seeing this also took hold of that box, and we went up and down with it, until the sea cast us among a people called Romranos [1] who are black Ethiopians, tall, without garment or clothing upon them, cannibals, like unto the beasts of the field.

2

And when we came to their country they took hold of us and, seeing that my companion was fat and healthy and pleasing, slaughtered and ate him, and he cried " Alas for me that I have been brought to this people and the Ethiopians will eat my flesh ", but me they took, for I was sick on board ship, and they put me in chains until I should get fat and well, and they brought before me all kinds of good but forbidden food, but I ate nothing and I hid the food, and when they asked me if I had eaten I answered, yes I had eaten.

3

And I was with them a long time until the Lord, blessed be He, performed a miracle with me, for a great army came upon them from another place, who took me captive, but they spoiled and killed them and took me along with the captives.

4

And those wicked men were fireworshippers and I dwelt with them four years, and behold, every morning they made a great fire and bowed down and worshipped it. And they brought me to the province of Azania.

5

And a Jew, a Merchant of the tribe of Issachar, found me and bought me for 32 gold pieces and brought me back with him to his country. They live in the mountains of the sea-coast[2] and belong to the land of the Medes and Persians. They fulfil the command " the book of this law shall not depart from thy mouth ". The yoke of sovereignty is not upon them but only the yoke of the law. Among them are leaders of hosts but they fight with no man. They only dispute as to the law, and they live in peace and comfort and there is no disturber and no evil chance. They dwell in a country ten days' journey by ten days, and they have great flocks and camels and asses and slaves, but they do not rear horses. They carry no weapons, except the slaughterer's knife, and there is not among them any oppression or robbery and, even if they should find on the road garments or money, they would not stretch forth their hand to take it. But near them are wicked men, fire-worshippers, who take their own mothers and sisters to wife, but them they do not hurt. They have a Judge, and I asked about him and they said his name was Nachshon, and they practice the four death penalties [3] according to the law, and they speak Hebrew and Persian.

6

And the sons of Zebulun are encamped in the hills of Paron and reach to their (i.e. Issachar's) neighbourhood and pitch tents made of hairy skins which come to them from the land of Armenia, and they reach up to the Euphrates, and they practice business and they observe the four death penalties inflicted by the court.

7

And the tribe of Reuben is over against them behind Mount Paron, and there is peace and brotherhood and companionship between them, and they go together to war and make roads and divide the spoils amongst themselves, and they go on the highroads of the Kings of Media and Persia and they speak Hebrew and Persian, and they possess scripture and Mishna, Talmud, and Haggadah, and every Sabbath they read the law with accents, the text in Hebrew and the interpretation (Targum) thereof in Persian.

8

And the tribe of Ephraim and half tribe of Manasseh are there in the mountains over against the city of Mecca, the stumbling block of the Ishmaelites. They are strong of body and of iron heart. They are horse-men and take the road and have no pity on their enemies, and their only livelihood comes of spoil. They are mighty men of war. One is match for a thousand.

9

And the tribe of Simeon and the half tribe of Manasseh live in the country of the Babylonians [4] six months' journey away, and they are the most

numerous of all of them, and they take tribute from
five and twenty kingdoms and some Ishmaelites
pay them tribute.

10

And in our country we say that it is a tradition
among us that ye are the sons of the captivity, the
tribe of Judah and the tribe of Benjamin under the
dominion of the heathen in an unclean land, who
were scattered under the Romans who destroyed
the Temple of our God, and under the Greeks and
the Ishmaelites, may their sword pierce their heart
and may their bones be broken !

11

We have a tradition from father to son that we,
the sons of Dan, were aforetime in the land of Israel
dwellers in tents and among all the tribes of Israel
there were none like us men of war and mighty of
valour. And, when Jeroboam, the son of Nebat, who
caused Israel to sin and made two golden calves,
arose over them, the kingdom of the house of David
was divided and the tribes gathered together and
said, " Come and fight against Rehoboam and against
Jerusalem." They answered, " Why should we fight
with our brothers and with the son of our lord David,
King of Israel and Judah ? God forbid ! " Then
said the elders of Israel, " You have not in all the
tribes of Israel mighty ones like the tribe of Dan."
At once they said to the children of Dan, " Arise and
fight with the children of Judah." They answered,
" By the life of Dan our father, we will not make war
with our brothers and we will not shed blood." At
once we children of Dan took swords and lances
and bows, and devoted ourselves to death to go forth
from the land of Israel, for we saw we could not stay,
" Let us go hence and find a resting place, but if
we wait until the end they will take us away." So

we took heart and counsel to go to Egypt to destroy it and to kill all its inhabitants. Our prince said to us, "Is it not written, ye shall not continue to see it again for ever? How will you prosper?" They said, "Let us go against Amalek or against Edom or against Ammon and Moab to destroy them and let us dwell in their place." Our princes said, "It is written in the law that the Holy One, blessed be He, has prevented Israel from crossing their border. Finally we took counsel to go to Egypt, but not by the way that our fathers went and not to destroy it, but only to go there to cross the River Pishon (Lower Nile) to the land of Ethiopia and, behold, when we came near to Egypt, all Egypt was afraid and sent to us asking, "Is it war or peace?" and we said, "For peace; we will cross your country to the River Pishon, and there we will find a resting place," and, behold, they did not believe us, but all Egypt stood on guard until we crossed their country and arrived in the land of Ethiopia. We found it a good and fat land, and, in it, fields, enclosures, and gardens. They could not restrain the children of Dan from dwelling with them, for they took the land by might and, behold, though they wished to kill them all, they had to pay tribute to Israel, and we dwelt with them many years, and increased and multiplied greatly and held great riches.

12

Afterwards Sennacherib, King of Assyria, arose and took the Reubenites and the Gadites and the half tribe of Manasseh captive, and took them to Halah and Habor and the River Gozan, and the cities of Media. And Sennacherib arose a second time and took captive the tribe of Asher and the tribe of Naphtali and led them to the land of Assyria, and, after the death of Sennacherib, three tribes of Israel, being Naphtali, Gad, and Asher, journeyed on their own to the land of Ethiopia and encamped in the wilderness until they came to their border, a twenty days' journey, and they slew the men of Ethiopia, and unto this very day, they fight with the children of the kingdoms of Ethiopia.

13

And these tribes, being Dan, Naphtali, Gad, and Asher, dwell in the ancient Havilah,[5] where gold is (and in goodly places in the kingdom of the Paravim, under the rule of Oreinos), and they trusted in their Maker, and the Lord helped them. These tribes placed their hands on the neck of their enemies and every year they make war with the seven kingdoms and seven countries. The names of these kingdoms are Tussina, Kamti, Kuba, Tariogi, Takula, Karma, and Kalom,[6] and they are on the other side of the rivers of Ethiopia. These four tribes have gold and silver and precious stones, and much sheep and cattle and camels and asses, and they sow and they reap, and they dwell in tents, and, when they will, they journey and encamp in tents, from border to border, two days by two days' journey, and in the place where they encamp there is no place where the foot of man enters, but they encamp in a place of fields and vineyards.

14

And their King's name is Uzziel and the name of their great prince Elizaphan, of the children of Aholiab, of the tribe of Dan, and their banner is white and written thereon in black is, " Hear, O Israel, the Lord our God is one God," and when they seek to go out to war the crier calls with the sound of the trumpet, and the lord of the hosts comes and the armies go forth one hundred and twenty thousand (?) with small white bannerettes. Every three months, a different tribe goes out to war, and the tribe remains three months away, and all that they bring from the spoil of their enemies they divide among their own tribe. But the descendants of Samson, of the tribe of Dan, are superior to all. They never run away, for that were a great shame to them. They are numerous as the sands of the sea, and have no employment but war and, whensoever they fight, they say it is not good for mighty men to flee, let them die young, but let them not flee, let them strengthen their heart unto God, and several times they say and cry all of them together, " Hear, O Israel, our God is one God," and then they all take heed.

15

And thus they do till their three months are over and then they return and they bring all their spoil to King Uzziel, and he divides it with all Israel, and this is their statute from King David until this day, and King Uzziel takes his share and the King gives a share to all the wise men, sages of the law, dwellers in tents, and afterwards all take their portion, and the lord of the host his share. Thus they do in the three months when Naphtali goes out, and in the three months when Gad goes out, and so (Asher); all of them until twelve months are completed, and then they repeat in succession.

16

As to the tribe of Moses our teacher, on whom be peace, the righteous servant of God whose name is called with us the tribe of *Janus*, for he fled from idolatry and clove to the fear of God, the sea surrounds them, three months' journey by three months. They dwell in glorious houses and fine buildings and castles, and train elephants for themselves in their times of joy. No unclean thing is to be found with them, no unclean fowl, no unclean beast, no unclean cattle, no flies, no fleas, no lice, no foxes, no scorpions, no serpents, and no dogs. All these were in the idolatrous land, where they had been in servitude. They have only sheep, oxen, and fowls, and their sheep bring forth twice a year. They sow seed twice a year ; they sow and they reap and they have gardens and olives and pomegranates and figs and all kinds of beans and cucumbers and melons and onions and garlic and barley and wheat, and from one comes forth a hundred.

17

They are of perfect faith and their Talmud is all in Hebrew, and thus they learn, " Thus taught us our Rabbis, from the mouth of Joshua the son of Nun, from the mouth of our father Moses, from the mouth of the Almighty." But they know not the Rabbis, for these were of the Second Temple and they did not reach them.

18

And they can speak only the Holy tongue and they all take ritual baths and never swear. They cry out against him that takes the name of God in vain, and say that by the sin of cursing your sons would die young. But they are long lived and live a hundred or 120 years and no son dies in his father's lifetime, and they reach three or four generations, and they sow and reap themselves, for they have no manservants or maidservants, and they are all equal, and do not shut their houses at night for that would be shame to them, and a young man goes with the flocks ten days' journey and fears neither robbers nor ghosts. They are all Levites and have not among them either Priest or Israelite, and they abide in the sanctity of Moses our teacher, the servant of the Lord.

Moreover, they see no man and no men see them except these four tribes, who dwell on the other side of the rivers of Ethiopia. There is a place where these can see each other and speak if they cry out, but the River Sambation is between them, and they tell, " Thus it happened to us in war time," and they tell all Israel what happened to them. When they want anything important, they have a kind of pigeon known among them and they write their letters and fasten them to the wings or to the feet of the pigeon, and these cross the River Sambation and the pigeons come to their Kings and their Princes. They also have very many precious stones and silver and gold, and they sow flax and they rear cochineal and make pleasant garments without end and are five times as numerous as those that came out of Egypt, for they are innumerable. The breadth of that river is 200 cubits bowshot, and the river is full of large and small stones and the sound of them rumbles like a great storm, like a tempest at sea and, in the night, the sound of it is heard a day's journey and they have with them six wells and they all unite into one lake and therefrom they irrigate their land, and therein are clean edible fish. The river runs and the stones and sand rumble during the six working days, but on the seventh day it rests and is tranquil until the end of Sabbath. And on the other side of the river, on the side where the four tribes dwell, is a fire which flames on Sabbath and no man can approach within a mile. And this is my name, Eldad ben Mahali ben Ezekiel ben Hezekiah ben Aluk ben Abner ben Shemaiah ben Hater ben Hur ben Elkanah ben Hillel ben Tobias ben Pedath ben Ainon ben Naaman ben Taam ben Taami ben Onam ben Gaul ben Shalom ben Caleb ben Omram ben Dumain ben Obadiah ben Abraham ben Joseph ben Moses ben

ELDAD THE DANITE

Jacob ben Kappur ben Ariel ben Asher ben Job ben Shallum ben Elihu ben Ahaliab ben Ahisamach ben Hushim ben Dan ben Jacob our father, on whom be peace and on all Israel.

These letters this Lord Eldad sent to Spain in the year 43 (883), and this Lord Eldad was full of law and commandments and, if a man sits with him from morning until evening, he does not cease to converse on the law in the Holy tongue and his words are sweeter than honey and the honeycomb. May the Lord give him a good reward in this world and in the world to come.

Here endeth the Book of Eldad the Danite.

CASE AS TO ELDAD THE DANITE

(according to the text printed at Constantinople in 1519)

This question the men of Kairouan asked of the Gaon Rabbenu Zemach with reference to Eldad the Danite of the tribes in ancient Havilah, in the land of Ethiopia, who had come unto them [after sundry greetings to the Gaon].

Be it known to your Lordship that a man has become our guest whose name is Eldad the Danite of the tribe of Dan, and he has told us that there are four tribes in one place, Dan, Naphtali, Gad, and Asher. Its name is the ancient Havilah where is the gold, and they have a Judge called Abdon, and they use the four methods of death penalty, and dwell in tents and journey and encamp from place to place. They fight with the five (? seven) Kings of Ethiopia and the extent of their land is seven months' journey. Five of those Kings surround them at the back and on two sides, and fight with them at all times, and whoever is faint-hearted is put into God's camp.[7] They possess the whole of the Bible, but they do not read

the scroll of the history of Esther, because they had
no part in that miracle, nor the scroll of Lamentations
so as not to break their heart. In all their lore no
sage's name is quoted as authority, but they assert
" Joshua said it, who had it from the mouth of Moses,
who had it from the Almighty." Every strong
man amongst them is put into their military camp,
and they keep at their work. These to war and the
others to study of the Torah. They are of the four
tribes but when they go forth to war they do not go
forth mixed. The strong men of Dan have three
fixed months. They go to fight on their horses and keep
on horseback all the week, but on the eve of the
Sabbath they alight wherever they may be and their
horses remain in their armour and their enemies do
not come upon them. They keep the Sabbath in
due form, but, if their enemies do come against them,
they fight them with all their arms and slay as many
of them as God enables them to slay.

There are also among them strong men descendants
of Samson, sons of Dalilah, and they like to go to
battle, and the smallest of them pursues many, and
the voice of every one of them is a mighty voice as
the roar of the lion and they call forth with their
great voice " Salvation is unto the Lord. Thy might
is with Thy people, the tribes of Jeshurun Selah ",
and they continue at war till three months are ended,
and when the three months are ended they come with
all their spoil to the King Addiel [8] and they divide it
equally among all the Israelites, and when the King
receives his portion he gives it to the wise men that
learn the law, and whoever is entitled to a portion
they give him a portion, and then they take their own
portion and so Gad and so Asher and so Naphtali
until the twelve months are over, and then the
rotation is repeated.

Their only language is the sacred tongue, and this

ELDAD THE DANITE

Eldad the Danite underſtands not a word of any other language, neither the language of Ethiopia nor the language of Ishmael, but Hebrew alone, and the Hebrew which he speaks contains words which we have never heard. Thus he calls a dove " tintar ", a bird he calls " requt ", for pepper he says " darmos ". Of such as these, we have written down many from his mouth, because we pointed the matter out to him and he told us the name in the sacred language, and we wrote it down, and after a time we again asked him each word and we found it the same as the firſt word he had given. Their Talmud is of a simple Hebrew and no wise man is mentioned therein, either Rabbi of the Mishna or Rabbi of the Talmud, but in every Halacha they say, " Thus have we learnt from the mouth of Joshua, from the mouth of Moses, from the mouth of God," and he tells of what is forbidden and what is permitted, and we have seen that it is the same law but slightly different, and we think it right to set forth to your Lordship matters written in part of their Talmud, which are surprising so that your Lordship may examine them. . . . [Here follow the laws expounded by Eldad.]

And he also told us that, when the Temple was deſtroyed, Israel went to Babylon, and the Chaldaeans rose up and said to the sons of Moses, " Sing to us of the songs of Zion." The sons of Moses arose and wept before the Lord, and cut their fingers saying, " These fingers with which we played in the Temple, how can we play with them in an impure land ? " and the cloud came and carried them with their tents and sheep and cattle and brought them to Havilah, and put them down in the night. Moreover he said to us, " Our fathers told us that our fathers had heard from their fathers that, in that night, there was a great noise, and in the morning they saw a big and mighty army, but they were surrounded by a river which ran with stones and dust to a place where there never had been a river before, and this river still flows with stones and dust without water, with a great rumbling and a great noise which would be scattered did it not meet a mountain of iron, and the river flows all the six weekdays with stones and dust, without a drop of water, but it rests on the Sabbath day, and, at the time when it gets evening at dusk, a cloud descends upon it and no man can touch it till the end of the Sabbath, and its name is Sambation and we call it Sabbatinus, and there are places in that river which are only 60 cubits wide. Those on one side of the river can talk with those on the other, but they are secluded because the river surrounds them, and we cannot go to them and they cannot get out.

And among them there are no wild beasts and no impure, but only cattle. There are no insects and no creeping things, but only their sheep and cattle. They reap and sow themselves, for they have no slaves, and they spoke together and told the sons of Dan of the destruction of the Temple of which they knew not.

But Naphtali and Gad and Asher, after the destruction of the Temple, came to Dan because aforetime they used to dwell with Issachar in their cities and they used to dispute with them, saying to them, "You are the children of the handmaids," and they feared lest war should fall out between them and journeyed and went until they reached Dan and the four tribes were united in one place.

And this is the reply which the Gaon Zemah gave to the men of Kairouan who asked concerning Eldad the Danite and the distinctions of his law :—

[OPINION]

With regard to Rabbi Eldad the Danite which you asked of us and what you have heard from him,

wise men tell us that they heard from Rabban Isaac
ben Mar and Rabban Simcha that they saw this
Rabbi Eldad the Danite and were surprised at his
words because some of them were according to
the words of the Rabbis and some of them
differed.

When we considered this matter, we saw that there
are passages which support our wise men because
when Sennacherib came up and took up the tribes
of Zebulun and Naphtali into exile in the eighth year
of King Ahaz (and from the building of the Temple
until the eighth year of Ahaz was about 64 years),
and when the sons of Dan, who were mighty men of
valour, saw that the King of Assyria had begun to
rule over Israel they went forth from the land of
Israel into Ethiopia and dwell in a land which is a
land of gardens and enclosures, fields and vineyards,
a wide land full of all good and their hearts prompted
them to serve the Lord with veneration and to do
all his commandments with love. And he granted
that they should be crowned with two crowns, that
of the law and that of the kingdom, even as this
Rabbi Eldad the Danite said.

And our sages have taught that there were ten
captivities in which Israel went captive, through
Sennacherib four, through Nebuchadnezzar four,
through Vespasian one, and one through Hadrian.
But the tribe of Dan is not mentioned in any of the
exiles because it went of its own accord to Ethiopia,
135 years before the destruction of the Temple.
It seemed to him that there was no flaw in this matter,
if Dan had not gone into exile before the third
captivity.

And Rabbi Eldad says that they practised the four
kinds of execution, stoning, burning, the sword,
and strangling, but death by strangling is not in
scripture, and the Rabbis interpreted that wherever

death is mentioned in scripture generally it means strangling.

And as to the sons of Moses being near them and the Sambation surrounding them, he spoke truth, for thus say our Rabbis in the Midrash, "Nebuchadnezzar sent into exile the Levites, the sons of Moses, sixty myriads," and when they came to the rivers of Babylon, they and their harps, it happened to them as Rabbi Eldad related to you.

And before our ancestors came into the land of Canaan, they were accustomed to fighting, and they forgot the Mishna which they had received from Moses, and even Joshua himself said as to this that he had doubts after the death of Moses, and of all the tribes who were throughout the land the tribes of Judah and Benjamin kept the law more strictly than any.

Do not be astonished at the variation and difference which you heard from Eldad, for it is a fact that the sages of Babylon and of Palestine study one and the same Mishna and they do not add to or take away from it, but sometimes these give one reason and those another reason, as when two wise men sit down to understand Scripture or Mishna, one finds one reason and another finds another reason, and even in Scripture, which is fixed in writing, there is a difference between Babylon and Palestine in the Massora as to defective and superfluous letters, as to open and closed sections, as to accents and as to the division of verses. Much more so in the Mishna, which is a closed matter, very, very deep. Who can cope with it ?

But it must be said that it is not far fetched to think that Eldad has erred and confused things in consequence of the many troubles through which he passed and the stress of travel wearying the body, but the Mishna is one law ; we cannot add to it nor diminish from it, and can admit no variation, neither variation in a great matter nor a small matter. But the Talmud is studied by the men of Babylon in Syriac and by the men of Palestine in Targum, and by the sages exiled to Ethiopia in Hebrew, which they understand. And as to there being no sages mentioned by name because in all the Mishna, which the Israelites learned in the Temple, the laws were general and no sages were quoted. But the law remains the same, whether in Mishna or Talmud, and all drink from one well, and it is not fitting to reveal everything, as it is said (Proverbs 25 (2)) " The honour of Kings is to search out a matter."

And as to what Eldad told that they prayed for the wise men of Babylon first and afterwards for all Israel in exile, they do well, for the chief sages and prophets were exiled to Babylon and they founded the law and they fixed the House of Learning (Jeshibah) on the River Euphrates, from the days of Jehoiakim, King of Judah, until this very day, and formed a chain of wisdom and prophecy and from them went forth the law to all the people and, as we have already told you, all drink from one well, therefore, keep ye diligently what the sages preach unto you and the Talmud which they taught you, turn not to the right or left from any of their words, for thus it is written (Deut. xvii, 11):—

" According to the sentence of the law which they shall teach thee and according to the judgment which they shall deliver thee thou shalt do."

THE EPISTLE OF R. CHISDAI, SON OF ISAAC (OF BLESSED MEMORY) TO THE KING OF THE KHOZARS (*ca.* 960) [1]

Chisdai Abu-Yusuf, the son of Isaac the son of Ezra, of the family of Shaprut, a physician, became Vizier to the Caliph Abd er-Rahman III (911–61) and his successor the Caliph Hakem (961–76). The Byzantine Emperor, Romanus II, driven into straits by the Abbaside Caliph at Bagdad courted the friendship of Abd er-Rahman and sent him a Greek medical manuscript of Dioscorides, in charge of a Monk, Nicolaus, to interpret the Greek into Latin. Nicolaus became Chisdai's friend. Chisdai was sent by Abd er-Rahman to Navarre and cured its deposed King Leon of obesity and helped to restore him to his throne of Navarre. Otto I, Emperor of Germany in 956, sent an embassy to the Caliph Abd er-Rahman, and Chisdai carried on the negotiations which led to a satisfactory treaty. As Nasi (Prince) or temporal head of the Jewish congregations of Cordova, Chisdai advanced Jewish interests and Jewish studies in Spain and elsewhere. He had heard from Oriental travellers that there was a Jewish kingdom in Asia ruled by a Jewish King. Once he was told by merchants from Choresvan (Khorasan) that such a Jewish kingdom did really exist and that the land was called Khozar. He had also heard of Eldad the Danite. Ambassadors from the Byzantine Emperor to the Caliph had told Chisdai that the merchant's story was true, Chisdai accordingly sent one Isaac ben Nathan with a letter, of which a translation follows, with a recommendation to the Emperor. Isaac remained six months in Constantinople, but went no further, the Emperor writing that the way to the land of Khozar was far too dangerous and the Black Sea only occasionally navigable. Chisdai thought of sending his letter to Jerusalem, where Jews had promised to forward it to Nisibis, thence to Armenia, from Armenia to Berdaa, and from thence to Khozar. But while he was considering this plan,

22

R. CHISDAI

Ambassadors came from the King of the Gebalim (Slavonians) to Abd er-Rahman, among whom were two Jews, Saul and Joseph. These offered to hand the letter to the King of Gebalim, who out of respect for Chisdai would send it to the Jews in Hungary, thence it would be forwarded to Roumelia and Bulgaria and so finally reach its destination. By these means the letter was delivered to Joseph the King of the Khozars, and the King sent him a reply of which a translation is also given. Chisdai is believed to have died in 1014. The authenticity of these letters, now generally accepted, was for a long time impugned by Buxtorf, Basnage and others. The great poet philosopher, Judah Halevi, in 1140 wrote the famous work *Cusari* which is based on the conversion of the King of the Khozars, who inhabited the Crimea, and of a portion of his people. This took place according to the Arabian historians in the second half of the eighth century.

I, CHISDAI, son of Isaac, son of Ezra, belonging to the exiled Jews of Jerusalem, in Spain, a servant of my Lord the King, bow to the earth before him and prostrate myself towards the abode of your Majesty, from a distant land. I rejoice in your tranquillity and magnificence, and stretch forth my hands to God in Heaven that He may prolong your reign in Israel. But who am I ? and what is my life that I should dare to indite a letter to my Lord the King and to address your Majesty ? I rely, however, on the integrity and uprightness of my object. How, indeed, can an idea be expressed in fair words by those who have wandered, after the honour of the kingdom has departed ; who have long suffered afflictions and calamities, and see their flags in the land no more ? We, indeed, who are of the remnant of the captive Israelites, servants of my Lord the King, are dwelling peacefully in the land of our sojourning (for our God has not forsaken us, nor has His shadow departed from us). When we had transgressed He brought us into judgment, cast affliction upon our

loins, and stirred up the minds of those who had been
set over the Israelites to appoint collectors of tribute
over them, who aggravated the yoke of the Israelites,
oppressed them cruelly, humbled them grievously
and inflicted great calamities upon them. But when
God saw their misery and labour, and that they were
helpless, He led me to present myself before the
King, and has graciously turned His heart to me,
not because of mine own righteousness, but for
His mercy and His covenant's sake. And by this
covenant the poor of the flock were exalted to safety,
the hands of the oppressors themselves were relaxed,
they refrained from further oppression, and through
the mercy of our God the yoke was lightened. Let
it be known, then, to the King my Lord, that the name
of our land in which we dwell is called in the sacred
tongue Sefarad, but in the language of the Arabs,
the indwellers of the land, Alandalus (Andalusia),
the name of the capital of the kingdom, Cordova.
The length of it is 25,000 cubits, the breadth 10,000.
It is situated at the left of the sea (Mediterranean)
which flows between your country and the great sea
(Atlantic), and compasses the whole of your land.
Between this city and the great sea beyond which there
is no farther habitable territory, are nine astronomical
degrees ; the sun advances one degree on each day,
according to the opinion of the astronomers ; each
degree contains 66 miles and two parts of a mile,
each mile consists of 3,000 cubits ; so that those
nine degrees make 600 miles. From that great
sea (Atlantic) the whole distance as far as
Constantineh (Constantinople) is 3,100 miles ; but
Cordova is 80 miles distant from the shore of the
sea which flows into your country (Mediterranean).
I have found in the books of the wise men that the
land of Khozar is 60 degrees longitude, making
270 miles (from Constantinople). Such is the journey

from Cordova to Conſtantineh. Before, however,
I set forth an account of it I will also premise the
measure of the length of its limits. Your servant is
not ignorant that the leaſt of the servants of my Lord
the King is greater than the wise men of our country ;
but I am not teaching, only recording.
According to mathematical principles we have
found that the diſtance of our city from the Equator
is 38 degrees, that of Conſtantineh 44, of your
boundaries 47. I have been induced to state these
facts because of my surprise that we have no account
of your kingdom, and I think this is only due to the
great distance of our kingdom from the realm of my
Lord the King. But I recently heard that two men,
inhabitants of our land, had arrived at the dwelling-
place of my Lord the King, one of them called Rabbi
Judah, son of Meir, son of Nathan, a prudent and
learned man, the other R. Joseph Haggaris, also a wise
man (happy they, and blessed their lot, whose fortune
it was to see the glorious majeſty and splendour of my
Lord the King, as well as the ſtate and condition of his
servants and miniſters), I thought that it was easy
in the sight of God in his great mercy to do a wonder
to me also, and to make me, too, worthy of seeing
the majeſty and royal throne of my Lord, and to enjoy
his gracious presence. I shall inform my Lord the
King of the name of the King who reigns over us.
His name is Abd er-Rahman, son of Mohammed,
son of Abd er-Rahman, son of Hakem, son of
Hisham, son of Abd er-Rahman, who all reigned
in succession except Mohammed alone, the father
of our king, who did not ascend the throne, but
died in the lifetime of his father. Abd er-Rahman
eighth of the Ommayads came into Spain while
the sons of al-Abbasī[2] ruled over it, neighbours of
those who are sovereigns in the land of Shinar at the
present time. Abd er-Rahman eighth of the Ommayads
liberated Spain when there was an insurrection againſt

it by the sons of al-Abbasi, son of Mu'awiya, son of
Hisham, son of Abd-el-Malik, who is called Amir al-
Muminim (Ruler of the Faithful), whose name is
universally known. Nor can any of the kings who
went before be compared with him. The extent of
Spain which is under the sovereignty of Abd ar-
Rahman, the Amir al-Muminim (to whom God be
propitious) is 16 degrees, making 1,100 miles. The
land is rich, abounding in rivers, springs, and
aqueducts ; a land of corn, oil, and wine, of fruits
and all manner of delicacies ; it has pleasure-gardens
and orchards, fruitful trees of every kind, including
the leaves of the tree upon which the silkworm feeds,
of which we have great abundance. In the mountains
and woods of our country cochineal is gathered in
great quantity. There are also found among us
mountains covered by crocus and with veins of
silver, gold, copper, iron, tin, lead, sulphur, porphyry,
marble, and crystal. It produces besides what is
called in the Arabic language *lulu*. Merchants
congregate in it, and traffickers from the ends of
the earth, from Egypt and adjacent countries, bringing
spices, precious stones, splendid wares for kings and
princes, and all the desirable things of Egypt. Our
king has collected very large treasures of silver, gold,
precious things, and valuables such as no king has
ever collected. His yearly revenue, I have heard,
is about 100,000 gold pieces, the greater part of
which is derived from the merchants who come
hither from various countries and islands ; and all
their mercantile transactions are placed under my
control.

Praise be to the beneficient God for his mercy
towards me ! Kings of the earth, to whom His
magnificence and power are known, bring gifts to
him, conciliating his favour by costly presents, such
as the King of the Germans,[3] the King of the Gebalim,

who are as-Saglab,[4] the King of Conſtantineh,[5] and others. All their gifts pass through my hands, and I am charged with making gifts in return. (Let my lips express praise to the God in Heaven who so far extends his loving kindness towards me without any merit of my own, but in the fullness of his mercies.) I always ask the ambassadors of these monarchs about our brethren the Israelites, the remnant of the captivity, whether they have heard anything concerning the deliverance of those who have pined in bondage and had found no reſt. At length mercantile emissaries of Khorasân told me that there is a kingdom of Jews who are called Khozars (and between Conſtantineh and that country is a sea voyage of 15 days, by land many nations dwell between us and them). But I did not believe these words, for I thought that they told me such things to procure my goodwill and favour. I was, therefore, hesitating and doubtful till the ambassadors of Conſtantineh came with presents and a letter from their king to our king, whom I interrogated concerning this matter. They answered me, " It is quite true ; there is in that place a kingdom Alcusari, diſtant from Conſtantineh a fifteen days' journey by sea, but many peoples are scattered through the land ; the name of the king now reigning is Joseph ; ships sometimes come from their country to ours bringing fish, skins, and wares of every kind ; the men are our brethren and are honoured by us ; there is frequent communication between us by embassies and mutual gifts ; they are very powerful ; they maintain numerous armies, which they occasionally engage in expeditions." This account inspired me with hope, wherefore I bowed down and adored the God of Heaven.

I now looked about for a faithful messenger whom I might send into your country in order that I might know the truth of this matter and ascertain the

welfare of my Lord and his servants our brethren.
The thing seemed impossible to me, owing to the very
great distance of the locality, but at length by the
will and favour of God, a man presented himself
to me named Mar Isaac, the son of Nathan. He
put his life into his hand and willingly offered to
take my letter to my Lord the King. I gave him a
large reward, supplying him with gold and silver
for his own expenses and those of his servants,
and with everything necessary. Moreover, I sent
out of my own resources a magnificent present to
the King of Constantineh, requesting him to aid
this my messenger in every possible way, till he
should arrive at that place where my Lord resides.
Accordingly this messenger set out, went to the
King and showed him my letter and presents. The
King, on his part, treated him honourably, and detained
him there for six months, with the ambassadors of
my Lord the King of Cordova. One day he told them
and my messenger to return, giving the latter a letter
in which he wrote that the way was dangerous, that
the peoples through whom he must pass were engaged
in warfare, that the sea was stormy and could not be
navigated except at a certain time. When I heard
this I was grieved even to death, and took it very ill
that he had not acted according to my orders and
fulfilled my wishes.

Afterwards I wished to send my letter by way
of Jerusalem, because persons there guaranteed that
my letter should be dispatched from thence to Nisibis,
thence to Armenia, from Armenia to Berdaa, and
thence to your country. While in this state of
suspense, behold ambassadors of the King of Gebalim
arrived, and with them two Israelites; the name of
one was Mar Saul, of the other Mar Joseph. These
persons understood my perplexity and comforted
me, saying, " Give us your letter, and we will take

care that it be carried to the King of the Gebalim, who for your sake will send it to the Israelites dwelling in the land of the Hungarians, they will send it to Russ, thence to Bulgar, till at last it will arrive, according to your wish, at its destination.

He who tries the heart and searches the reins knows that I did none of these things for the sake of mine own honour, but only to know the truth, whether the Israelitish exiles, anywhere form one independent kingdom and are not subject to any foreign ruler. If, indeed, I could learn that this was the case, then, despising all my glory, abandoning my high estate, leaving my family, I would go over mountains and hills, through seas and lands, till I should arrive at the place where my Lord the King resides, that I might see not only his glory and magnificence, and that of his servants and ministers, but also the tranquillity of the Israelites. On beholding this my eyes would brighten, my reins would exult, my lips would pour forth praises to God, who has not withdrawn his favour from his afflicted ones.

Now, therefore, let it please your Majesty, I beseech you, to have regard to the desires of your servant, and to command your scribes who are at hand to send back a reply from your distant land to your servant and to inform me fully concerning the condition of the Israelites, and how they came to dwell there. Our fathers told us that the place in which they originally settled was called Mount Seir, but my Lord knows that Mount Seir is far from the place where you dwell ; our ancestors say that it was, indeed, persecution, and by one calamity after another, till at length they became fixed in the place where they now dwell. The ancients, moreover, inform us that when a decree of fierce persecution was issued against the Jews on account of their transgressions, and the army of the Chaldaeans rose

up furiously against them, they hid the Book of the
Law and the Holy Scriptures in a certain cave. For
this reason they prayed in a cave and taught their
sons to pray there morning and evening. At length,
however, through distance of time and days, they
forgot, and lapsed into ignorance as to the meaning
of this cave and why they prayed in it ; while they
still continued to observe the custom of their fathers,
though ignorant of the reason for it. After a long
time there came a certain Israelite who was desirous
of knowing the true meaning of this custom, and when
he entered the cave he found it full of books, which
he brought out. From that time they resolved to
study the Law. This is what our fathers have related
to us as it was handed down from ancient times.
The two men who came from the land of Gebalim,
Mar Saul and Mar Joseph, after pledging themselves
to forward my letter to my Lord the King, told me ;
" About six years ago there came to us a wise and
intelligent Israelite afflicted with blindness, his name
was Mar Amram, and he said that he was from the
land of the Khoz, that he dwelt in the King's house,
ate at his table, and was held in honour by him." On
hearing this I sent messengers to bring him to me,
but they did not find him, yet this very circumstance
confirmed my hope.

Wherefore I have written this epistle to your
Majesty, in which I submissively entreat you not
to refuse my request, but to command your servant
to write to me about all these things, viz., what is
your State ? what is the nature of your land ? what
tribes inhabit it ? what is the manner of the government, how kings succeed one another—whether they
are chosen from a certain tribe or family or whether
sons succeed their fathers, as was customary among
our ancestors when they dwelt in their own land ?
Would my Lord the King also inform me as to the

extent of his country, its length and breadth? what
walled cities and what open towns it has ; whether
it be watered by artificial or natural means and how
far his dominion extends, also the number of his
armies and their leaders? Let not my Lord take it
ill, I pray, that I enquire about the number of his
forces ("May the Lord add unto them," etc.). My
Lord sees that I enquire about this with no other object
than that I may rejoice when I hear of the increase of
the holy people. I wish, too, that he would tell me
of the number of the provinces over which he rules,
the amount of tribute paid to him, if they give him
tithes, whether he dwells continually in the royal
city or goes about through the whole extent of his
dominions, if there are any islands in the neighbourhood, and if any of their inhabitants conform to
Judaism? if he judges his own people himself or
appoints judges over them? how he goes up to the
house of God? with what peoples he wages war?
whether he allows war to set aside the observance
of the Sabbath? what kingdoms or nations are on
his borders? what are their names and those of
territories? what are the cities near to his kingdom
called Khorasan, Berdaa, and Bab al Abwab? in
what way their caravans proceed to his territory?
how many kings ruled before him? what were their
names, how many years each of them ruled and what
is the current language of the land? In the time of
our fathers there was among us a certain Israelite,
an intelligent man, who belonged to the tribe of Dan,
who traced his descent back to Dan, the son of Jacob.
He spoke elegantly and gave everything its name
in the holy language. Nor was he at a loss for any
expression. When he expounded the Law he was
accustomed to say, " Thus has Othniel, son of Kenaz,
handed down by tradition from the mouth of Joshua,
and he from the mouth of Moses who was inspired

by the Almighty." One thing more I ask of my Lord, that he would tell me whether there is among you any computation concerning the final redemption which we have been awaiting so many years, whilſt we went from one captivity to another, from one exile to another. How ſtrong is the hope of him who awaits the realization of these events. And oh ! how can I hold my peace and be restful in the face of the desolation of the house of our glory and remembering those who, escaping the sword, have passed through fire and water, so that the remnant is but small. We have been caſt down from our glory, so that we have nothing to reply when they say daily unto us, " Every other people has its kingdom, but of yours there is no memorial on the earth." Hearing, therefore, the fame of my Lord the King, as well as the power of his dominions, and the multitude of his forces, we were amazed, we lifted up our head, our spirit revived, and our hands were ſtrengthened, and the kingdom of my Lord furnished us with an argument in answer to this taunt. May this report be subſtantiated ; for that would add to our greatness. Blessed be the Lord of Israel who has not left us without a kinsman as defender nor suffered the tribes of Israel to be without an independent kingdom. May my Lord the King prosper for ever . . .

THE ANSWER OF JOSEPH, KING OF THE TOGARMI, TO CHISDAI, THE HEAD OF THE CAPTIVITY, SON OF ISAAC, SON OF EZRA, THE SPANIARD, BELOVED AND HONOURED BY US

Behold, I inform you that your honoured epiſtle was given me by Rabbi Jacob, son of Eleazar, of the land of Nemez (Germany). We were rejoiced by it, and pleased with your discretion and wisdom, which we observed therein. I found in it a description

R. CHISDAI

of your land, its length and breadth, the descent of
its sovereign, Abd er-Rahman, his magnificence, and
majesty ; and how, with the help of God, he subdued
to himself the whole of the East, so that the fame of
his kingdom spread over the whole world, and the
fear of him seized upon all kings. You also told us
that had it not been for the arrival of those ambassadors
from Constantineh, who gave an account of the people
of our kingdom, and of our institutions, you would
have regarded all as false and would not have believed
it. You also inquired concerning our kingdom and
descent, how our fathers embraced the laws and
religion of the Israelites, how God enlightened our
eyes and scattered our enemies ; you also desired to
know the length and breadth of our land, the nations
that are our neighbours, such as are friendly and
hostile ; whether our ambassadors can go to your
land to salute your eminent and gracious king, who
draws the hearts of all men to love him and contract
friendship with him by the excellence of his character
and the uprightness of his actions, because the nations
tell you that the Israelites have no dominion and no
kingdom. If this were done, you say, the Israelites
would derive great benefit from it, their courage would
be reawakened, and they would have an answer and
occasion for priding themselves in reply to such as
say to them, " There are no Israelites remaining who
have a kingdom or dominion." We shall, therefore,
delighting in your wisdom, answer you with respect
to each of these particulars, concerning which you
have asked us in your letter.

We had already heard what you have written
concerning your land, and the family of the king.
Among our fathers there had been mutual intercourse
by letters, a thing which is written in our books and
is known to the elders of our country. We shall now
inform you of what happened to our fathers before

33

us, and what we shall leave as an inheritance to our children.

You ask, also, in your epistle of what people, of what family, and of what tribe we are? Know that we are descended from Japhet, through his son Togarma. We have found in the genealogical books of our fathers that Togarma had ten sons, whose names are these :—Agijoe, Tirus, Ouvar, Ugin, Bisal, Zarna, Cusar, Sanar, Balgad, and Savir.[6] We are of Cusar, of whom they write that in his days our fathers were few in number. But God gave them fortitude and power when they were carrying on wars with many and powerful nations, so that they expelled them from their country and pursued them in flight as far as the great River Duna (Danube ?), where the conquerors live to this day, near Constantineh, and thus the Khozars took possession of their territory . . .

As to your question concerning the extent of our land, its length and breadth, know that it is situated by the banks of a river near the sea of Gargal, towards the region of the East, a journey of four months. Near that river dwell very many populous tribes ; there are hamlets, towns, and fortified cities, all of which pay tribute to me. From thence the boundary turns towards Gargal ; and all those who dwell by the sea-shore, a month's journey, pay tribute to me. On the south side are fifteen very populous tribes, as far as Bab-al-Abwab, who live in the mountains. Likewise the inhabitants of the land of Bassa, and Tagat, as far as the sea of Constantineh, a journey of two months ; all these give me tribute. On the western side are thirteen tribes, also very numerous, dwelling on the shores of the sea of Constantineh, and thence the boundary turns to the north as far as the great river called Jaig. These live in open unwalled towns and occupy the whole wilderness (steppe) as far as the boundary of the Jugrians ; they are numerous as the sand of the sea, and all are tributary to me. Their land has an extent of four months' journey distant. I dwell at the mouth of the river and do not permit the Russians who come in ships to enter into their country, nor do I allow their enemies who come by land to penetrate into their territory. I have to wage grievous wars with them, for if I would permit them they would lay waste the whole land of the Mohammedans as far as Baghdad.

Moreover, I notify to you that I dwell by the banks of the river, by the grace of God, and have in my kingdom three royal cities. In the first the queen dwells with her maids and attendants. The length and breadth of it is fifty square parasangs together with its suburbs and adjacent hamlets. Israelites, Mohammedans, Christians and other peoples of various tongues dwell therein. The second, together with the suburbs, comprehends in length and breadth, eight square parasangs. In the third I reside with the princes and my servants and all my officers. This is a small city, in length and breadth three square parasangs ; this river flows within its walls. The whole winter we remain within the city, and in the month of Nisan (March) we leave this city and each one goes forth to his fields and gardens to cultivate them. Each family has its own hereditary estate. They enter and dwell in it with joy and song. The voice of an oppressor is not heard among us ; there are no enmities nor quarrels. I, with the princes and my ministers, then journey a distance of twenty parasangs to the great River Arsan, thence we make a circuit till we arrive at the extremity of the province. This is the extent of our land and the place of our rest. Our country is not frequently watered by rain ; it abounds in rivers and streams, having great abundance of fish ; we have many springs ; the land is fertile and rich ; fields, vineyards, gardens and orchards are watered by rivers ; we have fruit-bearing trees of every kind and in great abundance.

This, too, I add, that the limit of our lands towards the Eastern region is twenty parasangs' journey as far as the sea of Gargal, thirty towards the south, forty towards the west. I dwell in a fertile land and, by the grace of God, I dwell in tranquillity.

With reference to your question concerning the marvellous end, our eyes are turned to the Lord our God and to the wise men of Israel who dwell in Jerusalem and Babylon. Though we are far from Zion, we have heard that because of our iniquities the computations are erroneous ; nor do we know aught concerning this. But if it please the Lord, He will do it for the sake of His great name ; nor will the desolation of His house, the abolition of His service, and all the troubles which have come upon us be lightly esteemed in His sight. He will fulfil His promise, and " the Lord whom ye seek shall suddenly come to His temple, the messenger of the Covenant whom ye delight in : behold, he shall come, saith the Lord of Hosts " (Mal. iii, 1). Besides this we only have the prophecy of Daniel. May God hasten the redemption of Israel, gather together the captives and dispersed, you and I and all Israel that love His name, in the lifetime of us all.

Finally, you mention that you desire to see my face. I also long and desire to see your honoured face, to behold your wisdom and magnificence. Would that it were according to your word and that it were granted to me to be united with you, so that you might be my father and I your son. All my people would pay homage to you : according to your word and righteous counsel we should go out and come in. Farewell.

JUDAH HALEVI
(1085–1140)
HIS PILGRIMAGE TO ZION

Thine is my soul, Oh Lord ! in hope or dread :
To Thee alone I grateful bow the head.
A weary pilgrim I delight in Thee,
Throughout my wanderings, thankfully.
Alike when ship her gleaming wings o'erhead
Upon the sea, like fost'ring stork hath spread :
Or when the depths of Ocean moan below
And seem their sorrows from mine heart to know :
Alike what time the seething waters boil
And waves outhiss the cauldron's hot turmoil :
Or when the Christians sail in Moslem main
And Canaan's pirates threaten fierce campaign :
Or when the ship by monsters of the deep
Is chased, eager at their prey to leap—
Their prey, that from its troublous labour fain
Would seek escape, Alas ! it seeks in vain.
For me, altho' I thirst and long for food,
Thy praise in place of sustenance hath stood,
I ne'er the loss of all my wealth will mourn,
Of worldy goods bereft, and all forlorn,
My dearest kith and kin behind I leave,
Of only daughter sweet myself bereave.
Her son, my very heart, I will forget,
In mem'ry howso fast he once was set.
Child of delight, by mine own child begot,
Judah, by Judah even is forgot.
All else is nought. No love but God's is great
Thy holy Gates in joy approached, I wait
For death : My heart to Thee I sanctify
Upon Thine altar, love to testify.

BENJAMIN OF TUDELA
(1165–73)

Rabbi Benjamin ben Jonah of Tudela in Navarre was the most famous of Jewish travellers. He finished the travels he describes in 1173, and he must have been in Rome between 1165 and 1167. His travels have been translated into many European languages and a MS. in the British Museum, No. 27089, is almost contemporary.

The late Marcus Nathan Adler published a critical text, translation and commentary at the Oxford University Press in 1907, now unfortunately out of print. Pending the possible issue of another edition, his son, Mr. Herbert M. Adler, has been good enough to allow parts of the translation to figure in this volume and to permit a copy of the map of Western Asia, on which Benjamin's itinerary is marked, to be reproduced. Benjamin travelled from Tudela, in the north of Spain, through Rome and Otranto to Corfu across Greece to Constantinople, visiting the Archipelago, Rhodes and Cyprus on to Antioch. From Antioch, after a stay in Palestine, he proceeded to Damascus, Baghdad and Persia ; thence, across the Persian gulf, to India, Ceylon and perhaps China. He returned to Spain, by way of Aden, Assuan and overland to Cairo and Alexandria, crossing the Mediterranean to Sicily and Rome.

"THIS is the book of travels, which was compiled by Rabbi Benjamin, the son of Jonah, of the land of Navarre. His repose be in Paradise !

"The said Rabbi Benjamin set forth from Tudela, his native city, and passed through many remote countries, as is related in his book. In every place which he entered he made a record of all that he saw or was told of by trustworthy persons—matters not previously heard of in the land of Sepharad (Spain). Also he mentions some of the sages and illustrious men residing in each place. He brought this book with him on his return to the country of Castile, in the year 4933 (1173). The said Rabbi Benjamin is a wise and understanding man, learned in the Law and the Halacha, and wherever we have tested his statements we have found them accurate, true to fact and consistent ; for he is a trustworthy man . . .

" A three days' journey brings one to Abydos, which is upon an arm of the sea which flows between the mountains, and after a five days' journey the great city of Constantinople is reached. It is the capital of the whole land of Javan, which is called Greece. Here is the residence of the King Emanuel the Emperor. Twelve ministers are under him, each of whom has a palace in Constantinople and possesses castles and cities ; they rule all the land. At their head is the King Hipparchus, the second in command is the Megas Domesticus, the third Dominus, and the fourth is Megas Ducas, and the fifth is Oeconomus Megalus ; the others bear names like these. The circumference of the city of Constantinople is eighteen miles ; half of it is surrounded by the sea, and half by land, and it is situated upon two arms of the sea, one coming from the sea of Russia and one from the sea of Sepharad.

All sorts of merchants come here from the land of Babylon, from the land of Shinar, from Persia, Media, and all the sovereignty of the land of Egypt, from the land at Canaan and the Empire of Russia, from Hungaria, Patzinakia (Dacia), Khozaria, and the land of Lombardy and Sepharad. It is a busy city, and merchants come to it from every country by sea or land, and there is none like it in the world except Bagdad, the great city of Islam. In Constantinople is the church of Santa Sophia, and the seat of the Pope of the Greeks, since the Greeks do not obey the Pope of Rome. There are also churches according to the number of the days of the year. A quantity of wealth beyond telling is brought hither year by year as tribute from the two islands and the castles and villages which are there. And the like of this wealth is not to be found in any other church in the world. And in this church there are pillars of gold and silver and lamps of silver and gold more than a man can count. Close to the walls of the palace is also a place of amusement belonging to the king, which is called the Hippodrome, and every year on the anniversary of the birth of Jesus the king gives a great entertainment there. And in that place men from all the races of the world come before the king and queen with jugglery and without jugglery, and they introduce lions, leopards, bears, and wild asses, and they engage them in combat with one another ; and the same thing is done with birds. No entertainment like this is to be found in any other land.

This King Emanuel built a great palace for the seat of his government upon the sea-coaſt, in addition to the palaces which his fathers built, and he called its name Blachernae. He overlaid its columns and walls with gold and silver, and engraved thereon representations of the battles before his day and of his own combats. He also set up a throne of gold and of precious ſtones, and a golden crown was suspended by a gold chain over the throne so arranged that he might sit thereunder. It was inlaid with jewels of priceless value and at night time no lights were required, for every one could see by the light which the ſtones gave forth. Countless other buildings are to be met with in the city. From every part of the empire of Greece tribute is brought here every year, and they fill ſtrongholds with garments of silk, purple and gold. Like unto these ſtorehouses and this wealth, there is nothing in the whole world to be found. It is said that the tribute of the city amounts every year to 20,000 gold pieces, derived both from the rents of shops and markets and from the tribute of merchants who enter by sea or land.

The Greek inhabitants are very rich in gold and precious stones, and they go clothed in garments of silk with gold embroidery, and they ride horses, and look like princes. Indeed, the land is very rich in all cloth stuffs, and in bread, meat, and wine. Wealth like that of Constantinople is not to be found in the whole world. Here also are men learned in all the books of the Greeks, and they eat and drink, every man under his vine and his fig-tree.

They hire from amongst all nations warriors called Loazim (Barbarians) to fight with the Sultan Mas'ud, King of the Togarmim (Seljuks) who are called Turks ; for the natives are not warlike, but are as women who have no strength to fight.

No Jews live in the city, for they have been placed behind an inlet of the sea. An arm of the sea of Marmora shuts them in on the one side, and they are unable to go out except by way of the sea, when they want to do business with the inhabitants. In the Jewish quarter are about 2,000 Rabbanite Jews and about 500 Karaïtes, and a fence divides them. Amongst the scholars are several wise men, at their head being the chief rabbi, R. Abtalion, R. Obadiah, R. Aaron Bechor Shoro, R. Joseph Shir-Guru and R. Eliakim, the warden. And amongst them are artificers in silk and many rich merchants. No Jew there is allowed to ride on horseback. The one exception is R. Solomon Hamitsri, who is the king's physician, and through whom the Jews enjoy considerable alleviation of their oppression. For their condition is very low, and there is much hatred against them, which is fostered by the tanners, who throw out their dirty water in the streets before the doors of the Jewish houses and defile the Jews' quarter (the Ghetto). So the Greeks hate the Jews, good and bad alike, and subject them to great oppression, and beat them in the streets, and in every way treat them with rigour. Yet the Jews are rich and good, kindly and charitable, and bear their lot with cheerfulness. The district inhabited by the Jews is called Pera [1] . . . .

From the river Hiddekel (Tigris) at the foot of the mountains of Ararat it is a distance of four miles to the place where Noah's Ark rested, but Omar ben al-Khatab took the ark from the two mountains and made it into a mosque for the Mohammedans. Near the ark is the Synagogue of Ezra to this day, and on the ninth of Ab the Jews come hither from the city to pray. In the city of Geziret Omar are 4,000 Jews, at their head being R. Mubchar, R. Joseph, and R. Chiya.

Thence it is two days to Mosul, which is Assur the Great, and here dwell about 7,000 Jews, at their head being R. Zakkai the Nasi of the seed of David, and R. Joseph surnamed Burhan-al-mulk, the astronomer to the King Saif-ed-din, the brother of Nur-ed-din, King of Damascus. Mosul is the frontier town of the land of Persia. It is a very large and ancient city, situated on the River Hiddekel (Tigris) and is connected with Nineveh by means of a bridge. Nineveh is in ruins, but amid the ruins there are villages and hamlets, and the extent of the city may be determined by the walls, which extend forty parasangs to the city of Irbil (Arbela). The City of Nineveh is on the River Hiddekel. In the city of Assur (Mosul) is the synagogue of Obadiah, built by Jonah ; also the synagogue of Nahum the Elkoshite.

Thence it is a distance of three days to Rabbah, which is on the River Euphrates. Here there are about 2,000 Jews, at their head being R. Hezekiah, R. Tahor, and R. Isaac. It is a very fine city, large and fortified, and surrounded by gardens and plantations.

Thence it is a day's journey to Karkisiya, which is Carchemish, on the River Euphrates. Here there are about 500 Jews, at their head being R. Isaac and R. Elhanan. Thence it is two days to El-Anbar which is Pumbedita in Nehardea. Here reside 3,000 Jews and amongst them are learned men, at their head being the chief rabbi, R. Chen, R. Moses and R. Jehoiakim. Here are the graves of Rab, Jehuda and Samuel, and in front of the graves of each of them are the synagogues which they built in their lifetime. Here is also the grave of Bostanai the Nasi, the head of the Captivity, and of R. Nathan and Rab Nachman, the son of Papa.

Thence it takes five days to Hadara, where about 15,000 Jews dwell, at their head being R. Zaken, R. Jehosef and R. Nethanel.

Thence it takes two days to Okbara, the city which Jeconiah the King built, where there are about 10,000 Jews, and at their head are R. Chanan, R. Jabin and R. Ishmael.

Thence it is two days to Baghdad, the great city and the royal residence of the Caliph (Mustanjid) Al Abbasi of the family of Mohammed. He is at the head of the Mohammedan religion, and all the kings of Islam obey him ; he occupies a similar position to that held by the Pope over the Christians. He has a palace in Baghdad three miles in extent, wherein is a great park with all varieties of trees, fruit-bearing and otherwise, and all manner of animals. The whole is surrounded by a wall, and in the park there is a lake whose waters are fed by the River Hiddekel. Whenever the king desires to indulge in recreation and to rejoice and feast, his servants catch all manner of birds, game and flesh, and he goes to his palace with his counsellors and princes. There the great King, Al Abbasi the Caliph (Haft) holds his court, and he is kind unto Israel, and many belonging to the people of Israel are his attendants ; he knows all languages, and is well versed in the law of Israel. He reads and writes the holy language (Hebrew). He will not partake of anything unless he had earned it by the work of his own hands. He makes coverlets to which he attaches his seal ; his courtiers sell them in the market and the great ones of the land purchase them, and the proceeds thereof provide his sustenance. He is truthful and trusty, speaking peace to all men. The men of Islam see him but once in the year. The pilgrims that come from distant lands to go unto Mecca which is in the land Al Yemen (*sic*), are anxious to see his face, and they assemble before the palace exclaiming " Our Lord, light of Islam and glory of our Law, show us the effulgence of thy countenance ", but he pays no regard to their words. Then the princes who minister unto him say to him, " Our Lord, spread forth thy peace unto the men that have come from distant lands, who crave to abide under the shadow of thy graciousness," and thereupon he arises and lets down the hem of his robe from the window, and the pilgrims come and kiss it and a prince says unto them, " Go forth in peace, for our Master the Lord of Islam granteth peace to you." He is regarded by them as Mohammed, and they go to their houses rejoicing at the salutation which the prince has vouchsafed unto them and glad at heart that they have kissed his robe.

Each of his brothers and the members of his family has an abode in his palace, but they are all fettered in chains of iron and guards are placed over each of their houses so that they may not rise against the great Caliph. For once it happened to a predecessor that his brothers rose up against him and proclaimed one of themselves as Caliph ; then it was decreed that all the members of his family should be bound, that they might not rise up against the ruling Caliph. Each one of them resides in his palace in great splendour, and they own villages and towns, and their stewards bring them the tribute thereof, and they eat and drink and rejoice all the days of their life. Within the domains of the palace of the Caliph there are great buildings of marble and columns of silver and gold, and carvings upon rare stones are fixed in the walls. In the Caliph's palace are great riches and towers filled with gold, silken garments and all precious stones. He does not issue forth from his palace save once in the year, at the feast which the Muhammadans call El-id-bed (*sic*) Ramazan, and they come from distant lands that day to see him. He rides on a mule and is attired in the royal robes of gold and silver and fine linen ; on his head is a turban adorned with precious stones of priceless value, and over the turban is a black shawl as a sign of his modesty, implying that all this glory will be covered by darkness on the day of his death. He is accompanied by all the nobles of Islam dressed in fine garments and riding on horses, the princes of Arabia, the princes of Togarma and Daylam (Gilan) and the princes of Persia, Media and Ghuzz, and the princes of the land of Tibet, which is three months' journey distant, and westward of which lies the land of Samarkand. He proceeds from his palace to the great mosque of Islam which is by the Basrah Gate. Along the road the walls are adorned with silk and purple, and the inhabitants receive him with all kinds of song and exultation, and they dance before the great king which is styled the Caliph. They salute him with a loud voice and say " Peace unto thee, our Lord the King and Light of Islam ". He kisses his robe and stretching forth the hem thereof he salutes them. Then he proceeds to the court of the mosque, mounts a wooden pulpit, and expounds to them their law. Then the learned ones of Islam arise and pray for him and extol his greatness and his graciousness, to which they all respond. Afterwards he gives them his blessing, and they bring before him a camel which he slays, and this is their passover-sacrifice. He gives thereof unto the princes and they distribute it to all, so that they may taste of the sacrifice brought by their king ; and they all rejoice. Afterwards he leaves the mosque and returns alone to his palace by way of the river Hiddekel, and the grandees of Islam accompany him in ships on the river until he enters his palace. He does not return the way he came ; and the road which he takes along the river-side is watched all the year through so that no man shall tread in his footsteps. He does not leave the palace again for a whole year. He is a benevolent man.

He built, on the other side of the river, on the banks of an arm of the Euphrates which there borders the city, a hospital consisting of blocks of houses and hospices for the sick poor who come to be healed. Here there are about sixty physicians' stores which are provided from the Caliph's house with drugs and whatever else may be required. Every sick man who comes is maintained at the Caliph's expense and is medically treated. Here is a building which is called Dar-al-Maristan, where they keep charge of the demented people who have become insane in the towns through the great heat in the summer, and they chain each of them in iron chains until their reason becomes restored to them in the winter-time. Whilst they abide there, they are provided with food from the house of the Caliph, and when their reason is restored they are dismissed and each one of them goes to his house and his home. Money is given to those that have stayed in the hospices on their return to their homes. Every month the officers of the Caliph inquire and investigate whether they have regained their reason, in which case they are discharged. All

this the Caliph does out of charity to those that come
to the city of Baghdad, whether they be sick or insane.
The Caliph is a righteous man, and all his actions
are for good.

In Baghdad there are about 40,000 Jews and they
dwell in security, prosperity and honour under the
great Caliph, and amongst them are great sages,
the heads of Academies engaged in the study of the
law. In this city there are ten Academies. At the
head of the great Academy is the chief rabbi, R. Samuel,
the son of Eli. He is the head of the Academy Gaon
Jacob. He is a Levite, and traces his pedigree back
to Moses our teacher. The head of the second
Academy is R. Hanania his brother, warden of the
Levites ; R. Daniel is the head of the third Academy ;
R. Eleazar the scholar is the head of the fourth
Academy ; and R. Eleazar, the son of Zemach, is
the head of the Order, and his pedigree reaches to
Samuel the prophet, the Korahite. He and his brethren
know how to chant the melodies as did the singers
at the time when the Temple was standing. He is
head of the fifth Academy. R. Chisdai, the glory
of the scholars, is head of the sixth Academy.
R. Haggai is head of the seventh Academy. R. Ezra
is the head of the eighth Academy. R. Abraham,
who is called Abu Tahir, is the head of the ninth
Academy. R. Zakkai, the son of Bostanai the Nasi,
is the head of the Sium (i.e. the last or tenth Academy).
These are the ten Batlanim, and they do not engage
in any other work than communal administration ;
and all the days of the week they judge the Jews
their countrymen, except on the second day of the
week, when they all appear before the Chief Rabbi
Samuel, the head of the Yeshiba Gaon Jacob, who in
conjunction with the other " Batlanim " judges all
those that appear before him. And at the head of
them all is Daniel the son of Hisdai, who is styled

" Our Lord the Head of the Captivity of all Israel ".
He possesses a book of pedigrees going back as far
as David, King of Israel. The Jews call him " Our
Lord, Head of the Captivity ", and the Mohammedans
call him " Saidna ben Daud " and he has been
invested with authority over all the congregations of
Israel at the hands of the Emir al Muminin, the Lord
of Islam. For thus Mohammed commanded concerning him and his descendants ; and he granted
him a seal of office over all the congregations that
dwell under his rule, and ordered that every one,
whether Mohammedan or Jew, or belonging to any
other nation in his dominion, should rise up before
him (the Exilarch) and salute him, and that any one
who should refuse to rise up should receive one
hundred stripes.

And every fifth day, when he goes to pay a visit
to the great Caliph, horsemen, Gentiles as well as
Jews, escort him, and heralds proclaim in advance,
" Make way before our Lord, the son of David,
as is due unto him ", the Arabic words being *'Amilu
tarik li Saidna ben Daud*. He is mounted on a horse,
and is attired in robes of silk and embroidery with a
large turban on his head, and from the turban is
suspended a long white cloth adorned with a chain
upon which the cipher of Mohammed is engraved.
Then he appears before the Caliph and kisses his hand
and the Caliph rises and places him on a throne which
Mohammed had ordered to be made for him, and all
the Mohammedan princes who attend the court of the
Caliph rise up before him. And the Head of the
Captivity is seated on his throne opposite to the
Caliph, in compliance with the command of
Mohammed to give effect to what is written in the
law, " The sceptre shall not depart from Judah nor
a law-giver from between his feet until he come to
Shiloh : and to him shall the gathering of the people

be ". The authority of the Head of the Captivity extends over all the communities of Shinar, Persia, Khorasan and Sheba which is El-Yemen, and Diyar Kalach (Bekr) and the land of Aram Naharaim (Mesopotamia) and over the dwellers in the mountains of Ararat and the land of the Alani which is a country surrounded by mountains and has no outlet except by the iron gates which Alexander made, but which were afterwards broken. Here dwell the people called Alani. His authority extends also over the land of Siberia and the communities in the land of the Togarmim unto the mountains of Asveh and the land of Gurgan, the inhabitants of which are called Gurganim (Georgians) who dwell by the River Gihon, and these are the Girgashites who follow the Christian religion. Further it extends to the gates of Samarkand, the land of Tibet, and the land of India. In respect of all these countries the Head of the Captivity gives the communities power to appoint Rabbis and Ministers who come unto him to be consecrated and to receive his authority. They bring him offerings and gifts from the ends of the earth. He owns hospices, gardens and plantations in Babylon, and much land inherited from his fathers, and no one can take his possessions from him by force. He has a fixed weekly revenue arising from the hospices of the Jews, the markets and the merchants, apart from that which is brought to him from far-off lands. The man is very rich and wise in the Scriptures as well as in the Talmud, and many Israelites dine at his table every day." . . .

In Nihawand, there reside 4,000 Israelites. Thence it is four days to the land of the Mulahid. Here live a people who do not profess the Muhammadan religion, but live on high mountains, and worship the Old Man of the land of the Hashishim. And among them there are four communities of Israel who go forth with them in war time. They are not under the rule of the king of Persia, but reside in the high mountains, and descend from these mountains to pillage and to capture booty, and then retire to the mountains, and none can overcome them. There are learned men amongst the Jews of their land. These Jews are under the authority of the Head of the Captivity in Babylon. Thence it is five days to Amadia,[2] where there are about 25,000 Israelites. This is the first of those communities that dwell in the mountains of Chafton, where there are more than 100 Jewish communities. Here is the commencement of the land of Media. These Jews belong to the first captivity which King Shalmanezar led away ; and they speak the language in which the Targum is written. Amongst them are learned men. The communities reach from the province of Amadia unto the province of Gilan, twenty-five days distant, on the border of the kingdom of Persia. They are under the authority of the king of Persia and he raises a tribute from them through the hands of his officer, and the tribute which they pay every year by way of poll tax is one gold amir, which is equivalent to one and one-third maravedi. (This tax has to be paid by all males in the land of Islam who are over the age of fifteen.) At this place (Amadia) there arose this day ten years ago, a man named David Alroy of the city of Amadia. He studied under Chisdai, the Head of Captivity, and under the Head of the Academy Gaon Jacob, in the city of Bagdad, and he was well versed in the Law of Israel, in the Halachah, as well as in the Talmud, and in all the wisdom of the Mohammedans, also in secular literature and in the writings of magicians and soothsayers. He conceived the idea of rebelling against the king of Persia, and of collecting the Jews who live in the mountains of Chafton to go forth and to fight against all the nations, and to march and capture Jerusalem. He showed signs by pretended miracles to the Jews, and said, " The Holy One, blessed be He, sent me to capture Jerusalem, and to free you from the yoke of the Gentiles." And the Jews believed in him and called him their Messiah. When the King of Persia heard of it he sent for him to come and speak with him. Alroy went to him without fear, and when he had audience of the king, the latter asked him " Art thou the king of the Jews ? " He answered, " I am." Then the king was wrath and commanded that he should be seized and placed in the prison of the king, the place where the king's prisoners were bound unto the day of their death, in the city of Tabariſtan, which is on the large River Gozan. At the end of three days, whilſt the king was sitting and deliberating with his princes concerning the Jews who had rebelled, David suddenly ſtood before them. He had escaped from the prison without the knowledge of any man. And when the king saw him he said to him, " Who brought thee hither, and who has released thee ? " " My own wisdom and skill," answered the other, " for I am not afraid of thee, nor of any of thy servants." The king forthwith loudly bade his servants to seize him, but they answered, " We cannot see any man, although our ears hear him." Then the king and all his princes marvelled at his subtlety ; but he said to the king, " I will go my way," so he went forth. And the king went after him ; and the princes and the servants followed their king until they came to the river-side. Then Alroy took off his mantle and spread it on the face of the water to cross thereon. When the servants of the king saw that he crossed the water on his mantle, they pursued him in small boats, wishing to bring him back, but they were unable, and they said, " There is no wizard like this in the whole world." That self-same day he went a journey of ten days to the city of Amadia by the strength of the ineffable Name, and he told the Jews all that had befallen him, and they were astonished at his wisdom. After that the king of Persia sent word to the Emir Al-Muminin, the Caliph or the Muhammadans at Baghdad, urging him to warn the Head of the Exile, and the Head of the Academy Gaon Jacob, to restrain David Alroy from executing his designs. And he threatened that he would otherwise slay all the Jews in his Empire. Then all the congregations of the land of Persia were in great trouble. And the Head of the Captivity, and the Head of the Academy Gaon Jacob, sent to Alroy saying " The time of redemption is not yet arrived ; we have not yet seen the signs thereof ; for by strength shall no man prevail. Now our mandate is, that thou cease from these designs, or thou shalt surely be excommunicated from all Israel." And they sent unto Zakkai the Nasi, in the land of Assur (Mosul), and unto R. Joseph Burhan-al-Mulk the astronomer there, bidding them to send on the letter to Alroy, and, furthermore, they themselves wrote to him to warn him, but he would not accept the warning. Then there arose a king of the name of Saif-ed-din, the king of the Togarmin, and a vassal of the King of Persia, who sent to the father-in-law of David Alroy and gave him a bribe of 10,000 gold pieces to slay Alroy in secret. So he went to Alroy's house and slew him whilst he was asleep on his bed. Thus were his plans frustrated. Then the king of Persia went forth against the Jews that lived in the mountains ; and they sent to the Head of the Captivity to come to their assistance and to appease the King. He was eventually appeased by a gift of 100 talents of gold, which they gave him, and the land was at peace thereafter.

From this mountain it is a journey of twenty days to Hamadan, which is the great city of Media, where there are 30,000 Israelites. In front of a certain synagogue there are buried Mordecai and Esther. From thence (Hamadan) it takes four days to Tabaristan, which is situated on the River Gozan. Some (four) thousand Jews live there. Thence it is seven days to Ispahan, the great city and the royal residence. It is twelve miles in circumference and about 15,000 Israelites reside there. The Chief Rabbi is Sar Shalom, who has been appointed by the Head of the Captivity to have jurisdiction over all the Rabbis that are in the kingdom of Persia. Four days onward is Shiraz, which is the city of Fars, and 10,000 Jews live there. Thence it is seven days to Ghaznah [3] the great city on the River Gozan, where there are about 80,000 Israelites. It is a city of commercial importance ; people of all countries and tongues come hither with their wares. The land is extensive.

Thence it is five days to Samarkand, which is the great city of the confines of Persia. In it live some 50,000 Israelites, and R. Obadiah the Nasi is their appointed head. Among them are wise and very rich men.

Thence it is four days' journey to Tibet, the country in which forests the musk is found.

Thence it takes twenty-eight days to the mountains of Nishapur [4] by the River Gozan. And there are men of Israel in the land of Persia who say that in the mountains of Nishapur four of the tribes of Israel dwell, namely, the tribe of Dan, the tribe of Zebulun, the tribe of Asher, and the tribe of Naphtali, who were included in the first captivity of Shalmaneser, king of Assyria, as it is written (2 Kings, xviii, 11) : " And he put them in Halah and in Habor by the River of Gozan and in the cities of the Medes."

The extent of their land is twenty days' journey, and they have cities and large villages in the mountains ; the River Gozan forms the boundary on the one side. They are not under the rule of the Gentiles, but they have a prince of their own, whose name is R. Joseph Amarkala the Levite. There are scholars among them. And they sow and reap and go forth to war as far as the land of Cush by way of the desert.

They are in league with the Kuffur at-Turk, who worship the wind and live in the wilderness, and who do not eat bread, nor drink wine, but live on raw, uncooked meat. They have no noses, and in lieu thereof they have two small holes through which they breathe. They eat animals both clean and unclean, and they are very friendly towards the Israelites. Fifteen years ago they overran the country of Persia with a large army and took the city of Rayy,[5] they smote it with the edge of the sword, took all the spoil thereof, and returned by way of the wilderness. Such an invasion had not been known in the land of Persia for many years. When the King of Persia heard thereof his anger was kindled against them, and he said, " Not in my days nor in the days of my fathers did an army sally forth from this wilderness. Now I will go and cut off their name from the earth." A proclamation was made throughout his Empire and he assembled all his armies ; and he sought a guide who might show him the way to their encampment. And a certain man said that he would show him the way, as he was one of them. And the king promised that he would enrich him if he did so. And the king asked him as to what provisions they would require for the march through the wilderness. And he replied, " Take with you bread and wine for fifteen days, for you will find no sustenance by the way till you have reached their land." And they did so, and marched through the wilderness for fifteen days, but they found nothing at all. And their food began to give out, so that man and beast were dying of hunger and thirst. Then the king called the guide, and said to him, " Where is your promise to us that you would find our adversaries ? " To which the other replied, " I have mistaken the way." And the king was wroth, and commanded that his head should be struck off. And the king further gave orders throughout the camp that every man who had any food should divide it with his neighbour. And they consumed everything they had, including their beasts. And after a further thirteen days' march they reached the mountains of Nishapur, where Jews lived. They came there on the Sabbath and encamped in the gardens and plantations and by the springs of water which are by the side of the River Gozan. Now it was the time of the ripening of the fruit, and they ate and consumed everything. No man came forth to them, but on the mountains they saw cities and many towers. Then the king commanded two of his servants to go and inquire of the people who lived in the mountains, and to cross the river either in boats or by swimming. So they searched and found a large bridge, on which there were three towers, but the gate of the bridge was locked. And on the other side of the bridge was a great city. Then they shouted in front of the bridge till a man came forth and asked them what they wanted and who they were. But they did not understand him till an interpreter came who understood their language. And when he asked them, they said, " We are the servants of the king of Persia, and we have come to ask who you are, and whom you serve." To which the other replied : " We are Jews ; we have no king and no Gentile prince, but a Jewish prince rules over us." They then questioned him with regard to the infidels, the

sons of Ghuzz of the Kuffur at-Turk, and he answered,
" Truly they are in league with us, and he who seeks
to do them harm seeks our harm." Then they went
their way and told the king of Persia, who was much
alarmed. And on a certain day the Jews asked him
to join combat with them, but he answered, " I am
not come to fight you, but the Kuffur at-Turk, my
enemy, and if you fight against me I will be avenged
on you by killing all the Jews in my Empire ; I
know that you are stronger than I am in this place,
and my army has come out of this great wilderness
starving and athirst. Deal kindly with me and do
not fight against me, but leave me to engage with
the Kuffur at-Turk, my enemy, and sell me also the
provisions which I require for myself and my army."
The Jews then took counsel together, and resolved
to propitiate the king on account of the Jews who
were in exile in his Empire. Then the king entered
their land with his army and stayed there fifteen
days. And they showed him much honour, and also
sent a dispatch to the Kuffur-at-Turk, their allies,
reporting the matter to them. Thereupon the latter
occupied the mountain passes in force with a large
army composed of all those who dwelt in that desert,
and when the king of Persia went forth to fight
with them they placed themselves in battle array
against him. The Kuffur-at-Turk army was victorious
and slew many of the Persian host, and the king of
Persia fled with only a few followers to his own country.

Now a horseman, one of the servants of the King
of Persia, enticed a Jew, whose name was R.
Moses, to come with him, and when he came to the
land of Persia this horseman made the Jew his slave.
One day the archers came before the king to give
a display of their skill, and no one among them could
be found to draw the bow like this R. Moses.
Then the king inquired of him, by means of an

interpreter who knew his language, and he related all that the horseman had done to him. Thereupon the king at once granted him his liberty, had him clad in robes of silk, gave him gifts, and said to him, " If thou wilt embrace our religion I will make thee a rich man and steward of my house," but he answered, " My lord, I cannot do this thing." Then the king took him and placed him in the house of the Chief Rabbi of the Ispahan community, Sar Shalom, who gave him his daughter to wife. This same R. Moses told me all these things.

Thence one returns to the land of Khuzistan which is by the River Tigris, and one goes down the river which falls into the Indian Ocean unto an island called Kish. It is a six days' journey to reach this island. The inhabitants neither sow nor reap. They possess only one well, and there is no stream in the whole island, but they drink rain-water. The merchants who come from India and the islands encamp there with their wares. Moreover, men from Shinar, El-Yemen, and Persia bring hither all sorts of silk, purple and flax, cotton, hemp, worked wool, wheat, barley, millet, rye, and all sorts of food, and lentils of every description, and they trade with one another, whilst the men from India bring great quantities of spices thither. The islanders act as middlemen, and earn their livelihood thereby. There are about 500 Jews there.

Thence it is ten days' journey by sea to el-Katif, near Bahrein, where there are about 5,000 Jews. Here the bdellium [6] is to be found. On the 24th of Nisan rain falls upon the water, upon the surface of which certain small sea-animals float which drink in the rain and then shut themselves up and sink to the bottom. And about the middle of Tishri men descend to the bed of the sea by ropes and collect these shell-fish, then split them open and extract the pearls. This pearl-fishery belongs to the King of the country, but is controlled by a Jewish official.

Thence it is a seven days' journey to Khulam (Quilon) which is the beginning of the country of the Sun-worshippers. These are the sons of Cush who read the stars, and are all black in colour. They are honest in commerce. When merchants come to them from distant lands and enter the harbour three of the King's secretaries go down to them and record their names and then bring them before the King, whereupon the King makes himself responsible even for their property which they leave in the open unprotected. There is an official who sits in his office, and the owner of any lost property has only to describe it to him when he hands it back. This custom prevails in all that country. From Passover to New Year, that is, all during the summer, no man can go out of his house because of the sun, for the heat in that country is intense, and from the third hour of the day onward everybody remains in his house till the evening. Then they go forth and kindle lights in all the market places and all the streets, and then do their work and business at night-time. For they have to turn night into day in consequence of the great heat of the sun. Pepper is found there. They plant the trees thereof in the fields, and each man of the city knows his own plantation. The trees are small, and the pepper is as white as snow. And when they have collected it, they place it in saucepans and pour boiling water over it, so that it may become strong. They then take it out of the water and dry it in the sun, and it turns black. Calamus and ginger and many other kinds of spice are found in this land.

The people of this country do not bury their dead, but embalm them by means of various spices, after which they place them on chairs and cover them with fine linen. And each family has a house where it

preserves the embalmed remains of its ancestors
and relations. The flesh hardens on the bones, and
the embalmed bodies look like living beings, so that
every man can recognize his parents and the members
of his family for many years. They worship the
sun, and they have high places everywhere outside
the city at a distance of about half a mile. And every
morning they run forth to greet the sun, for on every
high place a solar disc is made of cunning workmanship, and as the sun rises the disc rotates with
thundering noise, and all, both men and women,
offer incense to the sun with censers in their hands.
Such are their superstitious practices. And throughout the island, including all the towns there, live
several thousand Israelites. The inhabitants are
all black, and the Jews also. The latter are good
and benevolent. They know the law of Moses and
the prophets, and to a small extent the Talmud and
Halacha.

Thence it is twenty-three days by sea to Ibrig,[7]
and the inhabitants are fire-worshippers and are
called Duchbin. Among them are about 3,000
Jews, and these Duchbins have priests in their several
temples who are great wizards in all manner of witch-
craft, and there are none like them in all the earth.
In front of the high place of their temple there is
a deep trench, where they keep a great fire alight
all the year, and they call it the deity. And they cause
their sons and daughters to pass through the fire,
and even their dead they throw into it. Some of the
great men of the country make a vow to die by fire."

.   .   .   .   .   .

"Thence (from Ibrig) to cross over to the land of
Zin (China) is a voyage of forty days. Zin is in the
uttermost East, and some say that there is the Sea
of Nikpa (Ning-po ?), where the star Orion pre-
dominates and stormy winds prevail. At times the

helmsman cannot govern his ship, as a fierce wind drives her into this Sea of Nikpa, where she cannot move from her place ; and the crew have to remain where they are till their stores of food are exhausted and then they die. In this way many a ship has been lost, but men eventually discovered a device by which to escape from this evil place. The crew provide themselves with hides of oxen. And when this evil wind blows which drives them into the Sea of Nikpa they wrap themselves up in the skins, which they make waterproof, and, armed with knives, plunge into the sea. A great bird, called the griffin, spies them out, and in the belief that the sailor is an animal, the griffin seizes hold of him, brings him to dry land, and puts him down on a mountain or in a hollow in order to devour him. The man then quickly thrusts at the bird with a knife and slays him. Then the man issues forth from the skin and walks till he comes to an inhabited place. And in this manner many a man escapes.

Thence to Al-Gingaleh is a voyage of fifteen days, and about 1,000 Israelites dwell there. Thence by sea to Chulan is seven days, but no Jews live there. From there it is twelve days to Zebid, where there are a few Jews. From there it is eight days' journey to India, which is on the mainland, called the land of Aden, and this is the Eden which is in Thelasar. The country is mountainous. There are many Israelites there, and they are not under the yoke of the Gentiles, but possess cities and castles on the summits of the mountains, from which they make descents into the plain-country called Lybia,[8] which is a Christian Empire. These are the Lybians of the land of Lybia with whom the Jews are at war. The Jews take spoil and booty and retreat to the mountains, and no man can prevail against them. Many of these Jews of the land of Aden come to Persia and Egypt.

Thence to the land of Assuan is a journey of twenty days through the desert. This is Seba on the River Pishon (Nile) which descends from the land of Cush. And some of these sons of Cush have a king whom they call the Sultan Al-Habash. There is a people among them who, like animals, eat of the herbs that grow on the banks of the Nile and in the fields. They go about naked, and have not the intelligence of ordinary men. They cohabit with their sisters and anyone they find. The climate is very hot. When the men of Assuan make a raid into their land, they take with them bread and wheat, dry grapes and figs, and throw the food to these people, who run after it. Thus they bring many of them back prisoners, and sell them in the land of Egypt and in the surrounding countries. And these are the black slaves, the sons of Ham.

From Assuan it is a distance of twelve days to Heluan where there are about 300 Jews. Thence people travel in caravans a journey of fifty days through the great desert called Sahara, to the land of Zawilah, which is Havilah in the land of Gana (Fezzan south of Tripoli). In this desert there are mountains of sand, and when the wind rises it covers the caravans with the sand and many die from suffocation. Those that escape bring back with them copper, wheat, fruit, all manner of lentils, and salt. And from thence they bring gold, and all kinds of jewels. This is in the land of Cush, which is called Al-Habash, on the western confines. From Heluan it is thirteen days' journey to Kutz, which is Kus, and this is the commencement of the land of Egypt. At Kutz there are 300 Jews. Thence it is 300 miles to Fayyum, which is Pithom, where there are 200 Jews ; and unto this day one can see ruins of the buildings which our forefathers erected there.

Thence to Mizraim is a journey of four days.

JEWISH TRAVELLERS

This Mizraim is the great city situated on the banks of the Nile, which is Pishon or Al-Nil. The number of Jewish inhabitants is about 7,000. Two large synagogues are there, one belonging to the men of the land of Israel and one belonging to the men of the land of Babylon. The synagogue of the men of the land of Israel is called Kenisat-al-Shamiyyin and the synagogue of the men of Babylon is called Kenisat-al-Irakiyyin. Their usage with regard to the portions and sections of the Law is not alike ; for the men of Babylon are accustomed to read a portion every week, as is done in Spain, and is our custom, and to finish the Law each year ; whilst the men of Palestine do not do so, but divide each portion into three sections and finish the Law at the end of three years. The two communities, however, have an established custom to unite and pray together on the day of the Rejoicing of the Law and on the day of the Giving of the Law. Among the Jews is Nethanel, the Prince of Princes and the head of the Academy, who is the head of all the congregations in Egypt ; he appoints Rabbis and officials, and is attached to the court of the great King, who lives in his palace of Zoan el-Medina, which is the royal city for the Arabs. All his subjects are called " Alawiyyim ", because they rose up against the Emir al Muminin al Abbasi (the Abbaside Caliph), who resides in Bagdad. And between the two parties there is a lasting feud, for the former have set up a rival throne in Zoan (Egypt).

Twice in the year the Egyptian monarch goes forth, once on the occasion of the great festival and again when the River Nile rises. Zoan is surrounded by a wall, but Mizraim has no wall, for the river encompasses it on one side. It is a great city and it has market places as well as inns in great number. The Jews that dwell there are very rich. No rain falls, neither is ice or snow ever seen. The climate is very hot.

The River Nile rises once a year, in the month of Ellul ; it covers all the land and irrigates it to a distance of fifteen days' journey. The waters remain upon the surface of the land during the months of Ellul and Tishri and irrigate and fertilize it.

The inhabitants have a pillar of marble, erected with much skill, in order to ascertain the extent of the rise of the Nile. It stands in the front of an island in the midst of the water and is twelve cubits high. When the Nile rises and covers the column they know that the river has risen and has covered the land for a distance of fifteen days' journey to its full extent. If only half the column is covered, the water only covers half the extent of the land. And day by day an officer takes a measurement on the column and makes proclamation thereof in Zoan and in the city of Mizraim.

RABBI PETACHIA OF RATISBON
(1170–87)

R. Petachia, son of R. Jacob, the brother of the Tosaphiſt, R. Isaac Halavan, and of R. Nachman of Ratisbon, was born there in the firſt half of the twelfth century. After settling for some years at Prague, he ſtarted thence on his travels through Poland, Kief, Crimea, Tartary, Armenia, Media, Persia, Iraq, Syria, Paleſtine, and Greece. His travels were only ten or fifteen years after those of Benjamin of Tudela and their accounts supplement each other. Petachia's references to the Karaïtes were the sole source of information about them until the ſtudies of Professor Trigland at the beginning of the eighteenth century.

Petachia muſt have been in Damascus between 1174 and 1187, because he reached that city after Saladin had captured Damascus and while the Crusaders were ſtill in Jerusalem. The account is described as a " *Sibbub* " or circular voyage. It is not Petachia's own account but a narrative put together from his notes by a contemporary, Rabbi Judah the Pious bar Samuel, who seems to have accompanied him on part of his way.

The text is based upon a manuscript which was printed in Prague in 1595 and translated into German at Altdorf in 1687, and into Latin by Wagenseil in the same year at Strasburg, into French by Carmoly in Paris in 1831, into English by Dr. Benisch in London in 1856 (with a second edition in 1861), and edited by Dr. Grünhut in Jerusalem.

THESE are the travels undertaken by Rabbi Petachia, who travelled through many lands. He set out from Prague, which is in Bohemia, going to Poland, and from Poland to Kiew in Russia. From Russia he went for six days on the River Dnieper. On the other side of the river he commenced his travels in the land of Kedar.[1] There they have no ships, but sew together ten extended horse hides, with a

64

thong round the border ; they then seat themselves
on the hides, placing thereon also the wagons and
all the luggage. They then tie the thong which is
on the border of the hides to the tails of the horses,
who start swimming, and thus they pass over the
water. They eat no bread in the land of Kedar,
but rice and millet boiled in milk, as well as milk
and cheese. They also put pieces of flesh under the
saddle of a horse, which they ride and, urging on
the animal, cause it to sweat. The flesh getting warm,
they eat it. They only travel in the land of Kedar
under escort. This is the manner in which the sons
of Kedar pledge their faith to each other. One man
thrusts a needle into his finger and invites the intended
companion of his journey to swallow the blood of
the wounded finger. He and that other person
become, as it were, the same blood and flesh. They
have another fashion of entering into this bond.
They fill a vessel of cast copper of the shape of a
human face and the traveller and his escort drink
thereout, after which they never prove faithless.
They have no king, but only princes and nobles.

Rabbi Petachia passed through the whole length
of the land of Kedar in sixteen days. The inhabitants
live in tents ; they are far-sighted and have beautiful
eyes, because they eat no salt and live among fragrant
plants. They are good archers, bringing down birds
whilst on the wing. They perceive and recognize
(objects) at more than a day's distance. There are
no mountains in their country, but all is level. And
a day's journey behind the land of Kedar extends
a gulf,[2] intervening between the land of Kedar and
the land of Khozaria.[3] There it is customary for women
the whole day and night to bemoan and lament their
deceased fathers and mothers. This they continue
until any of their sons or daughters or other members
of the family die, and the last (survivors) lament those

that preceded them in death. They teach their daughters lamentation. In the night they groan and howl. The dogs also whine and bark at their voice. The rabbi then travelled about eight days, and came where, at the extremity of the land of Khozaria, seventeen rivers [4] surrounding it unite, and whoever wishes to undertake a distant journey repairs hither. There is a sea there on one side, from which there arises a great stench,[5] whilst on the other side there is a sea which does not emit any offensive smell. There is about a day's journey between the two seas. If any individual passed the stinking sea he would die immediately. When the wind blows from the stinking sea to that not emitting any offensive smell many die. People only go there when the wind does not blow from it.

Rabbi Petachia passed into the land of Togarma.[6] From thence, and further on, people believed in the law of Mahomet. From Togarma he entered the country of Ararat. In eight days he journeyed as far as Nisibis, leaving the high mountains of Ararat at the right.

In the land of Kedar there are no Jews but only Karaïtes.[7] And Rabbi Petachia asked them : " Why do you not believe in the words of the sages ? " They replied : " Because our fathers did not teach them to us." On the eve of the Sabbath they cut all the bread to be eaten on the Sabbath. They eat in the dark and sit the whole day on one spot. Their prayers consist only of psalms. And when Rabbi Petachia imparted to them our ritual and prayer after meals they were pleased. They also said : " We have never heard of the Talmud."

In the land of Ararat he travelled in the mountains of Ararat as far as Nisibis and the city of the Hisn Kana [?] (that is, Strength of a Great Rock). At the extremity of the mountains of Ararat he travelled two days to the opposite side. At Nisibis there is a large congregation, also the synagogue of Rabbi Judah, son of Bethera, and two synagogues built by Ezra the Scribe. In one of them is a red stone, fixed in the wall, which Ezra had brought with him and which had been one of the stones of the Temple. From Nisibis and further extends the land of Assur. Khozaria has a language of its own ; Togarma has a language of its own (they pay tribute to the King of Greece [9]) ; and Kedar has a language of its own.

From Nisibis the rabbi journeyed in three days to New Nineveh.[10] The river Tigris flows before Nineveh. On the other side of the river he went a journey of three days more in a different direction to old Nineveh, which is desolate. The whole land of Nineveh is black as pitch. The site of Nineveh proper, where the city was, is overthrown like Sodom. There is there neither herb nor any vegetation. New Nineveh, opposite, is on the other side of the river. At New Nineveh is a large congregation numbering more than six thousand souls. It has two princes. The name of one is Rabbi David and of the other Rabbi Samuel. They are sons of two brothers and of the seed of King David. Everyone pays there annually a gold florin ; of that coming from the Jews half belongs to the king or sultan (whom they do not call king, but sultan), who is subject to the King of Babel (Caliph of Baghdad). The other half belongs to the princes ; they have fields and vineyards.

In those countries there are no precentors, nor have they any in the lands of Persia, Media, and Damascus. But among the households of the princes there are many scholars. Sometimes they call upon this man, and sometimes upon that, to recite the prayers. The prince has also a prison wherein he locks up the wicked. If a Gentile and a Jew have a dispute, he imprisons the guilty party whether Jew or Muhammadan.

R. Petachia fell sick at Nineveh, and the king's physicians said that he would not live. It is the custom there that when a Jew on his travels dies the sultan takes half of his property ; and because R. Petachia was dressed in beautiful clothes they thought that he was rich ; therefore the scribes of the sultan came thither to take possession of his property should he die. But R. Petachia gave directions, sick as he was, to carry him over the river Tigris. The river is broad and not crossed over in boats, for the current is swift and impetuous and would upset the boat. Therefore, they make rafts of reeds, which we call *floss*, upon which they put man and luggage. The waters being healing, he recovered immediately.

At Nineveh there was an elephant. Its head is not at all protruding. It is big, eats about two wagon loads of straw at one time ; its mouth is in its breast, and when it wants to eat it protrudes its lip (trunk) about two cubits, takes up with it the straw, and puts it into its mouth. When the sultan condemns anybody to death they say to the elephant : this person is guilty. It then seizes him with its lip, casts him aloft, and kills him. Whatever a human being does with his hand it does with its lip ; this is exceedingly strange and marvellous. Upon the elephant's back is set a structure like a citadel (howdah), within which there are twelve armed warriors ; when the beast stretches forth its lip they climb up, using it as a bridge.

At Nineveh there was an astrologer whose name was R. Solomon. There among all the sages in Nineveh, and the land of Assur, none as expert in the planets as he. R. Petachia asked him when Messiah would come. He replied, I have seen this often distinctly in the planets. But Rabbi Judah the Pious would not write it down lest he should be suspected of being a believer in the words of Rabbi Solomon.

The rabbi then embarked on the Tigris and went with the current of the river, in fifteen days, to the garden of the head of the academy [11] in Babel. The journey (would otherwise) take one month. From Nineveh, and further on, there are congregations in every city and village. He came to the garden of the head of the academy. In the garden there are all kinds of fruit. The garden is very large and there are mandrakes in it. These have the face of a human being and their foliage is broad. From thence he travelled in one day to Bagdad, in Babylon. Nobody ascends the River Tigris because its waters are swift and impetuous, but they employ camels and mules on dry land, tying inflated skins on the backs of the camels.

Baghdad is a metropolis. It is the seat of the Caliph or sultan. This is the great king [12] who rules and governs nations. Baghdad is very large, more than a day's journey from end to end. To go round it is more than three days' journey. In the city of Baghdad there are a thousand Jews. They walk about wrapped in cloth. Nobody there looks upon any woman, nor does anybody go into the house of his friend lest he should see the wife of that neighbour, who would immediately say unto him : insolent man, wherefor art thou come ? But he knocks with a tin (knocker), when the other comes forth and speaks to him. They all walk about wrapped in their praying scarves of wool with fringes. The head of the academy at Baghdad is R. Samuel, the Levite, son of Eli, head of the academy. He is the superior, full of wisdom both in the written and oral law and in all the wisdom of Egypt. Nothing is hidden from him. He knows the holy names, [13] and is profoundly versed in the Talmud. There is no one so ignorant in the whole of Babylon, Assyria, Media, and Persia, but knows the twenty-four books,[14] punctuation, grammar, the superfluous and omitted letters, for the preceptor does not recite the scripture lesson, but he that is called up to the scroll of the law recites it himself.[14] The head of the academy has about two thousand disciples at once, and more than five hundred sit round him, and they are all well-informed. But before they are ripe for the academy, they study in the city under other teachers, and when ripe they are brought before the head of the academy. The *Rosh Gola* (Exilarch) is Rabbi Eleazar, and under him is the head of the academy. The head of the academy occupies a large house, which is covered with tapestry ; he himself is clothed in garments adorned with gold. He is seated above and the disciples sit on the ground. He expounds to the interpreter, and the interpreter to the disciples. The disciples address their queries to the interpreter, and if the interpreter does not know the answer he addresses himself to the head of the academy. An interpreter expounds Tractate of the Talmud on one side, and another interpreter expounds another Tractate on the other side. The treatise to be expounded is first intoned, and afterwards the interpreter expounds it.

A year before the arrival of Rabbi Petachia, Rabbi Daniel, the head of the captivity, died. He is a higher authority than the head of the academy. They all possess a book of genealogy up to the founders of the tribes ; Rabbi Daniel descended from the house of David. The monarch appoints a head of the captivity only upon the recommendation of the principal men among the Jews. The only men eligible to be head of the captivity there are two princes of the house of David, and of these two some of the principal men prefer Rabbi David and some Rabbi Samuel. On this matter no understanding has yet been reached. They are both of them wise men. Rabbi Daniel had no sons, only daughters. Rabbi Samuel has a book of genealogy going back as far as Samuel of Ramah, son of Elkanah. He has no sons, but only one daughter. She is expert in Scripture and Talmud. She gives instruction in Scripture to young men through a window. She, herself, is within the building, whilst the disciples are below outside and do not see her. In all the land of Assyria and Damascus, in the cities of Persia and Media, as well as in the land of Babel, they have no judge that has not been appointed by Rabbi Samuel, the head of the academy. It is he that gives licence in every city to judge and to teach. His authority is acknowledged in all countries, and also in the land of Israel. They all respect him. He has about sixty beadles who hold the people in submission by means of rods. After the departure of the disciples, the elders derive instruction from Rabbi Samuel in the science of the planets and other branches of knowledge.

There are large cities in the land of Ararat.[15] There are few Jews there. In ancient times many Jews lived there. However, they slew each other and separated and went to the cities of Babel, Media, and Persia. But in the land of Cush [16] and Babel there are more than sixty myriads of Jews ; and there are as many in the land of Persia. But in Persia the Jews are subject to hard bondage and sufferings. Therefore, Rabbi Petachia visited only one city in Persia. Every Jew in Babel pays a gold florin annually to the head of the academy as a poll-tax. For the monarch requires no taxes, but only the head of the academy. The Jews in the land of Babel live in peace.

The monarch who reigned in the days of Rabbi Solomon, father of Rabbi Daniel, was a friend of Rabbi Solomon because the monarch was of the seed

of Mahomet, and the head of the Captivity descended
from King David. And he said to Rabbi Solomon
that he wished to see the prophet Ezekiel, who
performed miracles. And Rabbi Solomon said to
him : thou canſt not see him, for he is holy, nor muſt
thou uncover his grave. The monarch replied that
he would explore it. Then Rabbi Solomon and the
elders said to him, My lord and king, Baruch, son
of Neriah, his disciple, is buried near the enclosure
of the prophet. If it be thy will uncover his grave.
If thou canſt see his disciple then thou mayeſt try
to see his maſter. He then assembled all the princes,
and commanded them to dig. But everyone that dug
into the grave of Baruch, son of Neriah, fell down
immediately and died. There was there an old man,
an Ishmaelite, who said to the monarch : tell the Jews
that they should dig. The Jews replied : we are
afraid. But the king said : if you keep the law of
Baruch, son of Neriah, he will not hurt you, for every
Ishmaelite that dug fell down dead. Then Rabbi
Solomon said, Give us time, three days, that we may
faſt in order to obtain his pardon. After three days
the Jews dug, and were not hurt. The coffin of
Baruch, son of Neriah, was between two marble
ſtones, he being between the two. A portion of his
Tallith (praying scarf) [17] protruded between the ſtones.
The king said : no two kings make use of the same
crown [18] ; it does not become this righteous man to
be near Ezekiel. I will transfer him to another place.
They then carried away the marble ſtones together
with the coffin. When they had arrived at the
diſtance of a mile from the grave of Ezekiel, they could
not ſtir from the spot. Nor could any horses or mules
move the coffin from its place. Then said Rabbi
Solomon, Here the righteous man wishes to be buried,
and they buried there the coffin, and built a beautiful
palace over his grave.

Rabbi Samuel, the head of the academy, gave Rabbi Petachia a document with his seal, directing that he should have safe conduct whithersoever he should go, and that he should be shown the graves of the disciples of the wise and of the righteous. In the land of Babel they study the commentary of Rabbi Saadya Gaon, which he made on the whole of Scripture, and on the six orders of the Mishna ; as also the commentary of Rabbi Hai Gaon. Both of them are buried under Mount Sinai. They say that from thence to Mount Sinai is all one mountain range. It is near Baghdad. Rabbi Petachia carried the seal of Rabbi Samuel with him ; and the people did all that he required ; and they feared him. And Rabbi Petachia travelled to a city the name of which is Polos,[19] a day's journey from Baghdad. A distinguished priest lives there and all testify that he is of the seed of Aaron the priest, both from father's and mother's side, without any blemish. He also possesses a book of genealogy. Before that city is a grave over which a beautiful house is built. He was told that some rich man saw in his dream an apparition, saying to him : I am a Jew whose name is Brosak, one of the princes that went into captivity with Jeconiah. I am righteous. Thou hast no children. If thou wilt build a beautiful house over my grave thou wilt have children. He built over it a house, and he had children. They then put the question in a dream, to learn who was buried there, and he said : I am Brosak, I have no other name.

And the priest appointed about fifty youths, armed with spears and other weapons, who escorted him ; for there is a people in the neighbourhood of Babel which does not respect the king's authority. This people lives in the desert and is called Charamim (the accursed), because it robs and plunders every nation. Their faces are like the herb *grona*. They only believe in the God of Ezekiel, and thus all the Ishmaelites call them. About a day's or half a day's journey from Baghdad, in the desert, is the grave of the prophet Ezekiel. It is in the possession of the Charamim. The city (Kifl) is a mile from the grave. The Jews possess the keys. Round the grave of Ezekiel is a wall, and a large town, and a large enclosure. The Jews open the wicket, which is so low that those entering have to crawl on hands and feet. On the festival of Tabernacles, people from all countries resort hither, when the entrance becomes enlarged by itself so that they can enter it even on camels. About 60,000 or 80,000 Jews meet there, besides Ishmaelites. Tabernacles are erected in the enclosure of Ezekiel. Afterwards the entrance shrinks to its former dimensions. All can see that. Vows and free-will offerings take place over his grave. And whoever is barren, or whose cattle is barren, makes a vow, or prays over his grave. Rabbi Petachia was told that some person of distinction had a mare which had become barren,[20] and he vowed that if the mare would bring forth a foal he would give it to Ezekiel. His desire was gratified. But as the foal was beautiful, he wished to keep it for himself. But the foal left him of its own accord and went into the enclosure of Ezekiel, through the gate, which was enlarged for the purpose. The master searched for the horse everywhere without finding it. At last he supposed that, having vowed it to the righteous Ezekiel, it might have gone there to him, and there indeed he found it ; but when he desired to take the foal away he could not, for the entrance was too low. Then a Jew said to him : the horse came here in a miraculous manner ; you may, perhaps, have vowed it to the saint. He confessed, and said, yes, I did vow it to him. What shall I do to enable me to bring it out ? The Jew said : take money and lay it on his grave ;

if you lay down its value the horse will be able to go forth. He gradually increased the amount of the money until it reached the value, when the entrance became enlarged so that the foal could go forth.

Rabbi Petachia went to the grave of Ezekiel, and took with him gold, and gold grains, and the grains fell from his hands, and he said : my Lord Ezekiel, for thy honour have I come, and now the grains have dropped from my hands and are lost. Wherever they may be they are thine. And he saw what in the distance looked like a star. He thought it might be a precious stone. He then went there in that direction, and found the grains, and placed them on the tomb of Ezekiel. Every Ishmaelite that goes in pilgrimage to the tomb of Mahomet takes his way past the tomb of Ezekiel and makes some present or free-will offering to Ezekiel, making a vow and praying ; our Lord Ezekiel, if I return I will give thee such and such a thing. The journey by way of the desert takes forty days from the tomb of Ezekiel to the Sambation. Whoever wishes to go to a distant land deposits his purse, or his valuables, with Ezekiel, saying : our Lord Ezekiel, take charge of this valuable for me until I return, and let nobody take it but the rightful heir. And many purses with money lie there rotting because they have lain there many years. There were at one time books there, and a worthless person wished to carry away one of the books, but could not, for pain and blindness seized him ; therefore, everyone fears Ezekiel. Whoever has not seen the beautiful large structure over his grave has never seen a fine building. It is overlaid inside with gold. Over the grave is a mass of lime, as high as a man, and round the lime, and over it, is a structure of cedar wood, which is gilded ; the eye never saw the like. There are windows in it, through which people pass their heads and pray.

At the top is a large cupola of gold, and beautiful carpets cover the inside. There are also in it beautiful glass vases, and thirty lamps fed with olive oil burn there day and night. They are supplied with oil paid for out of the gifts deposited for the lighting of the thirty lamps. There are about two hundred overseers appointed for the administration of the gifts deposited on this grave, who discharge their office one after the other. From the money deposited on this grave, the synagogue requiring repair is repaired, orphans receive marriage portions, and destitute disciples are supported.

At Bagdad there are three synagogues, besides that built by Daniel on the spot on which the angel stood on the brink of the river ; one stands on each bank, as it is written in the book of Daniel.

Whilst Rabbi Petachia was at the grave of Ezekiel, he saw in the building a bird, the face of which was like that of a human being,[21] at which the overseer acting as doorkeeper grieved, for he said, It is a tradition with us, from our fathers, that every house wherein such a bird is found will become a ruin. But when the overseer observed that as the bird was going to quit the window it turned and died, he rejoiced greatly, for he said that since the bird was dead the doom was annulled. The head of the academy told Rabbi Petachia that formerly a column of fire rested over the grave of Ezekiel, but that wicked persons and come and desecrated the grave ; for there had come about 80,000 individuals to the feast of Tabernacles, among whom were unworthy persons, and the column of fire had disappeared. The tabernacles are erected in the same enclosure, close to the burial ground.

The River Euphrates and the River Chebar [22] join ; they can nevertheless, be distinguished. On the other side of the River Euphrates, about a mile, opposite to the grave of Ezekiel, are the graves of Hananiah, Mishael, and Azariah. Each is separate. Ezra, the scribe, is also buried there. Rabbi Petachia then returned, and in two days went as far as Nehardea. To go round that city takes about three days ; but everything is desolate. There is a congregation in a portion of the city. And when the rabbi produced the seal of the head of the academy they showed him the synagogue Shaf-Wyathib.[23] Its three walls are of stone, and the western wall is on the River Euphrates. No portion of the wall is built of either stone or brick, but consists entirely of the dust which Jeconiah brought with him. The synagogue has no roof, for everything is desolate. And the Jews told the rabbi that in the night they see a column of fire issue from it, extending as far as the grave of Brosak, before-mentioned. He then returned and came to a city called Mella,[24] where the grave of Rabbi Meïr is, the same Rabbi Meïr mentioned in the Mishna. Before the town, by the water, is a field, and in that field is the grave. And as the Euphrates, when it rose, overflowed the grave, they took the votive offerings of the Jews and Ishmaelites and built a city round his grave, with towers in the midst of the water. There is a beautiful house over his grave, which the Ishmaelites call Chinuk (Choking). The reason thereof is that one day the sultan came and took away one of the stones forming one of the steps leading to his grave. But in the night Rabbi Meïr appeared to him in a dream, seized him by the throat as though he was going to choke him, saying to him, Why didst thou carry away my stone ? Dost thou not know that I am righteous and beloved by God ? The sultan then begged the rabbi's pardon. But he replied : I will not pardon thee until thou carriest back the stone on thy own shoulder, before the eyes of all, saying : I was wicked in robbing my lord the righteous. In the morrow he carried the ſtone on his shoulder and put it in its former place, saying : I was wicked in robbing my lord the righteous. Therefore the Ishmaelites fear Rabbi Meïr, worship on his grave, make him presents, and vow that if they should return in peace they would give him this or that.

Wherever Rabbi Petachia showed the seal of the head of the academy, men armed with spears came immediately forward and escorted him.

From the grave of Ezekiel to that of Baruch, son of Neriah, is a diſtance of a mile, and from the grave of Baruch, son of Neriah, to that of Nahum, the Elkoshite, is about four parasangs. Between them, in the middle, is the grave of Abba Areka. The length of his grave is eighteen cubits ; five of the Amoraïm [25] are buried there. The mill which Raba had erected for the disciples is there, but it has no water. In his days they ground corn in it. There is a beautiful house over it. They have a tradition whereby they know graves of prophets and Amoraïm, 550 in number, like the number of *Sarim*. Where there exiſts a congregation near the grave of a righteous man, they spread a coſtly cloth over the grave, and when they remove thence they spread a mat over the grave on which there is no building. Underneath moſt of the cloths or mats covering the graves a serpent is coiled, which guards the graves. Therefore it is said : when thou raiseſt the mat beware of the serpent. The head of the academy wrote down for the rabbi the names of the Amoraïm buried there. Rabbi Petachia, however, forgot the liſt (and left it) in Bohemia, for he came from Bohemia hither. He related that ever since he set out from Bohemia he had travelled always eaſtward ; Bohemia being to the eaſt of Ratisbon, Russia to the eaſt of Poland. Thence he went eaſt again, and came in six days to the grave of our lord Ezra, the scribe. They said that in the days of old the grave of Ezra, the scribe, was in ruins. Then there came once a shepherd, who saw a mound and slept on it. One then appeared to him in a dream, saying to him, Tell the sultan I am Ezra, the scribe. Let him have me taken up by men who are Jews, and have me placed in such and such a spot. If not, all his people will die. However, the sultan did not attend to the matter, and so many people died. Whereupon the Jews were called upon, and they re-buried him with honour. The grave was of marble stone, and upon the marble was a tablet, upon which was engraven : " I am Ezra, the scribe." They buried him on the spot named to the shepherd and erected a fine structure over his grave. In the eleventh hour a column of fire ascends from his grave to the sky. This continues during the eleventh and twelfth hour. It is also seen in the first hour of the night. People can walk three or four parasangs by the light of the pillar. All the Ishmaelites worship there. The keys of the houses over the graves are in the hands of the Jews. They employ the proceeds of the votive offerings in giving marriage portions to orphans, supporting disciples, and repairing synagogues of the poor.

Before Rabbi Petachia set out for the grave of Ezra, the scribe, he spent eight days on a journey to Shushan, the former capital. There are only two Jews there and they are dyers. And he showed them the seal of the head of the academy, and they showed him the coffin of Daniel. Originally Daniel was buried on one side of the river, and there was there great plenty, prosperity, and blessing. Then those on the other side of the river said : because the righteous man is not buried in our portion therefore our district is not blessed. And there were constantly great wars between the two districts, during which the coffin was violently transferred from bank to bank. At laſt some elders came, who brought about a settlement between them, and they took the coffin and suspended it by iron chains on high iron pillars, erected in the middle of the river. The coffin is made of polished copper, conspicuous in the middle of the river, ten cubits above the water. At the diſtance it has the luſtre of glass. The Jews told him that any vessel passing underneath the coffin will proceed in safety if those in it be pious, but will founder if this be not the case. He was further told that underneath the coffin there are fish with golden pendants in their ears. He, however, did not pass underneath the coffin, but ſtood on the brink of the river looking at the coffin.

He then returned to Baghdad. There he was shown a flying camel.[26] It is low, and its legs are slender ; and if anybody wishes to ride on it he muſt tie himself to it leſt he should fall off. The rider traverses in one day the ground over which a man on foot would have to take fifteen. It would be possible to go even swifter if the rider could only ſtand it. In one second the flying camel gallops a mile. They also showed him the gates of Baghdad. They are a hundred cubits high and ten cubits wide. They are of polished copper and ornamented with figures so fashioned that no one can produce the like. A nail once fell out and no artificer is able to fix it again. Formerly the horses used to be ſtartled back at the sight of the gates for, seeing the brightness of the gates, they perceived, as it were, other horses running towards them, whereby they took fright and ſtarted off. They, therefore, poured boiling vinegar over the gates, and thus deadened the brightness of the polished copper, so that the horses should enter. However, the polish of the copper is ſtill partly to be perceived at the top, where no vinegar was poured.

These gates were once gates of Jerusalem. The head of the academy has many servants. They flog any one not immediately executing his orders ; therefore people fear him. He, however, is righteous, humble, and full of knowledge of the law. He is clothed in golden and coloured garments like the king ; his palace also is hung with coſtly tapeſtry like that of the king.

Rabbi Petachia travelled in two days from Baghdad to the boundary of Old Babylon. The house of Nebuchadnezzar is all desolate. Near his house is a pillar, and the house of Daniel looks as if it were new. On the place where Daniel used to sit there is a ſtone, and where his feet reſted a marble ſtone. There is also a ſtone at the top upon which the book lay out of which he used to write. In the wall between the house of Daniel and that of Nebuchadnezzar is a small window through which he threw writings. There are ſteps below, upon which three pious sages used to sit before him. On his right, by his seat, a ſtone is fixed, and they declared that there was a tradition that there the vessels from the holy temple were hidden. One day rulers who had heard of it came for the purpose of digging there but when they laid hold on the ſtone they all fell down dead, therefore they removed nothing. They then went from that room, and took the rabbi through the thickness of the wall to an upper room, wherein Daniel used to offer up his prayers. The entrance is so inclined that it is exaċtly opposite Jerusalem, and so cunningly contrived that nobody could point out where it was.

He then returned. He ſtated that he did not see any woman whilſt ſtaying in Babylon because they were all veiled and modeſt. Everyone has a bath in his courtyard ; and no one offered up his prayer before he had bathed. All travellers there travel in the night on account of the heat. Everything

JEWISH TRAVELLERS

grows there in winter as here in summer. Most
of their labours are performed during the night.
Babylon is, in fact, quite a different world. The
Jews are devoted to the study of the law and the fear
of God. The Ishmaelites also are trustworthy. When
a merchant arrives there he deposits his goods in
a house and goes away. The goods are then offered
for sale in the market-places. If the price demanded
by the merchant is given, it is good. If not, the goods
are shown to all the brokers. Should they become
spoiled they are sold. All this is done with honesty.

In Babylon there are thirty synagogues besides
that of Daniel. However, there is no minister there,
and he whom the head of the academy bids to do so
acts as precentor. It is done in this manner. Someone recites the hundred benedictions, and those present
say Amen ; then someone recites the prayer of
Baruch Sheamar with a loud voice, another rises and
recites all the Praises and in this is joined by the
whole congregation, his voice, however, being heard
above them all, that they should not recite too fast,
and they all follow him. He recites the prayer of
Yishtabach before *Vayosha*, and then goes on with
the other prayers. Thus the prayer is divided between
several precentors. No one talks to his neighbour
at synagogue ; all stand decorously, and they all
appear at synagogue without shoes, barefooted. If,
whilst practising, they should be mistaken in a tune,
the head of the academy gives them a sign with his
finger ; they then understand what is the tune. If
there be any young man having a pleasing voice he
recites a psalm. On the half-holidays they recite
the psalms to the accompaniment of musical
instruments, and they know by tradition the appointed
tunes. For the *Asor* they have ten tunes, and for
the *Sheminith* eight tunes ; they have several tunes
for each psalm. When Rabbi Petachia was in the

room of Daniel they showed him a very deep lions' den, and also a furnace half filled with water. Whoever is attacked by fever bathes therein and is healed. Whilst at Baghdad he saw ambassadors from the kings of Meshech (Khozaria), Magog is about ten days' journey thence. The land extends as far as the Mountains of Darkness. Beyond the Mountains of Darkness are the sons of Jonadab, son of Rechab. To the seven kings of Meshech an angel appeared in a dream, bidding them to give up their laws and statutes, and to embrace the law of Moses, son of Amram. If not, he threatened to lay waste their country. However, they delayed until the angel commenced to lay waste their country, when the kings of Meshech and all the inhabitants of their countries became proselytes, and they sent to the head of the academy a request that he would despatch to them some disciples of the wise. Every disciple of the wise that is poor goes there to teach them the law and Babylonian Talmud. From the land of Egypt the disciples go there to study. The rabbi saw the ambassadors visit the grave of Ezekiel when they heard of the miracles and that they who prayed there were heard.

Rabbi Petachia said that the mountains of Ararat are five days' journey from Babylon. The mountains of Ararat are high. There is one high mountain, behind which there are four others, two of which are opposite the two others. The ark of Noah was carried between these mountains and could not get out. However, the ark is not there, for it has decayed. The mountains are full of thorns and other herbs ; when the dew falls, manna is rained down upon these, but when the sun shines warm the manna melts. Whatever portion of it is gathered in the night, if it be kept, likewise melts. They, therefore, carry off the manna together with the thorns and herbs on which it has fallen, and which they are obliged to cut off, so very hard are they. The manna is white like snow. However, when boiled together with the manna they become sweeter than honey or any other sweet stuff. Were it boiled without the nettles the limbs of the partaker thereof would become disjointed for excessive sweetness. They look like small grains. They gave the rabbi a few to taste ; they melted in his mouth ; they were sweet ; penetrating into all his limbs, so that he could not bear the sweetness.

When Rabbi Petachia visited the grave of Ezekiel he saw the tower of the generation of the dispersed ; it is all fallen in, forming a high mountain, a mound for ever.

The king, who was contemporary with Rabbi Solomon, father of Rabbi Daniel, head of the captivity, and who saw the brightness ascending from the grave of Baruch, son of Neriah, and the beautiful and splendid praying scarf faintly visible between the marble stones, went afterwards to the city of Mecca, to the tomb of Mahomet; and behold there was a decayed and putrified corpse, from whose grave such a disagreeable smell arose that nobody could bear it. He then said to his people that there was no good either in Mahomet or his religion, for they knew that the body of Baruch, son of Neriah, was preserved, that his praying scarf protruded from his tomb, that he was a disciple to a prophet, and that the Ishmaelites who dug up his grave perished whilst, the Jews were not hurt ; and that, therefore, it might be known that the Jews hold by the law kept by Baruch, son of Neriah. He, however, had not time to become a convert and convert his people before he died, and thus the resolution he had formed of converting all his people came to nought.

Ezra, the scribe, is buried on the boundary of the land of Babylon.[27] When the pillar of fire is over his grave, the structure erected on it is not visible on account of the brightness over his grave. Behind the upper chamber of Daniel is a beautiful pleasure garden, wherein the palm-trees, as well as his well, are still in existence. Whoever of us stays in the place some little time understands their language, for it is nearly all allied to ours, or the Targum : for instance, *derech* becomes *droch*, *lechem*, *lechom*. In the land of Ishmael the gold grows like herbs. In the night its brightness is seen, when a mark is made with dust or lime. They then come in the morning and gather the herbs upon which the gold is found. Therefore, gold coins are found there, and they possess much gold.

Rabbi Petachia then turned west again, came back to Nineveh, and from Nineveh to Nisibis, where there is the synagogue which Ezra built ; upon the stone is engraved " Ezra, the Scribe." He then went to Haran, and to Aram Naharaïm (Mesopotamia), situate between two rivers. At Nisibis there are about 800 Jews. From thence he went to Hamath. He named all the cities ; and stated how many days it took him to travel from city to city. However, there is no occasion to write it down. From thence (he went) to Haleb [28] that is, Aram Zobah. Why is it called Haleb ? Because on the mountain was the flock of Abraham our father. Steps led down from the mountain, whence he was accustomed to hand milk to the poor. From thence he went to Damascus. This is a large city ; the King of Egypt rules over it. There are about 10,000 Jews there, who have a prince. The head of their academy is Rabbi Ezra, who is full of the knowledge of the law, for Rabbi Samuel, head of the academy of Babylon, ordained him. Damascus has goodly lands ; it lies in the midst of gardens and pleasure grounds. There are also high fountains from which the water pours, and many large pools. The Ishmaelites say, If Paradise be on earth, then Damascus is the Paradise, and if it be in heaven, then Damascus lies opposite it on the earth. Whosoever goes to Damascus sees Mount Seir in the vicinity, as also Mount Hermon and Mount Lebanon. In the land of Sihon and Og there is neither grass nor plant; it is as though it had been made desolate, like Sodom and Gomorrah. Rabbi Petachia saw a grave 80 cubits long. He was told that it was the grave of Shem, son of Noah. But the Jews did not tell him so. From here it is about two days' journey to Syria. The Jordan passes through a cave, people said, from Pameas (Banias). The rabbi then came to Tiberias ; at which place there is a congregation, for there are also congregations in the land of Israel, numbering, however, only one hundred, two hundred, or three hundred families. At Tiberias there is a synagogue which Joshua, son of Nun, built. At Sepphoris there is buried our Holy Rabbi.[29] A pleasing odour ascends from his grave. This odour is smelt at the distance of a mile from his grave. The graves in the land of Israel are in hollows, but not those of Babylon. For in Babylon water appears and, therefore, they cannot dig deep caves. Of the posterity of Rabbi Judah a descendant exists, whose name is Rabbi Nehorai. He has a son whose name is Judah, after Rabbi Judah, the prince. He possesses a book of genealogy going back to Rabbi Judah. Rabbi Nehorai is a physician and sells spices in the market. His children are with him in the shop. They are kept secluded that they may not look about. He is a disciple of the wise and righteous. Tiberias, Sepphoris, and all the cities in the plain belong to Lower Galilee. The rabbi also saw Usha and Shifrem, where Rabbi Gamaliel lived at the seat of the Sanhedrin. There are Jews at Acre. At Jabneh there is a spring which flows for six days of the week, but on the Sabbath not a single drop is found in it. In Lower Galilee there is a cave which is spacious and high within. On one side of the cave are buried Shammai and his disciples ; and on the other Hillel and his disciples. In the middle of the cave there is a large stone, hollow like a cup, which is capable of containing more than forty seah. When worthy men enter, the stone appears full of sweet water ; these may then wash hands and feet, and pray, imploring God for what they desire. The stone, however, is not hollowed out right through, for the water does not come up from beneath; it only appears in honour of a man who is worthy, and to an unworthy man the water does not appear. Though men were to draw from the stone a thousand jugs of water its quantity would not be diminished, but it would remain full as before.

Rabbi Petachia then went to Upper Galilee and stayed among the mountains. Nittai, the Arbelite, is buried there at Arbela. Har Gaash is very high; on it Obadiah, the prophet, is buried. The mountain is ascended by means of steps formed in it. In the midst of the mountain Joshua, son of Nun, is buried, and by his side Caleb, son of Jephunneh. Close by, a spring of good water gushes from the mountains ; there are beautiful palaces erected near the graves. Every building in the land of Israel is of stone. Near one of the palaces a foot-print is perceptible, like that of a human being treading on snow. This is that which the angel imprinted after the death of Joshua, son of Nun, when the land of Israel was shaken. Rabbi Petachia said that a compass round the whole land of Israel might be made in three days. From thence he went to the grave of Jonah, son of Amittai. There is a beautiful palace built over it. Near it is a pleasure garden, wherein all kinds of fruit are found. The keeper of the pleasure garden is a Gentile. Nevertheless, when Gentiles come there he gives

them no fruit, but when Jews come he gives them
a friendly reception, saying Jonah, son of Amittai,
was a Jew, therefore, it is due to you to partake of
what is his, and then gives to the Jews to eat thereof.
The rabbi then came to Rachel's grave, at Ephrath,
half a day's journey from Jerusalem. Upon her
grave are eleven ſtones, according to the number of
the eleven tribes ; and because Benjamin was only
born at her death there is no ſtone erected for him.
They are of marble. The ſtone of Jacob, however,
consiſting of one piece of marble, above all of them,
is very large, a load for many persons. A mile from
hence are the prieſts who took away the large ſtone
from the grave and placed it in a building for ſtrange
service.[30] In the morning, however, it was seen on
the grave as before. This was repeated several times,
until at laſt they abſtained from carrying it away.
On the ſtone is engraved the name of Jacob. He
also saw the ſtone over the well near Haran. Forty
persons could not move it from its place. The well
is about thirty cubits deep; there is, however, no water
in it.

Rabbi Petachia then went to Jerusalem. The
only Jew there is Rabbi Abraham, the dyer, and he
pays a heavy tax to the king to be permitted to remain
there. They showed him Mount Olivet, and he saw
that the pavement was three cubits high, which is
the breadth thereof. There is also a beautiful palace
which the Ishmaelites built in ancient times when
Jerusalem was ſtill in the hands of the Ishmaelites.
Then came worthless persons who brought to the
king of the Ishmaelites a slanderous report, saying :
there is an old man among us who knows the locality
of the temple and the court. Then the king grew
urgent with that old man until he pointed it out.
The king was a friend of the Jews, and said : I will
build here a temple, and none but Jews shall pray

therein. He built the temple of marble stone, a beautiful structure consisting of red, green, and variegated marble. Then came Gentiles and put images in it, but they fell down. They then fixed the images in the thickness of the wall, but in the Holy of Holies they could not place any. The hospice where the poor are is on another side. The ground is cleft, and is called Valley of the Son of Hinnom, where their burial-place is.

The circuit of the land of Israel may be made in about three days. The rabbi saw the Salt Sea of Sodom and Gomorrah. There is no herb there. As to the pillar of salt, he said that he did not see it and that it no longer existed. Nor did he see the stones which Joshua erected. He then went to Hebron. He saw over the cave a large palace, which Abraham, our father, built. There are in it large stones of twenty-seven or twenty-eight cubits. Every corner stone is about seventy cubits. He gave to the keeper of the key of the cave a gold piece to take him to the graves of the fathers ; and the keeper opened the door, and behold there was over the entrance an image,[31] and inside three cells. The Jews of Acre had told him previously : beware, for they have placed three corpses at the entrance of the cave and say that these were the patriarchs, but they are not. But the keeper of the cave said that they were. The rabbi, therefore, gave him another gold piece to take him inside the cave. The keeper then opened the (inner) door, saying, I never permitted a Gentile before to enter this doorway. The keeper then brought lights and they went inside and had to descend steps ; before they entered the inner cave they had to descend fifteen steps outside it. They then came to a very spacious cave. In the midst of the cave there is an entrance in the ground. The ground consists all of rock, and all the graves are in the hollow of the rock ; and over that entrance, in the middle, are placed very thick iron bars, the like no man can make by earthly means but with heavenly help only. And a storm-wind blows from between the holes between bar and bar. He could not enter there with lights. Then he understood that the fathers were there and he prayed there. Whenever he bent towards the mouth of the cave a storm-wind went forth and cast him backwards.

At Jerusalem there is a gate : its name is Gate of Mercy. The gate is piled up with stone and lime. No Jew is permitted to go there, and still less a Gentile. One day the Gentiles wished to remove the rubbish and open the gate, but the whole land of Israel shook and there was a tumult in the city until they abstained. There is a tradition amongst the Jews that the Divine glory appeared through this gate and through it would return. It is exactly opposite Mount Olivet. Mount Olivet is lower in height. Nevertheless, whoever stands on that mountain may see it. His feet will stand that day on Mount Olivet.[32] They shall see distinctly when the Eternal will return to Zion through that gate. Prayers are offered up there. The Tower of David still exists.

At Damascus there is a synagogue which Elisha built, also one built by Rabbi Eleazar, son of Azariah. It is large, and divine service is performed in it.

Among the oaks of Mamre, at a distance from there, dwelt an old man, who was near death when Rabbi Petachia arrived there, and he told his son to show Rabbi Petachia the tree under which the angels rested. He also showed him a fine olive-tree cleft into three parts with a stone in the middle. They have a tradition that when the angels sat down the tree was cleft into three parts, each resting under one part whilst sitting on the stone. The fruits of the tree are very sweet. By the tree is the well of

Sarah ; its waters are clear and sweet. By the well is the tent of Sarah. Close by Mamre is a plain, and on the other side it is about a hundred cubits from the well of Sarah to the well of Abraham ; its water is very agreeable. They also showed him a stone of twenty-eight cubits upon which Abraham, our father, was circumcised. The old man affirmed with an oath, now that he was quitting the world and would not utter a falsehood, but that one day, on the fast of the Day of Atonement, he had seen a fiery angel who was offering up his devotions and a fiery horse by the well of Sarah.

In Greece the Jews are subject to great oppression ; and even compelled to perform menial work in their own persons. There are youths among them who are expert in the use of the Divine name and can conjure evil spirits, but who are compelled to serve the Greeks like slaves. There are so many congregations in Greece, that the land of Israel could not contain them were they settled therein.

In the village of Usha is buried Jonah, son of Amittai ; in that of Bosra, of Babylon, is buried Ezra, the scribe. Rabbi Chana, the Baghdadi, who is mentioned in the Talmud, was of Baghdad, the great city mentioned before. At Babylon there are no stones, but everything is of brick.

End of the words of Rabbi Petachia, brother of Rabbi Isaac, Halavan, author of the Tosephoth, and of Rabbi Nachman, of Ratisbon.

RABBI JACOB BEN R. NATHANIEL HA COHEN
(Twelfth Century)

This short account of his journey to the East by a European Jewish pilgrim is only known from the unique MS. at the Cambridge University Library. It was edited by Dr. Grünhut as an appendix to his edition of Petachia. Steinschneider ascribes it to between the thirteenth and fifteenth centuries, and Dr. Grünhut to the middle of the thirteenth century. Inasmuch, however, as the author refers to the Crusaders in Jerusalem and Hebron, he must have visited Palestine prior to Saladin's capture of Jerusalem in 1187.

ACCOUNT of the journeys to places in the Holy Land and the tombs there of the righteous, composed by R. Jacob ben R. Nathaniel ha Cohen when he entered the Holy Land.

I
HEBRON

I, Jacob, the son of R. Nathaniel ha Cohen, journeyed with much difficulty, but God helped me to enter the Holy Land, and I saw the graves of our righteous Patriarchs in Hebron and the grave of Abner the son of Ner (near the well of our father Abraham), and of Jonah ben Amittai, the prophet, in Kiriath Arba, which is Hebron, and the grave of Hannah and the grave of Rachel at Ephrath, on the Jericho road on the way to Bethlehem. From these two villages it is a parasang and a half to Jerusalem. After that a man goes ten parasangs to Nob the city of the Priests, and from Nob to Ludd is four parasangs, and one parasang to Dudanim, two parasangs to Jabneh, two parasangs to Ashdod and four parasangs to

JACOB HA COHEN

Askelon. In Askelon there is a square wall of our father Abraham, two cubits from corner to corner. There are four caves there, a cave in each corner. Once the priests were washing in the Pool of Siloam, near Jerusalem, and a dish fell from the hands of a priest, and they found it in this well in Askelon, and the monks recognized it because of their writing thereon, and from Askelon to Gaza is four parasangs, and from Gaza to Gazaca two parasangs, and to Madon two parasangs.

II

EGYPT

From Succoth (El Arish) to Goshen is four days, and to Misr one day. In Rameses (Ain el Shams) there is a pyramid one hundred cubits long, and square, each breadth eight cubits. The tombs of Egypt are in Pharaoh's Court. In Alexandria of Egypt, I saw the College of King Alexander and therein are three hundred and sixty-five pillars, corresponding to the days of the solar year, and the middle pillar is thirty handbreadths thick and four cubits long, and there are two coffers, one above and one below, and upon them is a square image, the likeness of four living creatures, with a man's face, an eagle's face, a lion's face, and an ox's face. There Alexander used to learn of his teacher Aristotle, and there is a tower on the sea-coast called, in Arabic, Manara, and they put on the top a fire at night so that the ships should not go astray and this fire can be seen in Acre, in Africa, and in Provence. So beautiful and wide is this lighthouse that two knights on horses side by side can ascend it, and there is a water reservoir above which there is a promenade. And in the house of a Jew there is the statue of Bathia, the daughter of Pharoah, and its fellow at Rameses in the house of the *Chazan* (Cantor). The length

93

of the statue is twenty cubits and upon it is a robed
woman with a basket on her head and a little boy
in the basket, all of black stone; and the King ordered
that it should be taken outside and erected in the
street. At one time the water rose until almost all
Egypt was flooded, and the waters reached up to
her thighs and then subsided.

III

MERON

There are twelve tombs in a single stone and covered
also by a single stone. These graves are set one
opposite the other. It was built by Enoch, the son
of Jared, and a great and wise man told us, " Do not
fear or be afraid to enter, because it is righteous
magic." I immediately entered the cave and saw
two chambers of marble, those of Beth Shammai and
Beth Hillel, and two great caves under the hill with
doors. When a man enters he sees numberless
graves, but the only ones known are those of the son
of Isaiah, the prophet, and the grave of Jonathan
ben Uzziel, and the brook runs near his grave. I
asked the men of the place how could these graves
have been hewn in the hill, for the hill is all of stone.
Then they showed me the book, and we saw written
therein that for many years they neither sowed nor
reaped, as it is said, " And it shall bring forth fruit
for three years " (Leviticus xxv, 21), and in those three
years they built the caves. There are also about a
hundred other caves, but we know not what they are,
and all their burials are of stone like a box within
a room, and one stone covers many graves.

At Meron, R. Simeon ben Jochai and his son are
buried, and there are two monuments thereon, and
his College is still standing. From there it is three
parasangs to Kefar Hanan, and his Synagogue is
there hewn in the hill with only one wall built. Here

JACOB HA COHEN

R. Chalafta is buried with his son, and they have
monuments; and there are many other graves of the
unknown. Thence it is three parasangs to Har-
Gaash, where there are three Synagogues in one
building, and at the door of the third Synagogue
there are two fine trees. Near them are two graves,
one of our lord Joshua, the son of Nun, and one of
Caleb ben Jephunneh. Going back half a parasang
to Timnath Serah is the Synagogue of Joshua, the
son of Nun. It is a ruin, but there still remain the
gate, lintel, doorpost, and threshold. All the
monuments are of a single stone eight cubits long
and [?] broad. (At Arbela) R. Zera is buried,
and on his tomb is written, " Rabbi Zera," and near
him are the tombs of Reuben, Simeon and Dinah,
and their grave is so closed up that a man cannot
insert a hand. In one monument is a building like
a house built on the tomb of Seth, the son of Adam,
and the wall is inside the house. It is two parasangs
from there to the cave of Jochebed, and with her lie
buried eight righteous women. Thence it is half
a parasang to the cave of Rabban Jochanan ben
Zaccai with eight of his pupils, four on each side,
and he himself lies above them at the head of the cave
(one can enter into a corner there), and at his side
there are three coffins and on one side there are four
coffins with bones, and opposite is the grave of R.
Cahana, which is also full of coffins with bones. The
people of all nations kindle lights there, and sick
and barren come there and are healed.

IV

TIBERIAS

The tombs of our ancestors in Tiberias extend
about two parasangs and there are their caves as high
as a house, and the burials are four cubits by four,
like warp and woof joined with mortar, because the

Gentiles used to take the dead out of their graves because they wanted the golden threads with which their shrouds were sewn. Upon every coffin is written— "So and So, the son of So and So. God rest his soul."

When a knight from Provence came and saw that the uncircumcised lit many lights upon the grave, he asked who is this one, and they answered, it is a righteous Jew who heals the sick and helps the barren. He said to them, "Why do you thus in honour of a Jew?" and took a stone and threw it on the ground and raised his hand to throw another stone. He was on horseback but fell and died. Immediately the captains and monks gathered and said that he was not punished because of the Jew, but because he wounded the honour of the teacher of Jesus, and Jesus was wrath with him and killed him; and they said all this before the country folk.

The hot springs of Tiberias consist of some four baths on the shore of the Lake, and the waters taste sweet as honey, and the Jordan crosses the Lake and Miriam's Well is there. Thence it is two parasangs to a hill called Tur, and there our lord the prophet Ahiah, the Shilonite, is buried. From there it is three parasangs to where the Synagogue of our lord King Hezekiah stands and his name is written on the hill in the garden, and below there is a great cave and inside the cave is a little cave. Thus much is known, but there are countless other graves. From there it is half a parasang to Kefar Kanah where King Judah (i.e. Judas Maccabæus) is buried.

V

SHECHEM

Joseph the Righteous is buried in a cave where there are two coffins, and candles are lighted every evening. Once a knight came in with the uncircumcised and said, who is this. And they said, it is Joseph, the son of Jacob. And he had an axe in his hand and struck the grave, and behold a miracle. He died instantaneously and they took him out dead. There is a cave near there in which Baasha, king of Israel, is buried, and on a high hill in the forest is the grave of Zipporah, and a lion guards her and no man may enter or cut wood from the forest. Once a Gentile went in a wagon with two fat oxen. Unscrupulous, he took wood and returned home, but the lion followed and killed him and the two oxen, and then the lion returned to her grave. And there are also many graves there and a great cave, which some say is the grave of Jonah the son of Amittai, and there are unknown graves in other forests.

Thence it is four parasangs to Acre, and there in the middle of the gateway is the grave of Eliezer the Asmonean, and they say that the great church in Acre was his college; and in Cæsarea is the grave of the ten martyrs of the Romans, and on the place where they were killed there is a great marble stone in ruins. A Gentile was buried in front of the door of the cave and in a dream he came to the rulers of the province and cried to them, " Take me away, for I have no rest, for they smite me with iron rods heated in the fire," and he said to them that in this cave there are twelve dead men clothed in prayer cloaks (*tallith*), and they do not look like men but angels; but the Gentiles took no heed of his words. That Gentile was a fisherman and all the fishermen died, and they say that the great marble stone was the throne of Cæsar and never does any grass grow in the place where the righteous were martyred. In the middle of the old wall there is the grave of a righteous man, but they know not who he is.

VI

HEBRON

In Hebron, I, Jacob, entered in the guise of a Gentile into the cave which is the cave of Machpelah. The monks have built a structure upon it and falsely deceived the world. They have erected there a Church for their country folk. The first building had been erected by Joseph the Righteous, and others say that King Solomon buried him there, but this part is in ruins. There is the place out of which Adam, the first man, was created. They take earth from it and build houses with it, but it never grows less and is always full, and there are treasure stores built in the cave, and the monks say that these are the treasuries of the Matriarchs. When the Gentiles wish to enter there, each one goes alone and descends steps with a light, for it is a big descent. There are six graves there, three on each side, and they tell the Gentiles that these are the tombs of Abraham, Isaac, and Jacob, and those of Sarah, Rebecca, and Leah, but it is a falsehood, for there is a great wall strengthened with mortar and pottery between these new graves and the gate of the Cave of Machpelah, and they are not permitted to break into that wall, for once the monks made a small window therein and a strong wind came and killed them all and they closed the window; and the stone near the gate is the portion which King Solomon built. Like this also is the grave of our mother Rachel, in Ephrath, a tower built of hewn stones with four doors. There are eleven stones on her grave, for they say that Benjamin was small and could not bring his stone and the top stone was erected there by our father Jacob.

VII

JERUSALEM

In Jerusalem are the Tower of David and the Temple and the Sanctuary, and the western wall (but its upper ſtones are new), and King Solomon's quarries, and the Gates of Mercy, and the well in which the prieſts washed, and the Monument of Absalom, and below Mount Olivet, opposite the tower, is a tower upon a tower, and it is [?] cubits high, and no road passes it, and the waters of Siloam are over againſt Mount Zion and Jerusalem. Between Zion and Jerusalem there is nothing but one wall. These things are known and none knows more. I also saw the Valley of Jehoshaphat into which they throw ſtones, and every day at leaſt one hundred die and their bodies are brought from Benjamin's Gate down between the monument and the waters of Siloam, a great descent, until they come to Mount Olivet. Three big ciſterns are there, and I asked how is it that these ciſterns are not full, and they answered that the waters run away and it is not known where the water goes. Then said I, Jacob, to the Rabbis, "This is what our lord the prophet Isaiah said, (Isaiah xxx, 9) 'His fire is in Zion and his furnace in Jerusalem'", and I ſtood by the grave of Jesus four cubits from the place where he was ſtoned.

At sunrise on the same day a portent appeared on Mount Carmel like a wheel four cubits high, and it went back. I write of what I saw with my own eyes. On Mount Sinai, there is a mosque of the Ishmaelites, and there is a village under the hill, and the name of the village is Tursin.

As I have been privileged to write about the Holy Land, so may I be privileged to go there and die there.

Here end the words of me, Jacob ha Cohen, of all the sights I saw in the Holy Land.

THE CAIRO GENIZA
(Thirteenth Century)

The Cairo Geniza gives us a valuable indication as regards Indian Jews which confirms, and indeed explains, Benjamin of Tudela's references and the ninth century *Book of Ways*. It throws the most interesting light upon the commercial methods and activities of the Jews of his time. A fragment from the Geniza,[1] of which a facsimile is here given, though unfortunately incomplete, is sufficiently preserved to be intelligible. The Judæo-Arabic in which it is written is not easily intelligible to our co-religionists to-day.

A Jew in India writes to his business correspondent in Cairo, probably early in the thirteenth century or even before. He speaks in the third person, and is himself the " slave " referred to on line nineteen. The letter throws a welcome light upon the commercial relations of the Jews of India and Egypt, for whom Aden played the part of a port of exchange. The following is a translation :—

And he prays to God night and day
That he may give you health. His qualities are not concealed from you.
That he can be trusted with anything that one may wish. And thou art his lord.
And the greatest of men before him. And he is cheap in his commercial transactions.
He makes journeys from Malabar to Ceylon.
But his goods are the whole year in Aden. Now it is his intention to make a change, God willing, and to remove
For men cannot avoid misfortune and this matter is not hidden from thee.

If, therefore, thou wilt wait until the time of
his removal that is good
But if thou requireſt thy goods then send
A letter in thine own handwriting and he will
hand over the goods to him whom thou desireſt
Wishes . . . sending the account.
Five thousand Bahar as little thereof is to be
found in India.
And he possesses none of it. There is also but
little Baspas [2] in the market.
And coryphyllum coſts 40 per 10—I have not
voyaged to Aden this year. But ſtill I had
A little merchandise for thee which Sheikh
Joseph Ibn Abulmana took with him.
I wrote him a letter about it which he was to
send you
Should he be in Egypt, may my maſter support
him with the . . .
Due to me his slave
For I know that my lord is kind to the foreigners.
I know my lord from this point of view.
And I sent to thy Excellency full greetings of
peace as also to those in his circle.
Peace, and also to Sheikh Ibrahim.

It is difficult to fix the date of this intereſting letter, but from
the charaċter of the paper and script it can hardly be later than
the thirteenth century. That the Jews were great travellers
in those regions even earlier than that date is proved not only
by the Itinerary of Benjamin of Tudela but by no less a person
than Maimonides. His letter to Yemen is one of the moſt
intereſting of his minor works, but he himself was originally
a merchant in precious ſtones, trading with India, though, as
he expresses it, he ſtayed at home while his brother David did
the travelling for the firm. Graetz quotes Alkifti as his
authority for the faċt that David voyaged as far as India and,
indeed, loſt both his life and his jewels in the Indian Ocean about
1168. Though Maimonides grieved bitterly for his brother,

his loss proved Jewry's gain, for he gave up business after that and turned his attention to medicine and philosophy.

It is very striking to notice the natural prominence given to Yemen and the Aden Jews in all these adventures. And even to-day Yemen Jews, though despised and unnoticed, have done yeoman service to Judaism in connection with the Falashas of Abyssinia.

PLATE V

THE STORY OF JOSEPH WITH THE CARAVAN OF ISHMAELITE MERCHANTS

From an Italian Hagadah on vellum. XIV century

[British Museum Add. 27210]

ITINERARY OF RABBI SAMUEL BEN SAMSON IN 1210

R. Samuel ben Samson made a pilgrimage to Palestine in 1210 in company of the distinguished R. Jonathan ha Cohen for whom Samuel ibn Tibbon translated (from the Arabic into Hebrew) Maimonides' *Guide of the Perplexed* and Judah al Harizi translated Maimonides' *Commentary on the Mishna.* He is described in the traveller's account of the pilgrimage as " Resh Gola ", the head of the captivity. The text is that of the Parma MS. translated by Carmoly in his *Itinéraires,* pages 127 to 136.

The Traveller at the end of his narrative says that he carried a letter from the King of Jerusalem, i.e. John de Brienne and it is suggested that this letter recommended the emigration of Jews to Palestine and resulted in the famous pilgrimage of three hundred French and English Rabbis in the following year.

The Itinerary begins as follows :—

THESE words deserve to be written in order that we might know the places of the graves of our forefathers by whose merit the world exists. This appears from what I shall relate from the mouth of a man, who was in the Holy Land with Rabbi R. Jonathan ha Cohen, of Lunel. His name is R. Samuel ha Samson, who travelled with him in the land of Goshen, and crossed the desert with him and with him entered Jerusalem. This was in the year 4970 (= 1210).

I

We arrived at Jerusalem by the western end of the city, rending our garments on beholding it, as it has been ordained we should do. It was a moment of tenderest emotion, and we wept bitterly, [Rabbi Jonathan] the great priest of Lunel and I.

We entered by the [western] gate . . . as far as

the Tower of David, whence it is customary to proceed for prostration before the approach to the Temple. We fell on our faces before the Shechem Gate, beyond which is the road which leads to the fount of Etham, the bathing place of the priests. The gate opposite is in the western wall. At the base of this wall there is to be observed a kind of arch placed at the base of the Temple. It is by a subterranean passage that the priests reach the fount of Etam, the spot where the baths were.

From there we went to Mount Olivet, where in olden times the red heifer was burnt. We said our prayers there twice with a " minyan " (i.e. ten persons) and climbed the mountain. On the Sabbath day we recited the Afternoon Prayer on the spot where the uncircumcised had time and again set up a sanctuary with idols, whose presence the place would not endure, causing them to fall down again as fast as they were set up. It was one of the ten stations visited by the divine Majesty when He came [to earth] from His dwelling-place. The Ishmaelites venerate this spot. Only the foundations remain now in existence, but the place where the Ark stood is still to be seen.

We went on from there to the waters of Siloam ; and then next to Hebron. On our way to Hebron we came to the sepulchre of our mother Rachel.

Journeying on from that tomb we found the sepulchre of Nathan the prophet, where there is a Mosque.

From there we reached the spot where Abraham was circumcised. The Ishmaelites hold it in the highest honour. It is a rock in the form of a tomb of three hands-breadths.

After this we arrived at a fine edifice which king Asa caused to be built. It is magnificent. Thence we travelled on to the Oaks of Mamre, and saw there

the well of Abraham, where his tent stood, and
the tree under which he gave food to the three
angels stands opposite. Not far away is the well
of our mother Sarah. It all lies near to Hebron.

From here we came on to Hebron. The head
of the Captivity had in his hand the sealed permit
of the King, who by the mistaken law of Muhammad
is the Caliph. He entered alone, and we ourselves
did not dare to follow him. We betook ourselves to
the dyer—Rabbi Saadiah, Rabbi Tobiah, and myself—
and we said to him :

We are travellers from a far country, come hither
to pray in this place, and to prostrate ourselves where
our fathers once trod.

The man answered as :

Stay here until to-morrow, then, with God's help,
you shall enter in.

We stayed. And he went his way with his
companions. In the middle of the night the gate-
keeper came for us and we entered. We climbed
down twenty-four steps, a narrow stairway where
there could be no turning either to right or to left.
We saw there the site of the sacred place (an ancient
Synagogue), and remarked three monuments. The
building was erected six hundred years ago. It is
close to the cave. We prostrated ourselves and prayed
for mercy ; then we returned to Jerusalem.

After that we went on to Ramathaim (Rama) and
saw the sepulchre of the prophet Samuel there.

From there we proceeded to Beeroth ; we slept
the night there. It is all in ruins.

On the morning of the next day we took our way
at an early hour to Bethel and between Bethel and
Ai we saw the spot where Abraham erected his altar.

From Bethel we went on to Shiloh. We saw there
the sepulchre of Joseph the Just. We slept there
and kept a joyous Sabbath.

From there we went to Bethsean, and from Bethsean on to Tiberias. On the way we saw the tomb of Rabbi Meir, and just before reaching the city itself, the sepulchre of Rabbi Jochanan ben Nuri. Here a house is built. Under this house is a cave, and it was the rabbi himself who ordered the building of this house there, with his own money.

In front of the cave is the tomb of Rabbi Eleazar bar Simeon, and the sepulchre of Rabbi Cahana. Thence we journeyed to Kefar Hananiah, where we found a tomb. Nearly two parasangs further on along the road are the sepulchres of the Tribes [i.e. sons of Jacob], and in the midst of them the tomb of Dinah, their sister. On her tomb a myrtle grows. No one dare take anything from this tree, not even a single leaf. Nearby is said to be the monument of Seth. This we saw. From this place we came to Arbela, where we remarked the sepulchre of Nittai, the Arbelite, with a very beautiful monument upon it. We climbed up to Arbela, where stood the great synagogue which Nittai caused to be built there ; it is now, on account of our sins, in ruins. It lies in the centre of the town ; outside the town we discovered the tomb of Rabbi Zera. This sepulchre is devoid of monument, that which once stood there having fallen into ruins.

From here I went to the village of Hittin and there saw on the mountain side two sepulchres ; some say the tomb of Hosea [but some say, of Jethro], and the sepulchre of Zephaniah, the Prophet. We returned to Tiberias. All this ground we covered in a single day.

On our way back from Tiberias we went on to Kefar Hanan. In journeying there we came across the tomb of Habakkuk in Kefar Hakuk, from which place we came to the village of Lud, where we found the tomb of Rabbi Eliezer bar Jacob.

SAMUEL BEN SAMSON

Before reaching Kefar Hananiah itself we lighted in the fields upon the tombs of Rabbi Halafta and his son and grandson. Here we slept. From these monuments we took our way to Safed, where we discovered the cave of Rabbi Haninah ben Hyrcanus, in which there are sixteen recesses. We encircled them, weeping. There is a wall there for preventing the earth from falling in. Two Ishmaelites remain there continually to attend to the light and supply oil in honour of the righteous man.

I went alone with the head of the Captivity to Kefar Bar'am. Near the city we found the tombs of Honi ha-Me'agel [Onias the Circle Maker], and of his wife and children. These tombs have monuments. On our arrival in the city we found a synagogue, one of those which Rabbi Simeon, son of Jochai, had built, and which are as many as twenty-four in number. It is both beautiful and pleasant. Of the other synagogues of Rabbi Simeon, son of Jochai, some are destroyed, others exist still.

From there we came to Kefar Amuka, and we found there the sepulchre of Jonathan, son of Uzziel, on which there is a great tree. The Ishmaelites bring oil to it and have a light burning there in his honour. They make their vows there, too, to his glory.

On leaving Kefar Amuka we came to Kefar Nebarta [Akbara], where we found the tomb of Rabbi Meir. We returned from here to Safed, where we spent the Sabbath. In these places there are Jewish communities numbering in each case more than five times the "minyan" of ten.

From Safed we went to Gush Halab. On our way thither we came upon a city called Kisma. In Kisma we found the sepulchre of Rabbi José, son of Pedat, called from the name of the city, the man of Kisma.

II

From there we mounted to the village of Meron, and we found there the sepulchre of Rabbi Eleazar, son of Ḥisma. At Meron we found also the school of Rabbi Simeon ben Jochai ; it is four square, and in it he lies buried, and with him Rabbi Eleazar, his son. Two trees rise above his tomb ; it is a very beautiful spot. At the foot of the mountain we found the sepulchres of Hillel and of Shammaï, and thirty-six other tombs as well. Over these tombs is a cupola of a sort of white marble, the interior of which is adorned with reliefs representing branches of trees. Six wells are there. Here we prayed. We found that the firſt well on the right hand side was full of water, the second empty. On the left-hand side was a third well half-filled with water and the fourth completely full. In the hall in the centre of the hall on one side are three tombs, and on the other side three, and in each chamber of the hall there are three tombs, and above one a slab near these wells, of which one is full and the other empty. The head of the Captivity ordered a wax light to be lit and search made whence the water came into the basins, but we never found that out. We then threw out on to the ground a great quantity of their water, but there was no alteration in its amount. This water is as sweet as honey. It is a very marvellous thing.

Beyond the door of the cave is a great hall, where there are three coffins, one alongside the other, and the third above bigger than the other two.

In the city we found a tomb with a crown upon it as well as a very fine synagogue, the latter bears an inscription ſtating " This was built by Shalom ben Levi ". Coming away from the city we discovered the sepulchre of Rabbi Simeon ben Hulda, and a little further on the tomb of the Prophet Obadiah.

This latter is covered with a stone of white marble on which is engraved : " This is the tomb of Obadiah, the prophet, who feared God from his childhood up, and who died in the year 570 after the Exodus from Egypt." From there we came on to Gush Halab. Facing this city we found the sepulchres of Shemaiah and Abtalion. Alongside them are the tombs of Adrammelech and of Sharezer, the sons of Sennacherib, who became Jews and went to the Holy Land. We stopped at Gush Halab and celebrated the feast of Purim there. Its inhabitants are kind and benevolent. Wherever we came they assembled to meet us, as many as more than twice a " minyan " of ten, in honour of the chief of the Captivity.

From Gush Halab we journeyed to Alma. Before reaching that place we found the sepulchre of Rabbi Eliezer [ben Hyrcanus]. Two trees adorn his tomb; not a leaf of them may be removed from them by anyone. He is buried in a cave in the middle of the ground. A sort of hall is set up over his tomb. A stone having fallen from this monument, a root at once thrust out of the gap thus left and filled its place ; and a branch pushing through another place encircled the sepulchre in such a fashion that it was no longer possible for a stone of it to fall down. The Ishmaelites bring oil to burn there. It is a great and marvellous wonder.

A short distance within is the tomb of Rabbi Eleazar, son of Arach ; and further away, opposite the trees, the sepulchre of Rabbi Eliezer, son of Azariah. Upon this tomb stands a tree which surrounds it like a gridiron.

From there we climbed up to Silta, and there we found the sepulchre of Rabbi Judah ben Tema. Mounting higher still, we came upon the tomb of Rabbi José, the Galilean. From this place we went to

Kefar Bar'am and found there at the entrance of the city the tomb of Phineas ben Jaïr. It is adorned with a great monument in the form of a gridiron. Above this monument is built a very fine synagogue, the walls of which are ſtill ſtanding. We found here a place where there is a school. Beneath the tomb of Obadiah the Prophet, mentioned above, I found the tomb of Barak, the son of Abinoam.

From there we journeyed to Dan, where we saw the cave called Pameas [Banias], from which the Jordan issues. Beyond this city is the sepulchre of Iddo the Prophet. From Dan we travelled on to Damascus, and outside the city is a synagogue which Elijah had built. It is a very fine building, and we prayed there. From Damascus we went on to Nineveh (Mosul). Here is to be seen the tomb of Shem, son of Noah. It was built by himself. There is a very fine synagogue in this city. According to an inscription engraved on a marble slab therein it was built by the Rabbi Judan and by Rabbi Levi, son of Rabbi Asher.

(Signed)—Samuel Bar Samson.

Journeying from Jerusalem and from Galilee in the year 970 (= 1210). I have a firman with the seal of the King of Jerusalem atteſting the truth of the present writing.

JUDAH-AL-HARIZI, ca. 1216

Al Harizi was the great Hebrew satirical poet of the thirteenth century, and his *Tachkemoni* is a classic. The thirty-fifth and forty-sixth maqamath of that poem contain many references to the Jewish worthies whom he saw on his travels in the East. Like those of the Persian poets of his day, his expectations of lavish gifts for his poetry were generally disappointed, and it is the niggardliness of the notables which he found their distinguishing characteristic.

Professor Hirschfeld was fortunate enough to find among the Taylor Schechter fragments at Cambridge, discovered in the old hoard of Hebrew MSS. at Fostat, near Cairo, an Arabic poem which he identified as Al Harizi's and of which the following is his translation [1] :—

1 Al-Raqqa (Calneh) is rich in worthy men
  Their virtuous ways are known to all,
  Yet when I tested them
  I found their piety mixed with faults.

2 Tadmor (Palmyra) had given up its noblest
      man
  Whom people for his bounty call Simhah
  A man of riches, not regarding wealth
  A profit, ever in the fear of God.
  He loves to smile ; in times as dark as night,
  His shining appears as bright as morn.
  His children all their noble stock betray,
  As musk exhales its aromatic scent.
  Joshua well in letters trained his son,
  Doth conquer with the arrows of his wit.
  Writing when with enlightening pen his lines
  Thou seest chasing shades of night by his light.

3 Harran is blest with some distinguished people,
Of genial character and peaceful mood
There's none like him in intellect and lore,
Ben Zaki joins decorum to devoutness.
No praise, however lavish, can describe him.
As for the rest, greed closes up their hands,
And none can open them in east and west.
If any dare to blame them for their meanness,
They cut him short and say : " Thou art no
    friend "
We saw the noble man decrease in wealth,
But growing rich the mean and greedy fellow.

4 Edessa's land has cultured people,
Some e'en are marked for leadership
Precentor Josef is, indeed, a worthy,
And Hassan is his peer in merit.
The others, they do love cupidity,
And grant no space for noble deeds.
Ben Salim's is excessive meanness,
Though boasting of munificence
Rasing mountains, charity to evade,
Obstructing, as it were, his hands.

5 All Majdal's people knew enough
Of noble deeds and gentle breeding,
They value nothing more than goodness
Regarding virtue great as gain.

6 Industrious are Nasibin's (Nisibis) people,
Unscrupulous in amassing wealth ;
They love it and they yearn for it,
And flee from every noble deed.

7 Jazira's Jews between two waters
Are fairly good, yet rather hard
The stream of greed surroundeth them,
And like an isle they lie encircled.

8 A godly crowd are Sinjar's people.
Indeed, they are possessed of sense.
Abdul Sayyid, the victorious,
Knows all the ways of kindly doings,
Yet for cupidity pants his soul
As little birds pant for their nests.
Were he as gen'rous as he's clever !
But he is like a fruitless tree.

9 Abul Faraj ! thou art for bounty famous,
Thou labour'st to support the poor.
If other marts of help are bad
Thine of benevolence stands high.
Happy the land whose chief thou art,
Thou sheddest lustre over climes.
When the hand of time describes thy glory,
The morning is its paper, night its ink.
In praise thou'rt likened to an Indian sword [2]
Whose sheath is faith, whose belt is kindness.
There's none like thee in God's own land,
And none so noble in the universe.

In a manuscript at Jews' College, London, he also discovered
and published two poems referring to the poet's journey
through Mesopotamia which confirm the Arabic. These
Hirschfeld translates as follows :—

(Mosul)

This poem I wrote in Assur, concerning the
communities which I saw and observed in the lands
of the East.

" Hear wondrous things, ye children of the world,
Through them some wholesome knowledge ye
may gain.
To Alexandria I came, and camped
Among the people like a fish on dry land.
And citizens did I find in Kahira (Cairo),

But they allow deserving men to starve.
Thence to Damascus did I take my step,
To people, erring like abandoned lambs.
Their hapless state I soon forgot at Zobah (Aleppo),
Whose talk I likened to a two-edged sword.
Kalneh I scorn ; its people's hands are strong,
For nothing hold they firmer than their wealth.
In Assur (Mosul) then my memory lost them all ;
For brutes its people are and beasts of prey.
Should I the like find everywhere I go,
Then mankind only dwells beneath the earth."

This poem I composed concerning a man in
Calneh (Al Raqqa) whom I had praised in my song,
but he escaped to Harran from before me and was
hidden from my eye—

" O child of shame, O brother thou to meanness,
Combining every sort of avarice,
I sang his praises in two languages,
But came to grief through mouth and speech
    of mine,
And when I sought him I could find him not ;
For to Harran, they said, he took the road.
Now even though from me he's hid and gone,
His wicked name upon my staff he left,
Like to a mouse that in a hole took flight,
But in a weasel's mouth left out its tail."

Al Harizi travelled through Iraq and visited Ezra's grave
in the village of Maisan on the River Samura in the south corner
of Iraq, near the place where the Euphrates and Tigris unite.
He seems to have entered Mesopotamia at Al-Raqqa on the
Euphrates; turning to the north and passing Harran, Al-Ruha
(Edessa) Majdal, Nisibis, Al-Jazira, Sinjar and Mosul, and
thence down the Tigris to Nisar.

RABBI JACOB, THE MESSENGER OF RABBI JECHIEL OF PARIS

(1238–1244)

THESE are the journeyings of the children of Israel who wish to go to contemplate and pray at the graves of the Patriarchs, the righteous and the saints of the Holy Land, and to our holy and glorious Temple wherein our fathers prayed in Jerusalem. May it be rebuilt, and established soon in our days.

I

ACRE

Within a Sabbath day's journey of Acre there is a hill where there are Jewish graves. Some say that the grave of Deborah the Prophetess is there. In the City of Acre there is a gateway, on the sea coast of the Holy Land, which is called the Hasmonean Gate. From Acre to Haifa is a distance of four parasangs and the road leads by the seashore till we get to Haifa, where there is a cemetery at the foot of Mount Carmel. Here many great and pious Jews are buried who came over the seas. From Acre to Usha and Shiffrem are 4 parasangs and from Acre to Zippori (Sepphoris) is about 7 parasangs, and there is a cave in which R. Judah the Holy is buried. At the entrance to the cave is a marble door, about 40 cubits from which is the grave of his wife. From Acre to Kefar Hanan[1] is a day's journey to where are buried R. Eliezer ben Jacob, Author of the Kab-ve-Naki,[2] and R. Jacob, his father, and Abba Halaphta and his wife and children.

From Acre we go up to Jerusalem along Mount
Carmel. Jezreel is about half a parasang on the
left and Mount Ja'yer can be seen on the left in
the distance. There is also a land route 28 parasangs
along the sea coast by way of Ramah.

II

From Haifa we went four parasangs along Mount
Carmel and from there we ascended to Elijah's Altar
at the top of the hill. At the foot of the hill, opposite
the Altar, is the brook Kishon where Elijah slew the
prophets of Baal. The brook runs into the great
sea about half a parasang away from Haifa. It is
the place where Ahab went because of the rain,
and in the site of the Altar is a building where the
Moslems kindle lights to the glory of that holy place.
From there we go along the Megiddo road to Taanach
near the brook Kishon, as it is written in the war
with Sisera.[3] Thence we go to Shechem, but there
is another road by way of Samaria. The hills of
Samaria are wondrously beautiful. In Shechem is
the grave of Joseph with two marble pillars, the one
at his head and the other at his feet, and there is
a stone wall around the grave. There Mount Gerizim
and Mount Ebal face each other, and the city lies
between them in the Valley. Mount Gerizim is
a place of gardens, orchards, and vineyards, with
70 wells, and it is called the Mount of Blessing.
Mount Ebal is very dry and not a drop of water comes
from it and it is called the Mount of Cursing.
Perchance it is because of the blessings and curses
enjoined that they are so called. Here are Samaritans
who sacrifice the paschal offering every year on Mount
Gerizim. From Shechem we go up to a place called
Avarata, where there are two hills facing each other
and the road passes through the valley. The village
of Avarata is to the left as one goes up to Jerusalem,

and there is the grave of Ithamar the Prieſt, and it is a beautiful place. There is also another grave there, said to be the grave of Phineas, the son of Eleazar the Prieſt, and the Moslems have a place of prayer near to the grave. There is also in that village a cave in which seventy Elders are buried, and there the Ishmaelites have a house of prayer. And on the second hill to the right of the Jerusalem road is the grave of Eleazar, the son of Aaron the High Prieſt, and it is a very glorious building. From Shechem we go up to Jerusalem by way of the hill of Benjamin.

III

JERUSALEM

When we reach Zophim, we see Jerusalem and make one rent in our garments, and when we reach Jerusalem we go on one of the ruins and look at the Temple Mount and the wall of the Court of Women, and the Court of Israel, the site of the Altar, and the site of the Temple, and the Sanctuary, and we make a second rent in our garments for the Temple. From Jerusalem we go down to the brook of Siloam, the waters of which come out of the Temple Mount under earth until there. Thence they descend to the gardens of the City and there we bathe. It is said that the waters heal the sick and, therefore, the Moslems bathe there. Thence we ascend the Mount of Olives and some go by way of the valley, which is the Valley of Jehoshaphat, and there is the Jewish graveyard below the Temple Mount, and we follow along the valley until we reach a platform which is on the Mount of Olives, where the red heifer was slain, and we go uphill to the platform which faces the Temple gate. Thence we see the Temple Mount and all the buildings upon it, and we pray in the direction of the Temple.

The Valley of Jehoshaphat encircles the east and south of the Temple Mount. On the south is the graveyard we have mentioned, where many righteous are buried. Thence we descend the valley and enter, between two hills, a place called the Valley of ben Hinnom, and there in the Valley of Jehoshaphat is a tomb which is called Absalom's Monument. It is a high square building with many pillars around it, each of a single stone, and it is a beautiful building. In the Valley of Jehoshaphat, at the foot of the hill near the pool of Siloam, there is a square building, and it is said that a Christian Church used to be there. Above the pool of Siloam, on the hill, is Mount Zion, where there are the tombs of the Kings and an ancient building called David's Sanctuary, directed towards the Temple, and lights are kindled there in honour of the sacred place. They say it was built by David and was the place where the Ark was brought and kept by David till the Temple was built. Nearby is David's Tower, built of very large stones, obviously of ancient times, but it is now within Jerusalem. The wall of the court of the Temple is square and said to be 360 cubits long and 60 cubits high, perhaps the difference of 60 cubits between now and then is due to stones having been removed from the former building. The structure is of very great stones, and the corners are also of great stones and some are 30 spans long and 6 spans wide. Some hold that those stones belonged to Ezra's building. Round the *Eben Shethiah*,[4] the Ishmaelite Kings have built a very beautiful building for a house of prayer and erected on the top a very fine cupola. The building is on the site of the Holy of Holies and the Sanctuary, and in front of the Mosque towards the Altar is a structure of pillars and the cupola is at the top of these pillars and it would seem that this was the place of the outer Altar which was in the Court of Israel.

The Moslems gather there on their holy day in crowds and dance around it in procession as the Israelites used to do on the seventh day of the festivals, if we may compare holy things with profane. And there is a declivity in front of the big building, surrounded by a thick wall like the wall of the Court of Israel, and from the south there is a descent like the steps that used to be in the south, and there are caves opening into the wall of the outer Court and leading under the Temple Mount, and it is said that you can penetrate them up to the *Eben Shethiah*. To-day Jerusalem lies to the north-west of the Temple Mount, not as it used to be, on the south of the Temple Mount as it is said in Ezekiel xl, 2. "The frame of a city on the South," and in Psalms xlviii, 3, "Mount Zion on the sides of the north," and the cave of Zedekiah is there. Inside Jerusalem there is a Synagogue of Elijah the Prophet, and there is a niche in the wall for scrolls of the law and the ineffable name is engraved on the stone.

The cave of Simon the Just and his disciples is near Jerusalem and there, too, is the cave of the Prophet Haggai. On another side of Jerusalem is the Lion's cave where are the bones of the righteous who were slaughtered by the King of Greece for the sanctity of the name. He ordered that they should be burnt on the following day, but in the night the lion came and removed them one by one into the cave out of the nether pool which they had filled. And behold, in the morning the Greek King found the lion at the entrance to the cave with the slain, and then the King and all his people knew that they were saints and their bones have remained there till this day.

IV

BETHELEHEM, HEBRON AND RAMAH

About 2 parasangs from Jerusalem, on the Hebron road, is the tomb of Rachel, on the way to Bethlehem.

The tomb consists of 11 stones in pairs, each stone as broad as the grave, and two stones cover its length but the top stone is as broad and as long as the grave. Tradition has it that ten of Jacob's sons sent the ten stones and Jacob, their father, gave the top stone ; Benjamin did not give a stone as he was an infant just born, and Joseph did not give a stone because he was only about eight years old or because of his grief at having lost his mother. Near there is Tekoa, and there is a Saints' Cave, past which they go to Hebron. On the roadside there is Halhul, and another Saints' Cave, and in Hebron is the cave of Machpelah, where the Patriarchs are buried. Modern Hebron is near the cave ; ancient Hebron is at the top of the hill, where there are Jewish graves, and on one side there is a cave where Jesse is buried, but some say Joab, and in Hebron is also the grave of Abner, the son of Ner. About three parasangs from Hebron, on the Jerusalem road, there is on the left, near the hill, the Oaks of Mamre and there is the stone upon which Abraham sat after he had been circumcised, and people take dust from the stone to heal circumcision. On the right of the road is a hill, where the house of our father Abraham is open to the four winds of the world. Near it is a tree under which they say the angels partook of food and beneath it, in a cleft of the hill, is a well said to be the bath of our mother Sarah. The road leads in a valley between two hills of which it is said " so he sent him out of the Vale of Hebron and he came to Shechem " (Gen. xxxvii, 14). This proves our rabbis' saying that scripture must be taken literally, for it might have been suggested that Jacob had accompanied his son Joseph up to the valley and Joseph asked him why he troubled to descend all that hill and then have to go up again, seeing that he was an old man, and he answered, "Your company is both reward and punishment," and he then explained to him the law as to the beheaded heifer. Therefore, the wagons Joseph sent to him, which were drawn by heifers, were a reminder, and the Divine Chariot is called after them, but the literal explanation is best.

It is two parasangs from Jerusalem to Ramah and on the way there is a cave, which is really a cave within a cave, beautifully constructed, where many wise men are buried and also three graves of sons of the prophets, and in Ramah is the grave of Samuel of Ramah and the grave of Hannah his mother, in a very beautiful building. In front is a Moslem Mosque, and nearby a well which is said to be Hannah's bath. One can see Ramah from Rachel's tomb, about three parasangs away.

V

MERON

If one returns to Acre by way of Ramah, he goes from Ramah to a place called Zarephath with a little brook which runs between big hills. Perhaps it is the Zarephath where Elijah went to visit the widow woman. Thence one ascends the hill to Kefar Haras, which is Timnath Serah, and there Joshua, the son of Nun is buried, and his father Nun, and Caleb the son of Jephunneh, and from there to Avarata, where Eleazar and Ithamar and Phineas and the seventy Elders are buried, thence to Shechem and from there to Acre, whence it is about three parasangs to Kefar Hanan. There is the grave of Jacob of Kefar Hanan, and R. Eliezer, his son, that is R. Eliezer ben Jacob, the Author of Kab-ve-Naki, with about sixty cubits between them, and the graves of R. Halafta and his wife and son, R. José, one next to the other, and his pupils near to them. On the hill is a graveyard where R. Zachariah, the son

of the butcher, is buried and, below that, is a cave
in which there lie twenty-four of his disciples and
two other caves near each other, one open and the
other closed, and a synagogue of R. Simeon ben
Jochai is there. Thence it is two parasangs to Meron
and on the way near to Kefar Tanchum, about half
a parasang away, is the grave of Nahum Ish Gimzo,
and upon it is a beautiful monument, and the door
of the cave is closed and a stream of water runs
in front. Some say that he is buried in Kefar Raphadia
and some in Kefar Damin Pharuz. In Meron there
is the cave of Shammai and Hillel and their pupils,
thirty-two in all. There the Israelites meet on the
second day of Passover and pray and say hymns and,
when they find water in the cave, they all rejoice,
for it is a sign that the year will be blessed, but many
times they find no water, but when they pray the water
comes in a twinkling. There is the grave of R. Simeon
ben Jochai and upon it is a monument and near it
is that of R. Eleazar his son, and they say that
R. Simeon's Beth Hamedrash was there. Close by
R. Jose ben Kisma is buried, between the vineyards,
and another saint who is said to have been R. Judah,
and also R. Nachman Chatufa and R. Jochanan
the Cobbler. Here, too, is the Synagogue of R. Simeon
ben Jochai, which is a very glorious building and there
is a large stone hollowed from the top right to the
ground and they say this used to be an altar and that
the blood ran down through that hollow. From Meron
to Gush Halab is about a parasang and there are buried
Adrammelech and Sharezer, who slew their father
and came to the Holy Land and became Jews. Near
them are Shemaiah and Abtalion who were their
grandsons. There Rabbenu Meir Kazon[4] and his
wife are buried, and there, too, is a Synagogue of
R. Simeon ben Jochai, which is a very fine building
with an external wall and steps to go down into the

cave and many grottos. It is about two parasangs from Gush Halab to Kefar Bar'am, where the tomb of Obadiah the prophet is, with a great tree upon it which covers the whole length of the monument and near it is the Beth Hamedrash, a beautiful building; and there is the tomb of R. Phineas ben Jair and near is the tomb of Queen Esther, and the opening of the cave is at the top and a large stone covers it. Near there lies a saint who is said to be Nachman Chatufa, but some say that it is R. Isaac; and in the middle of the village is R. Simeon ben Jochai's Synagogue—a beautiful building made of large stones and large and long pillars. No man ever saw a building as beautiful as that.

We return to Gush Halab, two parasangs along the road, and half a parasang to the side is the grave of R. Zimra and there, in Alma, that of R. Eliezer ben Azariah under a tree. Higher up and near the said city are buried R. Azariah, his father, and R. Eleazar ben Arakh and R. Eliezer ben Hyrcanus under a tree, and R. Judah ben Tema on another side of the City. From Alma to Dalata is half a parasang, and at the head of the road is a cave full of water good to drink, which is called the cave of the Babylonians, where the righteous are buried who came from Babylon to the Holy Land, and near it is a cave in which Rabba, the son of R. Hunna, and R. Hamnuna and, in Dalata, in the village, R. José the Galilean are buried. Further on, towards Nebertin, near the valley at the foot of the hill near the road, is the grave of a righteous man, said by some to be R. Jacob Naburia, and further on towards Kiumia is the grave of R. José ben Yokrat, and there near the bottom is the grave of Jonathan ben Uzziel, under a fine big tree, finer than anyone ever saw in the world. Six parasangs thence is Shifrem, where Onias, the Circle Maker, and his wife, are buried, and near to the village is buried a righteous man whose name we know not. From there one can ascend a big mountain, near to the village, to be reached from the hillside opposite the spring. Abba Hilkiah is buried there, but some say Hanan Hanechba. Thence one goes to En Zatun where is the grave of R. Judah ben Ilai. Thence you go to Safed where is the cave in which R. Dosa ben Hyrcanus and his pupils are buried. Thence on the road to Akbara R. Nahorai, R. Jannai, and R. Doştai, are buried in the orchards. They are separated by rivulets of water two hand-breadths wide. From there one goes to Jakuk where is the grave of the prophet Habakkuk, upon which there is a fine monument between four party walls.

VI

From Jakuk one goes to Tiberias. At the top of the hill is a cave in which R. Akiba is buried, and below it is the burial ground of his pupils. Near it in the middle of the valley is the grave of R. Chiyya and his sons, and in that cave is buried R. Hunna of Babylon and a holy man whose name we know not. Near it is the grave of R. Cahana and near them that of Moses,[6] the son of R. Maimon, the Judge, and they say that a Gaon named R. Zemah is buried there.

On one side of the city on the mountain R. Meir is buried, and beneath it are the hot baths of Tiberias, and near there is the grave of Jeremiah the prophet and the monument upon it is very great, and on another side of the city is a very large cemetery in which are buried 24,000 pupils of R. Akiba, who died between Passover and Pentecoşt. About one mile from there Jochabed, the mother of our maşter Moses, is buried, and Miriam her daughter, and Zipporah, her daughter-in-law, and Elisheba, the daughter of Ammihud, and

four graves are there of men unknown. Less than
a parasang away is Arbela where is the grave of Nittai
of Arbela, upon which there is a fine building like
a cupola of large stones each as long as the cupola,
and lower down R. Zera is buried. On another side
of the city three sons of Jacob are buried with Dinah,
their sister, and on their monument is a very fine
myrtle tree. Near there is the grave of a saint covered
with dust with a building around it crossed by water
a cubit deep looking like a pit. They say that Seth,
the son of Adam, is buried there. Thence you go
to Kefar Hittin where Jethro, the father-in-law of
Moses, is buried, and there is a fine building upon it
which the Moslems have made into a prayer house,
for it is the custom of the Moslems to make their
prayer houses upon the graves of the righteous.
Thence you go to Araba where R. Hanina ben
Dosa and his wife are buried in one grave. And on
another side of the city R. Reuben, the Iztrobolite,
is buried. Thence you get to Sekhnin where R. Joshua
of Kefar Sekhnin is buried in a stone sarcophagus
with a fine stone cover and lower down in the field
is a saint whose name we know not. Thence you
go to Kefar Kanah where the sons of Jonah ben
Amittai are buried, and thereon is a fine building,
which is a prayer house for the Moslems. Thence
you go to Zippori where Rabbenu Judah, the holy,
is buried with some of his pupils in one cave, and in
another cave lower down his wife. From Zippori
you go to Ramah, where is the cave of Benjamin, the
son of the Patriarch Jacob, in a stone sarcophagus
with a marble cover, and it is a tradition among the
inhabitants that the Messiah will come from there.
Thence we go to Kefar Manda, where a saint is buried
who they say is Akabia ben Mahalallel. Between
Gath and Acre is the city of Jabneh, where the grave
of R. Gamaliel is. Upon it there is a fine cupola

and it is a prayer house for the Moslems, a fine building which they call Abuhadira. From there it is about four parasangs to Acre. May the Lord haſten to show us his signs and wonders in our glorious Temple. May it be speedily rebuilt in our days. Amen !

VII

TOMBS OUTSIDE THE HOLY LAND

And these are the journeys that they muſt make who journey from the Holy Land to outside and wish to go to pray in the holy Synagogues which were built in former generations and to spread their hands in prayer at the tombs of the righteous who were buried outside Paleſtine.

From Acre we go to Damascus and across the Jordan over a bridge built upon it. In Damascus is the Synagogue of R. Eleazar ben Arakh, a beautiful building in the midſt of the city. In the gardens also there is a Synagogue of Elijah the prophet, a very fine building and there are Amana (Abana) and Parpar, the rivers of Damascus—from Acre to Tyre the famous is two parasangs by sea or by land, and there is a Synagogue, a fine building and very beautiful —and from Tyre to Sidon is seven parasangs and Mount Lebanon is near Sidon and there is the Temple of the prophet Zephaniah, and from Sidon to Beeroth (Beyrout) is ten parasangs and from Beeroth to Jebel seven parasangs, where is a Synagogue of Elijah, a glorious building, and from there to Sinai is nine parasangs. All this either by sea or by land, and they are all fortified cities. From Sinai we go to Ludkia, where there are two fine Synagogues, one of Elijah and the second of Ezra, and from there it is three days' journey to Aleppo. Here there are three Synagogues, one of Moses, where four holy men are buried whose names we know not. And in the Tower of King David there is a house of our father Abraham. It is seven days' journey from there to Tarik (Taril) on the River Euphrates, and from there two days' journey to Hamath where there is a Synagogue of Elijah, and from there to Himaz one day's journey where there is a Synagogue of Elijah, and from there it is two days' journey to Baalath where are a Tower of King David and a Synagogue of R. Eleazar ben Arakh and also Elijah's cave, and from there it is one day's journey to Karak where is Noah's tomb twenty-four cubits long. One day's journey from Baalath at the top of the hill are the graves of Abel and Cain, and from Baalath it is two parasangs to Nebi Zerua where are the tombs of Eldad and Medad, and from Zerua it is one parasang to Edrei where is Job's tomb, and it is two days' journey from there to Eglon and at the top of the hill is the grave of Jephthah the Gileadite, and from there to Salt (es-Salt) and the tomb of Isaiah the prophet is a day's journey, and from there to Kefar Duna and Judah's tomb is half a parasang, and from there it is two parasangs to the Jordan and our father Jacob's bridge, and from there to Jericho is one parasang, and above Jericho are Sodom and Gomorrah, and it is three days' journey on the road thence to Mount Hor where Aaron is buried.

VIII

PALMYRA AND BAGHDAD

It is six days' journey from Damascus to Tadmor (Palmyra) where there is a tower of David and very great and wondrous buildings built by the Anakim, and there is the tomb of Joel, the son of Pethuel. It is five days' from Tadmor to Rahava where there is a ferry across the River Euphrates to Babylon, and it is three days' journey from Rahava to Shingar, and above Shingar are the hills of Ararat. It is three days' journey to Assur (Mosul) where there is a

notable Synagogue built of the dust of the Holy
Land, and there is the grave of Jonah's daughter
and near the city wall is the River Tigris, and thence
it is three days' journey to Arbel, and from Arbel
to Baghdad is twelve days' journey. In Baghdad there
is a very glorious Synagogue, built on the River Tigris,
and the Gates in the Prayer house of the Ishmaelites
are from David's Tower, and in two places " Holy
to the Lord " is written upon them, and there is the
Synagogue of the prophet Ezekiel, a very glorious
building and it is the place where he was circumcised.
From Baghdad to Babylon is two days' journey, and there
is the Tower of Nebuchadnezzar and the Synagogue of
Daniel, and from there to Hillah, where there is only a
ferry across the Euphrates, and from there to Al-Hanok
the grave of R. Meir Al-Hanok, and there is the
Synagogue of R. Keshisha and the scroll he wrote
with his own hand, and there is his grave and there is
the Synagogue of R. Zeira, and he is buried there.
All these Synagogues are very glorious buildings.
It is two parasangs thence to Shiraz, where there is
a tower built by Nimrod, and it is three parasangs
thence to Kutzurat, where is the Synagogue of Baruch,
the son of Neriah, where he is buried, and there are
the Synagogue and Temple of Joseph and the tomb
of the prophet Nahum the Elkoshite. It is a parasang's
distance from Kutzurat to the River Chebar and the
Synagogue of Ezekiel the prophet, a building more
beautiful than the eye of man has ever seen, and there
he is buried. It is two parasangs thence to the tombs
of Hananiah, Mishael, and Azariah, and it is eight
parasangs from Al-Hillah to Al-Kufa where is the
city first destroyed during the generation of the flood.
Thence it is a day and a half's journey to Sura, and the
tombs of the righteous R. Sherira, R. Hiyya, R. Zerah,
and R. Sabbatai. Four parasangs from Al-Kufa
is the place where Noah entered the Ark, and from

RABBI JACOB

Al-Hillah to Amsit is a six days' journey by way of the River Euphrates, and from Amsit to Barkoi and Samara is three days' journey to the Synagogue and tomb of Ezra. Thence it is two days' journey to Basra and from there to Susa, the capital, six days' journey, and here is the tower of Ahasuerus and the Palace of Queen Esther and the Tower of Haman. It is two days' journey from Susa to the place where Daniel is buried and it is fifteen days' journey from Susa to Persia and Media, where is Mordecai's Synagogue and he and Queen Esther are buried there, and outside the Synagogue are the tombs of Haggai and Zachariah. May the Lord support us and may we live in His presence. May He give us merit to see them alive speedily in our days !

THE ROADS FROM JERUSALEM

By Isaac ben Joseph ibn Chelo (1334)

THE HOLY CITY

For the love of *Jerusalem* I will not keep silence. For the love of *Zion* I will not rest, although I have already written to you twice or thrice.

The holy city possesses to-day four gates : the Gate of *Mercy*, at the east ; the Gate of David, at the west ; the Gate of *Abraham*, at the north ; the Gate of *Zion* at the south. Leaving the city by the Gate of Mercy, we climb the Mount of *Olives*, the mountain of oil, the place where of old the red calf was burnt. It is here that we find the valley of *Jehoshaphat*, the brook *Kedron*, *Bethphage*, and the *cemetery* of the Israelites.

Leaving by the Gate of David, we pass by the *Tower of David*, as it is called ; and from thence take our way down to the Valley of the *Rephaim*.

Leaving by the Gate of Abraham, we enter into the tombs of the Kings (to whom be salvation !). The cave of Ben Sirach,[1] the grandson of Jeremiah the prophet, is to be found here.

Leaving by the Zion Gate, we climb *Mount Zion*, and descend into the Valley of Hinnom. It is here that the spring of Siloam rises, the spring Gihon which King *Hezekiah* dammed up when *Sennacherib*, King of Assyria, came into the land of Judah.

On *Mount Zion* there stood formerly the fortress of Zion which King David (peace be with him !) took from the Jebusites and called with his name. It was on Mount *Moriah* that in the olden days the

Temple of Solomon (to whom be salvation !) was reared ; and from that august temple it received the name of the Mountain of the Temple. Alas, by reason of our sins, where the sacred building once stood, its place is taken to-day by a profane temple, built by the King of the Ishmaelites when he conquered Palestine and Jerusalem from the uncircumcised. The history of that event was in this wise :

The king, who had made a vow to build up again the ruins of the sacred edifice, if God put the holy city into his power, demanded of the Jews that they should make known those ruins to him. For the uncircumcised, in their hate against the people of God, had heaped rubbish and filth over the spot, so that no one knew exactly where the ruins stood. Now there was an old man then living who said : " If the King will take an oath to preserve the western wall, I will discover unto him the place where the ruins of the holy temple are." So the king straightway placed his hand on the thigh of the old man and swore by oath to do what he demanded. When the old man had shown him the ruins of the temple under a mound of defilements, the King had the ruins cleared and cleansed, taking part in the cleansing himself, until they were all fair and clean. After that he had them all set up again, with the exception of the western wall, and made of them a very beautiful temple, which he consecrated to his God.

It is this western wall which stands before the temple of *Omar ibn al Khattab*, and which is called the Gate of *Mercy*. The Jews resort thither to say their prayers, as Rabbi Benjamin has already related. To-day, this wall is one of the seven wonders of the Holy City, of which the names are : the Tower of David, Solomon's Palace, the tomb of Huldah the prophetess, the Sepulchres of the Kings, the Palace of Queen

Helena, the Gate of Mercy, and the Western Wall.

The first of these is the *Tower of David* mentioned above, near the gate of that name. It is of very ancient and very solid construction, and in the olden times the Jews used to dwell round about it. To-day there are no habitations in the vicinity but, instead, so many fortifications as to make this ancient stronghold quite impregnable in our time.

The second is an ancient building called *Solomon's Palace*. In former days, when the uncircumcised were in possession, this building was appointed to receive the sick of the holy city ; to-day a market of considerable importance is held there.

The third is the tomb of the prophetess *Huldah*.² This prophetess, to whom in the time of King *Josiah*, the Maker of Sacrifices, there went *Hilkiah*, *Ahikam*, *Achbor*, *Shaphan*, and *Asahiah*, was the wife of *Shallum*, son of *Tikvah*, son of *Harhas*, Keeper of the Wardrobe, who dwelt in Jerusalem. There she was buried, too, as was narrated by the great author in the following words : " They allowed no sepulchre in Jerusalem except the tombs of the House of David and that of Huldah, which have been there from the days of the earliest prophets."

The tomb of Huldah the prophetess, on the summit of the Mount of Olives, is very beautifully built. But the sepulchres of the House of David which were on Mount Zion are no longer known to-day either to Jews or Mussulmans ; for they are not the *Tombs of the Kings* about which we are now going to speak.

These latter sepulchres are the fourth of the wonders of the Holy City. They are, as we have already said, near the cave of Ben Sirach. They are of ancient and very massive construction, in form a masterpiece of sculpture. All the strangers who come to visit the

Holy City say they have never seen anything so beautiful.

The fifth of the curiosities to be seen is the *Palace of Queen Helena*, who came to Jerusalem with King Monobaz and was adopted into the Jewish religion there. This palace is a fine building inhabited to-day by the Cadi and his councillors.

The sixth is the *Gate of Mercy*, near the Temple. Formerly there were two gates, the one for wedding parties, the other for mourners, as we are told in the Chapters (Pirke) of Rabbi Eliezer the Great, the German Kabbalist, blessed be his memory! These two gates have been buried in the earth for the fulfilment of the Scriptures.

Finally, the last remarkable thing in the Holy City is the Western Wall, of which we spoke above.

The Jewish community in Jerusalem, God be gracious to her! is quite numerous. It is composed of fathers of families from all parts of the world, principally from France. The leading men of the community, as well as the principal rabbis, come from the latter kingdom—among others Rabbi Chaïm and Rabbi Joseph. They live there in happiness and tranquillity, each according to his condition and fortune, for the royal authority is just and great. May God re-establish her and raise her to the highest prosperity!

Among the different members of the holy congregation at Jerusalem are many who are engaged in handicrafts such as dyers, tailors, shoemakers, etc. Others carry on a rich commerce in all sorts of things, and have fine shops. Some are devoted to science, as medicine, astronomy, and mathematics. But the greater number of their learned men are working day and night at the study of the Holy Law and of the true wisdom, which is the Kabbalah. These are maintained out of the coffers of the community, because the study of the law is their only calling.

There are also at Jerusalem excellent caligraphists, and the copies are sought for by the strangers, who carry them away to their own countries.

I have seen a Pentateuch written with so much art that several persons at once wanted to acquire it, and it was only for an excessively high price that the Chief of the Synagogues of Babylon carried it off with him to Bagdad.

ROUTE I.—FROM JERUSALEM TO ARAD

Seven roads start in the Holy City and go through all the land of Israel. The first leads in a southerly direction to Arad, a town situated at the southern extremity of Palestine, and the places it goes through (or to) are seven : Ethain, Tekoa, Halhul, Hebron, Ziph, Ma'on, and Arad.

The first of these, *Ethain*, is the town that King *Rehoboam* caused to be fortified in order to secure himself against King *Jeroboam*, as it is written in the Scriptures. Later it was called *Ein-Etam (the fountain of Etam)* on account of its waters, which were brought from there to Jerusalem by solid pipes. To-day it is in ruins, its sole inhabitants some poor Jews, keepers of an old synagogue, one of the seven ancient synagogues which still exist in Palestine and which are attributed to Simeon, son of Jochai, blessed be his memory ! One of these keepers told me that every year, on the day of the giving of the Law, a voice is heard coming out of the Holy Ark which says : " Study the law, Oh, sons of Israel, and for the merit that shall thereby accrue to you God will have pity on you and restore you to your rights and your independence ; for the cause of all your troubles is that your ancestors abandoned the study of the law." This is the voice of Rabbi Simeon, who comes back every year into his synagogue.

From Etam we journey on to Tekoa, an ancient city from which came the woman sent by Joab to

David to entreat him to recall Absalom from his exile. Rehoboam fortified it at the same time as Etam, and Jeremiah the prophet speaks of it in his book. There is an ancient cave in this city, said to be the burial place of one of the seven prophets whose sacred bones lie buried in the Holy Land. According to some it is the tomb of the prophet *Amos* ; and according to others the sepulchre of the prophet *Isaiah.*

From there we reach Halhul, a place mentioned by Joshua. Here there are a certain number of Jews. They take travellers to see an ancient sepulchral monument attributed to *Gad the Seer.* It is the third tomb of the seven prophets.

From Halhul the road leads to *Hebron,* a place which bore formerly the name of *Kiriath-Arba,* the city of Arba, Father of the Anakim. He was a giant even among giants, and there still remains to this day at Hebron a skeleton of enormous stature said to be that of one of these giants.

The Jews, who are very numerous here, do a considerable trade in cotton, which they spin and dye themselves, as well as in all sorts of glass-ware made by them in Hebron. They have an ancient Synagogue and pray there day and night, for they are very devout. During the ten days of penitence they visit the tombs of *Jesse,* father of King *David,* and of *Abner,* son of *Ner.* There, with faces turned towards the Cave of Machpelah they implore that God will have mercy and restore this sacred place where the patriarchs are buried (Peace be with them !) into their hands, as in former days they used to be. On the eve of the day of the great pardon they all resort to the tombs of *Rachel* and of *Nathan the Prophet* to perform their devotions there.

I have visited these two tombs. The first is a monument composed of twelve great stones,

surmounted by a cupola also of stone. The second is
one single recumbent stone. I have prayed for you
and for myself on the sepulchre of our mother Rachel,
and I have prayed and wept for the health of my sick
son on the tomb of the prophet Nathan. (May God
grant my prayer!)

From Hebron the way leads to *Ziph*, a city
mentioned in Joshua. It was fortified by *Rehoboam*,
as was written in the Chronicles. To-day it is known
only for the miracles wrought at the tomb of *Rabbi
Ziphai*. The Arabs who have witnessed these miracles
maintain that this Rabbi Ziphai was a doctor of their
law. But every one knows that Rabbi Ziphai is
written of in the Talmud as a holy personage.[3]

From this place we proceed to *Ma'on*, a city
mentioned by Joshua. There is another *Ma'on*,
known in the story of *David* and *Abigail*. There
was here a learned man known as *Rabbi Sa'adiah*.
He was a man who was a worker of miracles. One day
during the hour of prayer a wall of the synagogue
fell down. At once the place where the wall had been
was filled with great flames, flaring up in all directions.
Then a great number of stars, remarkable for the beauty
of their colour and for their brilliancy, made a sort of
writing, which said: *Here lies Bar Cocheba (the son of
the Star) the anointed Prince.* Rabbi Sa'adiah, when he
knew whose tomb this was, threw himself on the
ground, praying and weeping for a long time, until
this vision had disappeared. Then he arose, had
stones and mortar brought, and himself rebuilt
the wall.

From Ma'on we come to *Arad*, one of the royal
cities of the land of Canaan. It was the King of Arad
who made war on the Children of Israel when they
came out of the land of Egypt, as it is written in the
holy law. It is a place of little importance to-day,
for it is only inhabited by a few poor Arabs and some

indigent Jews. The men of both races are shepherds and live by their few poor flocks. The rabbi even tends the sheep, and his disciples follow him into the open fields to receive their lessons in religion.

ROUTE II.—FROM JERUSALEM TO JAFFA

The road leading from the Holy City to Jaffa, at the furthest extremity of the tribe of Dan, is as follows :

From Jerusalem to Zorah, the home of Samson. To-day it is called *Zurah*, and the tomb of Samson is to be seen there. It is a very ancient monument, adorned with the jawbone of an ass with which he killed the Philistines.

From there the way leads to *Emmaus*, a place well known from the writings of our wise men, blessed be their memory ! Now it is no more than a poor village inhabited by some Ishmaelites who live in miserable dwellings. There is an ancient sepulchral monument at Emmaus, said to be the tomb of a Christian nobleman who fell in the war of the King of Persia.

From Emmaus we come next to *Gimzo*, the home of Rabbi *Nahum*, a citizen of *Gimzo*. This place, already mentioned in Holy Scripture, is still to-day well-peopled. The Jews have a beautiful and ancient synagogue there, attributed to Rabbi Simeon, son of Jochai. (May he have salvation !) In the time of the pure and holy Rabbi Nahum, a great worker .of miracles, the tyrannous Roman Government persecuted all Israel, particularly the pious and just ones of the nation. Rabbi Nahum was one of these pious and just men whom the Roman tyranny had chosen for its victims. Fleeing from his home, search was made for him everywhere. But love for his dear ones drove him to return to his family. On the way back, nearing his own city, he suddenly caught sight of a band of soldiers who had orders to seize him. He promptly hid himself in a cave nearby. At once God ordained that a spider should come and spin a web across the entrance of the cave. The soldiers on arriving at the spot and seeing this cobweb, went their way, saying : " He cannot have gone in there, for this cobweb would be broken ; let us seek him elsewhere." And they passed it by.

From Gimzo we come to *Ludd*, which is now no more than a village. At one time it was one of the principal cities of our wise men. (Blessed be their memory !) Ludd is the scene of the story of Ben Stada : he was a disciple of Rabbi Joshua, son of Perachiah, and went with him to Alexandria in Egypt. Later on Ludd became the seat of Rabbi Eliezer's celebrated school. When in the possession of the uncircumcised it was called *Saint George*, from the name of their chief ; but the Mussulmans have destroyed his temple and restored to Ludd its ancient name.

We next pass *Ramleh*, a city which had not come into existence either in the time of the prophets or of our wise men, with whom be peace ! It was built in the time of the Geonim, and is a fine city with many inhabitants. The number of Jews there is considerable ; and they are engaged in all sorts of professions. Among them I found a man from Cordova, and another from Toledo : both of them men of wealth and position. They have cotton factories.

Several persons have assured me that *Ramleh* was *Modin* ; others maintain that it is *Thimna*. In one author I have found that this city is called *Palestine*, in another writer that its name is *Rama*. God alone knows what the truth of the matter is.

From Ramleh we journey on to *Sarafand* : this is *Sariphin* mentioned in the Talmud. There is only one Jew living in this city ; he is a dyer, and has

fine works. But he has living with him in his home
a pious old man with several of his disciples, who form
a congregation of ten persons. This old man is a
great Kabbalist, and knows the seven kabbalistic
books by heart. His father was a disciple of Rabbi
Moses of Gerona (i.e. Nachmanides), and he told me
many marvellous things of that great man. (Salvation
be to him !)

From Sarafand we are next conveyed to *Jaffa*,
the belle of the seas. This is a place of considerable
commerce, with a rich and numerous population.
Among the things principally traded in at Jaffa may
be noticed olive oil, cotton thread, scented soap,
vases of glass, dyed stuffs, dried fruits, etc.

The Jews of this city have a beautiful synagogue,
filled with a great number of very ancient and very
beautiful books of the law. Alongside this synagogue
is a school and a library. But there are few learned
men at Jaffa, and the school has but a small attendance,
and the library is even less used. The library was
a gift to the community from a wise man of the olden
days who died in this place and attached to the gift
the condition that the community might not sell
it but must house it in a building near the synagogue,
for the building of which he bequeathed the money
necessary. (Blessings on the name of that just man !)

ROUTE III.—FROM JERUSALEM TO SHECHEM

The journey from the holy city to Shechem is
on this wise :

From Jerusalem to *Beth Hanina*, a village of the
tribe of Benjamin. An ancient tomb there is said to
be that of Rabbi *Hanina ben Dosa*. (Peace be to
him !)

Thence to *Ramah*, a place often spoken of in
Holy Scripture, where once a very bitter voice of
lamentation was heard : " Rachel mourning for her

children," and refusing to be comforted, because they
were not, as it was written in Jeremiah. During the war
between the Christians and the Mussulmans there
was enacted at Ramah a romance of which the story
deserves to be told here. A young Israelitish girl
of great beauty fell into the hands of a young Christian
nobleman who, when she offered resistance to his
evil designs, drew his sword and threatened to kill
her. The young girl boldly offered him her head
to cut off, whereat the young man, touched to the
heart by such virtue, threw himself at her feet and
asked to be forgiven for his barbarity. Then he sought
out her parents and took her home to them. But he
loved the young maid, and to obtain her hand in
marriage became an Israelite and one of the chiefs
of the Jewish community.

From Ramah the road leads to *Beeroth*, a city
mentioned in Joshua. It is known to-day as *Albera*.
There is another city of *Beeroth* besides this one.
It is outside the Holy Land and called now *Beyruut*.
Eliezer, citizen of Beratha, came from there.

Next, on to *Bethel*, the ancient *Luz*, in these days
called *Bethin*. Here there is an ancient sepulchral
monument said to be the tomb of the prophet *Ahijah
the Shilonite*, who foretold to *Jeroboam*, his accession
to the throne, the division of the twelve tribes, and
the sad end of his son. A very striking miracle was
performed at this tomb. In the time of the Emperor
Hadrian, a Roman nobleman who was a mortal
enemy of the Jews embarked with the greatest zeal
and ardour on a persecution of the sons of Israel.
He went through Palestine at the head of his troops,
breathing slaughter and carnage. But, behold! a
miracle! When he was near the tomb of Bethel,
a sepulchral voice was suddenly heard saying :
" Wretched man, what are you about to do ? Know
you not that the victims whose lives you are seeking

are the children of the friend of God, of Abraham (Peace be with him!)." This voice made such an impression on him that on the instant he resolved to become a Jew. A venerable old man then appeared to him, speaking with the same sepulchral voice he had heard, and told him to go to Babylon to receive there the sign of the Covenant, which he did, as it is all told in the *Midrash*.

From Bethel we journey to *Geba*, which is the *Gibeah of Benjamin* mentioned in the Judges. The Arabs who live there to-day call it *Djibia*. They have a fine mosque there which was formerly a church of the uncircumcised. There are not many Jews at Gibeah.

The next stage of the journey is *Shiloh*, called *Sailon*, where the sepulchres of the high priest *Eli*, and of his two sons *Hophni* and *Phineas*, are a very remarkable sepulchral monument, where lights are kept perpetually burning by both Jews and Mussulmans. An old man, a Kabbalist, lives near this monument. He is a German, and lives by making copies of sacred books, such as those of *Sefer-ha-Bahir*, of Rabbi *Nechunia ben ha-Kana*, of *Sefer ha-Bittachon*, of Rabbi *Judah ben Bethera*, of *Sefer-ha-Yezirah*, attributed to Rabbi *Akiba*, and of others as well.

From Shiloh we come at last to Shechem, the renowned city. It was called in the time of our wise men (Peace be with them!) *Neapolis* ; to-day it is called *Nablus*. People come from afar to visit the tomb of *Joseph the Pious*, and the well of *Jacob the Patriarch*, a fountain dug out by our father Jacob (Salvation be his!). There are few real Jews at Nablus, but many Samaritans. They are *Cuthim*, and come from *Cutha*, a city of Iraq. They have a temple on Mount *Gerizim* which they look upon as the only place where it is permitted to sacrifice to God.

Facing this mountain, which is also called the Blessed Mount, is Mount *Ebal*, called the Accursed Mount, for Joshua, when the children of Israel entered into the land of Canaan, by God's command pronounced blessings from Mount Gerizim and curses from Mount Ebal. Though they rigorously observe the law of Moses, an idol in the form of a pigeon has been found among them. Four letters of our Hebrew alphabet are wanting in theirs, the *alef*, the *hé*, the *het*, and the *aïn*. Their writing also differs from ours, so that it was impossible for me to read a single word of their pentateuch, which they showed me.

ROUTE IV.—JERUSALEM TO ACCO OR ACRE

The fourth road from the Holy City leads to Acco, through the cities we have just enumerated, as far as Shechem ; the following places are passed through [next].

Sebaste, otherwise *Samaria*, the first town met on leaving Shechem. It is in ruins, its only inhabitants now a few poor shepherds.

From these ruins we journey on to other ruins called *Bether*, for this is the famous city of Bar Cocheba. We know that Rabbi Akiba was the standard-bearer of that prince who desired to rebuild the House of God. But, alas ! unless the Lord build the house, their labour is but lost that build it. Bar Cocheba fell, and with him the hope of Israel.

After passing these ruins, in the midst of which stands the tomb of Rabbi *Eleazar Modein*, we arrive next at *Arsuf*, formerly a considerable city, now a village of little importance. It is inhabited by only a few boatmen, who convey travellers to Kaisarieh. I engaged to take me there one of these boatmen, a good man and a God-fearing one. He told me how, in his father's day, when his boat was in danger from a violent and furious tempest, a young and beautiful woman who was with her husband in the boat fell into the sea. Inconsolable at her death, the husband was the prey of utter despair, and nothing could assuage his affliction. A wise rabbi, however, who had learnt of his grief, came to seek him out, telling him : I can call back your darling to life, provided you are willing to furnish me with the things necessary for this operation. The husband, full of joy, replied that all his fortune was at his disposal. But the rabbi answered him that all he required was the name of only one person of his acquaintance to whom no single misfortune had ever happened in his life, so that he could write the name on a stone and throw it into the sea at the place where his wife had fallen into it. He could not find one such person, though he sought through all his memory, and consoled himself in the end with the thought that no one altogether escapes unhappiness in this world.

Kaisarieh is the city of Caesarea, situated on the sea shore. In the time of Rabbi *Akiba* it was the seat of the Roman Government, and it was here that that just man fell by the hand of the tyrant. The place is still shown where he was executed, as well as the tomb which holds his sacred body.

In this city also is the sepulchre of Rabbi *Abahu* and that of his son. Both are placed not far away from the synagogue. As in the days of R. Benjamin there are few Jews at Kaisarieh, but there are no Samaritans there any more.

From Kaisarieh we go on by sea again to *Kalmun*, an ancient city in ruins. The foundations of the buildings and temples which formerly adorned the city are still to be seen. To-day there is nothing there but a few wretched houses and poor cabins.

From Kalmun we come next to *Haifa*, opposite Mount Carmel. It is the native place of Rabbi

Abdimi. In this city there is a Jewish congregation renowned for its piety. Its graveyard, which is at the foot of Mount Carmel, is visited by all those who come to the Holy Land, because there are interred within it many wise men of Israel and of all countries, who have died at Acco (Acre).

For centuries, indeed, this laſt city has been a refuge for many wise men, such as Rabbi *Yehiel of Paris,* Rabbi *Moses of Gerona,* Rabbi *Menachem the German,* and others. To-day ſtill the city holds many learned foreigners and pious rabbis from France and Germany.

Acco or *Acre* is a celebrated seaport. It is spoken of as a city of the tribe of Asher in the Book of Judges. It ſtands at the foot of Mount Carmel, not far from the cave of Elijah of pious memory. There is a great trade carried on there and its inhabitants are numerous and rich.

ROUTE V

This is the road from Jerusalem to Tiberias by way of Acco (Acre).

Abelin, inhabited by the Jews, is the firſt place passed along this road. It is *Jabneh,* the home of *Levitas,* a citizen of Jabne, and of *Ela,* a wise man of Jabne. To-day it is known only on account of a magnificent erection there, said to be the tomb of Rabban *Gamaliel.* At Abelin I found a disciple of Rabbi Samuel of Acco, deeply versed in Kabbaliſtic lore, and he showed me ancient writings such as the *Book of Rabbi Chamai,* the *Pirke Rabbi Ishmael,* and others.

From Abelin the way lies next to *Kefar Manda.* This village is renowned for its possession of an ancient sepulchral monument said to be the tomb of Rabbi *Akabia,* son of *Mahalallel.* (Blessed be his memory !)

From there Sepphoris is reached. It is the capital of Galilee, very often spoken of in the books of our

wise men. (May they rest in peace !)   Here sleep
Rabbenu ha-Kadosh and his two sons, Rabban *Gamaliel*
and Rabbi *Simeon*. (Blessings on their memory !) Over
the door of the cavern where Rabbenu ha-Kadosh
is buried a stone tablet is placed on which is engraved
this epitaph : *This is the sepulchre of our Rabbi the Holy ;
he is resting on his bed.*

The caves holding the tombs of his sons are about
half a league further on.   Each rests in a grotto apart.
Around these caves are many tombs of the great ones
of Israel.

From Sepphoris the road leads next to *Gathahepher*,
to-day called *Meshed*.   It was the home of the prophet
Jonah, son of Amittai, as Holy Scripture saith.   According to the Talmud, the prophet Jonah was of the
tribe of Zebulun on his father's side and of the tribe of
Asher on his mother's side.   Gathahepher is an
insignificant place inhabited only by some poor
Mussulmans.

From there we arrive next at Kefar Kanah, a village
containing the tomb of the prophet Jona, son of
Amittai.   The Arabs have had a beautiful mosque
built over the sepulchre of this man of God.   Jonah
is one of the seven prophets buried in Palestine whose
tombs are known.   A Mussulman lord, enemy of the
Jews, formerly dwelt at Kefar Kanah.   He came forth
one day from his palace filled with evil designs against
the sons of Israel.   Passing near the tomb of the
prophet, he suddenly beheld before him a man in
armour of terrifying aspect.   At once this lord threw
himself at his feet, as if he had come before his judge :
" Jonah, lord and master ! " he cried out, " you have
taken shape in this armed man ; why do you thus
affright me ? "   " I *am* Jonah, and have come hither
to keep you from harming my people," he was
answered.   Such was the effect of this vision that the
lord did no more harm to the Jews but became their
greatest friend, as it is written.

JEWISH TRAVELLERS

After *Kefar Kanah* we come to *Kefar Sekhnin,* a village in ruins. A sepulchral monument of a great beauty is shown there. According to some, it is the tomb of *Joshua of Sekhnin,* according to others, that of Rabbi *Simeon Chasida.* Kefar Sekhnin contains other ancient sepulchres as well, but time has effaced the inscriptions on them.

[Tiberias] Tebarieh is reached next, a town whose name comes from that of Tiberius. There we find the hot baths of Tebarieh quoted in the writings of our sages. (Upon whose memory may benedictions rest!) The Jewish community has a fine synagogue there, attributed to Caleb, son of Jephunneh.

[Tiberias] Tebarieh bears five different names, to wit : *Tebarieh, Hamath, Mesia, Rakat,* and *Asdoth ha-Pisga.* It is situated on the lake of Gennesaret called the lake of Tebarieh. Since the destruction of Jerusalem it has become one of the most important cities of the land of Israel. Here there were thirteen synagogues and a great number of schools. It was in this place that *Rabbenu ha-Kadosh* composed the Mishna. And that Rabbi *Aaron ben Asher* published the Massora. To this day still this city has in its midst a holy congregation, which studies the law day and night.

People come from afar to visit the tombs of Tebarieh; they are very many in number. The best known are the sepulchres of the disciples of Rabbi *Akiba* ; the caves of Rabbi *Jochanan,* son of *Zakkai* and of *Rab Cahana* ; the tombs of Rabbi *Jonathan,* son of Levi, and of Rabbi *Moses,* son of *Maïmon,* the grottoes of Rabbi *Chiyya,* of Rab *Huna,* of Rabbi *Meir,* and of Rabbi *Zemach Gaon.* (Upon whose memory be blessing !)

ROUTE VI : FROM TIBERIAS TO SAFED

Between Tiberias and Safed lies the sixth route to the Holy City, and the following seven places are to be found along this road.

146

ISAAC CHELO

The village Chitim or Chitin appears to be the *Kefar Chittin* or *Isim* of the Mishna or the *Kefar Chitia* of the Talmud. It is known only for two ancient funeral monuments said to be the tombs of Jethro, father-in-law of Moses, and of *Jacob of Kefar Hittaia.* (May he have salvation !)

From there the way lies to Arbela, the home of *Nittai of Arbela.* (Peace be with him !) There still exist the ruins of the synagogue of this great man.

Arbela contains several celebrated sepulchres, such as those of *Nittai,* of Rabbi *Zera,* of *Dinah,* of *Jochabed,* etc. These tombs are very fine monuments in stone : their names are engraved on them. That of Dinah bears another name also, which I have not been able to read by reason of its great age. There is another ancient sepulchre at Arbela as well, believed to be that of *Seth,* son of *Adam.* Whether this is so, God knows !

From Arbela we reach *Kefar Nahum* or Capernaum, which is the *Kefar Nahum* spoken of in the writings of our sages. (Upon whose memory be a blessing !) It is a village in ruins, where there is an ancient tomb said to be that of *Nahum the Old.* At one time there was in this village a number of *Minim,* all great sorcerers as we know from the history of *Chanina,* nephew of Rabbi *Joshua.*

From this place the road leads next to *Kefar Ilanan,* the *Kefar Hanania* of the Mishna. It is the home of Rabbi *Halafta,* a citizen of Kefar Hanania. He is buried there with his wife and children. Other ancient sepulchres adorn this village, as those of Rabbi *Jacob,* of Rabbi *Eliezer,* his son, etc. (Blessed be the memory of them all !)

From Kefar Hanan we come to *Shezur,* the birthplace of Rabbi *Simeon Shezuri.* (Peace be with him !) His tomb is still shown there, as well as that of his son, Rabbi Eliezer. These tombs are foursquare and

built of stone ; round about them some pistachio-
trees are growing.

The next place on the road is Meron, the abode of
Rabbi Simeon, son of Jochai. Here the school, the
synagogue, and the tomb of this great man are to be
seen. Two beautiful palm-trees shade the tomb,
which is of hewn stone. The school is to the right
and the synagogue to the left of this sepulchral
monument.

At *Meron* repose also *Hillel* and *Shammai*. Their
tombs, and the tombs of their disciples, are in a cave
in the mountain side. The miracles and marvels
wrought on the tombs of these holy ones are known
throughout all the land of Israel.

Among other sepulchres of our wise men (of blessed
memory!) found in this place must be reckoned the tombs
of Rabbi *Eleazar*, of Rabbi *José*, of Rabbi *Jochanan*,
of Rabbi Judah and others. (Upon whose memory
may blessing fall!) The Jewish community at Meron
is of no great importance ; most of its members
belong to the holy congregation of Safed. It possesses
a fine synagogue, however.

Safed, just mentioned, is a city peopled by Jews
from all parts of the world. In this place Rabbi
Shemtob of Soria composed his numerous works.
Although the wise men, followers of the truth, have
much criticized this learned man, they have never
ceased to copy him and to receive his traditions.
The synagogue is beautiful and ancient and so also
is the public school.

At Safed there is a cave celebrated for its tombs.
It is attributed to *Hanina ben Dosa* by some, and to
Hanina ben Hyrcanus by others. Another cave is
shown also in this town, that of Rabbi *Dosa ben
Hyrcanus*, who is buried there with his disciples.
A carob-tree stands at the entrance to the cave.

ISAAC CHELO

The laſt road from the Holy City leads through diverse cities of the tribes of Asher and of Naphthali. The firſt of these is *Gush Halab*, not far away from Safed. In it there is a holy congregation of Jews, rich, beneficent, and generous folk, by whom a great trade in oil and wine is carried on with remote countries. They have an ancient synagogue with a school, in which they entertain a great number of disciples of the wise men. In this place are the tombs of *Shemaiah* and of *Abtalion*, as well as those of Adrammelech and of Sharezer, their anceſtors, who were sons of Sennacherib, and became Jews. Their sepulchral monument is beautiful old work ; it is of hewn ſtone. Other tombs and several caves which contain ancient sepulchres are to be found at *Gush Halab*. (May God in His mercy, have their occupants, with other juſt men, in his remembrance ! *Amen.*)

From *Gush Halab* we come next to *Sa'sa'*, a village of the tribe of Asher. The Jewish community there is in considerable force ; it possesses an ancient synagogue attributed to Rabbi Simeon ben Jochai, as well as a fine school attributed to the same rabbi. (Blessed be his memory !) In the said school are preserved several ancient writings, among others the *Sefer-ha-Taggin* and the *Sefer Shiur Komah*.

I have heard it said that Sa'sa' was the home of Rabbi *Sisai*, and indeed tombs are shown there said to be those of Rabbi *Sisai*, of Rabbi *Levi*, son of Sisai, and of Rabbi *José*, son of *Sisai*. (What the truth of this matter is, God knows !)

From Sa'sa' the road leads to Fararah, a village which contains a Jewish congregation. In this village there is an ancient sepulchral monument said to be the tomb of Rabbi Nahum the Mede. This ancient tomb is shaded by a great elm.

The next place passed is *Dalata*, a village where there is a little Jewish community and a great number of tombs and sepulchres of our wise men. (Blessings on their memory !) Among the tombs worthy of mention are those of Rabbi *Eliezer*, of Rabbi *Ishmael*, of Rab *Hamnuna*, of Rabbi *Judah*, Rabbi *José*, etc. All these sepulchres are in caves round about Dalata. Not far from this village, on the road to *Alma*, is a vast cave named the *cave of the Babylonians*, because it is filled with tons of bones of the just from Babylonia.

Alma, just mentioned, possesses a holy association of Jews. Three tombs of three wise men of the Israelites, all three bearing the name of Rabbi *Eleazar*, are the glory of this place. These ancient tombs lie in the shadow of some beautiful pomegranate-trees. Every Friday evening lights are lit on these tombs by the Jews and the Mussulmans. Now it happened one Friday evening that the number of lights was so great their flames set on fire one of these trees, the pomegranate overhanging the tomb of Rabbi Eleazar, son of Arach. Everyone refused to extinguish the flames : the Jews in order not to profane the Sabbath, the Ishmaelites in imitation of the Jews. The tree burnt, therefore, the whole night through, and on the morrow when they came to visit the sacred tomb it was seen with astonishment that neither the trunk nor the branches of this tree had received any hurt. It was a miracle to behold, as it has been written.

From Almah we reached *Kedesh*, which is the *Kedesh of Naphtali* of the book of Judges. There are not many Jews living there, and most of those who are live there only to act as keepers of the Jewish tombs which are there and to receive the strangers who came to visit these. Among these tombs may be remarked that of *Barak*, son of *Abinoam*, and that of Deborah, his wife.

From Kedesh we arrived at *Balneas*, which is *Dan*. It is called also *Banias* or *Paneas*.

ELIJAH OF FERRARA
(1434)

FEARING that my previous letters may not have reached your hands, I take up my pen again to acquaint you with the woes we have suffered on our journey—woes that have devoured, have broken me.

In the first place, by the loss of one most near and dear, the desire of my eyes, the joy of my heart. Hardly a breath of life was left in me when, alas, he died— my Jacob, my grandson, whom I mourn in my soul with sighs and secret tears. Woe is me ! Oh, my head, my head ! Young head so prepared for the study of the moral sciences, all thy bent and disposition to philosophy. Whatever was perfection in my eyes, he possessed it all.

While still plunged in the depths of this first affliction, fresh sorrows were even then on their way to assail me. On my arrival in Egypt, my son Menahem fell ill and died. My soul rejects all consolation for the death of this beloved son, for he was the child of my old age. Alas, I was hoping that he would be a rock to my heart, my refuge in troubles ; and behold, he has left me, he has departed hence : grief is added to grief.

My well-beloved son Isaac, too, always so faithful to me, he, too, went hence a few days after Menahem.

Then, through grief for my losses so many and so cruel, I myself fell ill and came nigh to death's door. But thanks be to God, the Physician, who exacts no reward, He sent his angel to me and gave me strength to come on here to Jerusalem, the holy city, where I arrived on the 41st of the *Sephirah*,[1] in the year 194.[2] My weakness was still, however, extreme, either because I had not yet entirely recovered from my sickness, or by reason of my afflictions and much grieving. The days of my mourning were not yet over, and my sorrow still lay heavy upon me, when the notables of the community came to visit me and besought me to expound to them, in the synagogue, the chapters of Maimonides, according to their custom, and from that time they imposed upon me the charge to expound publicly to them three times a day the ethics of the Fathers in the synagogue, *Halachah* with *Tosafoth* in the *Beth Hamidrash* (college) and again *Halachah* with *Rashi's* commentary in the synagogue towards evening. In addition to all this, I am charged with the duties of religious adviser in this city, and of giving response upon questions of law from Misr, Alexandria, Damascus, and other remote cities. After all this, you will hardly be able to believe it, but, with the help of the Almighty, I have found strength for all. For all this labour and toil, however, I receive but a small reward, yet one which has enabled me so far to live in plenty, because provisions are plentiful and abundant and cheaper to buy (God be thanked !) than in any other place where I lived in the West.

It is not necessary for me to recommend to your care the orphaned children of your brother, your senior in years and in merits. (May his soul rest in peace !) The same I say unto you as regards the respect which you owe to the wife of your aged father. May the Holy One give you grace to maintain and increase your virtues !

There is a great plague ravaging these countries, in Egypt, in Damascus, and in Jerusalem. Close on ninety victims have perished here, and five hundred at Damascus ; but now (Praised be the Physician without reward !) the mortality has ceased.

That you may know how fathers of families earn their living here, some engage in business and sell in shops ; others again work as carpenters and chemists. They have no adept knowledge of the art of preparing drugs and other matters pertaining to pharmacy, they simply buy them and sell them again. I need hardly say that they know nothing of medicine, but are for the most part asses. Many of them carry on the work of goldsmiths or shoe-makers ; some deal in silks, the men doing the buying and selling, the women the actual work.

The Jews ply their trades side by side with the Ishmaelites, and no jealousy between them results such as I have remarked in other places.

Meseems I have already imparted to you heretofore what a young Jew has told me concerning those men of his own country and religion, who are their own masters, and owe no dependence to any one. These (Falashas) dwell among a great nation called Habesh (Abyssinia), they make a show of Christianity, wearing on their faces chain and filament ; they are constantly at war with them and only now and again with other Jews.

These Hebrews have a language of their own. It is neither Hebrew nor Ishmaelite. They possess the Law and a traditional commentary upon it. They have neither our Talmud nor our codes. I have obtained information from this young Jew about several of their precepts. In some they follow our doctrine ; in others they conform to the opinions of the Karaïtes. They are in possession of the Book of Esther. But they have not the feast of Chanukah.[3] They are a three months' journey distant from us, and the river Gozan (Nile) flows through their regions.

A Jew from Basra told me that his country was nearly a two days' journey from New Babylon. Hosea the son of Beeri is buried there. Not far away is Susa, the capital, where Daniel and his companions lie buried. At Babylon itself are the graves of Ezekiel and Baruch, the son of Neriah. Old Babylon is a day's journey farther on. Here were aforetime the tower which the children of Adam built, and Ur of the Chaldees, and the furnace into which was thrown our father Abraham, of blessed memory.

An old man informed me that he had been in India, which is in the far East, facing Cush (Ethiopia) to the West, a sea and a desert separating them. Now in India there is a king,[4] very mighty and powerful, reigning over the Jews only; the rest of the country is governed by peoples rejecting every form of belief : peoples who kill no living creature for food. Their adoration is given principally to the sun, moon and the stars.

The children of Moses live upon an island situated near the river Sambation ; the tribe of Manasseh live opposite them. Beyond this river are the tribes of Dan, Naphthali, Gad, and Asher. The tribe of Issachar live in a province occupied by themselves alone, and hold no communication with anyone else whatsoever. They are marvellously learned in the Law, and their languages are Hebrew, Arabic and Persian, and around them dwell the fire worshippers.

The tribe of Simeon live to the extreme south. They too are governed by their own kings. The tribes of Zebulun and Reuben live on the banks of the Euphrates, the former on this side, the latter on the farther side of the river. They have the *Mishnah* and the Talmud. Their languages are Hebrew and Arabic. The tribe of Ephraim live to the south of Babylon. They are a fighting race, warriors who live on the booty they capture, and their language is Hebrew.

I will not speak to you now of the miracles and marvels constantly manifested at the tombs of the prophets and of the pious men of Galilee and beyond Jordan, as well as in other places of the country of

ELIJAH OF FERRARA

Israel, because, with God's help, I hope to go there and see them for myself. I will make them known to you next year. May God protect you, my beloved sons! Give greetings from me to my sons-in-law, my daughters and their children. May they all be blessed. I make my prayer to God before His sacred temple, that He may cause you to grow and multiply in the pure fear of Himself : then God, in His mercy, will bless you as He has promised. Forget not to call me to the remembrance of my dear and well-beloved brothers. Remember and forget not, my dearly beloved brother, desire of my eyes, what I have spoken unto you, and your duty to occupy yourself strenuously in the work I imposed on you. The beginning is difficult, but its end will be very great, and may peace be with you.

ELIJAH,
Your father and brother.

In the week [5]: " He shall pour the water out of his buckets " (5195.)

[*At the back of the letter.*]
To the hands of my beloved friends Israël Chaïm and Joseph Baruch : May their Creator and Saviour, by whom they have salvation at Jerusalem, grant them His protection ! I pray my lords and brethren of the Holy Synagogue of Ferrara, to transmit this letter to my sons (May their Creator and Saviour have them in His keeping !) wherever they may be. It shall be counted to them for merit and their reward therefor shall be complete.

To FERRARA.

RABBI MESHULLAM BEN R. MENAHEM
OF VOLTERRA
(1481)

[From a unique Florentine MS. first published in 1882 at Vienna by Luncz in " Jerusalem I "]

I
RHODES

ON the 4th May, 5241 (1481), we reached Rhodes which has a harbour and occupies the valley and the hill, and at the top of the hill is the house of the Gran Maeſtro of Rhodes. The city is very beautiful and the knights are beautifully caparisoned.

I saw the Gran Maeſtro face to face. He is a handsome man, ſtraight as a reed, of French origin with a long beard, about 55 years old. I also saw all the premises of the Synagogue with rooms in the College of R. Abraham Daphne, a German, who resides with a Jewish Notable.

I saw how the Turks had laid the city waſte especially the giudecca (Jewish quarter) to the left, for the chief fighting was there.

They overthrew all the houses and the house of Monsieur Galeon of Rhodes and of R. Azariah the Physician and other houses, and the walls near the Synagogue fell down. And one day, they say, more than 10,000 Turks got on the wall, and threw the Gran Maeſtro from the wall but the Lord confounded them, each man ſtriking his brother and his relative, and their hearts failed them, for the Lord helped the people of the city. And now they have made new walls and

156

renewed the whole city, more beautiful than any I have seen, and they have also erected two moats at the foot of the wall, one on either side, and a Synagogue between in the place where the miracle happened, and the Gentiles besought the Gran Maestro to remove the Synagogue, but he would not listen to them, for the Keeper of Israel neither sleepeth nor slumbereth.

The circumference of the Island of Rhodes is 300 miles from Chios to the City of Rhodes and there are many villages on the Island and the Jews live there in perfect tranquillity.

To-day the 2nd June, 1481, we journeyed from Rhodes and on the left about ten miles from Rhodes in the Gulf of Rositalia we saw the hills of Turkey.

On Tuesday, the 5th June, 1481, 310 miles from Rhodes in the morning there were great winds from all sides raging one against the other, and we wished to lower the great sail and we were in great danger of snapping our ropes on the left, and the ship went round in a circle and we thought to drown, but with God's help the wind ceased in a single hour.

II

ALEXANDRIA

On Wednesday, the 6th June, we reached our goal of Alexandria, but, as our pilot had died in the battle and the anchor master was wounded and bed-ridden, we were obliged to appoint one of the sailors master and when we entered the harbour the vessel grounded and was nearly wrecked. There was a great cry in the ship, and the Genoese came out of Alexandria to help us in another galley and cast anchor, and after they had fastened our ship to them with ropes and wanted to pull her off the sailors gave a mighty heave and the towing rope of the galley broke, though it was strong and as thick as my arm. Finally, after much trouble they got her out and we stopped about a mile from Alexandria because Alexandria is rocky and big ships cannot get near the city, but God helped us and saved us this time, for we were in great danger. The same day I landed at Alexandria. It is in a valley to the right and it has towers with sea between them, and there was a galley there like those of Rome but not so big. When you enter Alexandria, you find a fort beautiful with twenty-two turrets and a wall ten cubits thick between turret and turret and surrounding them like a crown on one side of the city. They could easily put the fortress on an island, but the Sultan does not wish to do this because there is now a hidden approach from the city. I never saw so fine a fortress only three years old, and eight hundred mamelukes sleep there every night, for such is the law; and the mamelukes wear a red cap on their heads and a stick in their hands. Near the fortress there are twenty mosques and when we got to the gate we were taken hold of and they found our money upon us, although it was under the soles of our feet, and they took about ten per cent of it, and although they found money upon me which I had not declared they returned me the balance. Jews pay nothing for merchandise, but Gentiles pay ten per cent, and it is impossible to avoid the tax because they search everybody even Jews and women.

I inquired about the usages of Alexandria and their mode of life and found that they are very extraordinary in all their ways. The women see but are not seen, for they wear a black veil on their faces which has small holes and they wear on their heads a turban of muslin folded many times embroidered and ornamented and upon it a white veil which reaches to their ankles, and covers their bodies. The Ishmaelites also wear cotton garments and constantly sit on straw mats or rugs, and they go with bare feet and legs and wear only a cotton garment with a girdle, and the garment reaches up to the middle of the thigh, and the women wear breeches and the wives of the Turks go to the barber once a week. But on the contrary the men wear no breeches and do not have their hair cut but they shave their head with a razor without washing the head except with a little water.

When a man marries a wife he gives her a dowry and from thenceforward he is only obliged to feed her, eating and drinking alone, but not clothing, for she must dress herself from her own money and also, when she has children, she is bound to feed them and when she is expecting a child he must not touch her, therefore they marry twenty-three wives and there are Ishmaelites who have twenty sons and daughters born in a single year. Everybody rides upon donkeys and mules for nobody, not even a Moslem, may ride a horse except only the mamelukes. Their donkeys are very fine indeed and fat and they carry valuable "bardili" and "soli" as ornaments. I saw one donkey's bardili, which were worth more than 2,000 ducats, made of precious stones and diamonds with golden fringe which they put upon it and especially the front of the bardili in front of the donkey. The Ishmaelites are like camels and oxen; just as the camel is never shod, so they go without shoes. The camel crouches and eats on the ground, so they crouch and eat on the ground without a cloth but only red leather. The camel sleeps in its harness, so they sleep and crouch on their legs and on their clothes and never undress at night. The Jews do like the Ishmaelites in all the lands and provinces of the Sultan. They have neither bed not table nor chair nor lamp, but they eat, drink and sleep on the ground always, and all their work is on the ground.

Alexandria is as big as Florence. It is well built and the city walls are high and fine, but all the city is very dry and it has more ruins than buildings. The houses are beautiful, and in each house you will find a courtyard paved with white stones and with a tree and in the middle a cistern. Each house has two cisterns, one for new water and one for old water, for the Nile comes up every year in the month of August and waters all Alexandria and the ponds get filled up when the water comes in and replenishes the cisterns, for Alexandria is hollow in consequence of the said cisterns. The fruit of Alexandria is very good and cheap, bread and meat and all kinds of fowls are cheap, but timber is very dear, and oil, honey and wine are very dear because they have to pay a heavy tax, about 24 per cent. The flax of Alexandria is very good and their linen garments fine and cheap. Rain never falls in Alexandria, except a very little in the winter. Their fruits ripen and increase very much in consequence of the quantity of dew. I never saw so much dew in my life. It looks like rain, but when the sun comes out it evaporates. The cause of the cheapness of poultry is that they hatch them in ovens. They warm the ovens and put therein cattle and horse dung and they put in 1,000 or 2,000 eggs and consequently in about three weeks they have live chickens and get no end of fowls.

III

In the months of June, July and August the air is very bad in Alexandria, and this because an evil wind rages then called the *borea* which attacks people like the black plague, God forbid! or makes them blind so that for five or six months they cannot see at all. Therefore it is that in Alexandria many people are found whose eyes are diseased, and the notables of the city at that season go to other places and do not stay in Alexandria. Particularly foreigners who come from other lands and who are not accustomed to the climate are injured and killed mostly in these three months. It is very bad to eat fruit during this season. The reason why Alexandria is ruined is that the King of Cyprus fought against it and captured it and reigned over it for three years; then the Sultan, King of Egypt, fought him and attacked and burned the city and captured the King of Cyprus. The King of Cyprus undertook to pay the King of Egypt a tribute of 10,000 dinars every year and the King of Egypt let him return to Cyprus and thus he continued to pay it until the Venetians captured Cyprus and from thenceforward the Sultan received the said tribute from the Venetian King of Cyprus year by year. Therefore it was the intention of the Sultan to help the King of Cyprus and he sent to King Firnati (Ferdinand) on behalf of his son to give him his daughter in order that the men of Cyprus should not rebel against him but pay him tribute as before. The Venetians agreed in this and they now pay the tribute to the Sultan in coins with the effigy of the King's daughter upon them, although she dwells outside Cyprus. This is the truth, for it was told me by the Gran Maestro of the Order who acted for the said Princess in Alexandria.

THE JEWS IN ALEXANDRIA

Last, but not least, there are in Alexandria about sixty Jewish householders with no Karaïtes or Samaritans among them, but only Rabbanites. Their habit of clothing is like that of the Ishmaelites. They wear no shoes but sit on the ground and enter the Synagogues without shoes and without trousers. Some Jews there are who remember that in their time there were about 4,000 householders, but they have become less and less, like the sacrificial bullocks of Tabernacles. They have two Synagogues, one big and the other small, and all the Jews testify that the small one was

built by Elijah the Prophet and he used to pray
there ; and therein there is an ark and near it a chair,
and there is always a light burning inside ; and the
Synagogue has two beadles, the one R. Joseph ben
Baruch and the other R. Halifa. They appointed
themselves beadles of the Synagogue and they told
me that in the year 1455, on the eve of the Faſt of
Atonement, they were left to sleep in the Synagogue,
they and two others, and behold they all saw at
midnight what looked like an old man sitting on the
chair and they determined to go before him humbly and
bowing down beg something of him, but, when they got
near and approached him, they looked up and he was
no more, for God had taken him. And they told me of
many wonders which they had seen in the Synagogue,
and with my own eyes I saw the MS. of the twenty-four
books of the Bible on parchment in four volumes in
very large script more beautiful than I have ever seen,
and also a scroll of the law which Ezra the Scribe had
written with his signature, and he left it as a
legacy for this Synagogue of Elijah the Prophet, and
he enjoined a curse upon the man who should remove
it from the Synagogue. I also saw other manuscripts
in that Synagogue.

In Alexandria I saw four large fondaks, one
for the Franks and another for the Genoese and their
Consul and two for the Venetians and their Consul,
and they are all on the right hand of one ſtreet as you
approach Alexandria, and opposite them in the middle
is the great fondak of the Ishmaelites. I also saw the
Admiral who had a pigeon and, whenever he wished
to send a message to the Sultan, he placed it in the
pigeon's mouth or faſtened the letter to it and the
pigeon took it to Misr (Cairo) and brought it to the
window of the Sultan's house and there was always a
man waiting in the window on the look out. And
this is really the truth and there is no doubt about it.

MESHULLAM BEN R. MENAHEM

In Alexandria all the Gentiles pay 13 ducats each on entry to the city and they cannot go out unless they pay it, but the Jews pay nothing, but every Jew must get permission from the Emir when he leaves it to go abroad, and they go in a great caravan.

IV

EGYPT

To-day, Tuesday, the 12th June, we left Alexandria, I and my companion Raphael, with the suite of Monsieur Antonio. We obtained a permit from the Gran Maestro and the Queen of Cyprus to go to Misr. We rode on donkeys and took in our company a mameluke to protect us on the way to Rosetta, where one reaches the Nile. But when we were about three miles away from Alexandria the said mameluke rose up to slay us, for he had found excuse and he carried bow and arrows and a sword and we had no weapons. He compelled us to give him eight ducats, three I and my companion paid, and Monsieur Antonio and his three companions paid five, and there was also a *mokro* with our camel which carried our things, but he also played us false and was in league with the said mameluke.

On Wednesday, the 13th June, we reached Rosetta. It is a fine city. We left the donkeys which we had ridden outside the city on the main road, for it is the custom of the Ishmaelites not to allow anybody to bring mules and asses into the city, but when you come to the said place you must leave them and an Ishmaelite immediately comes and takes them in charge, for they are appointed for that purpose. We alighted from our donkeys outside the city, because neither Jew nor Gentile is permitted to ride in the city even on donkeys. The Jews wear a yellow turban on their heads throughout the provinces of the Sultan's realm. In Rosetta we hired a boat to go to

Fohar, which is 60 miles distance from Rosetta, and we journeyed on the Nile. There was a good strong wind on the Nile, and although we were going against the current we were able to carry sail. We arrived after 23 hours' journey and found on the Nile from Rosetta to Fooah all the cities whose names I will give you. They are all on the river bank right and left. They are not walled cities, but they are bigger than the city of Frati in Tuscany, besides villages which are on the banks of the Nile. From Alexandria to Misr there are forty such villages.

On the river banks they cultivate sugar and rice in very great quantities. About a mile from Rosetta there is a large palm tree between which and Fooah are the following cities :—[Here follow 23 names, including Saideeyeh, Kelyoob and Bulak.]

While we were on the Nile dolphins pursued *mavani* (flying fish), which fled before them and glided along the water. Forty of them jumped into our boat and remained there, and at night we ate them roasted at Fooah. In the Nile I saw on many islets big serpents which are as large as human beings with very short legs and very hard skin-like scales. No man can kill them with any kind of weapon, but in the winter when they sleep on an island and sprawl on the ground with their belly upwards one can shoot them in the belly from a boat with arrows and then kill them. The Ishmaelites cut off their head and tail, although their tail is very short. They leave the lower jaws, but eat the flesh and say that it is very good to eat. The Ishmaelites call this serpent *altamsa*. It only feeds on fishes. In our language they call it crocodile, and Pliny says that it grows to 18 feet, but I saw such a serpent 5 feet long, bigger than myself or Raphael, my companion. These serpents have no lower hole, and cannot let forth their excrement, but the Lord created a fowl prepared for that purpose. This fowl is like a goose, quite white, and its head and beak is sharp and long, and it has a long but soft horn in the head and a flapper which it can raise or lower at will. When the serpent wishes to get rid of its excrement it opens its mouth. Its teeth are as sharp as a dog's, but as soon as he opens its mouth some hundreds of these birds come. The bird puts his flapper into the mouth of the serpent and raises its horn, so that the serpent cannot bite it, and eats its excrement, and when the bird is full and the serpent wants to void more another bird comes and does likewise, until the whole of its excrement has been removed through its throat. The serpent cannot live without the bird, and the bird cannot feed itself except from the excrement of the serpent. The name of the bird in the Ishmaelite tongue is apis, and in our language we call it *plinio tirkilo*, and although I know that people that hear this will not believe me, I cannot omit to write it, and I swear by God Almighty that I have seen more than a hundred of these serpents and more than a thousand of these birds ; and now let us return to our journey. We reached Fooah and there we hired a boat to go to Misr, and inasmuch as this boat belonged to one of the lords of the land, and it is their custom to arrange between themselves who should journey with whom, and the more important the greater his right. He takes the passengers with their luggage by force, and puts them in his boat, and the traveller is forced to go with him against his will. It happened to us that we hired a boat for 30 mijori up to Misr, and a deed was drawn up by an Ishmaelite scribe, for if you do not do this when you arrive they will seek twice double pay and will deny the bargain that you made with them; and after we had written out the contract and it was in our hands the owner of the boat took all our moveables into his boat and said : " You are coming with me," and he asked of us 10 ducats, but

we did not wish to pay more than 10 mijori, and
wanted to take another boat. He brought us before
the Cadi of the place and before the Emir, and said
to him in Arabic that he was a servant hired by the
Queen's Exchequer, and the Emir knew that the
Queen was in Misr at the King's request, and therefore he ordered the owner of the boat to return us our
property or else to accept the 10 majori, but we were
forced to give him another 10 majori, and we went
to Misr, and reached there on Sunday, the 14th
June, 1481.

V

I have seen Misr (Cairo) and inquired about the
people to know their ways, and, if I were to write and
describe the glory and wealth of the city and the men
therein, this book would not suffice, and I swear that
if it were possible to place all the cities of Rome,
Milan, Padua, and Florence together with four other
cities, they would not, the whole lot of them, contain
the wealth and population of the half of Misr, and this
is true. For Misr is divided into twenty-four quarters,
together with old Misr, which the natives call
Babozinia Fostat, which adjoins new Misr, which
is Cairo, half a mile away from it, and that quarter
has 30,000 householders, and in one house there are
three or four to a household. The circumference of
Misr is more than 80 miles, and if I were asked
whether I have examined Misr or counted the houses
and all this people, as though I were deceiving him,
I would answer that by heavens I swear that the
Chief Interpreter of the King, whose name is Sagri
Vardi, himself told me all this. He told me that every
night the Chiefs bring him in writing the number of
all the births and deaths in the city, and I can bring
faithful witnesses who were with me at the time when

he told me this, and particularly R. Raphael, my companion, and R. Joseph ben Hezekiah Ashkenazi, who were at the interview, and if you asked how could I converse with the interpreter—my friends, I went to visit him at the orders of the Nagid because the interpreter is of Jewish descent and came to Misr to return to Judaism, and he is a Spaniard; the Pregadino placed a mesh on all the land of Spain and all the Jews were captured in it, and this man, in order to remain free, changed his religion and became a Moro (Musulman). He knows seven languages—Hebrew, Italian, Turkish, Greek, Arabic, German, and French. At the Sultan's Court they talk Turkish. He gave me much benefit and privileges. I never had to pay any duty on the precious stones which I bought in Misr on which people pay 10 per cent, and he also wrote to the interpreter at Jerusalem and gave orders that they were to take nothing from me, although the Jews there pay 3 ducats a head.

To return to the first point, old Misr, which is called Babozinia, is all in ruins and few people live there. It has a synagogue of Elijah the Prophet, like that of Alexandria, and on the other side of the Nile there are three great treasure chambers, like a city rising to a diamond point. These are the pyramids, of which I have seen nothing so big, even in Rome. They are very much higher than the foundation-base, and if a man stands on top of the pyramid in the middle and throws a stone, he cannot throw it outside the structure. They are built out of stones great beyond measure. Near them is the Synagogue of our Patriarch Moses, in which he used to sit and pray before he went to speak to Pharaoh, and the river between the treasure chambers and Cairo and the place is called Rames, and many Jews tell me that wonders are seen there every day, and the treasuries of Joseph are also near them. New Cairo has also a circumference of about 80 miles, and there is not even a single house in it in ruins, and the lanes of the city are short and narrower than the lanes of Venice, and the tops of the houses meet one another and some have the road shaded with palm-trees because of the great and terrible heat. Without this it would be impossible to live there.

In Misr are to be found more than 10,000 men, appointed constantly to sprinkle water in the city, in order to lay the dust. They put the water into many receptacles, and at every moment one can see more than 4,000 men carrying a cistern of water like a vessel which has a linen pipe, and they sell the water to anybody for 1 filipo to drink in good vessels, as much as he pleases ; and if he wishes to drink from other men after he has given the filipo to one water-seller and gone elsewhere, he gives some solidi to the man for himself and takes the water from him, and they can tell whether he has originally paid his filipo. Every hour and every moment you can find water to drink. They have also scented water, which you can drink if you like, and they drink Nile water, that comes from that river. There is nothing so good as that water, and a man may drink his bellyfull of it and never be hurt, for it is as sweet as honey and comes from the Garden of Eden. The women wear breeches, but not the men, just as in Alexandria, and they carry on the cords or laces of the breeches precious stones and pearls, and in their ears they have ten or eight holes, and they thread in them precious stones. The Moorish women do not wear golden rings, but silver, with precious stones and pearls set therein. They ornament their skin with colours, which are not removed by water in six months, although they go every day to the baths. There are no baths as fine as those of Egypt, and there are lavatories there. The saddles of the donkeys are worth very much, and the mamelukes wear on their horse saddles many precious stones, pearls, and also on the bridles, beyond description. They are very clean in their person, and the Moorish rider wears a fine white garment, and the mameluke also wears clean clothes, but in their feeding they are pigs. They sit on the ground or the carpet or a linen box without a cover. They put neither a cloth nor knife nor salt on the table, they all eat out of one vessel, both servants and master, they eat with their fingers, and most are always squatting, and when they want to show honour to anybody they bring raisin wine a thousand times stronger than malmsey. You have to drink twice before they give you anything to eat except fruit. Finally you have to drink to all those who are sitting round, and everyone that drinks says to his neighbour " To your honour ", and takes a fruit and puts it in his hand, and says " For life and healing ", and everyone does the same, and you have to wait two hours before you come to the meal, and I had already drunk twice and they had also drunk; and if you do not drink it is an insult to the host. It happened to me several times, although I knew it before, and so I made it a condition before I went and said to them that I cannot possibly drink because I have a bodily illness, and so I guarded myself from that drinking, but my companion Raphael took my place, and certainly he could not tell the difference between cursed Haman and blessed Mordecai, but that drinking was for me not compulsory.

To return to our former subject. In Misr there are big fondaks, with a street between them, and round the street the houses are shops with two, three, or four doors, which are closed every night, and there are always watchmen there; and in the fondaks there are all kinds of goods, and the merchants and craftsmen sit near their shops, which are very small, and show samples of all their goods ; and if you wish to buy from them, a matter of importance, of some value they bring you into their warehouse, and there you can see the wonderful goods they have, for you could hardly believe that there are one thousand and more warehouses in each fondak; and there is nothing in the world that you do not find in the fondaks in Misr, even the smallest things. The roads in Misr are short and dark, but when you go into the houses you can see wonderful mosaics, and most people dwell in the basement.

On Friday, the 22nd June, 1481, I saw the Sultan face to face. He is an old man of 80, but straight as a reed, tall, and good looking, clothed in a white garment. He was riding, and more than two thousand mameluke soldiers were with him. They said that a treasure had been found in the city and the King went to inspect it. Anyone who wishes to see the Sultan can see him easily. He has a fine large fort in the city, and he sits on the front on Mondays and Thursdays openly in the company of the Governor of the city, and his Dragomans at his side, and mamelukes all round, more than three hundred to protect him. If anybody wishes to complain of any violence or theft which the princes or lords had done to him he can then complain, and this is the reason why the nobles of the land take care to do nothing improper.

Rain never falls in Misr, but the dew is wonderful. It falls on the ground every day, on the gardens and orchards in Misr, and from Bulak on the Nile they water the gardens by means of canals; and in Bulak is a place which you ascend by steps, and they have marks upon it on the ground from step to step, and when the Nile rises it covers the steps and they have a sign to mark whether the year is plentiful or moderate or the reverse, and it is this : If the water rises sixteen steps and not more, it is a year of much famine, but if it rises to eighteen steps it is a medium year; and if it rises to twenty steps it is a year of plenty, and if it rises to twenty-two steps it is a year of the utmost prosperity and cheapness, and the Nile never exceeds this mark ; and every day they proclaim in Misr that the Nile has risen so and so much, and, when it ceases to rise any more, the King goes with a big crowd to that place with songs and timbrels and harps, and the Sultan himself begins to dig in that place (in order to make a trench for the water to irrigate the gardens), and after that his servants dig trenches and the water goes forth on the face of all the land, and waters all Egypt ; and this is generally at the end of the month of August.

VI

THE JEWS IN CAIRO

In Misr there are about eight hundred Jewish householders, and about as many Karaïte house-holders, and fifty Samaritan householders. You know already that the Karaites observe the written law and the Samaritans part of the written law, but they are idolators. Their script is different from all others, and they have not the letters ע, ה, א or ח, ב, צ, and when you say Ja'aqob they say Jaqob. Isaac they pronounce Issak, and so on, and their law and all their books are in their own script. Three times a year they ascend Mount Gerizim, and they have an altar there and they carry a golden dove and place it on the altar. They do not go up to Jerusalem, for they say that Mount Gerizim is the Mount of Jerusalem, and they sacrifice a lamb for Passover and do not break its bones. They live in a quarter of their own, and they have a Synagogue of their own, and they keep Sabbath till midday, and then they profane it. Also the Karaïtes have two Synagogues of their own, and the good Jews (the Rabbanites), who keep both written law and oral law like we do,

also live apart, and they have six synagogues; and the
Sultan has placed over the Jews, the Karaïtes, and the
Samaritans, a Jewish lord, rich and learned and much
honoured. His name is R. Solomon ben R. Joseph.
He is a native of this country, and his father was also
Nagid and the Sultan's physician. The Nagid has
power over the Jews in all the Sultan's dominions;
both in criminal and civil matters his word cannot
be contradicted. He has four Judges, and their names
are R. Jacob ben R. Samuel Rabakh, R. Jacob al
Fabuya, R. Samuel ben Achil, and R. Aaron Meppi,
and two clerks named R. Judah Aruba and R. David
Alhamar, who keeps a prison. On the second day
of my arrival in Misr R. Parisilah of Rosetta sent
for me and the Nagid, who showed me very
much honour, and this because there was a Jew there,
a great dealer in precious stones, called R. Moses
di Villa. Rialah, who introduced me to him, for twenty-
two years ago he was in our house in Florence, and
our father of blessed memory honoured him
particularly in our estate called Polveroso. He
remembered the kindness done him by our father,
and told the Nagid of our father, and of me that we
were rich then and owned more than 100,000 ducats,
and he praised us very much. And so from that day
onwards I was forced to sit next to the Nagid in the
Synagogue, between him and the Judges, and was
also forced to eat with him very many times; and
seeing that he honoured me in the presence of all
the Jews they all honoured me also, and many of the
notables and particularly R. Jacob de Baro, the richest
and most honoured man in the city, and he and his
father looked upon me as though I were a king, and
they invited me to their house to eat and drink with
them with the permission of the Nagid. This because
no man may presume to invite any Jew to eat and
drink with him, after the Nagid has honoured him with

an invitation to his table, in order that it may not seem as though he wanted to be Nagid like the Nagid; and not only this but the Nagid made me find favour in the eyes of the Sultan's great dragoman who is called Tagri Vardi, and is of Jewish descent, as I have said above, and when I travelled from Misr to go to Jerusalem the Holy City, the dragoman wrote a letter to the dragoman of Jerusalem, and the Nagid wrote to the Vice-Nagid in my favour, so that I was received there with much honour, as I will write, D.V., when speaking of Jerusalem, I did not pay the dragoman the tax which the Jews pay, and the Vice-Nagid gave me a house full of all good things for my dwelling.

Among the Jews there are many honoured people, and particularly those whom I have mentioned, and the counsellors who stand by the Nagid, whose names are R. Samuel Rabakh and R. Jacob, his son, and R. Joshua Alhamar, R. Zedakah b. Obri, R. Abraham, the disciple, for he says that he was the disciple of R. Moses Fisi, R. Jacob al Fabuya, R. Suleiman Inso, and particularly R. Samuel Rabakh and his son. He is a great man, and very, very charitable, and the King loves him, and he is physician to the King, the Sultan; and also R. Jacob, his son, walks in the way of his father. He is 35 years old, God-fearing, and free from vice ; none are as good as they in Misr. They honoured me in their house, with the Nagid's permission, several times, and there my companion Raphael got well drunk. From him I received a list of all the goods which come into Egypt twice a year, which the Gentiles take to Christian countries. There are 3,300 different kinds of goods, mostly spices and medicines. The Moslems are bad to people, and sin against God. They are only to be trusted, because of their fear of the Government. No Jew or Gentile may point with his second finger or the Moslem might cut it off or kill him, God forbid, nor may they go to the mosque. The Moslems when they go to the mosque, bathe, and every mosque has a fountain in order that they can wash therein five times a day, and they keep their Sabbath on Friday ; but they only keep it holy two hours while they are in their house of prayer. They have two feasts in the year, and they fast thirty days consecutively once a year. This fast of theirs is like the Jewish fast, and it is with reference to them that the Author of the prayer, Oleinu Leshabéah, says that they worship vanity *habel* (*h*) for their five daily washes, (*b*) for their two annual feasts, and (*l*) for their thirty days' fast.

VII

We left Misr on the 4th July, 1481, may it be the Almighty's will that I may reach Jerusalem and fulfil my vows, and that he may let me go back to my house in life and joy and peace. The same day, when we were five miles distance from Misr, we saw on the left-hand of the road a small pyramid of a single stone, and opposite a garden in which they make spices ; and I saw that in that garden there are about one hundred very small trees, and they have thin branches, and their foliage is small like that of gum-trees, but greener and thinner ; and in the garden there is a fountain of running water, and they sprinkle the trees with this water, and also the ground around the trees every day. The trees only grow in that garden. The Moslems have already tried to remove some trees with their earth and plant them in another place, but only so long as they water them with that water do the trees remain alive and full of sap, though giving very little balsam; but if they put other waters upon them the trees dry up. They make balsam in the following way : They remove the bark from the tree and cut the small branches, whence the balsam issues into a vessel placed beneath, and although the garden is surrounded by a wall, every tree has five guards so that nobody can touch them. All the juice they extract they carry once a year to the Sultan, and he gives a little of it to those who are of the first rank in the kingdom ; and, as sure as I live, I saw in the house of the great dragoman that he had a little which the Sultan had given him, and he had a friend called Muhammad who was cutting wood, and the axe fell on his foot and struck the big toe of his left foot, and the toe was nearly cut off. He placed on the wound a little of this balsam, and in three days it was healed, and no sign of the wound remained. I never saw anything so wonderful in all my days. This oil is thick, and like castor oil, and if anyone tells you that he has brought this balm to Tuscany do not believe him, because it is impossible that any man should get hold of it other than lords, and very few of them.

On the same day we went with my dragoman, called Behar Joseph bar Hezekiah, to a big city surrounded by a wall called Alhanika, that is Rephidim. It is two miles distance from Misr, and there are twenty Jewish householders there. There the caravan of the Islam dragoman waited in order to speed us on our journey. We left Alhanika on Friday morning about dawn of the 12th July, with a caravan, about one hundred and twenty Ishmaelites and Turks with camels. The desert begins there, and when we were about six miles distant, near the place called Baro, an Arab on horseback lying in wait came to meet us, but when he saw that we were many and strong, and with bows and riding on horseback, he fled. The same day we reached a city like Alhanika, called Bilibis, that is Goshen. There are three Jewish householders there, honoured workpeople. They prepared for us a bed and table and chair and candle in a chamber near the synagogue. One honoured Jew, called R.

Melammed Cohen, and R. David, his son, took me
and my friend on the Sabbath to eat with them ;
may the Lord reward him for his kindness to us.
Whilst we were still in Misr some time ago we saw
with our eyes that the Sultan sentenced a man called
Orbano to death because he was a robber chief. They
flayed his skin from him, and began to flay him from
his ankles. And so his brother rose up to avenge his
blood, and went into the desert with five hundred
men mounted on horses and with bows, and they rob
everybody ; and we had to be afraid of them and stop
at Bilibis, and the caravan did not start until the
Sabbath after night, when a caravan of about four
hundred Turks reached Bilibis all on horseback and
armed with bows who were going to Lamin. We left
Bilibis on Sunday, the 13th, with the two said
caravans, and in two days we reached a small place
called Hatara, where no Jews live. We entered the
desert, and all the way wore white turbans on our
heads like Ishmaelites or Turks, with the permission
of the chief of the caravan, although he knew that
we were Jews, because Jews and foreigners pay a
heavy tax, and although the people of the place spoke
with me and I could not understand their language,
they thought that I was an inhabitant of Turkey
because all my ways were like their ways. The Turks
and the Ishmaelites have the same faith, and speak
a different language, and do not understand each
other. We left Hatara on Monday, the 14th July,
1481, and arrived at a place called Salahia, a small
place like Hatara, and there we paid the same tax
as Turks, for the inhabitants are appointed by the
Sultan to guard the roads and the riders ; and they
may take from each horse half a majori, called *brix*,
which is like our dinar, but from Jews and foreigners
they take more than they should, as robbers do, and
after we had paid the tax an Ishmaelite betrayed that

our dragoman was a Jew, and they called us back; and all the men of the place rose up against us and asked two ducats from us, but the Turkish lord, the chief of the caravan, rose up in anger and said : "It is true he is a Jew, but I have bought him, and he is my slave"; and he saved us from their hands by his strength, although they uttered great cries, and we remained free, thank God.

We left Salahia on Tuesday, the 15th July, and reached the city of Rivayrar, and there we paid the tax like Turks. It is a place like Hatara. Rivayrar means a well. We left there on Wednesday the 16th, and reached Kastaia, a fine city, with many palm-trees, more than one can count. It is not surrounded by a wall. It is the residence of the Admiral, called the Emir. There everyone of us paid a tax, whoever he might be, and also for every camel, because this Emir pays to the Sultan every year for this passage and the palms and the fruit of the palms a thousand golden ducats per annum. We should have had to pay more than the two ducats, but providentially my dragoman is a great friend of the Emir and therefore we only paid a majori; and as we could not stop and spend the Sabbath in the desert if we went with the caravan, we left them on the Thursday and stayed at Kastaia until the Sabbath; but, close on 24 o'clock of the Friday, a caravan of Turks all armed with bows arrived, and were delayed overnight. Thank God for our good fortune, in that He has enabled us to go up to Jerusalem and return home in life and peace. Seeing that the Emir was a friend of R. Joseph, our interpreter as mentioned, he sent two mamelukes to speak to the head of the caravan to allow us to go with him as far as Gaza and entrusted us to his care. The noble lord, the head of the caravan, replied that we should wear a white sash like the Turks and Moslems, and fear nobody, for he would be responsible, and please

God he would bring us safe to our destination.
We left Kastaia on Sunday, the 18th July, 1481, with
the said caravan of Turks, and on the same day we
arrived at a place called Bir-Debur, that is Eber's
Well. It is a small place where there is brackish
water, and we came to a place called Sabri, and there
we stayed till midday, and in the morning we arrived
at a placed called Arari. All these places have custom
houses, and we were kept there till night after the
great heat had passed, and at midnight the head of the
customs came to me and asked me in Arabic, but I
did not know what to reply, but the head of the
caravan quickly said : " Do not speak with him for
he does not understand your language, as he is a
Turk," and so the Moslems did not get to know that
I was a Jew. We left there on Monday, the 19th, and
arrived at a place called Malhasin. It is a small
place also, and there we stayed all day until
21 o'clock ; and there a big toll is demanded, and on the
same day we journeyed also, and came to a place
called Harish, that is Succoth, for in Arabic *harish*
means hut. This is the place built by our father
Jacob, peace to his memory, and there is only one
little house there in ruins and a well of brackish water ;
and behold, at night there came upon us a swarm
of insects found in the sand of the desert, as large as
two flies and rather red. They say that these are
the lice with which Pharaoh was plagued, and they
bit me big bites, but fortunately we had lemons which
we brought with us from Misr, because we knew
about them, that there was no remedy to their bite
except lemon juice, for the juice prevents the wound
festering in man's flesh, and I swear that in all my days
I never had so much pain as that night, and my
companion, Raphael, was also afflicted like me,
and some of the Turks of our caravan were also
plagued. We left there on Tuesday, the 20th, and

arrived at a place called Asika, in Arabic called Azan, and there we found a little sweet water. It is a place as small as Succoth, and there we ſtopped in the morning to eat, and our soul was sated with these waters because in all the desert we had only found brackish water ; and there we ſtayed till evening, and we paid cuſtoms as in the other places. It is about four miles from the sea, and the Moslems keep guard there because of the corsaires from the sea. They are moſtly corsairs of Rhodes who come moſtly to levy booty from the travellers there. At nightfall we left the place and arrived at midnight at a place called al-Khan. It is a big fondak building, but there was neither man or woman there because on the previous night four fishing-boats had come from Rhodes and captured sixty men who were passing in big companies. And those who were in al-Khan fled when they heard them and left all their property and went to Gaza ; and the corsair robbers were about four hundred men and they wanted to capture the men of the fondak, but they only found their tools and clothes and they took all the spoil and went away. God was good to us that we did not reach there earlier else we should have been captured, God forbid, thanks be to the Lord.

VIII

GAZA

We journeyed from al-Khan on Wednesday, the 21st, and reached Gaza, and when we were about a mile from Gaza we heard that the robbers (Orbano's followers) were about, and nobody left his house door, for they had slain three men near Gaza and taken from them two camels laden with merchandize. When we heard this the fear of the robbers fell upon our hearts and upon the hearts of all the caravan, until we arrived at the place where our father Abraham said to his servant, "Wait ye here with the ass"; and there we heard that the way was safe up to Gaza, but we were not to leave Gaza until we had a caravan of four to five thousand men, and thank God we reached Gaza in peace and when we approached the city we saw the fondak called Al-Khan, and this is the place where the troops or caravans stop. It has very large courts and behind them the men stay behind curtains, and we saw that the places were full of men here and there, for all the caravans which had reached there had stopped because of the disturbance, and there were more than seven thousand men and ten thousand camels in Gaza who were going to Damascus; and we passed a khan near to Jaruca and we there heard that the whole city was in anxiety for the Niepo, that is, the lord of the place, who had gone against the said Orbano to assist the Niepo of another city called Ramleh or Gath, because the men of Orbano had attacked Gath and consumed it with fire; and then it was not known what would be the result, and, therefore, all the caravans stopped there.

Gazza is called by the Moslems Gaza. It is a fine and renowned place, and its fruits are very renowned and good. Bread and good wine is to be found there, but only Jews make wine. Gaza has a circumference of four miles and no walls. It is about six miles from the sea and situated in a valley and on a hill. It has a population as numerous as the sands of the sea, and there are about fifty (sixty) Jewish householders, artisans. They have a small but pretty Synagogue, and vineyards and fields and houses. They had already begun to make the new wine. They showed us much honour, especially R. Moses bar Judah Sephardi, who stutters a little, and R. Meir Sephardi, the money changer, the father-in-law of R. Moses, of Villa Marina Riale. The Jews live at the top of the hill. May God exalt them. There are also four Samaritan householders who live on the hillside. At the top of the Judecca (Jewish quarter) is the house of Delilah in which the mighty Samson dwelt, and about one-eighth of a mile beyond it at the top of the hill I saw a great group of buildings which by his strength and might he caused to fall. Those houses are now ruined and desolate, but to this very day it can be seen that the court was in truth very great. From Misr to Gaza is 298 miles, thanks be to the Lord, who has protected us from the dangers between Misr and Gaza.

And in order, my friends, that you may know the things we had to do and everyone has to do who takes this route, I will briefly relate them. From the balsam garden to Gaza and also close up to Jerusalem it is all desert, and every man must carry on his beast two sacks, one of biscuits and the other of straw and fodder, also water skins, for there you cannot find sweet water, but only salt. You must also take with you lemons because of the insects which I wrote about above, and you must go in a big caravan because of the robbers who frequent the desert, and you must go slowly for two reasons; the one because in the desert there is much dust and sand and the horses sink in it up to their knees and go with difficulty, and secondly because the dust rises and gets into a man's mouth and makes his throat dry and kills him with thirst, and if he drinks of the hot brackish water he is troubled worse than before. Moreover, a man who does not know Arabic must dress like a Turk in order that he may not be taken for a Jew or Frank, else even a Jubilee would not set him free from paying much money to the coffre, that is, taxes ; but you must wear a white cover on your head like the Turks and Moslems do, and there is great danger, lest, God forbid, anyone of the caravan should tell that you are

a Jew or Frank; and if you have escaped all these
you will always find people lying in wait on the road
who are hidden in sand up to their necks, two or
three days without food or drink, who put a stone
in front of them, and they can see other people but
the others cannot see them, and when they see a
caravan rather smaller and weaker than their own
they go out and call their fellows and ride on their
horses swift as leopards, with bamboo lances topped
with iron in their hands, which are very hard. They
also carry a pirate's mace in their hands and bucklers
made of parchment and pitch, and they ride naked
with only a shirt upon them, without trousers or shoes
or spurs, and they come upon the caravans suddenly
and take everything, even the clothes and horses,
and sometimes they kill them; but generally they rob
but do not kill them, therefore it is good to be in
a caravan of Turks who are all good bowmen, and
the robbers fear them because they are naked and
cannot shoot, and two Turks could put ten Ishmaelites
to flight. And if you escape them there is another
great danger from corsairs. These are all foreigners
who come in *Schioppette* (sloops) and are armed, and
they are good fighters and wear Turkish clothes. When
you come to the custom houses if you do a single
thing not according to their usage they will at once
understand that you are not a Turk or an Ishmaelite,
and they are always on the watch, and if you ask
me what their manner is and what to do it is necessary
that when you reach those places you must immediately
take your shoes off and sit on the ground and bend
your legs under you and never let your legs appear
or stand upon them at all, but you must eat on the
ground, and if crumbs fall from the bread pick them
up, but do not eat the bread until you have put it
on your head, and you must give to the people around
you a little of all you eat, even if they are not eating

with you; and you muſt never take any of your clothes
off, but you muſt sleep in them at night, and if they
pass you anything to eat you muſt ſtretch forth your
hand to take it with a bow, and, when you go to relieve
yourself, take care not to lift up any of your clothes
and keep close to the ground. You muſt never go
to the house of anybody with shoes and never speak
to anybody except seated with your legs bent beneath
you, and even if you have only one loaf of bread and
one cup of wine and a man comes and takes it and eats
and drinks you muſt let him do so, for even if they take
from Kings there is no redress and nothing to do,
and it is their cuſtom when they go to eat to sit in
a circle, and they all eat out of one vessel, slaves and
maſters are all alike, and they place their hands into
the dish and take a handful out and do not place
before them either a napkin or a knife or salt; and
they never wash their hands except after eating,
when they wash their arms up to the elbow. Some
people clean their hands in fine white duſt somewhat
scented, which in Arabic they call *raihān*. It is also
their cuſtom to give no fodder to donkeys and nothing
to drink, only all the caravan together, for it is by
their law a great sin that the other horses or small
donkeys should see one of them eat, because that would
hurt those that are not eating, and that is cruelty
to animals; and, therefore, every man muſt be careful
not to transgress their cuſtoms lest, God forbid,
they find out that he is a Jew or Frank, and unlucky
is he that falls into this trap.

And even if you escape all these dangers yourself
it often happens to people that the horses on which
they ride die, or they are nearly dead when they reach
Jerusalem, because of the brackish water they drink,
and the great heat and the duſt which comes into their
mouths, and the sand in which they go up to the
knees in great pain and also because of the want of

food and the long journey; therefore a man mu&t be very careful in his ways and add wisdom to wisdom so as to save himself from all these many evils, and to be always cleaving to the Lord and to pray that he will deliver him from them. So be it, Amen. In this desert heaps and heaps of bones of camels, horses, and asses are to be found who have died there, as above stated and no pa&ture can be found in the wilderness; and every man mu&t take with him a long piece of iron with a point (campanelli) on its head in order to push it into the ground so as to fa&ten horses or ass to it; for there is nothing else to fasten them to, not even a shrub, for they do not grow there, and the irons mu&t be long because the sand does not hold the iron unless it goes two cubits into the ground, and even then it is difficult to pull it out.

We were also forced to delay in Gaza because of the fear of the robbers, who are Orbano highwaymen, as we saw with our own eyes in Egypt; for the Sultan ordered Orbano the Robber Chief to be beheaded and to fill his skin with &traw and to have him carried through the city on a camel, and Orbano's brother went forth to avenge him with some of his companions, and they are a hard lot who go hither and thither robbing people; and the King sent a large force after him but could not prevail, and the Orbanians began to become very &trong, especially now that the Sultan has few mamelukes because King Asampik, called Uzun Hasan, had made war upon him and conquered three cities and killed thirty thousand mamelukes and also killed the great Rergvira, that is, his deputy who governs the land; and all the Orbanians feared him more than the Sultan, for he executed punishment on them, so now they have found a place and time to do whatever they care to do. But the Emir of Gaza, as said above, went to prote& the Emir of Ramleh and went afield, as I

myself saw, but the Orbanians prevailed over him
on the same day and killed all his force and all the
troops of the Niepo of Gaza, twenty three thousand
in number, and only he alone escaped and about
one hundred men and some horses; and had not
other Orbanians come to his assistance, who were hostile
to the others, he also would have met with his death.
He returned to Gaza mourning and having his head
covered. All the roads are very, very dangerous.
and we do not know what to do and may the Lord
help us.

In Gaza we stayed until Monday, the 27th July,
1481, and the same day we found in Gaza the Niepo
of Hebron, that is, its great Lord, and he had to return
to Hebron, and with him were more than two hundred
horses and their riders; and we went with him in
safety, for we had no reason to fear the Orbanians,
for they all love him seeing that he is the Lord of the
cave of Machpelah, and the Orbanians honour that
place more than other people do, and we arrived there
in peace.

IX

Hebron is like Gaza, but in a valley. It has no walls
and is in a fat and rich valley. I saw the cave of
Machpelah which is where the ground rises and it
looks like this : the cave is in a field in the midst
of Hebron and the Moslems have built a mosque
upon it, as is their custom, and they have made a
wall over the cave and in it is a small window where
the Jews pray and throw into it money and spices.
I also prayed there. The Moslems honour the place
very much and give thirteen thousand loaves every
day to the poor in honour of Abraham, Isaac, and
Jacob, and especially in honour of Abraham; and they
put the bread in mustard and tender veal, such as
Abraham gave to the angels, and in honour of Isaac

they give venison and delicacies such as he loved, and in honour of Jacob bread and a mess of pottage such as he gave to Esau, and this constantly every day without fail. About twenty (*l.v.* 80) Jewish householders live there and no more, and from them I heard that in the mosque opposite the graves of Abraham and Sarah there is a golden candlestick with precious stones, and opposite the tombs of Isaac, Jacob, Rebecca, and Leah, there is a silver candlestick with precious stones, and on their graves are silk and embroidered garments. They know this from their women, for many of them go into the mosque, as they are not recognised because of the black veil they wear on their faces, and the guards of the caves think they are Moslem women; and from the mouths of these women I also heard that the cave derives income from the lands near the cave and owns vineyards and olives and houses too numerous to count which the Moslems give for their dead to atone for them, and their revenue from people is more than five hundred thousand golden ducats every year.

We left Hebron on Tuesday, the 28th July, and went in the company of two good and honoured mamelukes, because there are only occasionally caravans of Christian *macinatori* from Hebron to Jerusalem, for the caravan does not go to Jerusalem. So we were obliged to accompany these two men, and with them there was a bastard whose intention was to kill us. His name is Ali and he was a Moslem. We took our lives in our hands and went with him. At nightfall we reached a village called Halibi, and that bastard went into the village and induced three robbers, companions of his, to rob us on the journey, and that man Ali came and deceitfully spoke to us and said that we should go with him and two of the mamelukes and he would bring us by an indirect path so that we should not have to pay tolls until

MESHULLAM BEN R. MENAHEM

Jerusalem. The mamelukes believed him and so did we. We journeyed forth at midnight and he brought us in a circle to a place ten miles from Hebron, where there was a house in ruins and a cave where Jesse, the father of David, was buried ; and they say that this cave reaches to the cave of Machpelah, and the cursed man led us by ways which nobody had passed before into a great wood on the hills, and when we reached the middle of the woods the cursed Ali said, " I now want the two ducats which you have promised me." My companion, the dragoman, said, " We only promised you one golden ducat. Anyhow, we shall give you what you want when we reach Jerusalem, and now we shall give you half a ducat because we have no more " ; and the bastard wished to see our money and, therefore, he made excuses. He had a bow and arrows and was riding on a fine horse, a jennet, and he left us and went and called in the woods, and when the mamelukes saw this they went after him and spoke to his heart, and Joseph, the dragoman, said to them, for God had put the words in his mouth, " Know that if this man does any wrong to us or kills us you will not escape, for the Jews know the matter, for we went with the Niepo from Hebron and they will seek us through him, and the Niepo knows that we went with you and he will seek us at your hands, and what will you reply ? " And the good mamelukes, who had no intention to harm us, replied to him, " By our lives we will kill him," and they also had bows and arrows and they went after the man and they brought him back, and R. Joseph, the dragoman, went after them in stealth in order to hear their words, and I and Raphael, my companion, were left alone in the middle of the wood, and the dragoman heard Ali say, " Let me do this because I have three companions with whom I have spoken at night in Halevi, and we will kill them and take their horses and all that they have got and divide equally, because they are very rich and who will seek them at our hands ? " Then the mamelukes replied, " Do not think so, for it is our duty to guard them, for the Lord the Niepo of Hebron has entrusted them to our hands, and it is for us to account for them." Then the bastard answered, " You tell the Niepo that you left them near to Jerusalem or that Orbanites slew them, and that you fled with their good horses and they pursued you, because they recognised that you were mamelukes, and you were not able to save them and are guiltless." All this the said Joseph heard when he went behind them in order to find out whether the mamelukes would consent after all the talk, and when the mamelukes saw that Ali would not listen to them they said to him " Choose one of two things : either die here, for we will slay you, or come with us, because we do not wish you to call your companions, because of the responsibility for this rests upon us. If you come with us we swear by the life of our King that we will not betray your secret to anybody " ; and for this reason he returned against his will, and the mamelukes said to us, " Let us go in front with this cursed fellow and you go behind us near to us. Then there was much talk between them, and the mamelukes placed him between them so that he could not flee, and thus we went at night by moonshine until dawn, and when Ali saw that it was dawn he said to the mamelukes, " I wish to leave my horse here in a village," because he was afraid to enter Jerusalem for fear that the mamelukes would betray him to the Emir of Jerusalem. So he made himself scarce, and we went hurriedly to Bethlehem, and from there on the high road we found Rachel's tomb. It is a high monument of stones and the Moslems have placed above her grave four pillars and an arch above. They honour her and both

Jews and Moslems pray there. God protected us
from the hands of that betrayer, and robber, and we
gave to the mamelukes each a ducat instead of to the
villain, and anyhow, we paid no tax because of the
roundabout journey we made, for there are seven toll
houses between Hebron and Jerusalem.

On the same day we arrived in Jerusalem, the Holy
City, in peace, thanks be to the Lord, who sent us
those two mamelukes to save our lives from death.
On the way we found at the well of Bekr (the Virgin)
more than ten thousand men who were proceeding
against the Orbanites and none could go out and none
could come in. You see, therefore, that if we had
delayed a single day we should not have been able
to get through and should have been in great danger.
Blessed be He and blessed be His name who doeth
good unto the undeserving.

X

JERUSALEM

On Wednesday, the 29th July, we reached the
Holy City of Jerusalem, and when I saw its ruins I
rent my garments a hand breadth, and in the bitterness
of my heart recited the appropriate prayer which I had
in a small book.

Now Jerusalem has no walls except a little on one
side where I entered, and although through our sins
it is all in ruins there are ten thousand Moslem householders and about two hundred and fifty Jewish
householders. The Temple, may it be restored
speedily in our days, is still surrounded by a wall.
On the east side are the Gates of Mercy made of brass
and embedded in the ground. The gates are closed
and on the sides of the gates are Moslem graves.
Opposite this is the site of the Temple of King Solomon
and a Moslem building upon it. The huge stones
in this building are a wondrous matter, and it is difficult

to believe how the strength of man could have moved them into their present position. Near the sanctuary is a great vaulted building with pillars surrounding the large pavement which covers the Temple area. The circumference of the Temple seems about half a mile. On the western side of the pavement there is a place about three fingers high which is said to be the Eben Shethiah, and there is a great cupola beautifully gilded, about twenty or perhaps thirty cubits square. It is very high, and the Ishmaelites have covered it with lead, and they say that this is doubtless the Holy of Holies. On the border of the Holy of Holies there is a place about two and a half cubits high, and at its four corners there are stones to get up to it. Here there is a well of running water and near it the cupola is built. The Moslems only go inside after bathing five times, and they do not approach a woman three days previously. Many Moslem servants in a state of purification are there and they light seven lamps inside. I know, my friends, that there can be no doubt about this, because every year when the Jews go to Synagogue on the eve of the 9th of Ab all the lamps in the Temple Court go out of their own accord, and cannot be kindled again, and the Moslems know when it is the 9th of Ab, which they observe somewhat like the Jews because of this. This is clear and known to everyone without any doubt. On the southern side, inside the temple area, there is a large and beautiful house also covered with lead called Solomon's College, and in the middle of the temple area there are about ten olive trees ; and now by the King's command they are building inside a place for him when he wishes to go up to Jerusalem. The walls round the temple area where it was broken down and burnt have been built up by the Ishmaelites, and it is now completely surrounded, although very bare. The walls are not as high as they originally were because of our transgressions, and the Moslems who dwell in their houses opposite the walls overlook them. The temple area has twelve gates, of which five are closed; two are the Gates of Mercy, in one of which bridegrooms enter, and in the others mourners. They are of iron closed and embedded about two cubits in the ground and project about four cubits above the ground, and the other three gates are built in the wall, for they were built by the Moslems and their character is evident; and before all these gates you will find wide and goodly roads vaulted with houses on either side, in which pilgrims once dwelt, but now through our iniquities the Moslems make in them shops for all kinds of merchandise.

The temple area is on Mount Moriah in the place where our father Abraham bound his son Isaac for sacrifice, and opposite, to the east, is the Mount of Olives, and the Valley of Jehoshaphat in between. This valley begins a little to the north of the temple area, and the Mount of Olivet is steep and narrow at the beginning but it afterwards rises and broadens out very much above; and at the top of the hill is the cave of Huldah the prophetess, and she is buried there, and there is a tomb near upon it and a large building; but the house is somewhat in ruins, and when one descends down the hill one comes to the grave of the prophet Haggai, may his rest be honoured, and about three steps from there is the grave of the prophet Habakkuk, peace be with him. This is opposite the temple area. Below there, in the valley, somewhat to the south, is the monument of Absalom. It is built of large stones round it and made " punte de diamanti." It is very beautiful, like a high tower surrounded by pillars, and the whole structure is of single stones, even the pillars. Round the tower are many caves of saints who are buried there to the south, and a little more to the south is the cave of the prophet Zachariah, may peace be with him, and on the cave is a tower like Absalom's but the entrance to the cave can be seen ; and the cupola of the tower is in two parts, and near the cave are many caves of saints buried there, and one cave has a house built of a single stone. All who pass Absalom's monument, even the Moslem, throw a stone on his grave because he rebelled against his father, and at the side there is a very great heap of stones, and every year the heap is removed.

On the southern side is Mount Zion, that is the city of David, and above it, near to David's tomb, there is a church of the Franciscans. The place of David's burial is a house which has a great iron door, and the Moslems take care of the key and honour the place and pray there. Going down from there on the slope of the hill is the valley of the son of Hinnom, which goes down to the valley of Jehoshaphat ; and on the west is Millo, which is a plain near the city where people go out to walk, especially the Jews. On this road, if you go to the west about two miles, a little distance from the road bed to the right on the way to Jerusalem you find a cave with a door of hewn stone by which you enter. It is all covered up and has many caves, cave upon cave, very beautiful, those of the seventy Sanhedrin, and I prayed in that place ; and if you go another two miles you come into a valley where there is a great bridge of stones, in which place David slew the Philistine. After that I ascended a big hill about two miles away, about six miles or a little more distance from Jerusalem, that is Ramah, the place of our Lord the Prophet Samuel, on whom be peace, and about half a mile before I reached Ramah I found two pools, that is, the upper pool and the lower pool. They are empty, and with no water, and when I ascended to Ramah at the top of the hill I saw a fortified town with high turrets in ruins, and the single house shut up which the Jews hold as a house of prayer, and the beadle of the Synagogue, whose name is R. Moses bar Samuel, opened the door to me. It is beautiful and has a high vaulting, and I then entered a room which was as broad and big as the first, or a little less; and in that room there was a stone staircase going down to the cave, with a door also closed, and there is a synagogue in which a perpetual light is burning. Here is the tomb of our Lord Samuel, the prophet, on whom be peace, and his father Elkanah, and his mother, Hannah, and his two sons. The Jews gather there every year and come even from Babylon, from Aram Zobah, which they call Aleppo, from Hamath, and from Gaza, and from Damascus, and Misr, and other places, so that the foreigners by themselves are more than one thousand in number who come there every year on the 28th of the month of Iyar to mourn and to pray in this cave; for on that day his soul was bound up in the bond of life, and all the Jews who come there are accustomed to buy oil to light in that Synagogue, and I, poor man, prayed in that place and put oil there as is the custom, and I had a great and heavy burning ague when I prayed, and this was at the end of the month of July, 1481. I also saw a bath of water under a small cave near to Ramah, about one-eighth of a mile away, which was the bath of the righteous Hannah, the Mother of Samuel of Ramah; and when I returned to Jerusalem about a mile to the north I saw the grave of Simeon the righteous in a cave, and all round Jerusalem there are many caves and in them are buried many pious and saintly people without number, but we do not know who they are except those marked; but it is a tradition amongst us from mouth to mouth from ancient times that there is no doubt as to their truth, and we see that the Moslems also honour all these places and that they have the same traditions about them as we. They ask the Jews " Why do you not go to the grave of such a saint or such a prophet ? " The Moslems have many a time sought to have these graves closed up and to have them dedicated as *wakuf* in their hands, but God has opposed their intention and would not listen to them, for the keeper of Israel neither sleepeth nor slumbereth.

The buildings of Jerusalem are very fine and the stones are larger than in the buildings of the other places that I have seen. The land flows with milk and honey although it is hilly and ruined and desolate, and everything is cheap ; its fruits are choice and very good. There is a *Karob* honey which is called dipirasciativo, also date honey, and the honey of bees, and wheat and barley and pomegranates and all kinds of fruits good and fine; and they have good olive oil, but they only eat sesame oil, which is very fine. The Moslems and also the Jews of this place are pigs at their eating. They all eat out of one vessel with their fingers, without a napkin, just as the Cairenes do, but their clothes are clean. They also have asses whose saddle is worth a lot of money, for they place upon it precious stones and gold threads. The customs of the Moslems are diverse from all people, for everyone marries twenty or thirty wives as he pleases, but they do not see them until they go home; and the men give dowries to the women, and from the day of marriage the man is only bound to give her food, but her clothes and all other things she requires she has to make herself; and when she is with child Moslems do not touch her till two months after the child is born, for that would be a great sin, and the wife is bound to pay for the food and clothes of all her sons and daughters; therefore they are all openly harlots, and when they do not wish to stay with their husbands they go to the Niepo, the Lord of the City, and say that their husband does not give them food and they are believed, and the husband muſt divorce his wife; for the Moslems give divorce like the Jews. All men and women and children, Jews as well as Moslems, have these cuſtoms. They sleep in their clothes, and these cuſtoms are usual in the whole Kingdom of the Sultan, and not in Jerusalem only. I wrote this when I was in Alexandria of Egypt, but I forgot to write of some of their cuſtoms. They are all alike.

I was ill in Jerusalem from the day I arrived until I left to go to Damascus, and I was near to death's door, but by the mercy of God an Ashkenazi called R. Jacob Kolvarani, he and his wife and his mother-in-law, gave me food after our cuſtom, although I was ſtaying at the house of the Vice Lord by command of the Lord of Misr. I have already written about this above at full length, but at any rate I could not eat and enjoy their dishes, for they are different to our people's and ſtrange to a healthy man, much more so for a sick man like myself; but the said Jacob and his household did not leave me day and night, and they cooked for me and for my companion, Raphael; for he also was ill, but only through dieting and God's help we got ſtrong again. Also Joseph, the dragoman, was on the point of death, and we left him ill. It is not to be wondered at that foreigners who go there get ill; the wonder is that they do not all die. This is caused by the troublesome journey and the great heat one has to endure on the way. In Jerusalem there are draughts every day, summer and winter, different winds from the four corners of the earth such as I have never seen. They get into a man's limbs and kill him, and all the time we were there one or two Jews died a sudden death, and they are buried in the lower ground in the valley of Jehoshaphat, which is the Israelite cemetery; but the Lord helped me and did not forsake me, and I saw all the places in Jerusalem within two days, for they are all close together. The notable Jews are R. Joseph of Mantagna, an Ashkenazi, the Warden, R. Jacob ben Moses Coucy Nagid, Haham Amram, Zedekiah ben R. Obadiah, Samuel Rakbas ben R. Mordecai, Halaftan Rakbas ben R. Jacob, Joseph ben R. Obadiah, Abraham ben R. Nathan, Samuel bar Joseph, Obadiah bar Samuel. These are the Judges and Elders of Jerusalem, and the learned among them are R. Salmon Ashkenazi, who is a Rabbi, R. Nathan, a Rabbi, and three or four other Rabbis whose names I do not know; and the Judges are Sheik Moses, Sheik Samuel, Sheik Halfa, Sheik Sevillano, Sheik Nissim. All these go every year with the congregation behind them to Mount Zion on the ninth of Ab to mourn and weep, and thence they descend to the valley of Jehoshaphat and go upon Mount Olivet, whence they see the whole of the Temple area and mourn for the destruction of the temple. There are still olives on Mount Olivet, and the Moslems call the whole surroundings of Jerusalem and Mount Zion, El Kuds, that is, the holy land. May it be the will of our Father in heaven that it may be rebuilt speedily in our days. Amen.

XI

FROM JERUSALEM TO BEYRUT

To-day, the 26th August, 1481, we journeyed from Jerusalem on our way home. May it be God's will that we may arrive at our destination in peace, and may his salvation be our shield. On the same day we arrived at a city all in ruins somewhat down the hill, that is, Nob, the city of Priests, distant from Jerusalem a parasang, that is, twelve miles. There we ate and stayed till the end of the day because of the great heat, and especially because I had a heavy and strong ague. On the same day we journeyed on, but I had so great a headache that I could not stay on my horse. At midnight we reached a city called Ramleh, once called Gath. Ramleh is like Gaza, it has no walls. We stayed a little there until after morning in an inn, or fondak, where foreigners and the caravans that go to Damascus stop, because it is on the road from Misr to Damascus; and on the day we arrived there I saw the brother of the Turkish King, who is now King in Constantinople, for he had fled before his brother, mourning and with covered head, and about four hundred men were with him, and he was penniless. He is a young man twenty-three years old or so, of short stature and fat, and by command of the King all the lords of Jerusalem came to greet him, and really there were then more than thirty thousand men in Gath, besides the citizens who came to see him, and they struck on timbrels more than four cubits round; and they have no musical instruments but this.

On Monday, the 28th, we arrived at Jaffa, which is six miles distance from Gath. Jaffa is a place all in ruins. It is on the sea in the valley at a little height. There is a tower there over the sea. The sea there is rocky and here we met the Niepo of Jerusalem, and the King's dragoman who lives in Jerusalem, who had come on Saturday, and the Niepo with about four hundred of his friends and with a company of pilgrims who were going to the Holy Sepulchre on Mount Gilboa, which is in Jerusalem, and the Italians call Bolseano; and in order to enter there they pay fourteen ducats a head, and therefore they have to make themselves into a company in order that they may go safe from Orbanians or others. On the same day we entered a fishing smack of the pilgrims, and the owner of the smack was called Augustini Comantarino. He concealed from the pilgrims that I and my companions were Jews, and they all believed that we were Gentile merchants, God forbid ! I knew that they were all wicked Germans and Frenchmen, but strong nobles and lords, and I showed them many favours so that they might not presume to injure me, even if they did know afterwards that I was a Jew. As I thought so it was, for after they heard that I was a Jew, they were much astounded, but still because of their former love for me they could not change their attitude.

On Monday, at three hours before sunrise, we raised sail to go to the harbour of Beyrut, for the master of the fishing boat had business there in spices come from Damascus, and he wished to take them to Venice. May the Lord help us that we may go in peace and reach our house alive and well, so may it be, and let us say Amen.

On Tuesday morning, the 29th, we arrived at Beyrut. It is a little city all in ruins without walls, situate on the sea. It is a spiaggia scogliosa (rocky shore), and accordingly we could not get nearer than half a mile from Beyrut, and we went to land in a skiff, but the master of the boat did not find his goods. He was very angry, and immediately after eating he sent his mate with two companions and with me and my companion, and we rode on mules and asses to go to Damascus, and two mamelukes went with us and the owner of the beasts. We travelled to Damascus in two days and a half. There are no roads so bad in all the world. The hills are steeper than the Alps of Bologna, and it is particularly difficult because people are obliged to travel on foot because beasts cannot carry them this way, and we arrived there on Sunday, the 3rd September, 1481.

XII

DAMASCUS

The city of Damascus lies in a valley between two hills, and in the whole world there is no city as beautiful as Damascus, a wide and beautiful country surrounds it, and its fruits are esteemed as of the greatest merit. It is not surrounded by a wall, and so far as my eyes can judge the circumference of the city is fifteen miles, and the houses of the city are very beautiful; and in everything it surpasses and humbles Misr and all the other cities I have seen till to-day, for I have seen nothing like it for its beauty and the merchandize therein. There is a mint there where they make sarafi and majori and other coins. The foundry is in a courtyard with a great pavement, and in the middle of the pavement is a spring which gushes forth in the midst of two peach-trees. The courtyard has two large gates, and by the back door there is a big shower bath very beautiful with mosaics and jasper wonderful to behold. There are also four large bazaars in Damascus: one for precious stones, and pearls, the second for all kinds of spices, the third for all kinds of silk, and the fourth for Damascene goods of brass inlaid with gold and silver; and there are gates to each bazaar and guards stand there day and night. It is wonderful to behold the merchants of the city and their goods. There are also in Damascus four hundred and fifty Jewish householders, rich and honoured merchants all of them, and at their head is a wise, honoured, and pious Jew, R. Joseph, the Physician. I do not know his father's name, and there are many other honoured Jews whose names I do not know. The said R. Joseph and others also of the city showed me much honour. On Wednesday, the 6th September, we journeyed from there and returned to Beyrut without merchandize. I know not the reason, and we arrived there on Friday at dawn on the 8th, and on the same night we went on our way in peace.

XIII

RETURN TO ITALY

On Saturday at midnight, the 9th September, a ship of three hundred tons from Venice came to meet us, and when it approached, our Captain approached the cabin officer and told him to watch with open eyes to see whose was the ship which was approaching; but the officer was drunk and said it is nothing but a tower on land, and when the boat came near to us the Captain of our ship cried to the officer that he should go to the helm (and turn aside), but the ships collided because they thought that they had a fair way, and half of our cabin was broken and there was also a great and bitter cry; but the Lord helped us for the wind was not strong and we did not collide so very violently. But for this it would not have been possible for us to be saved, and we should have been drowned, God forbid.

On Sunday, the 10th September, 1481, we reached Cyprus. It is an island seven hundred miles in circumference, full of all good things. Its fruits are much praised and of the finest kind. It is like Venice but its air is much worse because of the various winds that always blow there. It has a Governor and many fine cities, and these are their names: Famagusta (the best of them), Nikosia, Papi, and Lomeso. They are all on the right, and there is another city there called Biskofia. It is three hundred miles from Jaffa to Cyprus.

On Monday, the 11th, we left there, and the wind was very strong, levante mistral, and the same day we passed an island belonging to King Fernati and upon it is a strong fortress called Castel Rivo. We then passed an island called Capo Hazididonia, which belongs to the Turks. It is at the head of the Gulf

Gistalia, and the distance from the island of Cyprus to Capo Hazididonia is two miles.

On Tuesday, the 12th September, one of the intermediate days of Tabernacles, we arrived at Rhodes, and I have already above spoken of Rhodes and its buildings, and so I shall not enlarge upon them now. We stayed there all Wednesday, the 13th. On Thursday, the 14th, at morning, we left Rhodes and we sighted on the left an island one hundred and twenty miles distant from Rhodes, with a circumference of one hundred miles, where there are Greeks who call it Sacraponto. It is on the Turkish side of the Mediterranean, which is in the centre of the world, as sailors say. On Friday, the 16th, we passed an island, Standia, which is one hundred and twenty miles from Sacraponto and it is inhabited by Greeks, and on the same day we arrived in peace at Candia. Candia is an island seven hundred miles in circumference and has many cities and villages upon it, and it is fine and rich and full of good things. It has a very large and fine harbour and lies in the valley and on the hill. On the left and opposite are the Turkish cities, and it has fine sorts of fruit and bread and malvoisey wine and meat and fish, all of the best, and at the front of the city outside the gate is a very large and fine castle. Most of the inhabitants of the city are Greeks, and there are about six hundred Jewish householders, and they have four Synagogues on the main road, and all the passers-by can see them. The men of the community live in a separate quarter and most of them construct their tabernacles by the road, and they are merchants and handicraftsmen; and it is surprising that they are not stoned by the Greek Gentiles, who are very anti-Jewish because of the synagogues and tabernacles on the road. To show you their hostility I know that it is forbidden for a Jew who buys anything to touch the goods or fruit of the vendor, for if his hand touched the goods he would be forced against his will to buy and to give him anything he asked. On that day God showed me a great miracle, namely, when at night I went on a skiff from the dock in order to speak with the ship's captain and I wanted to get out of the skiff, the skiff slipped under me and I fell into the sea and sunk more than ten cubits with all my clothes and with my silk guibetto, and in my girdle I had all the jewels and precious stones which I had bought in Egypt bound up in a little tapestry. The skiff turned completely turtle and the oars fell into the water, but thank God the master of the ship saw that I had fallen into the water and ordered his sailors to jump into the water and get me out; and Marco Sacrivanilo was the first to go after me and I leaned my hands and feet upon him and he got me up out of the water and took hold of me by his right hand, and four other sailors who were on the skiff helped me and removed my cloak from me with all their strength, and then they got me on to dry land and God saved me. Blessed be he and blessed be His great name; and because I had swallowed such a lot of water my inside was smitten with a consumption and with a fever for two days and three nights in the house of the honourable Gedaliah Lamirov, and there was a Jewish doctor there wise, honoured, rich, and great, called Monsieur Moses, and he was of former times an Ashkenazi, and he did not leave me day or night, and gave me medicine, and I was restored to my former strength. From Rhodes to Candia are three hundred and ten miles.

On Monday, the 19th September, 1481, we left Candia to go to Moron, and another great miracle was wrought to me by the Almighty; for I was sitting under the mast of the ship and got up, I do not know why. Immediately afterwards a timber fell from the mast on the place where I had been sitting, and the people wondered when they saw the miracle that God had wrought by giving me the idea to get up and save my life, for if I had not moved from there, God forbid, I could not have escaped because of the weight of the timber. Blessed be He who doeth wondrously and who did not permit the destroyer to injure me. May His name be blessed from now and evermore.

On the same day I saw in the hills of Turkey on the right a place called Capo San Vicento, one hundred and eighty miles from Candia. On Tuesday, the 24th, we reached at eventide an island on the left, thirty miles in circumference, about two miles from Moron, called Spanizia, and in half an hour we reached Moron, a small city on the seaside to the left with rocks and they have a fine strong fort outside the gate; and about 300 Jewish householders live round the fort, all engaged in handicrafts and trade. They honoured me in their houses, particularly R. Abraham Cohen, the son of Matathias, the righteous priest, and R. Eliezer, and R. Matathias, and R. Zachariah, the sons of the said R. Abraham, all very honoured, and there are other honoured Jews such as R. Abraham Machiri, R. Mordecai Vensura, R. Nathan, and his sons, and many besides, whose names I do not know. Moron is not an island, but on the mainland. On Thursday, the 26th September, we left Moron and went into a skiff in order to join our ship. We were three men, and two Gentiles, and the skiff was small, and two youths rowed it; but they rowed one against the other so that the skiff overturned and we all fell into the water, but God willed that my left hand already clutched the ladder of the galley and I did not get into the water except to the neck, but the others fell right in, but they came up again because they could swim, and when I wished to clasp the ladder of the galley I had a ring with a very beautiful cameo on the finger next to my thumb which had been pledged with me for six ducats by Moses Piero, the interpreter of the galley; and the ring came off my hand and fell into the sea, and I was obliged to pay him twenty ducats, as is explained in the decision in my hand which was given by three arbitrators, and I was also in danger of death. Blessed be He that saveth and delivereth.

On the same day when we were near another island called Prodeno on the left with the Turkish hills on the right a sirocco levante arose, and when we were near there four ships of corsairs pursued us, and the head of the corsairs was called Filosino; and we fled to another island called Portogiunchi, for they wished to capture us because Monsieur Augustino Contarino, the master of the Pilgrim Ship, had aforetime had a quarrel and dispute with Monsieur Filosino, and therefore we were afraid, and fled before him to the Turkish territory on the right.

XIV
CORFU

To-day, Tuesday, the 2nd October, 1482, we arrived at Corfu. It has a rocky shore to the left. It is an island with a fine big fortress. It is built in a valley and on a hill, and is surrounded by a wall. It has two fine and very strong castles, one opposite the other. The market is in front of the fort, and most of the schiavoni and butergi come from there to Venice. There are three hundred Jewish householders in Corfu honoured and rich. The Turkish hills lie opposite Corfu at about four miles distance, and extend to Durabo. Turkey is all on the mainland and Corfu lies opposite as I have said. We left Corfu on Wednesday, the 3rd October, 1481, to go to our destination in peace. We were in the Gulf of Venice, but in the night a strong tempest arose which was the mistral levante, and we lowered the *artimoni* and mizzen and travelled all that night with *trichito* (with small sail) one hundred and five miles. During the day we passed another island called Lasursa, the place where the King France lay in wait with his armada against the Turks. We were about twelve miles off it and two miles distance from Otranto, and as the *artimoni* had been lowered by the orders of the captain a strong wind tore it from top to bottom, and water covered the ship from one side to the other, and we shipped much water, until we arrived at Ragusa, where we stayed. We entered Ragusa that night. It is a very beautiful city and I have seen none to equal it for beauty and pomp. One can almost say that it is like Florence. The men of Ragusa are extremely rich and great merchants and dress like lords, but no Jews live there. From Corfu to Ragusa is three hundred miles. It is on the right and a free city like Florence. On Thursday, the 4th, we journeyed from there and found to the left, forty miles from Ragusa, an island called Lamliga, and further on an island called Lagusta, and another called Haschiabo. They are subject to Venice, and we passed by way of the canal which starts from Ragusa. That canal is a mile wide and the wind does not blow there, but when we left it the wind did blow and we nearly ran on the rocks because of the strong wind, and the trincati was torn. As I live I was only half a cubit from the rocks. Blessed be He that doeth wonders. On Friday, the 5th, we passed the mainland on the right, and upon it was a city called Zara, that is, Hascobonia, and we passed a city also on the right called Nona, and opposite to the left an island called Lissa, with a small city surrounded by a wall. That night we entered a canal about a quarter of a mile wide and 30 miles long, with the mainland to the right, and to the left a beach called San Piero Animo, about 30 miles distance from Nona and half a mile away from Romitorio, called San Piero Animo. On

Saturday, the 6th October, 1481, we wished to go
to a small but pretty city to the right, one hundred
and thirty miles distance from San Piero Animo,
but a great storm arose so that we returned to San
Piero Animo and stayed there all Tuesday, the
15th October, 1481 ; and on Wednesday before dawn
we made sail and at mid-day when we were in a canal
a quarter of a mile wide in Campi Sapula, the canal
being five miles long, and some of the sailors wished
to hoist the big sail and other sailors said that this is
not the time to hoist because the wind is strengthening;
and there was a dispute between them, and finally
they decided to hoist the sail, but they could not,
and the *artimoni* was torn again and the mast was
almost shifted, and all the sailors and we and all
the pilgrims took hold of the mast but were not able
to keep it upright, and we were in very great danger,
but the Lord helped us and our arms succeeded in
putting it in position. May the Lord be blessed for
all the good that He has done.

On the same day, at night, there was thunder and
lightning and heavy clouds on the mountains, and
rain pouring on the ground with a deafening east
wind like I have never seen in my life, and a sea came
upon us when we were near the sail and we were nearly
stranded ; but the Lord helped us, because in an hour
the sea abated and at that time the wind drove us to
within ten cubits from the shore, and I swear that I
heard the sailors say that never since they had been
at sea had they seen so powerful and evil a wind
as that, for the waves passed over all sides and every
corner of the ship, and it went under water and then
came out; but God saved us from that tempest, may
His name be ever blessed, and how many kindnesses
has God shown us ? After an hour before night we
entered the harbour of Pola and there we cast
anchor, and stayed there on Thursday and Friday

until the great storm on the sea had passed. It was
God's will that we should stay in port, for on the
Thursday a ship laden with four hundred casks
of malvoisy was wrecked, and it was near us but
could not enter, and it sank at sea   The name of the
ship was *Algarili* and only one man was saved who
mounted a cask, and the sea drove him with the cask
to another ship. Blessed be He that saveth and
delivereth.

Pola is a very small city to the right, and in the
middle of it there is a very large and fine mansion
evidently new, and it is good to see the gardens and
flower beds in it. No Jews live there except outside
the city. On Sunday morning, the 14th October,
1481, we arrived at a beautiful city about ten miles
distance from Parenzo, called Rovigno, and on the
same day we arrived at Parenzo at midday, but
previously we had been in great fear because of the
strong wind on the sea, but by God's mercy we arrived
there in peace. In Parenzo there is a very large harbour
made like this [plan]. On three sides there is the mainland with olives and other trees, and the harbour is fine
to look at, for it is not made by man's strength,
but by nature, and in the middle of the harbour one
thousand ships can lie in case of need, so wide and deep
is the port. Parenzo is a small city, but very beautiful.
It is to the right somewhat in a valley, and everything
that man can ask for is to be found there, but there
are no Jewish inhabitants, most, if not all, come from
Venice.   There we stayed until the 18th October
because of the storm at sea, and the sea journey from
Parenzo to Venice is very dangerous because of the
numerous rocks, and there are also places where the
sea is very shallow and any one not acquainted with
the place can come to grief with his ship or his vessel
by grounding or striking the rocks ; therefore it is
forbidden to any master of a vessel or ship to leave

the place or go to sea without taking a pilot with him from Parenzo. At his orders the ship and vessel must go. He stands at the head in the place of the captain. We also took a pilot and journeyed that night and came at 7 o'clock within eight miles of Venice. The pilot became drunk and the wind prevailed against us before we struck anchor, so that the vessel of Monsieur Piero Lando, who was in his cabin, was nearly wrecked. It was a close thing and we had nearly been in very great danger. On the same day we arrived in Venice, that is, to-day, the 19th October, 1481, well and hearty, thanks be to God. From Parenzo to Venice is one hundred miles.

From this it follows that from Naples to Jerusalem the holy city is two thousand eight hundred and seventy three miles, from Jerusalem to Damascus two hundred and eight miles, and from Damascus to Venice five thousand seven hundred and three miles. The total of the journey which R. Meshullam, the son of R. Menahem of Volterra, made when he went to Jerusalem, the holy city, that is, from Naples to Venice is eight thousand seven hundred and eighty-four miles. May the Lord send us the righteous Redeemer to deliver us and bring us to Jerusalem speedily with all Israel our friends, and let us say Amen!

THE LETTERS OF OBADIAH JARÉ DA BERTINORO

(1487–90)

Obadiah Jaré of Bertinoro in Italy was one of the moſt diſtinguished Italian Rabbis of his time. His Commentary on the Mishna known as "The Bertinoro" remains a ſtandard work. As will be seen from the three letters, of which translations follow, he migrated to Paleſtine in 1487. The firſt two of these letters are found in manuscripts in the Gunzburg Library bought for Jerusalem but ſtill impounded by the Soviet Government. The laſt is from a copy of the British Museum contemporary MS. This copy was formerly in the E. N. Adler collection and now belongs to the Jewish Theological Seminary, New York. The firſt two were published with a German translation by Dr. Neubauer and with an English translation, here reproduced, in *Miscellany of Hebrew Literature*, London, 1872.

The Hebrew text of the laſt was edited by Professor Alexander Marx, of New York, in the *Paleſtine New Year Book*, 2 *and* 3, at Tel-Aviv, in 1926 and again by Eisenſtein.

Obadiah appears to have resided in Jerusalem until his death, about 1500, and a subsequent traveller says that he was the leading Jew of Paleſtine in his time.

I

My departure has caused you sorrow and trouble, and I am inconsolable because I have left you at a time when your ſtrength is failing ; when I remember, dear father, that I have forsaken your grey hairs I cannot refrain from tears. But since I am denied the happiness of being able to serve you as I ought, for God has decreed our separation, I will at leaſt give you an account of my journey from beginning

209

to end in the way in which you desired me to do
in your letters, which I received in Naples about this
time laſt year, by describing the manners and cuſtoms
of the Jews in all the places I have visited and the
nature of their intercourse with the other inhabitants
of these cities.

On the firſt day of the ninth month (Kislev, 1486),
after having arranged all matters in my place of
residence, Citta di Caſtello, I repaired to Rome,
and thence to Naples, where I arrived on the 12th of
that month and where I tarried for a long time, not
finding any vessel such as I wished. I went to Salerno,
where I gave gratuitous inſtruction for at leaſt four
months and then returned to Naples.

In the fourth month, on the faſt day (the 17th of
Tammuz), 1487, I set out from Naples, in the large
and swift ship of *Mossen* [1] *Blanchi*, together with
nine other Jews ; it was five days, however, before we
reached Palermo, owing to a calm.

Palermo is the chief town of Sicily, and contains
about 850 Jewish families, all living in one ſtreet,
which is situated in the beſt part of the town. They
are artisans, such as copper-smiths and iron-smiths,
porters and peasants, and are despised by the Chriſtians
because they wear tattered garments. As a mark of
diſtinction they are obliged to wear a piece of red cloth,
about the size of a gold coin, faſtened on the breaſt.
The royal tax falls heavily on them, for they are obliged
to work for the king at any employment that is given
them ; they have to draw ships to the shore, to
conſtruct dykes, and so on. They are also employed
in adminiſtering corporal punishment and in carrying
out the sentence of death.

The Synagogue at Palermo has not its equal in
the whole world ; the ſtone pillars in the outer courtyard are encircled by vines such as I have never before
seen. I measured one of them and it was of the

thickness of five spans. From this court you descend
by stone steps into another which belongs to the
vestibule of the Synagogue. This vestibule has three
sides and a porch in which there are large chairs for
any who may not wish to enter the Synagogue, and a
splendid fountain. The entrance is placed at the
fourth side of the Synagogue which is built in the form
of a square, 40 cubits long and 40 cubits wide. On
the eastern side there is a stone building, shaped like
a dome, the Ark. It contains the rolls of the law which
are ornamented with crowns and pomegranates of
silver and precious stones to the value of 4,000 gold
pieces (according to the statement of the Jews who live
there) and are laid on a wooden shelf, and not put into
a chest as with us. The Ark has two doors, one towards
the south, and one towards the north, and the office
of opening and shutting the doors is entrusted to two
of the congregation. In the centre of the Synagogue
is a wooden platform, the Theba, where the Readers
recite their prayers. There are at present five Readers
in the community ; and on the Sabbath and on
Festivals they chant the prayers more sweetly than I
have ever heard it done in any other congregation.
On week-days the number of visitors to the Synagogue
is very small, so that a little child might count them.

The Synagogue is surrounded by numerous
buildings, such as the hospital, where beds are
provided for sick people, and for strangers who come
there and do not know where to pass the night ;
and again a large and magnificent mansion, where
those who are elected sit in judgment and regulate
the affairs of the community. There are twelve of
these, and they are chosen every year ; they are
empowered by the king to fix the taxes, to levy fines,
and to punish with imprisonment. There is nothing
to be said in favour of this arrangement, for men
of no name and of bad character frequently prevail

upon the Governor, by means of gifts, to appoint them members of this body. They then indemnify themselves for their presents by taxing the Synagogue and congregation, so that the poor people are over-burdened with imposts ; for this elected body is supported by the Governor and has absolute power, and the cry of misery from the oppressed is exceedingly great.

In Palermo I noticed the following customs : When anybody dies, his coffin is brought into the vestibule of the Synagogue and the Ministers hold the funeral service and recite lamentations over him. If the departed is a distinguished man especially learned in the law the coffin is brought into the Synagogue itself, a roll of the law is taken out and placed in the corner of the Ark, while the coffin is placed opposite to this corner, and then the funeral service commences and lamentations are recited ; the same thing is done with all the four corners of the Ark. The coffin is then carried to the place of burial outside the town and on arriving at the gate of the town the Reader begins to repeat aloud the 49th and other Psalms till they reach the burial ground.

I have also noticed the following customs : On the evening of the Day of Atonement and of the Seventh Day of Tabernacles (Hoshana Rabba), after the prayers are finished, the two officials open the doors of the Ark and remain there the whole night ; women come there in family groups to kiss the roll of the law and to prostrate themselves before it ; they enter at one door and go out by the other, and this continues through the whole night, some coming and others going. . . . . . .

I remained in Palermo from Tammuz 22nd, 5247, till Sabbath Bereshith, 5248 (i.e. from about July to October). On my arrival there the chief Jews invited me to deliver lectures on the Sabbath before the Mincha-prayer (Afternoon Service). I consented, and began on the Sabbath of the New Moon of Ab (5247). My discourses were very favourably received, so that I was obliged to continue them every Sabbath ; but this was no advantage to me, for I had come to Palermo with the object of going on to Syracuse, which is at the extreme end of Sicily, for I had heard this was the time when Venetian ships going to Beyrut, near Jerusalem, would touch there. The Jews of Palermo then got many persons to circulate false rumours to dissuade me from my intention, and succeeded in taking me in their net, so that I missed the good crossing for the ships to Syracuse ; I therefore remained in Palermo to give lectures to the people, about three hours before the Mincha. In my discourses I inveighed against informers and other transgressors, so that the elders of the city told me that many refrained from sin, and the number of informers also decreased while I was there ; I do not know if they will go back to their old ways. But yet I cannot spend all my life among them, although they honour and deify me, for indeed they treated me as the Gentiles treat their saints.

The common people said that God had sent me to them, while many wanted a piece of my garments for a remembrance ; and a woman who washed my linen was counted happy by the rest. They calculated that I would remain at least a year there, and wanted to assign me an extraordinary salary, which, how-ever, I declined, for my heart longed to reach the Promised Land.

On the eve of Tabernacles, 5248 (1487), a French galley came to Palermo, on its way to Alexandria. The worthy Meshullam [2] of Volterra was in it, with his servant, and I rejoiced to travel in his company. The night after Sabbath Bereshith we embarked, and on Sunday at mid-day we left Palermo. All day and night we had a favourable wind, so that in the morning we were close to the Pharos of Messina ; we got safely paſt this and were in Messina on Monday at noon. This town is a place of trade for all nations ; ships come here from all parts ; for Messina lies in the middle of the Pharos, so that ships from the eaſt and the weſt pass it by, and its harbour is the only one of its kind in the world ; the largeſt vessels may here come close to the shore. Messina is not so large as Palermo, neither has it such good springs ; but the town is very beautiful and has a ſtrong fortress. There are about 400 Jewish families in it, living quietly in a ſtreet of their own ; they are richer than those in Palermo, and are almoſt all artisans ; there are only a few merchants among them. They have a Synagogue with a porch, open above but enclosed on the four sides, and in the middle of it is a well with spring water. There is an adminiſtration consiſting of persons who are chosen every year ; and this, as well as other arrangements, resembles that of the Jews of Palermo. At a wedding which took place near my residence I witnessed the following ceremony. After the seven blessings had been repeated, the bride was placed on a horse and rode through the town. The whole community went before her on foot, the bridegroom in the midſt of the elders and before the bride, who was the only one on horseback; youths and children carried burning torches and made loud exclamations, so that the whole place resounded ; they made the circuit of the ſtreets and all the Jewish courts ; the Chriſtian inhabitants looked on with pleasure and no one diſturbed the feſtivity.

On the eleventh of Marcheshvan (Oɡober) we left Messina to go to Rhodes ; we were joined in the ship by a Jewish merchant from Sucari,[3] with his servant, three Jewish leatherworkers from Syracuse, and a Sephardic Jew with his wife, two sons and two daughters, so that together we were fourteen Jewish souls on board. We passed the Pharos in safety, sailed through the Gulf of Venice, and thus reached the Archipelago. The Archipelago is full of small islands. Corfu, Candia, Negropont, Rhodes, and Cyprus are reckoned among its islands, and altogether it is said to contain about 300 inhabited and uninhabited islands. For four days we had a favourable wind ; on the fourth day, towards evening, we were thrown back by a storm and could only escape the fury of the waves by remaining in a little natural harbour in the mountains, into which we were thrown ; these mountains are full of St. John's bread and myrtle-trees, and here we remained for three days.

After three days, on Sunday, the 18th of Marcheshvan, we left this place and came within 60 miles of Rhodes. All the way we saw islands on both sides, and the Turkish mountains were also visible. But we were driven back 80 miles ; and the ship had to cast anchor on the shores of the island Longo, which is under the dominion of Rhodes, and there we had to remain ten days, for the wind was unfavourable. During our stay here, one of the sailors used insolent language to the worthy Meshullam, who complained of it to the master. The master himself went in search of the sailor ; the others tried to hide him, but in vain. He commanded him to be tied to the mast and severely flogged, and when the beater seemed to spare him he took the rope himself and continued to punish the insolence of the sailor. He also desired him to make a public apology to the worthy Meshullam. The whole ship's crew were very much annoyed that all this should have happened on account of a few abusive words spoken against a Jew, and from this time they began to hate us and no longer treated us as they had done before.

The worthy merchant, Meshullam, took advantage

of a small ship that was coming from Rhodes and
going to Chios to leave our vessel, intending to go to
Chios and thence to Constantinople, for he had given
up his intention of accompanying us to Alexandria.
On the second day after Rabbi Meshullam had left
us we met a small ship by which we were made aware
that a well-armed Genoese man-of-war was coming
towards us. This news alarmed the master, for we
had no wind ; otherwise, if the wind be favourable,
the galley does not fear a multitude of other ships,
for there is no safer vessel than this. The master
therefore made for a little town, Castel San Giovani,
on the Turkish mountains, which is under the supremacy
of Rhodes, and is the only place in Turkey that has
remained in possession of the Christians. It is small
but very strongly fortified, and its extreme environs
already belong to the Turks. We arrived there on
Friday, the day of the new moon, Kislev (November),
5248, and were in safety. On Saturday, towards
noon, God caused a favourable wind to blow so that
we were able to leave the place and to sail all day
and night ; and on Sunday, Kislev 3rd, 5248, we
arrived joyfully at Rhodes, after 22 days sail.

The inhabitants of Rhodes welcomed us gladly,
for the master of our ship was a friend and relative of
the Governor. The chief men of the Jewish community
of Rhodes soon came to our ship, and received us with
kindness ; for the merchant Meshullam, who had
been with us in the ship, was the brother of the
physician R. Nathan, the most distinguished man
among the Jews of Rhodes. A fine room, provided
with all necessities, was assigned to me, while the
other Jews who accompanied me were accommodated
as well as it was possible, for the Jewish houses in
Rhodes had been almost entirely destroyed by the
siege of the Turks, under their first Emperor, undertaken by him in the year of his death. No one who

has not seen Rhodes, with its high and strong walls, its firm gates and battlements, has ever seen a fortress. The Turkish Emperor [4] in the year of his death sent a besieging army against it, bombarded the town with a multitude of stones, which are still to be seen there, and in this way threw down the walls surrounding the Jewish street and destroyed the houses. The Jews here have told me that when the Turks got into the town they killed all before them until they came to the door of the Synagogue, when God brought confusion among them, so that they began at once to flee and slay one another. On account of this miracle the Governor built a church on the spot and gave the Jews another building instead of it. While I was in Rhodes, he granted them 100 ducats from the revenues of the town to build a new synagogue.

Not many Jews have remained in Rhodes; altogether there are twenty-two families, all poor, who subsist with difficulty on vegetables, not eating bread or meat, for they never slaughter nor do they buy any wine, for fear of getting into disputes with the Greeks who dwell there. When they buy in the market, they touch nothing that belongs to the Greeks ; and they observe the law against wine just as strictly as against pork. The Jews here are all very intelligent and well educated ; they speak a pure dialect and are very moral and polite ; even the tanners are neatly dressed and speak with propriety. They all allow their hair to grow long and are beautiful in person. Nowhere are there more beautiful Jewesses than in Rhodes ; they occupy themselves in doing all kinds of handiwork for the Acomodors (the nobles of the land), and in this way support their husbands. The Acomodors hold the Jews in high esteem, often coming into their houses to chat awhile with the women who work there.

When anybody dies there is no coffin made for him,

he is buried only in his shroud ; an impression of a human form is made in the ground where he is to be buried, for the earth there has never been cultivated so that it receives any impression ; the dead body is laid in this cavity, a board is placed over it, and then it is covered with earth. The air in Rhodes is purer and more agreeable than I have yet felt it in any other place, the water is sweet, the soil is clean but poor, and moſt of the inhabitants are Greeks who are subjeƈt to the Acomodors.

In Rhodes we remained from the 3rd of Kislev to the 15th of Tebeth (December), because the Governor would not allow the ship to sail to Alexandria, fearing leſt the King of Egypt would keep it there. For the Governor had accepted 120,000 gold pieces from the Egyptian King, promising to deliver up to him the brother of the Turkish Emperor, Dschem by name, who was detained a prisoner in France ; but he had not been able to keep his promise from fear of the Turkish Emperor ; for this reason he was afraid that the Egyptian King might seize the ship, which contained a vaſt amount of treasures, together with all the men in it. When, however, time wore on, the maſter having consulted with the merchants of the ship, thought better to set sail in spite of all danger. On the 15th of Tebeth, therefore, we left Rhodes, and after six days we were before Alexandria ; the maſter would not sail into it until he had learnt how matters ſtood. We therefore remained at Bukari, a place between Alexandria and Rosetta, on the way to Cairo ; the water was not deep here but the place was large, and we caſt anchor about four miles from the shore. We had a vessel of 200 tons with us, as tender, which the maſter had bought and loaded with grain to sell in Alexandria.

The Emir, i.e. the representative of the King of Egypt, who had his seat in Alexandria, sent an assurance to the master that the ship and all that was in it might come there in safety, but the latter placed no faith in this promise, and himself sent ambassadors to the king. He was willing, however, to send the smaller ship with wheat and a small crew to Alexandria on the word of the Emir. The Jews therefore resorted to this ship on Friday, expecting to reach Alexandria on the Sabbath. But the Emir would not allow this because the master had refused to place confidence in him, and so we Jews remained in this ship, about a bow-shot removed from the galley.

A considerable time elapsed and the messengers had not yet returned from Cairo ; our victuals began to be exhausted, we had no water, and would already have preferred death to life.

On the 8th of Shebat (January), about midnight, a dreadful storm arose; two anchors of our ship suddenly broke, only the weakest remaining. The sailors were terrified and threw many things overboard to lighten the ship; they signalled to the other ship, by firing guns, to send off the boat with men ; but nobody heard and nobody answered, for those in the galley were occupied with their own safety and, indeed, it would scarcely have been possible for a bark to have approached us, for the sea was too stormy. It drove us, with the damaged anchor which still remained, on to a whirlpool ; the waves went over us, we were tossed hither and thither, and the ship threatened to be wrecked every moment, for it was old and damaged, so that the water penetrated on all sides, and the sea in that part was full of rocks. For about twenty-four hours we were in such danger that we expected death every moment. We had each a pail in our hands to empty out the water which flowed abundantly into the ship ; and we tearfully filled our pails and emptied them, till God took mercy on us, and we happily escaped the storm almost miraculously. When the storm was over, the master sent for the people from the damaged vessel, and on the morning of the second day we entered into the large ship and remained there till the ambassadors returned bringing a guarantee from the king. There was now again a calm, and the ship could not leave Bukari. The merchants and the Jews in the large ship preferred to go ashore in a bark, that their lives might be in safety. We then travelled on foot (not being able to get asses) for 18 miles of the way, and we reached Alexandria on the 14th of Shebat, tired and weary. Here God gave us favour in the eyes of a generous man who was very much beloved even by the Arabs, by name R. Moses Grasso, dragoman to the Venetians. He came to meet us and released us from the hands of the Arabs who sit in the gate and plunder foreign Jews at their pleasure. He took me in his house, and there I had to remain while I stayed in Alexandria. I read with him in a book on the Cabbala, which he had in his possession, for he dearly loved this science. By thus reading with him I found favour in his sight and we became friends. On the Sabbath he gave a dinner, to which he invited the Sephardi who had come with me ; his two sons were also there when he brought me into the dining-room.

The following is the arrangement of the Sabbath meal customary to Jews in all Arabian countries. They sit in a circle on a carpet, the cup-bearer standing near them near a small cloth which is spread on this carpet ; all kinds of fruit which are in season are then brought and laid on the cloth. The host now takes a glass of wine, pronounces the blessing of sanctification (*Kiddush*), and empties the cup completely. The cup-bearer then takes it from the host, and hands it successively to the whole company, always refilled, and each one empties it, then the host takes two or three pieces of fruit, eats some, and drinks a second

glass, while the company say "Health and life".
Whoever sits next also takes some fruit, and the cup-
bearer fills a second glass for him, saying, "To your
pleasure," the company join in with the words
"Health and life", and so it goes round. Then a
second kind of fruit is partaken of, another glass is
filled, and this is continued until each one has emptied
at least six or seven glasses. Sometimes they even
drink when they smell the flowers which are provided
for the occasion ; these flowers are the *dudaim*, which
Rashi translates into Arabic by jasmine ; it is a
plant bearing only blossoms which have a delightful
and invigorating fragrance. The wine is unusually
strong, and this is especially the case in Jerusalem,
where it is drunk unmixed. After all have drunk
to their heart's content, a large dish of meat is brought,
each one stretches forth his hand, takes what he wants,
and eats quickly, for they are not very big eaters.
R. Moses brought us confectionery, fresh ginger,
dates, raisins, almonds, and confectionery of coriander
seeds; a glass of wine is drunk with each kind. Then
followed raisin wine, which was very good, then malmsey
wine from Candia, and again native wine. I drank
with them and was exhilarated.

There is yet another custom in the country of the
Arabs ; on Friday all go to bathe, and on their return
the women bring them wine, of which they drink
copiously ; word is then brought that the supper is
ready, and it is eaten in the day-time, before evening.
Then they all come to the synagogue, cleanly and
neatly dressed. They begin with psalms and thanks-
giving and evening prayer is read until two hours
after dusk. On their return home they repeat the
Kiddush, eat only a piece of bread of the size of an
olive, and recite the grace after meals. In this whole
district the Mincha prayer is read on Friday in private,
except in Jerusalem, where the Ashkenazim (Germans)

have done away with the custom, and the Mincha and evening prayer are said with *Minyan* as with us, and they eat at night ; the evening prayer is not begun, however, until the stars are visible. In these parts the Sabbath is more strictly kept than in any other ; nobody leaves his house on the Sabbath, except to go to the Synagogue or to the Beth Hamidrash (house of study). I need scarcely mention that nobody kindles a fire on the Sabbath, or has a light that has been extinguished rekindled, even by a Gentile. All who are able to read the Holy Scriptures read the whole day, after having slept off the effect of their wine.

In Alexandria there are about twenty-five families and two old Synagogues. One is very large and somewhat damaged, the other is smaller. Most pray in the smaller, because it bears the name of the prophet Elijah ; and it is said that he once appeared to somebody in the south-east corner, where a light is now kept constantly burning. I have been told that twenty years ago he again appeared to an old man. God alone knows the truth ! In all Arabian countries no man enters the Synagogue with shoes on his feet ; even in paying a visit the shoes are left outside, at the door, and everybody sits on the ground on mats or carpets.[5]

Alexandria is a very large town surrounded with a wall and encircled by the sea, though two-thirds of it are now destroyed and many houses uninhabited The inhabited courts are paved with mosaic ; peach- and date-trees are in the middle of them. All the houses are large and beautiful, but the inhabitants are few on account of the unhealthy atmosphere which has prevailed here for many years. It is said that those who are not accustomed to the air, and remain long here, die or at least fall sick. Most of the inhabitants are subject to the diseases of the eye. Merchants come from all parts, and at present there are four consuls here : for Venice, Genoa, Catalonia and Ancona, and the merchants of all nations have to treat with them. The Christians are obliged to shut themselves in their houses every evening ; the Arabs close up the streets from without, and open them again every morning. It is the same on Friday from noon till the evening ; while the Arabs tarry in the house of prayer, the Christians have to stay in their houses, and whoever is seen in the street has himself to blame if he is ill-treated. The King of Egypt receives an immense sum of money by the export and import duties paid on wares which come to Alexandria, for the tax is very high ; even current money that is brought in has to pay two per cent. As for me, by the help of God I was not obliged to pay entrance duty for my money. Smugglers are not subjected to any special punishment by the Egyptian tax-collectors.

I spent seven days in Alexandria, leaving my effects, which were very few, in the large ship, which was still detained in Bukari by the calm. It happened just at this time that there was a man in Alexandria who had made a vow to celebrate the passover-feast in Jerusalem with his wife and two sons ; I joined myself to him, and travelled with him on camels. I commissioned R. Moses Grasso to bring my things from the large ship and send them to Cairo. At Rosetta, on the Nile, we got into a ship. On both sides of the Nile there are towns and villages which are beautiful, large and populous, but all unfortified. We remained two days in Fooah, because the wind was not favourable ; it is a large and beautiful place, and fish and vegetables can be got almost for nothing. We came next to Bulak, which already forms the beginning of Cairo. On the Nile I saw the large species of frog which the natives call El Timsah (the crocodile) ; it is larger than a bear and spots are visible on its skin. The ship's crew say that there are some twice as big. These are the frogs which have remained from the time of Moses, as Nachmanides mentions in his commentary. The Nile is wide and its waters are very sweet but turbid. The part on which we sailed forms merely a branch, for the other goes to Damietta, where it flows into the sea.

Before coming to Bulak we observed two very old dome-shaped buildings which lay on the same side of the ſtream ; it is said that they are the magazines which Joseph built. The door is above in the roof. Although they are now only ruins, yet it is easy to see that they have once been magnificent buildings ; the diſtrict is uninhabited. Twelve days before Purim, towards evening, we came to Cairo ; it was the time of the great harveſt, and the severe famine which had prevailed in the whole diſtrict of Cairo was on the decrease. The barley ripens sooner here than elsewhere by the influence of the waters of the Nile, and the harveſt appeared to be very good. In the following month there was great plenty, so that there was no more thought of famine. The inhabitants and their fields are to this day subject to the king, who takes a fifth part of the produce, and sometimes more. Egypt is the only place in the world where the fields are thus subject to the king to the present day.

I shall not speak of the grandeur of Cairo and of the multitude of men to be seen ſtreaming there, for many before me have described them, and all that has been said of the town is true. It is not completely surrounded by a wall, though there are several places here and there protected in that way. The town is very animated, and one hears the different languages of the foreigners who inhabit it. It is situated between the Red Sea and the Mediterranean, and all merchants come from India, Ethiopia, and the countries of Preſter John [6] through the Red Sea to Cairo both to sell their wares, which consiſt of spices, pearls, and precious stones, and to purchase commodities which come from France, Germany, Italy and Turkey, across the Mediterranean Sea through Alexandria to Cairo. In the Red Sea there are magnets ; hence the ships which come through it have no iron in them, not so much as a nail. The place where the sea was divided for our forefathers is said to have been identified, and many priests go to visit it, but I have heard of no Jew who has been there. The harbour where the ships coming from the Red Sea unload their cargoes, and from whence the wares are brought to Cairo by means of camels is said to be not far distant from Mount Sinai, which is only five days' journey from Cairo. The Christian ecclesiastics live here in a convent and come daily to Cairo, making the journey there and back more frequently than any other people, even than the Arabs, for it is known that they carry no gold with them ; the whole way is infested by Bedouins, who rob and plunder at their will in the wilderness ; they do no injury, however, to these ecclesiastics who have made an agreement both with the king and with the Bedouins. It is said, indeed, that the Bedouins keep their word to strangers who dwell among them.

In Cairo there are now about seven hundred Jewish families ; of these fifty are Samaritans, called also Cutheans, one hundred and fifty are Karaïtes, and the rest Rabbanites. The Samaritans have only the five books of Moses, and their mode of writing differs from ours—the sacred writing. Maimonides remarks that this writing was customary among the Israelites before the time of the Assyrian exile, as already related in tractate *Sanhedrin* ; but their Hebrew is like ours. Wherever the tetragrammaton occurs in scripture they write Ashima [7] ; they are an abomination to the Jews because they offer up sacrifices and frankincense on Mount Gerizim. Many of them left Cairo with us to bring the passover-offering to Mount Gerizim, for they have a temple there ; they celebrate the Sabbath from the midday of Friday till the midday of Saturday. There are very few of them in existence now : it is said scarcely 500 families in all the world.

The Karaïm, as you know, do not believe in the words of our sages, but they are familiar with all the Bible. They fix the day of the new moon according to the appearance of the moon [8] consequently the Karaïm in Cairo keep different days for Rosh Hashana (New Year) and the Day of Atonement, from those in Jerusalem, maintaining that there is nothing wrong in this. Every year they send to Jerusalem to observe the month of spring ; and when they see that it is necessary to have a leap-year (Ibbur) they add an intercalary month. They do not think it any harm if the Karaïm in Cairo add a month and those in Constantinople do not, for every place fixes its calendar according to its own judgment : they fast on the 7th and 10th of Ab. It is well-known that they always celebrate Shabuoth (Pentecost) on Sunday ; they hang the Lulab (palm branch) and the other plants (mentioned in Leviticus xxxiii, 40) in the midst of the Synagogue ; they all look upon them, and this they consider sufficient ; they have no fire in their houses on the Sabbath, either by day or night ; the five rules respecting Shechita (slaughtering animals for food) are the same with them as with us, although not expressly mentioned in the Torah ; they also observe the regulation to kill with a very sharp knife, free from all notches, and the law respecting wine they keep even more strictly than the Rabbanites. In all the districts through which I passed, I have noticed that the law respecting wine is most strictly kept ; there is even a doubt as to whether the honey may be used which the Arabs prepare from the grapes ; it is very good, and in preparing it the grapes are not trodden in the same way as in making wine. I was asked to allow the use of it, for there are so many arguments in its favour, but my predecessors had not done it, and I did not wish to make innovations. There is not a single man who would drink wine that had been touched by an Arab, much less by an idolater. The Karaïtes observe all the laws of purification ; if anybody dies they all leave the house and hire poor Rabbanites to carry away their dead, for they will not touch a corpse. I have seen some of their commentaries, such as that of Japhet, which is quoted by Ibn-Ezra, and those of R. Aaron, the Karaïte ; every day they make new explanations of the Torah, and maintain that even a fundamental law which has been established by the ancients may be altered if it does not appear to one of their wise men now living to agree with the text of the Bible, and they decide everything by the letter of the Torah. In all this they do not consider that either old or living scholars do any wrong. They have a synagogue in Cairo ; most of their prayers consist of psalms and other biblical verses ; in recent times they have made a rule to read from the Torah on Mondays and Thursdays, which was not done formerly ; they have Priests and Levites, and it is said of a very rich and honourable Karaïte in Cairo, Zadakah by name, that he is really descended from the family of David ; he wanted to lay before me his genealogy, attested by witnesses of every generation, but I had not time to meet him.

The Samaritans are the richest of all the Jews in Cairo, and fill most of the higher offices of state ; they are cashiers and administrators ; one of them is said to have a property of 200,000 pieces of gold. The Karaïtes are richer than the Rabbanites, but there are opulent men even among the latter. The custom of the Jews is always to represent themselves as poor in the country of the Arabs ; they go about as beggars, humbling themselves before the Arabs ; they are not charitable towards one another ; the Karaïtes mix among the Rabbanites and try to become friendly with them.

In Cairo there are about fifty families of forced apostates (Marranos) from Spain, who have all done penance ; they are mostly poor, having left their possessions, their parents, and relatives, and come here to seek shelter under the wings of the Lord God of Israel. Among the Jews in Cairo there are money changers and merchants, for the country is large, and some branch of industry is open to everyone. For trade there is no better place in the world than Cairo ; it is easy to grow rich ; hence one meets there with innumerable foreigners of all nations and languages. You may go out by night as well as by day, for all the streets are lighted with torches ; the people sleep on the ground before the shop. The Jew can buy everything that is necessary, such as meat, cheese, fish, vegetables, and in general all that he requires, for everything is sold in the Jews' street ; this is also the case in Palermo, but there it is not the same as in Cairo, for in the latter place the Jews cook at home only for the Sabbath, since men as well as women are occupied during the whole week and can therefore buy everything in the market. Wood is very dear ; a load of wood, not so large as the load of a pair of mules, costs upwards of two-thirds of a ducat, and even more ; meat and fruit are also dear ; the former is very good, however, especially the tail of the sheep. The Karaïtes do not eat this, for according to them it belongs to that kind of fat which the Torah has forbidden. I have seen nothing cheap in Cairo except onions of the Nile, leek, melons, cucumbers, and vegetables. Bread is cheap in years of plenty—it is made in the form of a cake and is kneaded very soft.

The Jewish *Nagid* who has his residence in Cairo is appointed over all the Jews who are under the dominion of the King of Egypt ; he has all the power of a king and can punish and imprison those who aɕt in opposition to his decrees ; he appoints the Dayyanim (judges) in every community. The present prince lived formerly for a long time in Jerusalem, but was obliged to leave it on account of the Elders, the calumniators, and informers who were there. He is called R. Nathan ha-Cohen, is rich, wise, pious, old, and is a native of Barbary. When I came to Cairo he showed me much honour, loved me as a father loves his son, and tried to dissuade me altogether from going to Jerusalem on account of the informers there ; all scholars and rabbis formerly in Jerusalem left the city in haɕte in order to preserve their lives from the oppressions of the Elders. The Jews who were in Jerusalem, about three hundred families, disappeared by degrees on account of the great taxes and burdens laid upon them by the Elders, so that the poor only remained, and women ; and there was scarcely one to whom the name of man could juɕtly be given. These grey-haired criminals went so far as to sell all the scrolls of the law with their covers, the curtains, the pomegranates, and all the sacred appurtenances which were in Jerusalem, to Gentiles, who were to carry them away into foreign lands ; they sold the numerous books, such as the Talmud and Codices, which were deposited by the Ashkenazim in Jerusalem, so that nothing of value was left there. The *Nagid* told me he could not well put a ɕtop to this because he feared that the Elders would speak evil againɕt all the Jews to the King, and the " throat of the King is an open sepulchre, and his eyes are not satisfied ". About the same time disturbances took place in Egypt ; for the King wanted to raise money to give to his generals, who were to fight against the Turkish Emperor in Aleppo ; and he imposed the heavy tax of seventy-five thousand pieces of gold on the Jews in Cairo, viz. the Samaritans, Karaïtes, and Rabbanites, and the same on Christians and Arabs, for he wanted to raise an immense sum of money. In Purim of that year there was, therefore, sorrow, fasting and weeping among the Jews ; yet I did not lose my courage, my heart was fixed on God.

On the 20th of Adar, I left Cairo in company with the Jew who came from Alexandria, and we came to Chanak ⁹ which is about two miles distant from Cairo. Before I left New Cairo I went to Old Cairo, called Mizraim Atika, which is also inhabited, though not so closely as New Cairo, and both are quite close together. On the way thither we saw the place where the King sends people every year to prepare a dam against the rising of the Nile, which takes place in the month of Ab (August). I have heard many things about the rising of the Nile, which, however, would be too wearisome to write down, especially as I have not seen it with my own eyes. I saw rain in Cairo, but not much ; and while there I felt severe cold at the time of Purim. The people, indeed, wondered and said that it had not been so cold for many years, for according to all accounts Egypt is very warm.

In Old Cairo there is a very beautiful synagogue built on large and splendid pillars ; it also is dedicated to the prophet Elijah, who is said to have appeared there to the pious in the south-east corner, where a light is kept continually burning. In the north-east corner is a platform where the scroll of Ezra used to be placed. It is related that many years ago a Jew came from the west, and bought it from the temple servant ; he set sail from Alexandria, carrying with him the roll of the law, but the ship was not far from Alexandria when it sank, and he was lost, together with the roll of the law. The temple servant, who had sold it to him for 100 gold pieces, became an apostate, and died shortly afterwards. The case of this roll is still in the Synagogue and a light is always kept burning before it. Last year the King wanted to take the pillars on which the Synagogue is built for his palace because they are large and very beautiful, but the Jews redeemed them for 1,000 gold pieces. According to the date on the wall of the Synagogue, it was built thirty-eight years before the destruction of the second temple. Near to it there is another fine, large Synagogue, but not equal to the former ; prayers are offered up here every Sabbath, and the Jews hire a person to watch over it.

I was not so fortunate as to get to Dimo,[10] a place outside Cairo, where Moses is said to have prayed ; here there are two Synagogues, one belonging to the Rabbanites and one to the Karaïtes ; Divine Service is often held here on Sabbaths and on feast days. I was told that the mamelukes of the King feed their horses on the way to it, and that it would, therefore, be very dangerous for a Jew to go there for the mamelukes were at this time in the habit of beating and plundering Jews as well as Arabs.

In Chanak we remained two days, and there hired five camels, for two men and two women had joined us in Cairo. It is said that this is Goshen, where the Jews sojourned in Egypt. We then came to Salahia where we remained over the Sabbath, waiting for a passing caravan, since the way through the wilderness begins here and it is not safe to make the journey with only five camels. Not a Jew lives on the way from here to Gaza.

We were three days in Salahia when an Arab caravan of eight camels arrived, with which we travelled as far as Katiah, a town in the middle of the wilderness, where no vegetation is to be seen except date-trees. The wilderness between Egypt and Palestine is not large, for from one day's journey to another there are places of encampment for the camels, erected principally for travellers ; yet it is all sand, and no vegetation whatever is to be seen except date-trees in certain well-known places. Water is found after every two days' journey, sometimes even after one day's journey, but it is rather brackish.

In the wilderness we came to Arish, said to be the former Succoth. The caravans going through the wilderness either encamp at mid-day and journey in the evening till midnight, or travel from midnight into the first third of the day ; this depends on the will of those who have charge of the caravans. Generally speaking, they travel by night rather than by day. Thus we journeyed from place to place in the wilderness, till we came to Gaza, without misadventure. Gaza is the first town that we found on coming out of the wilderness leading to the land of the Philistines. It is a large and beautiful city, of the same size as Jerusalem, but without walls, for among all the places under Egyptian dominion, which now extends over Palestine, the country of the Philistines and Syria, Alexandria and Aleppo alone are surrounded by walls. If the account of the Jews living there be correct, I saw in Gaza the ruins of the building that Samson pulled down on the Philistines. We remained four days in Gaza ; there is now a Rabbi from Germany there, by name Rabbi Moses, of Prague, who fled thither from Jerusalem; he insisted on my going to his house, and I was obliged to stay with him all the time I was in Gaza. On the Sabbath all the wardens were invited to dine with us. Cakes of grapes and fruit were brought ; we partook of several glasses before eating, and were joyful.

On Sunday, the 11th of Nisan (April), we journeyed
from Gaza on asses ; we came within two miles of
Hebron, and there spent the night. On Monday
we reached Hebron, a small town on the slope of the
mountain, called by the Turks Khalil.[11] It is divided
into two parts, one beside the Cave of the Patriarchs ;
the other opposite, a bow-shot farther away. I was
in the Cave of Machpelah, over which the mosque
has been built ; and the Arabs hold the place in
high honour. All the kings of the Arabs come here
to repeat their prayers, but neither a Jew nor an Arab
may enter the Cave itself, where the real graves of the
Patriarchs are ; the Arabs remain above, and let
down burning torches into it through a window,
for they keep a light always burning there. All who
come to pray leave money, which they throw into the
cave through the window ; when they wish to take
the money out they let down a young man who is
unmarried by a rope, to bring it up—so I have been
told by the Jews who live there. All Hebron, with
its fields and neighbourhood, belongs to the Cave ;
bread and lentil, or some other kind of pulse, is
distributed to the poor every day without distinction
of faith, and this is done in honour of Abraham.
Without, in the wall of the Cave, there is a small
opening, said to have been made just after the burial
of Abraham, and there the Jews are allowed to pray,
but none may come within the walls of the cave.
At this little window I offered up my prayers. On
the summit of the opposite mountain is a large cave,
said to be the grave of Jesse, the father of David.
We went there also to pray on the same day. Between
the grave of Jesse and the Cave of the Patriarchs is
a well, which the Arabs call the well of Isaac, said
to have belonged to the patriarch Isaac. Near to
Hebron, between rocks, there is a spring of fresh
water, distinguished as the well of Sarah. Hebron

has many vineyards and olive-trees, and contains
at the present time twenty families, all Rabbanites,
half of whom are descendants of the forced Apostates
who have recently returned to their faith.

On Tuesday morning, the 13th of Nisan, we left
Hebron, which is a day's journey distant from
Jerusalem, and came on as far as Rachel's tomb,
where there is a round, vaulted building in the open
road. We got down from our asses and prayed at
the grave, each one according to his ability. On the
right hand of the traveller to Jerusalem lies the hill
on which Bethlehem stands ; this is a small village,
about half a mile from Rachel's grave, and the Catholic
priests have a church there.

From Bethlehem to Jerusalem is a journey of about
three miles. The whole way is full of vineyards and
orchards. The vineyards are like those in Romagna,
the vines being low, but thick. About three-quarters
of a mile from Jerusalem, at a place where the mountain
is ascended by steps, we beheld the famous city of
our delight, and here we rent our garments, as was
our duty. A little farther on, the sanctuary, the desolate
house of our splendour, became visible, and at the
sight of it we again made rents in our garments.
We came as far as the gates of Jerusalem, and on the
13th of Nissan, 5248, at noon, our feet stood within
the gates of the city. Here we were met by an
Ashkenazi who had been educated in Italy, Rabbi Jacob
Calmann ; he took me into his house, and I remained
his guest during the whole time of the Passover.
Jerusalem is for the most part desolate and in ruins.
I need not repeat that it is not surrounded by walls.
Its inhabitants, I am told, number about 4,000
families. As for Jews, about seventy families of the
poorest class have remained ; there is scarcely a
family that is not in want of the commonest necessaries;
one who has bread for a year is called rich. Among the

OBADIAH DA BERTINORO

Jewish population there are many aged, forsaken widows from Germany, Spain, Portugal and other countries, so that there are seven women to one man. The land is now quieter and happier than before ; for the Elders have repented of the evil they had done, when they saw that only the poorer portion of the inhabitants remained ; they are therefore very friendly to every newcomer. They excuse themselves for what has happened, and assert that they never injured anyone who did not try to obtain the maſtery over them. As for me, so far I have no complaint to make againſt them ; on the contrary, they have shown me great kindness and have dealt honourably with me, for which I daily give thanks to God.

The Jews are not persecuted by the Arabs in these parts. I have travelled through the country in its length and breadth, and none of them has put an obſtacle in my way. They are very kind to ſtrangers, particularly to anyone who does not know the language ; and if they see many Jews together they are not annoyed by it. In my opinion, an intelligent man versed in political science might easily raise himself to be chief of the Jews as well as of the Arabs ; for among all the inhabitants there is not a wise and sensible man who knows how to deal affably with his fellow men, all are ignorant misanthropes intent only on gain. . . . .

The Synagogue here is built on columns ; it is long, narrow, and dark, the light entering only by the door. There is a fountain in the middle of it. In the court of the Synagogue, quite close to it, ſtands a mosque. The court of the Synagogue is very large, and contains many houses, all of them buildings devoted by the Ashkenazim to charitable purposes, and inhabited by Ashkenazi widows. There were formerly many courts in the Jewish ſtreets belonging to these buildings, but the Elders sold them, so that not a single one remained. They could not, however, sell the buildings of the Ashkenazim, because they were exclusively for Ashkenazim, and no other poor had a right to them. The Jews' street and the houses are very large ; some of them dwell also on Zion. At one time they had more houses, but these are now heaps of rubbish and cannot be rebuilt, for the law of the land is that a Jew may not rebuild his ruined house without permission, and the permission often costs more than the whole house is worth. The houses in Jerusalem are of stone, none of wood or plaster.

There are some excellent regulations here. I have nowhere seen the daily service conducted in a better manner. The Jews rise an hour or two before day-break, even on the Sabbath, and recite psalms and other songs of praise till the day dawns. Then they repeat the *Kaddish*; after which two of the Readers appointed for the purpose chant the Blessing of the Law, the Chapter on Sacrifices, and all the songs of praise which follow with a suitable melody, the " Hear, O Israel " being read on the appearance of the sun's first rays. The Cohanim repeat the priestly benediction daily, on weekdays as well as on the Sabbaths ; in every service this Blessing occurs. At the morning and afternoon service supplications are said with great devotion, together with the Thirteen Attributes of God ; and there is no difference between Mondays and Thursdays, and the other days of the week except that the Law is read on the two former.

Jerusalem, notwithstanding its destruction, still contains four very beautiful, long bazaars, such as I have never before seen, at the foot of Zion. They have all dome-shaped roofs, and contain wares of every kind. They are divided into different departments, the merchant bazaar, the spice bazaar, the vegetable market, and one in which cooked food and bread are sold. When I came to Jerusalem there was a dreadful famine in the land. A man of moderate means could have eaten bread the weight of a drachma at every meal, which in our money makes a bolognino of old silver, and he would not have been satisfied. I was told that the famine was less severe than it was at the beginning of the year. Many Jews died of hunger, they had been seen a day or two before asking for bread, which nobody could give them, and the next day they were found dead in their houses. Many lived on grass, going out like ſtags to look for paſture. At present there is only one German Rabbi here who was educated in Jerusalem. I have never seen his equal for humility and the fear of God ; he weaves night and day when he is not occupied with his ſtudies, and for six months he taſted no bread between Sabbath and Sabbath, his food consiſting of raw turnips and the remains of the St. John's bread, which is very plentiful here, after the sugar has been taken out of it. According to the account of a truſtworthy man, Jericho, the " city of palms ", is only half a day's journey from Jerusalem, and there are at the present day scarcely three palm-trees in the town.

Now, the wheat harveſt being over, the famine is at an end, and there is once more plenty, praise be to God. Here, in Jerusalem, I have seen several kinds of fruits which are not to be found in our country. There is one tree with long leaves, which grows higher than a man's ſtature and bears fruit only once ; it then withers, and from its roots there rises another similar one, which again bears fruit the next year ; and the same thing is continually repeated. The grapes are larger than in our country, but neither cherries, hazel-nuts, nor cheſtnuts are to be found. All the necessaries of life, such as meat, wine, olives, and sesame-oil can be had very cheap. The soil is excellent, but it is not possible to gain a living by any branch of industry, unless it be that of a shoe-maker, weaver, or goldsmith ; even such artisans as these gain their livelihood with great difficulty. Persons of various nationalities are always to be found in Jerusalem from Christian countries, and from Babylonia and Abyssinia. The Arabs come frequently to offer up prayers at the temple, for they hold it in great veneration.

I made enquiries concerning the Sambation, and I hear from one who has been informed, that a man has come from the kingdom of Prester John and has related that there are high mountains and valleys there which can be traversed in a ten days' journey, and which are certainly inhabited by descendants of Israel. They have five princes or kings, and have carried on great wars against the Johannites (Abyssinians) for more than a century, but, unfortunately, the Johannites prevailed and Ephraim was beaten. The Johannites penetrated into their country and laid it waste, and the remembrance of Israel had almost died away in those places, for an edict was issued against those who remained prohibiting the exercise of their religious duties as severe as that which Antiochus issued in the time of the Hasmoneans. But God had mercy. Other kings succeeded in India who were not so cruel as their predecessors ; and it is said that the former glory of the Jews is now in a measure restored ; they have again become numerous, and though they still pay tribute to the Johannites they are not entirely subject to them. Four years ago, it is said, they again made war with their neighbours, when they plundered their enemies and made many prisoners. The enemy, on the other hand, took some of them prisoners, and sold them as slaves ; a few of these were brought to Cairo and redeemed by the Jews there. I saw two of them in Cairo ; they were black (Falashas ?) but not so black as the negroes. It was impossible to learn from them whether they belonged to the Karaïtes or the Rabbanites. In some respects they seem to hold the doctrine of the Karaïtes, for they say that there is no fire in their houses on the Sabbath ; in other respects they seem to observe Rabbanism. It is said that the pepper and other spices which the negroes sell come principally from their country.

It is universally known here that the Arabs who make pilgrimages from Egypt to Mecca journey through a large and fearful desert, forming caravans of at least 10,000 camels. Sometimes they are overtaken in the wilderness by a people of gigantic stature, one of whom can chase a thousand Arabs. They call this people El-Arabes, that is, children of the Almighty, because in their battles they always invoke the name of Almighty God. The Arabs assert that one of these people is able to bear the burden of a camel in one hand, while in the other he holds the sword with which he fights ; it is known that they observe the Jewish religious customs, and it is affirmed they are the descendants of Rechab.

No Jew may enter the enclosure of the temple. Although sometimes the Arabs are anxious to admit carpenters and goldsmiths to perform work there, nobody will go in, for we have all been defiled (by touching bodies of the dead). I do not know whether the Arabs enter the Holy of Holies or not. I also made enquiries relative to the *Eben Shethiah* where the Ark of the Covenant was placed, and am told that it is under a high and beautiful dome built by the Arabs in the court of the Temple. It is enclosed in this building, and no one may enter. There is great wealth in the enclosure of the temple. We hear that the monarchs build chambers there inlaid with gold, and the king now reigning is said to have erected a building, more splendid than any ever before built, adorned with gold and precious stones. The temple enclosure has still twelve gates. Those which are called the gates of mercy are of iron, and are two in number ; they look towards the east of the temple and are always closed. They only reach half-way above the ground, the other half is sunk in the earth. It is said that the Arabs often tried to raise them up but were not able to do so.

The western wall, part of which is still standing, is composed of large, thick stones, such as I have never before seen in an old building, either in Rome or in any other country. At the north-east corner is a tower of very large stones. I entered it and found a vast edifice supported by massive and lofty pillars ; there are so many pillars that it wearied me to go to the end of the building. Everything is filled with earth which has been thrown there from the ruins of the temple. The temple-building stands on these columns, and in each of them is a hole through which a cord may be drawn. It is said that the bulls and rams for sacrifice were bound here. Throughout the whole region of Jerusalem, in fields as well as vineyards, there are large caves connected with one another.

On the Mount of Olives are the graves of the Prophet Haggai and Huldah the Prophetess and more than ten caves, one leading out of the other. The sepulchre of the seventy Elders, which lies about 2,000 cubits from Jerusalem, is splendid, especially that of Simon the Just. Everywhere, outside and inside, both in fields and houses, the caves are innumerable.

The waters of Siloam flow underground in the valley of Jehoshaphat. Siloam is not exactly a stream, but rather a spring which rises up every morning till about noon, then falls and flows under the mountain to a place near which there is now a large ruin. It is said that this building was built by Solomon as a mint ; now it is used for a tanyard. The vale of Jehoshaphat is small. It runs along between the temple mount and Mount Olivet. At the foot of the slope of the temple mountain are Jewish graves ; the new ones are at the foot of the Mount of Olives, and the valley runs between the grave-yards. Not far from here are the monuments of Absalom and of the Prophet Zachariah ; at the latter place, prayers are offered up on faſt days ; and on the 9th of Ab lamentations are repeated.

The Mount of Olives is lofty and barren ; scarcely an olive-tree is to be found on it. From the top, Sodom and Gomorrah may be seen in the diſtance ; they now form a salt sea. I heard from people who were there that the ground was everywhere covered with salt. Of Lot's wife nobody could tell me anything ; for pillars of salt are innumerable, so that it is impossible to diſtinguish which is Lot's wife.

Mount Abarim, where Moses is buried, is visible from Jerusalem. The diſtrict beyond the Jordan, including the lands of Reuben, Gad and Manasseh, and of the sons of Ammon, the Mountain of Moab, and Mount Seir, are now waſte places. Not an inhabited city is to be found there ; for the Bedouins deſtroy everything. They come even up to the gates of Jerusalem, ſteal and plunder in the open roads, and no one can interfere with them, they are so numerous. For this reason the diſtrict is all waſte, without inhabitants ; and there is neither ploughing nor sowing. Jericho is a small village, consiſting of about twenty to thirty houses. Bethar, formerly a large city, is now a place for cattle, and contains about twenty houses ; it is half a day's journey from Jerusalem. Nearly all the houses that were formerly great are now waſte places.

They continue to bear the same names, but are uninhabited.

In all these districts, in the valleys and mountains, there are toll-collectors, who represent themselves as overseers for the security of the way, and are called Naphar [13] in Arabic. These men take as many taxes as they like from the Jews with perfect impunity. From Cairo there are twenty toll bars ; and I for my part paid them altogether about a ducat. The Jews who come from Cairo to Jerusalem have only to pay ten silver denarii at the city gate, while, on the other hand, those who come by way of Jaffa have to pay a ducat. The Jews in Jerusalem have to pay down every year thirty-two silver pieces per head. The poor man, as well as the rich, has to pay this tribute as soon as he comes to the age of manhood.

Everyone is obliged to pay fifty ducats annually to the Niepo,[13] i.e. the Governor of Jerusalem, for permission to make wine, a beverage which is an abomination to the Arabs. This is the whole amount of annual taxation to which the Jews are liable. But the Elders go so far in their iniquity that, in consequence of alleged deficits, they every week impose new taxes, making each one pay what they like ; and whoever refuses is beaten by order of a non-Jewish tribunal until he submits.

As for me, so far God has helped me ; they have demanded nothing from me as yet, how it may fare with me in the future I cannot tell.

The Christians in Jerusalem are divided into five sects—Catholics, Greeks, Jacobites, Armenians, and Johannites (Abyssinians) ; each one declares the faith of the others to be false, just as the Samaritans and Karaïtes do with respect to the Rabbanites. Each sect has a separate division in the Church of the Sepulchre, which is very large and has a tower surmounted by a cupola, but without a bell. In this

Church there are always two persons of each sect who are not allowed to leave it.

On Mount Zion, near the Sepulchre of the Kings, the Franciscans have a large Church. The Sepulchre of the Kings also belonged to them a long time ago, but a rich Ashkenazi, who came to Jerusalem, wished to purchase the graves from the King, and so involved himself in strife with the ecclesiastics, and the Arabs then took the graves away from them and have ever since retained them in their own keeping. When it became known in Venice that the graves had been taken from the Catholics through Jews who had come from Christian lands, an edict was published that no Jew might travel to Jerusalem through Venice ; but this edict is now repealed, and every year Jews come in the Venetian galleys and even in the pilgrim ships, for there is really no safer and shorter way than by these ships. I wish I had known all this while I was still in those parts, I would not then have remained so long on the journey. The galleys perform the voyage from Venice here in forty days at the most.

I have taken a house here close to the Synagogue. The upper chamber of my dwelling is even in the wall of the Synagogue. In the court where my house is there are five inhabitants, all of them women. There is only one blind man living here, and his wife attends on me. I must thank God, who has hitherto vouchsafed me His blessing, that I have not been sick, like others who came at the same time with me. Most of those who come to Jerusalem from foreign countries fall ill, owing to climatic changes and the sudden variations of the wind, now cold, now warm. All possible winds blow in Jerusalem. It is said that every wind before going where it listeth comes to Jerusalem to prostrate itself before the Lord. Blessed be He that knoweth the truth.

I earnestly entreat that you will not despond nor suffer anxiety on account of my having travelled so far away, and that you will not shed tears for my sake. For God in His mercy has brought me to his holy dwelling, which rejoices my heart and should also delight you. God is my witness that I have forgotten all my former distresses, and all remembrance of my native country has passed away from me. All the memories which I still retain of it centre in your image, revered father, which is constantly before my eyes. Mine eyes are dimmed when I remember that I have left you in your old age, and I fear lest your tears will recall the sins of my youth.

Now, I beseech you, bestow your blessing upon your servant. Let this letter atone for my absence, for it will show you the disposition of your son and you will no longer be displeased with him. If God will preserve me, I shall send you a letter every year with the galley, which will comfort you. Banish all sorrow from your heart. Rejoice with your dear children and grand-children who sit around your table. They will nourish and sustain your old age. I have prayed for their welfare and continue to do so in the sacred places of Jerusalem, the restoration of which, by means of the Messiah, God grant us to witness, so that you may come joyfully to Zion. Amen.

Finished in haste in Jerusalem, the Holy City. May it soon be rebuilt in our days.

From your Son,

OBADIAH JARE.

On the 8th Ellul, 5248 (1488).

II

How precious are your words to me, my brother. They are sweeter than sweet spices. Your three letters came to me on the 15th Ellul, through the master of the pilgrim ship, together with the long

letter from the worthy Signor Emanuel Chai of
Camerino. I shall answer them generally, and in
a few points more explicitly.

First of all I praise the Almighty and thank you
for the good news that our aged father, whom I never
cease to love tenderly, still lives. May God continue
His mercy and preserve him to us in strength and
health for a long time to come. But my joy was very
much saddened by the death of your eldest daughter
and of your son who was born to you after I had
left you. What God determines is ever for the best,
however, and there is nothing left for us to do but
to pray for those who still remain to us, that God
would grant them His blessing and preserve them.

You ask me about the miracles which are said to
take place at the temple-mountain and graves of the
pious. What can I tell you, my brother, about them?
I have not seen them. As for the lights on the site
of the temple, of which you have heard that they
always cease to burn on the 9th of Ab, I have been
told that this is the case, but I cannot speak with
certainty respecting it ; I need not say that the story
about the Sephardi is all deception and falsehood ;
but intelligent men like you, my brother, must inquire
into such stories and not trust to false reports.

I have not yet had time to go anywhere since I
came here, therefore I can only tell you by hearsay
of the environs of the Holy City and the other
adjoining districts. It is said that the Jews live quietly
and peaceably with the Arabs in Safed, in the village
of Cana, and in all Galilee, yet most of them are poor
and maintain themselves by peddling, and many go
about the villages seeking scanty means of subsistence.
In Damascus, on the other hand, I hear the Jews are
rich merchants and in every respect there is no place
so blessed as Damascus. It has beautiful houses
and magnificent gardens, such as are scarcely to be

seen elsewhere. The air, however, is not very pure, and
strangers going there become sick. People come
hither from Egypt, Damascus, Aleppo, and other
places to prostrate themselves before the Lord.
Jews have come here from Aden. Aden is said
to be the site of the garden of Eden : it lies S.E. of
Ethiopia, but the Red Sea separates them. These Jews
say that in their country there are many large Jewish
communities. The king is an Arab and is very
kindly disposed to the Jews, and that the country
is very large and beautiful, bearing many splendid
fruits, of kinds which are not to be found among
us. Where Paradise was actually situated they
do not know ; they sow in the month of Adar
(March) and reap in Kislev (December). The
rain season there is from Passover to the month
of Ab (August). It is in consequence of the great
quantity of rain that falls there that the Nile rises in
the month of Ab. Its inhabitants are somewhat black.
The Jews do not possess the books of the Talmud ;
all that they have are the works of R. Isaac Alfasi,
together with commentaries on them, and the works
of Maimonides. They are all, from great to small,
well versed in the works of Maimonides, for they
occupy themselves principally with studying them.
The Jews told us also that it is now well-known through
Arabian merchants that the river Sambation is fifty
days' journey from them in the wilderness, and
like a thread, surrounds the whole land where the
descendants of Israel dwell. This river throws up
stones and sand and rests only on the Sabbath, therefore no Jew, who is travelling in that country is
likely to violate the Sabbath. It is traditional among
them, that the descendants of Jacob dwell there.
This river throws up stones and sand and rests only
on the Sabbath, therefore no Jew can cross over it,
for otherwise he would violate the Sabbath. It is

traditional among them that they are all descendants of Moses, all pure and innocent as angels, and no evil-doer in their midst. On the other side of the Sambation the children of Israel are as numerous as the sand of the sea, and there are many kings and princes among them, but they are not so pure and holy as those who are surrounded by the stream. The Jews of Aden relate all this with a certain confidence, as if it were well-known, and no one ever doubted the truth of their assertions.

And old Ashkenazi Rabbi, who was born and educated here (Jerusalem), tells me that he remembers how even in his youth Jews came from Aden, and narrated everything literally as these do. The Jews of Aden also say that the Israelites dwelling on the borders of their territory, of whom I wrote in my first letter, are now at war with the people of Prester John (the Abyssinian), and that some of them have been taken prisoners and brought to Cairo. I have seen some of these with my own eyes ; these Jews are a month's journey in the wilderness from the others who live on the Sambation. The Christians who come from the territory of the Johannites relate that the Jews there, who are at war with the people of Prester John, have suffered great defeats, and we are very anxious to know if these accounts are really true, which God forfend. May the Lord always protect his people and his servants !

I live here in Jerusalem in the house of the Nagid, who has appointed me ruler of his household, and twice a month I hold discourses in the Synagogue in the Hebrew tongue, which most of the people here understand. My sermons sound in their ears like a lovely song, they praise them and like to listen· to them, but they do not act in accordance with them. Yet I cannot say that anybody has done me an injury : even the Elders have done me no wrong; they have not yet burdened me with any tax, as is generally done here every week. They even would not have me pay the poll-tax the firſt year, from which no one is exempt. So I remain here as by a miracle. God knows how it will go with me in the future !

The honoured Emanuel Chai of Camerino sent me one hundred Venetian ducats at my requeſt, the profits on the capital I left with him, and he has promised to do so every year. I give ten per cent. to the maſter of the ship, who brings me the money. The worthy Emanuel also added twenty-five ducats, partly for oil for the synagogue lamps and partly to give to the poor. As for me I live contentedly in Jerusalem wanting nothing from anyone. Every morning and evening we meet together to ſtudy Halacha (law). Two Sephardic pupils take uninterrupted part in my inſtruction and we have now also two Ashkenazic Rabbis here. And perchance the Promised Land may now be rebuilt and inhabited, for the king has issued a decree of laſting validity, that the Jews in Jerusalem shall pay only the poll-tax imposed on them. Formerly the Jewish inhabitants had to pay four hundred ducats annually, without reference to their number, and thus all suffered. Now each one pays his own poll-tax, and has nothing to pay for the others. This is a decree such as has not been made in Jerusalem for fifty years. Hence many who left Jerusalem are returning. May it please God that the city and the temple be rebuilt, and that the scattered of Judah and Ephraim may come together here and proſtrate themselves before God at the holy mountain. I muſt now conclude for the present, for I am much occupied.

Sent in haſte from Jerusalem, Ellul the 27th, 5249 (1489).

From your Brother,

OBADIAH JARE.

III

Honoured Sir,[14]

May the Almighty give you mercy and length of days, and may you acquire the merit to see the Sanctuary and Temple. Amen.

When the Florentine Ambassador came here with my Lord's pleasant letters, I was not in Jerusalem, the Holy City, for I had gone to Hebron and dwelt there many days. My stay there seemed somewhat dearer to me than at Jerusalem, for the Jews there are few and good and not bad like the men of Jerusalem. There are about twenty householders living in a closed courtyard, and no Ishmaelite or unclean man comes among them, and it is a tradition in all the country that it is better to be buried in Hebron than Jerusalem.

Here in Hebron, on the tomb of the Patriarchs, is a very old building of almost incredibly great stones, and on the old building is a new building of the Ishmaelites, and the place where the angels revealed themselves to Abraham is still called Mamre and there is a small cave there and a stone upon which it is said that Abraham was circumcised, and a distance away from the City is a large well which the Ishmaelites call Bir Ibrahim and a little further on is another well, Bir Ishaq, and a bow-shot or more away is the brook of Eshcol, still so called, and the grapes near the brook are to this very day larger than all the grapes of the country around, and there are still many villages around Hebron called by their names, as mentioned in the Books of the Prophets. And now as to the great city of Damascus, about which my Lord asks whether it is in the Holy Land. It is well-known from the words of all the wise men, and particularly of those of Maimonides in Hilchot Terumot (81–9), that it is reckoned as of Syria, and to this day all the inhabitants of Galilee agree as to this, but they say that the borders of the Holy Land are very near it. Safat and Banorsa (probably Tafas and Mzerib), the big city of Galilee, are near Damascus and their borders reach close to Damascus. But Tripoli, of Syria, a harbour for ships and a mart of nations, is on the border of Palestine and well spoken of, for it is blessed with fruit and all things that come from all the cities of the Holy Land, and travellers come there from the ends of the earth. At present there are about a hundred Jewish householders who dwell peacefully there. Many say that if a prudent man from Italy were to come there he would become very rich in a short time by trading with the merchants of Italy who constantly arrive there.

The war of the King of Turkey with the King of Egypt is by now forgotten and many think that, two years ago, they made a treaty not to harm each other, and the King who lives there is the same King neither dead nor changed. It is twenty years that he has reigned over the kingdom of Egypt, and he is very old, and no enemy of the Jews, though he takes from them heavy taxes, as he does also of the Ishmaelites and the uncircumcised who dwell in his land.

I have nothing new to tell my Lord to-day, except that I meditate on the tombs of our saintly fathers, and every day I pray towards the Temple that thy peace may be as a river and that thy fair house may have peace, and that the Lord may bless thee in all thy doings according to thy wish and wish of thy servant.

OBADIAH JARE

Citizen of the Holy City of Jerusalem.
Here, Hebron, 22nd Tebeth, 1250 (1490).
In haste.

DAVID REUBENI

(1522–1525)

The following account of David Reubeni's diary, from 1522 till 1525, is translated from a unique MS. in the Bodleian Library, Oxford. This MS. was acquired with others from the Michael Collection in 1848, and a photographic facsimile and plain copy was made a few years later. The facsimile remained at the Bodleian and the plain copy was acquired by the Breslau Jewish Seminary. Since 1867 the original of the MS. has disappeared.

To judge by the facsimile, it may very well have been the autograph of Reubeni's Secretary, Solomon Cohen of Prato. It will be observed that it ends abruptly and does not tell of David's subsequent adventures in Spain and Flanders and Italy, and his negotiations with the Emperor Charles V.

The MS. has been repeatedly published, notably by Dr. Neubauer in the *Anecdota Oxoniensia*, an extract published by Dr. Biberfeld, with a German translation, at Leipzig in 1892. The present translation is from the somewhat abbreviated text adopted by Eisenstein, with a few additions, notably at the end.

I

I am David, the son of King Solomon (may the memory of the righteous be for a blessing), and my brother is King Joseph, who is older than I, and who sits on the throne of his kingdom in the wilderness of Habor (Khorgbar), and rules over thirty myriads of the tribe of Gad and of the tribe of Reuben and of the half-tribe of Manasseh. I have journeyed from before the King, my brother and his counsellors, the seventy Elders. They charged me to go first to Rome to the presence of the Pope, may his glory be exalted. I left them by way of the hills, ten days' journey,

251

till I arrived at Jeddah, where I was taken with
a great sickness and remained five weeks, until I
heard that a ship was going to the land of Ethiopia.
I embarked on the ship in the Red Sea and we went
three days, and on the fourth day we arrived at the
city of Suakim, in Ethiopia. I took a house and
stayed there two months, but I was ill, and being
cupped lost fifty pounds of blood; for in order to get
better I had more than one hundred applications of
hot nails. Afterwards I met many merchants who
were travelling by way of Mecca to the Kingdom of
Sheba, and I called the chief of them, a descendant
of the Prophet of the Ishmaelites named Omar Abu
Kamil. I took two camels to journey with them, and
they were a great multitude with more than three
thousand camels. I improved in health daily, and
we passed through great deserts and forests and
fields in which there are many good herbs and good
pasturage and rivers, a journey of two months, until
we arrived at the capital of the kingdom of Sheba
in Ethiopia, where resides King Omara, who dwells
on the Nile. He is a black king and reigns over black
and white, and the name of his city is Lamula, and
I stayed with him ten months. The King travels
in his countries, every month a different journey.
I travelled with the King and had as my servants
more than sixty men of the sons of the Prophet
riding on horses, and they honoured me with great
honour. All the time that I stayed in the country
of Ethiopia with the King I fasted daily, when I
lay down and when I got up, and I prayed day and
night and I stayed not in the company of scoffers
or of merrymakers. On every journey they prepared
for me a wooden hut near the King's house. The
King has maidservants and menservants and slaves,
most of them naked, and the Queen and the concubines
and the ladies are dressed in golden bracelets, two

on the hands and two on the legs; and they cover their
nakedness with a golden chain, hand-embroidered,
and a cubit wide round their loins closed before and
behind. But their body is quite naked and bare,
and they wear a golden wreath in their noses. The
males and females eat elephants and wolves, leopards,
dogs, and camels, and they eat human flesh. The
King called me every day before him and said, " What
askest thou of us, thou son of the Prophet; if thou
desirest slaves, camels, or horses, take them"; and
I replied to him, " I want nothing of thee, but I have
heard of the glory of thy kingdom and I have brought
thee this gift with love and pleasure, and behold,
I give thee a garment of silk and seven hundred
ducats, florins of gold," and I said, " I love thee
and I grant thee pardon and forgiveness and a full
title to paradise, to thee and to thy sons and daughters,
and all thy household, and thou shalt come to us next
year to the city of Mecca, the place for the atonement
of sins." After these things an Ishmaelite came from
the city of Mecca and slandered me before the king,
and said, " This man in whom thou believest is not
of the sons of the Prophet, but from the wilderness
of Habor." When the King heard this and sent
for Abu Kamil and told him the words and the
slander, and Abu Kamil answered and said, " I know
neither one man nor the other, but I have seen that
the first man is honourable and fasts every day and
fears God, and does not go after merriment nor after
women and does not love money. But the other man
loves money and does many evil things and talks a
great deal"; and the king said, " Thy words are true,"
and Abu Kamil left him and told me these matters.
After that the king's wife heard the words of the
slanderer and sent for me and said to me, " Do not
remain in this country for this new man who has come
from Mecca has slandered thee to the king in words

unfitting, and he is taking counsel with many men to seek from the king to slay thee." And I said to her, " How can I go away without the king's permission ? " But the Queen replied, " The king comes to-night to my house and I will send for thee, and thou shalt come before me and before the king and thou shalt ask permission from the king, and I shall help thee and thou shalt go to-morrow on thy way in peace." So when I came before the king I burst forth and said, " What is my transgression, and what is my sin ? Have I not come before thee with gifts and love and kindness, and desired not to receive from thee, either silver or gold or slaves or maid-servants or men-servants; but this knave who has slandered me to thee loves money and speaks falsehood, and behold, I have been with thee ten months. Call thy servants and thy lords and let them tell thee if they have found in me any sin or transgression or any fault. Therefore, in thy kindness and for God's sake, give me permission to go on my way and I shall pray for thee and bless thee." And the Queen also said, " Give him per-mission that he may go on his way, for he is honourable and trusty and we have found no blemish in him, but only good report." And the king answered and said to me, " What needest thou, slaves, or camels, or horses ? Take them and go in peace "; and I said to the king, " I want nothing but permission from thee that I may go to-morrow at dawn, for I know that I have wicked enemies against me; therefore may it be good in thy sight to send with me one of thy honoured servants to the place of the house of Abu Kiamil." Then the king called one of his servants and ordered him to go with him and gave us two horses and we rode to the house of Abu Kiamil, and on the way we crossed many rivers and the feeding ground of elephants. There was one river of mud and water in which horses, when crossing it, sank in the mire up to their bellies, and many men and horses had been drowned in this place. But we crossed it on horseback, and thanked God we were safe. We travelled eighteen days until we arrived at Senaar, and next morning I and my servant journeyed on further five days on the River Nile until I reached the city of Sheba, but it is in ruins and desolate, and there are wooden huts in it, and Abu Kiamil came to me and said, " How art thou come from the king and he did not give thee slaves ? I know that the king loves thee, therefore ſtay in my house and I will go up to the king and will beg him for thee "; and I said, " I will do so." But that night I dreamt in the house of Abu Kamil, and I saw my father, on whom be peace, and he said to me, " Why haſt thou come to this far land ? Go hence to-morrow in peace and no evil will come upon thee, but if thou waiteſt until Abu Kamil returns, know that thou wilt die "; and when I woke from my sleep I said to Abu Kamil, " Let me go, I do not wish thee to go to the king for me," and in the morning I journeyed from Sheba, and Abu Kamil sent his brother with me, and we went ten days' journey to the kingdom of Elgel. Elgel is in the kingdom of Sheba and under the rule of Omara, and the name of the King of Elgel is Abu Akrab, and we came before him and Abu Kamil's brother said to him, " The king has ordered us to conduct this our lord, the son of the Prophet, by this way "; and I ſtayed before that king three days, and afterwards I journeyed on, I and my servant, till we came to Mount Takaki, and I ſtood before a great lord called Abd Alohab, and he wished me to go by way of a short desert to the land of Dongola, and I ſtayed in his house six days and gave him twenty ducats and garments. They filled me six water skins and placed them on three camels, and I journeyed on, I and my servant and the servant of Alohab, ten days by the desert way, and we found many men on horses, and I said to the servant of Alohab, "Lead me to Masah, five days' distance from this land, which is at the end of the kingdom of Sheba, on the River Nile ; " and he said to me, " I will do according to thy words, and if thou wishest I will go with thee to Egypt." Then I bowed myself down before the King of heaven and earth, when I heard the words of the man, for I feared to remain in the land of Sheba, and I and he went through the beginning of the desert, where there is much sand, and we went on the sand as upon hills and I fasted three days consecutively until I reached the city of al Habor; and afterwards I reached the River Nile and behold, there was an old Ishmaelite of the lords of Egypt in front of me, and he came and kissed my hands, and said, " Come, O blessed of the Lord, O lord the son of our lord, do me kindness and come into my house and I will take thy blessing. I have food and provender and place to lodge," and I went with that man whose name is Osman. He had a wife and children, and prepared the house for me and my servant, and then I sent away the servant of Alohab to his country, and I gave him ten ducats and he went home.

And in that land five young men came to me from the two tribes and gave me two little lions, and I took them to bring them to Egypt, and they returned to their country; and I stayed in the house of the old man with my servant one month, and the honoured old man said to me, " Behold thy camels are very weak and cannot travel in this desert, thou wilt have to feed them two or three months until they get fat and then they can travel the three days' journey in the desert, where camels can find neither grass nor food nor anything to eat until you get to Girgeh, on the River Nile near to Egypt." I bought from the old man a she-camel, good and fat, for twenty ducats, and the old man bought for me two strong camels for seventy ducats, and the camels which I had I gave at camel price in exchange, and afterwards the lords of that city and its surroundings came and brought me flour, barley, rye, lambs, and bullocks, by way of tithe to the house of the old man, and they filled his house. But of what they gave me I only took what the camels eat and the remainder I gave to the old man and to the poor as a gift, and I said to the old man, " Come with me to King Mehmel," and I went with him before the king and his servants, and he was drinking date-wine and eating mutton without bread. The king was pleased with me and said, " This day is blessed on which our lord, the son of our lord the Prophet, has come before us, and it is my will that thou shalt remain in my house and, if thou wilt, I will do thee honour and glory," and I said to the king, " Be thou blessed before the Lord, I will pray for thee and I will give thee pardon and atonement for all thy sins."

On the 14th day of the month of Kislev I journeyed with my servant from the house of the old man, with many men by way of the great desert, and I was always fasting and praying to God, when I lay down and when I got up, and when I went forth and when I journeyed; and I determined not to eat nor drink, save only once in every three days and nights, and did not eat between one oasis and another, for in this desert even wells three days' distance from each other are reckoned near, and some wells are four days' journey apart, and some wells five days. We could only drink the water which was on our camels until we arrived at the city of Girgeh, after forty-five days, and we had a man with us who knew the way in the desert like a pilot in the sea, by way of the stars by night and through his knowledge by day, for this desert is like the great sea. That wise man said to me, " Come

257

with me to my house until I find thee a way to go to Egypt"; and the man's name was Shalom, in Arabic Selim. His house was a mile from the end of the desert and I went with him to his house, which is on the Nile, and he gave me a hut and bed, and one of his servants to do for me. My servant and I ſtayed with the man twenty days, and I sold my camels for one hundred golden florins and I sailed in a small boat on the River Nile until I reached the Gates of Egypt. There the Ishmaelite Turks detained me, and wished to examine my ſtuff and boxes in order to take tithe from me, and they wanted twenty florins for the servants. But when the Turks saw the two lions I had with me, they asked them of me as a present, and they would free me from the cuſtoms and the tithe. So I gave them the lions and I had no other expenses, and they honoured me with great honour and their joy was very great, for they said they wished to send the lions to the King of Turkey.

II

CAIRO AND PALESTINE

I entered Cairo on the New Moon of Adar, 5283 (1523). I had journeyed with a man who had friends in Cairo, who said to me, " Come to my house to-night and ſtay till morning, and to-morrow I will seek for you a suitable lodging." I went with this man, I and my slave, and all my ſtuff.

It was a big house with large trees, and they gave me a room and placed before me bread and cheese. I said, " I cannot eat cheese, give me eggs," and I ate and slept till the morning. That morning I took out my pieces of gold and said, " Come with me to sell the gold to the Jews, because they are better versed in business than the ordinary people." He came with me to the Jewish quarter, and I ſtood in front of the door of a shop in which were Jewish

money changers. I asked them in Hebrew, " Who
is the chief among you ? " so that the Ishmaelites
should not understand. The Jew said, " I will come
with thee," and I and he went till we came to the
house of R. Abraham (De Castro), Chief of the
Mint. He was the most esteemed in Cairo. I said
to him, " I am a Jew, and wish to stay with thee
three or four days, and I will tell you a secret. Put
me on the way to go to Jerusalem. I want neither
silver nor gold nor food from you, but only lodging."
R. Abraham answered, " I cannot let thee come to
my house, because thou hast come disguised as an
Ishmaelite, and if thou didst stay in my house it would
do me harm." I said to him, " Do me this kindness for
the love of God and the love of the Elders, for one
good deed leads to another." He answered, " It
would be good for me and all the Israelites that live
in Egypt if thou dost not come to my house." So
I left his house and went with the Ishmaelite and came
to the house of an Ishmaelite merchant, whose name
in Hebrew was Zachariah and in Arabic Jahia, the son
of Abdallah. Then I sold my Ethiopian slave to
the merchant for 200 broad florins, and travelled with
several merchants from Cairo to Gaza. We came to
a big khan like an encampment, and they gave me
one of the upper rooms and in my room a Jewish
merchant from Beyrouth was staying, called Abraham
Dunaz. I stayed in that room two days and spoke
nothing to him ; all day I prayed and spoke to nobody.
After that I called him and asked his name, and I
asked, " What do you pray for at this season, for rain
or dew ? " He replied, " For rain," and also told
me that he had seen many Ishmaelites, and even
descendants of the prophet, but never saw a man as
wise as me. I said to him, " I know by calculation
that to-day is a festival of yours, the day of Purim."
He replied, " Yes, that is true," and asked me,

"Who told you all this?" I replied that in my country there are many Jews and wise men, and their houses are near to my house, and I have friends among them who eat at my table of fruit but not meat, and they love me and I love them." And he said to me that in his country Jews cannot talk with any Ishmaelites nor any descendants of the prophet, for they hate us and they love dogs more than Israelites. I told the Jew, "Fear not nor be dismayed, for speedily the end will come for you and the Almighty will humble the wicked to the ground and raise up the lowly upon high, and speedily make you see great matters and much confusion among the kings. Now, Abraham, do me a kindness and seek for me merchants to conduct me to the Temple in Jerusalem, but first to Hebron." He told me that he would do so, and went and found a donkey man and made the bargain between him and me. I did not wish to reveal my secret to him, but when starting on my journey told him the beginning of the matter. The money changer, Joseph, the shopkeeper, came to me with his brother, Jacob, and their old father, who was still living. They were with me about two hours and I told them no more of my business than the barest headings. Through the Jew, Abraham, the Jews sent me meat and bread, and I stayed at Gaza five days.

HEBRON

On the 19th Adar, 5283 (1523), I journeyed from Gaza to Hebron, and travelled day and night until I arrived at Hebron at the site of the cave of Machpelah on the 23rd Adar at noon. The keepers of the cave came to kiss my hands and feet, and said to me, "Come in, O blessed of the Lord, our lord, the son of our lord"; and two of the guardians of the Mosque of Abraham, who were wise and great and appointed over all the guardians and Judges in Hebron, took

me by the hand and brought me to one grave and said
to me, "This is the grave of Abraham, our father,"
and I prayed at that place; and then they showed me
on the left hand a small chapel and therein is the
tomb of Sarah, our mother, and between them is the
Ishmaelites' praying chapel. Above Abraham's tomb
is the tomb of Isaac in the great Mosque, and near
to his tomb is Rebecca's, above the tomb of Sarah;
and at the foot of Abraham's tomb is a plan of
Jacob's tomb in another great Mosque, and near the
plan of his grave is Leah's, alongside of Sarah's.
I gave them ten florins charity to buy olive oil for the
lamps and said to the guardians that this plan is not
true, for Abraham, Isaac, and Jacob are in one cave
underground, and they are not buried on the surface.
They replied, "Thy words are true," and I asked them
to show me the cave, and I went with them. They
showed me a well with a lamp therein burning day
and night, and lowered the lamp into the well by a
rope, and I saw, from the mouth of the well, a door
of man's height. I believed that this was the real cave
and rejoiced in my heart, and sent the Ishmaelites
away and prayed by that well until I had finished my
prayer. After that I called the oldest of the guardians
and said to them, "This is not the door of the well,
but there is another door," and they replied, "It
is so. In olden days the door of the cave was in the
middle of the great Mosque, in which is the plan of
Isaac's tomb." I asked them to show me the place of
that door and went with them. They removed the
carpets from the floor of the Mosque and showed me
the place of the door, closed by big stones and leaden
weights, and no man can remove that overburden.
I told them to cover the ground again with the carpets,
and asked them if they knew who built the door of
the cave. They took out a book and read out before
me that a king, the second after Mahommed, built

the gate of the cave after the Ishmaelites had taken the holy place from the Christians. That king sent four men into the cave, each with a candle in his hand, and they stayed an hour in the cave and came out. Three of them died immediately after they came out, but the fourth survived for three days. The king asked what they had seen in the cave and the survivor replied, " I saw these forms: our father Abraham in his coffin in the place of the upper plan, and round Abraham's tomb many lamps and books and a covering of beautiful cloths over it; and near to our father Abraham, our mother Sarah and Isaac and Rebecca above at their head, and our father Jacob and our mother Leah at their feet; and there were lamps round each tomb, and on each was an image, a man's on a man's tomb, and a woman on a woman's. The lamps in our hands were extinguished, and in the cave shone a great light like the light of the sun, and in the cave there was a pleasant odour like that of incense. When we passed Rebecca's tomb the man's image on Isaac's tomb called out to us in a great voice, and we remained breathless until we left the cave." The king commanded that the gate should be closed and it remains closed to this very day.

I stayed to pray at the mouth of the well and watched the door of the cave on Sabbath eve until dawn, and in the morning I stayed to pray until the evening, and on the Sunday night I prayed and did not sleep until the morning. The two Elders had told me that on the third day I should find a sign and I remained, wondering what I should see. On the Sunday morning the guardians called me with great joy and said to me, " Our lord and prophet, rejoice with us for we have had a great joy. Water has come to the bath of the Mosque, and it is now four years since water came to it"; and I went with them to see the water. It was good and clear and came to the bath from a distant land.

DAVID REUBENI

I journeyed from Hebron on the 24th Adar and came to Jerusalem, and there were robbers on the way. My companions said to me, " Our lord, son of the Prophet, there are enemies before us"; and I said to them, " Fear not nor be dismayed, they are afraid and you are safe." I was still speaking when, behold, the Turkish judge had come from Hebron with many servants. The robbers saw him and all of them fled, and I journeyed with him to Jerusalem. I entered it on the 25th Adar, 283 (1523), and that day I entered the house of the Holy of Holies, and when I came to the sanctuary all the Ishmaelite guardians came to bow before me and to kiss my feet, and said to me, " Enter, Oh blessed of the Lord, our lord, the son of our lord," and the two chief among them came and took me to the cavern which is under the *Eben Shethiah*, and said to me, " This is the place of Elijah the prophet, and this the place of King David, and this King Solomon's place, and this the place of Abraham and Isaac, and this the place of Mahomet." I said to the guardians, " Now that I know all these places go ye on your way, for I wish to pray, and in the morning I will give you charity." They went away and I knew at once that all their words were false and vain. I prayed until all the Ishmaelites came to prayer. They left the Temple court after their prayer two hours after dark. I went below the *Eben Shethiah*. Then the guards extinguished all the lights in the Court except four, and before they closed the gates they searched to see if any man were sleeping in the cavern, so as to turn him out. They found me, and said, " Leave this place, for we are the guards and may allow no one to remain to sleep here. We have so sworn to the King, and if thou wilt not go we shall ask the Governor to remove thee against thy will." When I heard these words, I came out of the court and they shut the doors, and I prayed outside the court all night, and fasted, and this was my fourth day. In the morning, when the Ishmaelites came to pray in the court, I entered with them, and when they had finished their prayer, I called out with a loud voice, "Where are the guards? Let them all come before me"; and I said to them, "I am your lord, and the son of your Lord, the Prophet. I have come from a distant country to this holy house and my soul desireth to remain therein to pray and not to sleep." And after that four of the guards came to expel me, and I said to them, "I am your lord, the son of your Lord, if you wish peace wish me well and I will bless you ; but if not I will be avenged of you and will write to the King of Turkey your evil deeds." They replied, "Forgive us this time for we wish to serve thee and to be thy slaves as long as thou remainest in the holy house, and will do thy will." Then I gave them ten ducats for charity, and stayed in the sanctuary and fasted in the Holy of Holies five weeks. I ate no bread and drank no water except from Sabbath eve to close of Sabbath, and I prayed below the *Eben Shethiah* and above it. Afterwards ten messengers from King Joseph, my brother, and his elders came before me, and they recognized and stood before me in the sanctuary.

The Ishmaelites have a sign on the top of the cupola of the court, and this sign is like a half moon turned westward ; and on the first day of Pentecost of 283 (1523), it turned eastward. When the Ishmaelites saw this they cried out with a loud voice, and I said, "Why do you cry?" and they replied, "For our sins, this sign of the half moon is turned eastwards, and that is an evil sign for the Ishmaelites"; and the Ishmaelite workmen went on the Sunday to restore the sign to its place, and on Monday the sign again

turned eastward while I was praying, and the
Ishmaelites were crying and weeping, and they sought
to turn it round but they could not ; and our elders
had already told me, " When thou seest this sign go
to Rome," and I saw the gates of mercy and the gates
of repentance, and walked in the sanctuary. It is
a big structure like the upper buildings, and I did
that which the Elders ordered me underneath the
sanctuary, out of man's reach, and the turning of
the sign took place after I had done what the Elders
commanded beneath the sanctuary. I went up the
Mount of Olives, and I saw two caves there and
returned to Jerusalem and ascended Mount Zion.
There are two places of worship there in the town ;
the upper place is in the hands of the Christians and
the lower in that of the Ishmaelites. This the
Ishmaelites opened for me and showed me a grave,
and told me that it was the grave of King David,
on whom be peace, and I prayed there. Then I left
and went to the upper place of worship, which the
Christians opened for me. I entered it and prayed
there and returned to Jerusalem, and went to the house
of a Jew called Abraham Hager. He was smelting
near the synagogue, and there were women there
cleaning the candlesticks of the Synagogue. I asked
him his name and he said, "Abraham"; and I sent the
Ishmaelites away and said to them, " I have work to
do with the smelter." They went away and I asked
him, " At this season do you pray for rain or dew ? "
and he said, " Dew," and was astonished, and I spoke
a good deal with him but did not tell him I was a Jew.
But on the third time that I went to his house before
leaving Jerusalem, I said to him, " Make me a model
showing Venice, Rome, and Portugal." He made
me such a model, being a Sefardi, who had come
from there and I said I wished to go to Rome, and
he said, " Why ? " and I answered, " I am going for

a good cause, but it is a secret which I cannot reveal, and I want thee to advise me how I should go "; and I then gave him a letter which I had written to Jerusalem and said to him, " Give this letter into the hand of R. Isaac the Nagid."

I left Jerusalem on the 24th Sivan, 5283, and a number of Ishmaelites came on horseback to accompany me five miles. I went on my way and arrived in Gaza in the month of Tammuz at the place where I ſtayed on the firſt occasion. An old Jew, a dealer in spices, called Ephraim, came to me and I said to him, " Go summon unto me Joseph, the money changer, and let him bring with him weights for gold and silver and piƈtures of coins, and come together to me in the presence of the Ishmaelites." The old man did so, and two of them came to me and I asked Joseph, the money changer, as to the health of his old father, and his brother, Jacob, and he said, " They are well." Afterwards four old men came before me, and I said to them, " I am a Jew, and my father is King Solomon, and my brother, Joseph, who is my elder, is now King over thirty myriads in the wilderness of Habor." We ate and drank wine that night, though from the day I journeyed from the wilderness of Habor I had drunk no wine till that night. Afterwards I went with old Ephraim that night to the house of a Jew called R. Daniel. He is the richeſt of the Jews in Gaza and honeſt and pious, and he told me of all the Turkish Governors who had come to Gaza. R. Daniel has a son valiant and handsome, called Solomon, but the Jews hate him because they say he is wild. I summoned him and rebuked him between ourselves and said, " Turn from thy evil ways before Jerusalem is taken ; if thou doſt not repent, thy blood be on thy head," and he swore that he would repent. Then the Rabbi, R. Samuel, sent me through old Ephraim a thousand greetings and begged me to take the Sabbath meal with him that night. I did so and stayed with him till midnight, and asked them to show me their Synagogue, and I went and prayed therein about two hours. I returned to the house of the Rabbi R. Ishmael and said to him, " If thou wilt do me a favour for the sake of God and thy love of the elders and the rest of Israel, find me speedily a ship going to Alexandria." They told me that a ship was starting that week for Damietta with Jews from Jerusalem therein and this old man, R. Ephraim, would accompany me. I said to them, " Be blessed of the Lord, remove from you causeless hate and return to the Lord in order that he may speed our redemption and the redemption of the house of Israel, for thus said the Elders." I journeyed from Gaza on the 15th Tammuz, 5283, and in two days reached Damietta, where I took a house, and then I went to the house of a Jew called R. Mordecai, whose brother, R. Samuel, lives in Cairo. I stayed with him over Sabbath, and on Sunday he took me to the sea-shore, and we rode on a camel for twenty days along the shore. I embarked on a ship and reached Alexandria on the 24th Tammuz, and went to the khan, and the learned Kabbalist, R. Mordecai, came to me and I said, " I am a Jew, the brother of the King of the wilderness of Habor, and I wish thee to direct me by sea to Rome." R. Mordecai said to me, " Go to the Consul and he will advise thee what to do, for he is an honourable man. Tell me what he tells thee." I went to the Consul and said to him, " I am the brother of the king of the wilderness of Habor, and I have come by the command of my brother, King Joseph, and the advice of the seventy elders, and I wish to go to the Pope and then to the King of Portugal. Therefore advise me what I shall do and find me the ship in which I shall go." The Consul replied, " There is a ship going to Puglia,

but I fear evil will come to me because of thee ; therefore, I advise thee to wait till a galley goes to Venice,
and the Ishmaelites will direct thee." I returned to
my place and went to the house of the said Rabbi
Mordecai. A young man called Joseph, whose father
and mother were of Naples, and who had a wife from
Turkey, came there, and I asked R. Mordecai to
let the young man go with me to Rome. He said to
me, " Go, this young man will be thy interpreter in
Rome." Then I went home and stayed until the eve
of the New Year, 5284, and prayed in the little
synagogue on New Year's eve. The name of the
landlord was Isaac Bucapzi, and he and a Jew called
R. Benjamin joined me in prayers. I stayed there
the two days New Year, and then went home, and
during the feast of Tabernacles I went to the house
of R. Mordecai to stay with him the first two days.
I remained in Alexandria until I heard the galley
was about to start for Venice, and I went to the great
Turkish Pasha to get his permission. There were
mighty lords with him and I said to him, " I seek
a kindness from you because of my love and the love
of the Prophet, and I will pray to the Prophet for you
that he may give you a right to Paradise ; speak to
the captain of the galley and order him to conduct
me in the ship to Venice." They did so, and they
sent with me their servants and ordered the captain
accordingly, and the captain said," So will I do."

III

ALEXANDRIA TO ROME

I and my servant, Joseph, travelled from Alexandria
in the middle of Kislev, 5284 (November, 1523), and
I fasted all day and prayed day and night, and took
with me from Alexandria all kinds of food for Joseph.
But it was no use, for all became mixed up with the

food of the Christians. He ate from their utensils, and I cried out against him, but he cared not. When I reached Candia I bought many kinds of food, and the Christians and the Captain complained to me of Joseph that he stole bread and wine from the people on the ship. I was ashamed of him but could not speak with him, for he regarded not my word. When I reached Venice I went to the Captain's house, where he gave me room, and I fasted in his house six days and six nights, and when I had finished prayers I saw a man behind me, and said to him in Hebrew, "Who art thou?" He replied, "I am a Jew," and I asked him who told him I was here. He replied, "Thy servant Joseph says that thou art a holy envoy." I asked him his name, and he replied Elchanan. Another time this Elchanan returned with another Jew called R. Moses Castilis, a painter. I said to R. Moses, "I am greatly in need of seven ducats, for my servant Joseph is poor and sick, and I have spent for him and in Alexandria much money." I went with R. Moses to the Ghetto (the place of the Jews) and a respected Jew called R. Mazliah came to me, and I spoke to him as to the expense, and he said he would go to the house of R. Hiyya. We went there and I said to him, "I am a Jew from the wilderness of Habor, a holy envoy sent by the seventy Elders." I was in his eyes as one who mocked, so I said to him, "I require seven ducats; speak with the wardens and find out if they will give this." He replied, "If the rest of the Jews will give, I will give my share." I told him this was the sixth day of my fast and I was only eating at nightfall, and asked him to send me some wine. I returned to my lodging at the Captain's house, but he sent me nothing. So I only ate eggs, bread and water, but the respected R. Mazliah had done his best, and R. Simon ben Asher Meshullam came to me and said, "I hear that you are a holy envoy from the seventy elders and going to Rome ; tell me wherefore they have sent you and I will send two Jews with you and pay all the expenses." I said to him, " I am going to the Pope and can say nothing more than that I am going for the good of Israel. If thou wilt send two men with me to Rome, thou wilt have a share in the good deed, and they will bring you back good tidings." Afterwards I and R. Moses, the painter, went to the captain's house and took leave of him, and took all my things and went to the Ghetto to the house of R. Moses, the painter : and R. Mazliah came to me and I asked him to find me a ship for Rome. He did so and that night I got into a small boat, and from there into the ship, and I fasted. I and Joseph started on our journey on Friday, the new moon of Adar, 5284 (about March, 1524), and stayed over Sabbath on the ship until I reached Pesaro. Here I stayed in the house of R. Foligno, and said to him, " Do me the kindness to put me on my way to Rome, as I do not wish to sleep here over-night." He went and found me horses, and I and Joseph rode to another city where there were Jews ; and so every evening from journey to journey, with many Jews, until we arrived, on the eve of Purim, at midday at Castel Nuovo, near Rome, at the house of a Jew called R. Samuel, and I stayed with him over Purim ; and on that day I bought the skipping hoop [1] with which I did what the Elders had ordered me and next day I left and arrived at Rome, thank God!

IV

I, David, the son of King Solomon, of righteous memory, from the wilderness of Habor, entered the gate of the City of Rome on the 15th day of Adar, 1524, and a Gentile from Venice came to me and spoke with me in Arabic, and I was angry with him. I

went to the Pope's palace, riding on horseback, and
my servant before me, and the Jews also came with
me, and I entered the presence of Cardinal Egidio ;
and all the Cardinals and Princes came to see me,
and with the said Cardinal was R. Joseph Ashkenazi,
who was his teacher, and the physician Rabbi, Joseph
Sarphati ; and I spoke to the Cardinal, and my interpreter
was the learned man who came with me, and the Jews
heard all that I spoke to the cardinal, and I said to
him that to the Pope I would complete my message.
I stayed with the Cardinal all day till the eve of
Sabbath, and he promised to bring the matter before
the Pope to-morrow. I went away with R. Joseph
Ashkenazi and with R. Raphael, the old man who
lived in the same house, and we took our Sabbath
meal and slept till the morning; and I went with them
to the Synagogue in order to pronounce the blessing
of deliverance from peril before the scroll of the
Law. Men, women, and children came to meet us
all the way until we entered the house of the said
R. Raphael, and I fasted on that Sabbath day. All
day long men and women, Jews and gentiles came
to visit me until evening. Cardinal Egidio sent for
R. Joseph Ashkenazi to tell me that the Pope was very
pleased, and wished to see me on Sunday before 11.
And so in the morning, before prayers, they gave me
a horse and I went to Borghetto Santo Gile to the house
of an old man, the brother-in-law of R. Joseph
Sarphati, before morning prayer; and I prayed there,
and many Jews came to me, may God keep them and
multiply them a thousand fold ! At eight o'clock
I went to the house of the Pope and entered Cardinal
Egidio's room, and with me were about twelve old
and honoured Jews. As soon as the Cardinal saw me,
he rose from his chair and we went, I and he, to the
apartment of the Pope, and I spoke with him, and he
received me graciously and said, " The matter is

from the Lord"; and I said to him, "King Joseph
and his elders ordered me to speak to thee that thou
shouldst make peace between the Emperor and the
French King, by all means, for it will be well with thee
and them if thou makest this peace, and write for me
a letter to these two Kings, and they will help us
and we will help them; and write also for me to King
Prester John (i.e. the King of Abyssinia). The Pope
answered me, "As to the two kings between whom
thou askest me to make peace, I cannot do it, but
if thou needest help the King of Portugal will assist
thee, and I will write to him and he will do all, and his
land is near to thy country and they are accustomed to
travel on the great sea every year, more than those in the
lands of those other Kings"; and I replied to the Pope,
"Whatever thou wishest I will do, and I will not turn
to the right or left from what thou biddest me, for
I have come for God's service, and not for anything
else, and I will pray for thy welfare and good all the
days of my life." And the Pope asked the Cardinal,
"Where does the Ambassador lodge?" and he
answered, "The Jews asked him to go with them,"
and the honourable Jews who were with the
Pope told him, "Let the Ambassador stay with us,
for we will honour him for the sake of thy honour,"
and the Pope said to them, "If you will do honour to
him I will pay all your expenses"; and I said to the
Pope, "I wish to come before thee once every two days,
for to see thee is as seeing the face of God"; and the
Pope answered me that he ordered Cardinal Egidio
to come with me every time I came to see him, and
I took leave of the Pope and went from before him,
and I went with the Jews and rejoiced and was glad
of heart. I returned to the old man's house by way
of Santo Gile, but Aaron, the warden, was angry
that I went to the old man's house, and told the
Cardinal that the wardens and the whole congregation

had prepared a house for the ambassador and provided servants for him, because I could not remain alone; the Cardinal wrote me that I should go with them, and I went with them. They prepared for me a fine dwelling with three big good rooms, and the master of the house was called Joseph, and he had three sons, the eldest Moses, the second Benjamin, and the third Judah; and they all waited on me, and I stayed in their house six weeks, and I went to the Cardinal's house five days consecutively, for the other Cardinals went to his house and they consulted me from morning to evening, and I fasted in that house six days consecutively; and on Friday they boiled some water for me and put in it many herbs. They did all this for the love of me, because they said that it was medicine after the fast, but my soul was weary, and I wished to drink water, and they gave me the boiled water and I drank a stomach full. This water caused me a great and strong pain in the stomach, for I was not accustomed to drink hot water after a fast. I fasted in Jerusalem six times, seven days and nights, and in Venice, six days and nights, and after all these fasts I drank nothing but cold water with much sugar, and that did me no harm; but they only did it for my good, to give me hot water, because they did not know my constitution, may the house-holders and the warden be blessed ! A great sickness came upon me and I said to them, " Find me a bath of hot water for I wish to go there "; and a man came called Yomtob Halevi, and he prepared me a bath and a good couch to sleep upon, and I entered the bath and slept there, and that day I let much blood, cupping all my limbs, and then I sent for the physician, R. Joseph Sarphati, and said to him, " Look how I am; if thou wishest to get a great name, let me stay in thy house and remain with me until my sickness leaves me." He did so, and I stayed in his house three months, and he paid all the expenses and for all I required, may the Lord bless him and his household ! He gave me to eat and gave me various kinds of remedies, and boiled wine for me to drink and heated herbs and placed them on my feet, and washed my feet and anointed me, and took olive oil and put it in a big vessel; and I entered and washed in that hot olive oil, and I came out from the hot oil and lay on a good bed, and they changed the sheets each time, and I lay on the bed like a dead man; and they saw that there was gravel in my water, which is a bad sign, and I told them that I would not die from this illness until I had brought Israel to Jerusalem, built the altar, and offered sacrifice; but I got no sleep and was in great pain and lay between life and death, and they said to me, " Wilt thou make confession, for that will neither bring death near nor keep it away "; and I was angered with them, and said, " Go in peace, I do not wish to say the confession, for I trust in God, that he will stay with me and save me." They were astonished at my good constitution and pleased, and God sent a great sweat on me on that day and I was healed from the great sickness. My servants were with me, Haim, and the Cantor, and Mattathias, and Yomtob, and David Pirani, and Simcha, and Solomon Gabani, and an Arab Jew, Shua, and his brother Moses, and a third called Sabbatai; and they all stayed in the house of R. Joseph Sarphati, day and night, and waited on me and slept in the house, and I called R. Joseph Sarphati and said to him, " Find me a hot bath," and he prepared a bath in the Synagogue of the Sephardim, and I got in and out; and Judah Kutunia prepared for us a great feast, an hour after the bath. Then I returned to the house of R. Joseph-Sarphati, but did not wish to reside there because of the sick men in the house, and I called the physician, R. Moses Abudarhin, to find me another house; and he replied that he had a good room in his house, and said to me that he had three sons, Joseph, Samuel, and Isaac, who would wait upon me. I ſtayed in his house from Wednesday until after Sabbath; and he had a grown up daughter, who could read Scripture, and who prayed daily morning and evening prayer, and on the Sabbath she had great rejoicing and danced from joy, and on the Sunday she was ſtricken with the plague; and a wise woman called Rabith, a teacher of infants, and the teacher of that girl, came to me and said, " Pray for the daughter of R. Moses Abudarhin, for the fever is come upon her laſt night "; and, as soon as I heard the words of the woman, I called R. Moses and said to him, " Find me a garden, for I wish to go into the garden "; and I sent for my servants and the three sons of R. Moses, and went with them into a garden, and we ſtayed there all that day until night, and then I sent Joseph with R. Moses to tell his father that I could not go into his house until eight days had passed and his daughter was healed from her sickness. Joseph went and returned, and said that his father had prepared a room in the house of R. Isaac Abudarhin, his uncle, and all that was needful for me, and I went with him to his uncle's house, which was an evil house and an evil smell in it; but R. Isaac had a worthy wife, whose name was Perna, who spoke Arabic, and was wise, and I ſtayed with them, and also the three sons of R. Moses ſtayed there until their siſter's sickness had ceased. They all waited on me and all expenses were paid by R. Moses Abudarhin, and his brother, Abraham, visited me weekly with gifts; and the daughter of Moses Abudarhin died that week, and her brothers ſtayed in my house until forty days had elapsed. Three months I ſtayed in this house, only because of my affection for them, for the house was very evil, and the Chriſtian lords came to visit me in a house which was not fitting. After that I sent a letter to the Cardinal to tell him that I had left the house of Joseph Sarphati because of the illness that had come upon me in that house, and that I was now staying in a house which was not fitting nor proper; and immediately he sent to the wardens and requested them to prepare a good and proper house for the needs of myself and four servants. The wardens hired or rented for me four rooms and paid six months rent, and my servants prepared all the rooms nicely with a nice bed, and in the big room they made a synagogue with a scroll of the law and thirty lamps lighted therein. The servants waited on me for the love of God, and asked no wage of me and vowed to come with me anywhere that I should go, and my scribe, R. Elijah, the teacher, the son of Joab, and his brother, Benjamin, the Cantor, remained with me and waited on me all the time that I remained in Rome. To the servant who came with me from Candia, that wicked Joseph, I gave clothes and money and sent him to his father in Naples, because every day he made quarrels and strife with the other servants and wanted to rule over them. He also slandered me to Don Miguel, the Ambassador of the King of Portugal, saying that I had come hither to bring the Marrano Jews back to their Judaism, and the Marranos in Rome heard this and sought to slay him, and I begged them to do him no harm and sent him away, and I stayed in this house until the new year.

Cardinal Egidio went to Viterbo and I wondered who would help me and stand between me and the Pope. I saw a man whose name was R. Daniel, of Pisa, who used to frequent the Pope, and lived in a house near the Pope's, a very rich man and a Kabbalist, and I decided to ask him. I spoke and said to him, " I see that you are honoured and considered by the Pope and all the Cardinals. I want you to be interpreter between me and the Pope, and to advise me and show me the good way, for the love of God and the love of the house of Israel and the love of King Joseph, my brother, and his elders of the wilderness of Khabor; and God will show you more honour than you have yet had if you do this in His service. I have come from Eaſt to the Weſt, for the sake of God's service and the love of Israel, who are under the dominion of Edom and Ishmael." I then told him all the secrets of my heart and the hints and the secrets told me by my brother King Joseph ; there was nothing I did not tell him, because I saw that he was good and upright in the eyes of man and God; and then I said to him, " God's secret is to them that fear him." The said R. Daniel vowed that he would not journey or move from Rome until he had received letters from the Pope for me, and he would be interpreter between us; and he also vowed not to leave me on the road, but to go with me on the ship I was to enter; and he forthwith wrote a letter to the Pope, and I sent him by Chaim, my servant, to Ratieri, and he said to him, " The Ambassador gives thee a thousand greetings and sends this letter to you to hand to the Pope, and he wishes to know at what hour he can get an answer to the letter." He took the letter and said to Chaim, " Go in peace, and come back for the answer in eighteen hours." Next day I sent Chaim to the Ratieri, and as soon as he entered he said, " Go call thy lord, the ambassador, and let him come speedily before the Pope, because he summons him." Then Chaim, my servant, returned with the servant of R. Daniel of Pisa, brought me a horse, and I went to the Pope with all my servants; and they opened all the rooms for me; and I entered the room neareſt the Pope and I said to the guards of the Pope's rooms that I did not wish to appear before the Pope until R. Daniel of Pisa should come, because he is interpreter

between us; and when R. Daniel came I said to him,
" Go thou first before the Pope"; and he entered and
returned to me and I went with him and I spoke to
the Pope as follows, " I have stood before thee for
nearly a year and it is my will for God's sake and thy
honour that thou shouldst write me the letters which
I asked of thy Holiness for Prester John, and also
all the Christians whose lands I shall traverse, whether
great or small"; and R. Daniel spoke to the Pope, who
said, " I will do all that the ambassador desires."
Then I and R. Daniel of Pisa left the Pope, happy and
of good courage, and we went in peace to my home;
but there were then in Rome four or five slanderers,
and God put repentance in their hearts that they
should return from their evil way; and there were also
strong Jews in Rome and Italy, mighty and lion-
hearted for all work, and suitable for war, but the
Jews who are in Jerusalem and Egypt and Iraq, and
all the Moslem countries, are faint hearted and prone
to fear and fright and not fitted for war like the
Italian Jews. May the Almighty increase them a
thousand fold, and bless them ! . . .
Within a few days the letters came from the Pope
and R. Daniel gave them to me. That night many Jews
came to my house in order to rejoice with me that I had
received the letters. Four notables, the heads of the
Roman congregation, R. Obadiah of Sforno, and
R. Judah of Ascoli, the Physician, and two others came
to me. But there were in my house slanderers and
spies whom I did not recognize, and they wished
to read the brief and the letters which the Pope had
written, that they might profit by remembering them ;
and I was very angry with them, for men told me that
they were spies and would go before the scribes of
the Pope repeating the words, in order to spoil my
business ; they caused me much worry and thought.
Afterwards the Pope sent for R. Daniel of Pisa and

spoke with him about me whether I wished to go, for he would give me leave, and ordered that I should come before him at eighteen o'clock on the 24th of the firSt Adar, and I and R. Daniel went before him, and I Stayed with him about two hours. He spoke to me saying, " I have given you a letter to King PreSter John, and I have also written to the King of Portugal, and I have written to the ChriStians whose country thou wilt pass so that they should help thee, and honour thee for God's sake and my sake; and he further said, " Be Strong and of good courage and fear not, for God is with thee", and I said to him, " There is none before me but the Almighty and thou, and I am prepared to serve thee all the days of my life, and also King Joseph my brother and all my people's sons are inclined to thee"; and the Pope ordered that they should give me a sign and shield to show to King Joseph my brother, and he also gave me one hundred golden ducats. I would not take the money, but only under compulsion when he said, " Take it for thy servants," and I left the Pope and returned home in peace and joy and a good heart. Then I went to Don Miguel, the King of Portugal's Ambassador, in order to get a safe conduCt from him for the journey, and he said, " If thou wisheSt to go to Pisa, I will write and send thee to Pisa the safe conduCt." But he did this by way of trick, and I left his house in anger, and the Pope heard the matter and said to Don Miguel, " Write for him a safe conduCt, for I too have written to the King of Portugal"; but he did not obey the Pope, and left Rome for hunting and Stayed away a week and returned. I asked a second time for a safe conduCt, and he said that he would send it after me to Pisa at any rate, and I believed his words and I went home and R. Daniel went with me, and I said to him that it was my desire to leave Rome to-morrow, in the middle of the month of Nisan, as our fathers left Egypt; and

I ſtayed in Rome till mid-day of the 15th of Adar
to arrange my matters and see who of all my servants
should go with me. Two went, one called R. Raphael
ha Cohen, who sang in my home from the day I arrived
in Rome, a ſtrong man and warlike, and the second,
Jacob ha Levi, even ſtronger than Raphael Cohen,
and he was my servant from the day I arrived in Rome;
and I gave each of them in Rome five ducats in order
that they should arrange all their affairs, and R. Daniel
was with me and promised to give me other servants,
and he gave me a third servant, Tobias.

V

We left Rome at mid-day, the 15th of the Second
Adar, juſt as we entered Rome at mid-day on the 15th
of Adar, so that we ſtayed in Rome a full year. The
Jews of Rome came to accompany me on thirty
horses for five miles, and I found at Roncelin an army
of the King of France with five hundred horses,
thank God ; they showed us great honour. At laſt
I arrived at Viterbo, and with me were my servants
Raphael Cohen and Joseph Levi and Tobias; but
R. Daniel ſtayed on in Rome, saying he would follow
us, and ordered Joab to go with me to Pisa to the
house of R. Jechiel of Pisa (Author of *Minchat
Qenaoth*) and we ſtayed in Viterbo at the house of
R. Joseph Cohen. He is an honourable Jew, and has
several sons and his mother, who did all necessary for me.
The Jews of Viterbo came to me and there was a
dispute and quarrels and causeless hatred between
them, but I made peace between them by the good
words I spoke to them. Afterwards the Grand Maſter
of Rhodes sent for me, and R. Jechiel and R. Moses
came with me before him, and I spoke a great deal to
him. He is an old and honourable man. When I
left Viterbo, Jews on ten horses accompanied me and
we ſtayed at Bolsena over sabbath in the house of the

said R. Joseph, and remained there until Sunday, and they showed us great honour, more than proper. Thence we journeyed to Siena and came to the house of the honourable Ishmael of Rieti, who took us and made room in his house, and prepared for me a bed and separate room. He has a large dwelling and is very rich, and I said to him, " What desireſt thou more, Jerusalem or thy own place ? " and he answered, " I have no desire in Jerusalem but only in Siena "; and I was much surprised at him that he cannot do meritorious deeds with the wealth that God has given him. " He that loveth silver shall not be satisfied with silver." He promised to do kindness unto my servants, but repented and did not keep his promise and did not desire to earn a good name before all Israel.

We journeyed from Siena on the Monday and arrived at Pisa in the house of R. Jechiel, may he be remembered with a thousand times a thousand blessings, he and his mother Signora Laura and his grandmother Signora Sarah, may they be blessed among women. Amen !

He was like an angel of God, wise in the Torah and Talmud, humble, pious and charitable; his heart cleaves to Jerusalem, the holy city, and his house is open to all the poor of Israel, and all who come to his house eat at his table. Every day he does charity to the poor and likewise his mother and grandmother do charity, for they all do kindness and truth ; and, with my own eyes, I saw all their good deeds, more than I saw throughout Italy. We ſtayed in their house seven months and I sent my servants back to Rome because they had been slandering, but only Tobias, who was my cook, remained as my servant. Don Miguel, bad man, did not send me the safe conduct he had promised to send, but wrote to me that the King does not wish me to come to him to Portugal this year. This was false and a lie, and I had great pain

from it, and fasted six times six days and nights, and
I also fasted three days and nights in forty days. The
household of R. Jechiel gave me all kinds of food and
spices and flowers and apple water, and served me with
all the delicacies of the world, and did all kindness and
truth with me and sent me great presents and silk
robes, and gave money to all my servants and, on the
great fast, they came to me with honour to the house
of R. Jechiel. His wife, called Diamante, the daughter
of R. Asher Meshullam, of Venice, and the mother
of R. Jechiel, Signora Laura, and her mother, Signora
Sarah, and other young women used to dance in the
room where I was and the wife of R. Jechiel played
the harp, and they said to me, " We are come here for
your honour's sake, and in order that the sorrow may
go from the fast and that you may rejoice "; and they
asked me if I had any delight in the sound of the harp
and in dancing and I answered, " You are very kind,"
but God knows my thoughts that I did not wish to
listen to the sound of the harp and the flute and
rejoicings. The Gentiles of Pisa came to me to
R. Jechiel's house and blew trumpets and made great
sounds in order to get money, and the said R. Jechiel
wrote a scroll of the law with his own hand, and I
made the blessing over that scroll several Sabbaths.
It was very well written and the Signora Benvenida,
the wife of Samuel Abarbanel, sent me from Naples
to Pisa a banner of fine silk on which the ten commandments were written in two columns, with golden
embroidery old and antique. She also sent me a
Turkish gown of gold brocade to wear for her sake,
besides having sent me money three times when I
was in Rome. I heard that she fasts every day, and
had also heard of her fame when in Alexandria and
Jerusalem; how she used to ransom the captives, and
had ransomed more than a thousand captives, and
gave charity to every one that asked of her, may she be

blessed before the Lord ! Signora Sarah, of Pisa, gave me a golden signet ring and said to me, " Let this be a witness between me and thee." She also gave me a big manuscript of Psalms, Job, Proverbs, and the five Scrolls on parchment, and she wrote with her own hand at the beginning of the book her advice " Never be angry or hasty." She also gave me a prayer book, saying, " Pray in this for my sake."

After a few days the King of Portugal sent to Rome as Ambassador Don Martin instead of Don Miguel, and as soon as Don Martin arrived in Rome he wrote to me to Pisa that " the King of Portugal has heard about thee that thou has come to serve him; he is glad and will do thee kindness, therefore prepare and go with this ship." There was a big ship in Leghorn going to Portugal, and the captain was detained in Rome as he had business with the Pope, and I waited until the captain came, and I sent for R. Daniel from Pisa to Florence; and he came to me to Pisa and I consulted him and he said to me, " I do not wish thee to go with the letters sent by Don Martin, but I will send a messenger to Rome to Don Martin and he shall give thee other letters." After that I sent my servant to Florence in haste to R. Jechiel that he should come to me at once, as the captain of the ship had come and wished to sail speedily. But neither R. Daniel nor R. Tobias came to me three days, and the ship captain said to me, " If thou wishest to come with us know that we are certainly sailing to-morrow anyhow ; we have prepared for thee a fine room in the ship and all that thou requirest until thou comest to the King in Portugal." On the Monday I arranged all my things and placed them on mules and sent them to Leghorn and journeyed with R. Jechiel and R. Reuben and his sons and Joseph Levy and David the Rumanian with me, and we reached Leghorn and with all our stuff stayed at a hostel, and I fasted all that night and it

was the second night of the three days and in this
hostel I had great pain and worry, because Tobias
had gone to R. Daniel and neither had come here, and
the captain told me that they were sailing very early
to-morrow morning. R. Daniel sent me a young man
called Benzion of Curio, and after midnight came to
me ; he had pursued us up to Leghorn. I was greatly
rejoiced when I saw him, and slept till morning, and
R. Daniel gave me as a gift from the Pope a gabardine
of red damask and a black velvet cap, and R. Daniel
also gave me for myself a double gabardine of black
and green. May he be remembered for good! R. Daniel
also ordered Solomon Cohen of Prato to come with
me and paid his wages, twelve ducats, and to Tobias
he gave ten ducats, and the captain came to the house
and said, " If thou needest three or five hundred
ducats I will give them to thee until thou reachest
the King, and then thou wilt return them to me.
I have bought for thee all that thou requirest, bread
and eggs and fowls," and after that R. Daniel gave me
one hundred and twenty ducats and said, " Take this,
for the sake of my love of thee," and I took all my
stuff and took them to the big ship, and Tobias blew
the trumpet and R. Daniel and R. Jechiel stood on
the seashore and we were on the big ship ; then
R. Daniel and R. Jechiel came to see me and stayed
with me a little and blessed me and went their way,
and I and Solomon Cohen and Tobias and David the
Rumanian journeyed from Leghorn with a good will.
May the Lord preserve us. Selah !

VI

PORTUGAL

Thence we went with a good wind westward to
the King of Portugal through the great sea
(Mediterranean). We arrived close to Cadiz, in the

Kingdom of the Emperor, and I sent Tobias to the
magistrate with the Pope's letter to ask him to allow
us to leave the ship and stay in his city for one day,
but the magistrate was not willing. Tobias said
that the men of the city spoke evil things of us to the
magistrate and said that the Jewish King had sent to the
King of Portugal, who was of small account (compared
with the Emperor). They thought we were going
against the Emperor and advised him to come and
arrest me and get horses to send me before the
Emperor, but I was emboldened in my mission and
rejoiced in all that God had done, for it would be for
my good and the good of Israel to appear before the
Emperor, but my servants were afraid and terrified,
and I said to them, " Do no fear or be terrified." After
that the ship captain came to me and said, " Better
that you should leave this ship for another ship
belonging to the King of Portugal," so we left that
ship at midnight and left all our stuff in the cabin
and closed it, and got into a little boat, which took
us to the King of Portugal's ship, on which we
embarked. The captain of that ship was asleep,
but when he heard that we had come on board he got
up from his bed and we came to him to his cabin and
showed him the letter of the King of Portugal (John
the III) and our ship's captain spoke with the captain
of the King's ship at length as to the words of the
magistrate and the nobles in the city of Cadiz and we
stayed there till dawn. Then we went to the City of
Elmira, and the two ship captains went before the
magistrates and notables, and my servants Tobias
with them, and Tobias returned and said that the
magistrates and notables had quarrelled with the
captains because they wanted to arrest us. Afterwards
our ship captain asked permission for us to go to
Tavira, which is at the extremity of the Kingdom of
Portugal, and gave us the stuff, which they had

brought from the big ship to the other ship belonging
to the King of Portugal, and I paid seventy-five ducats
to the captain of the firSt ship for his trouble, and he
left. We Stayed in the King's ship until midnight
and then entered a ship, laden with wheat, which was
going by sea to Tavira and I sent, by my servant
Tobias, the Pope's letter and that of the King to the
Judge of Tavira, who is an officer of the King of
Portugal. Immediately Tobias returned with two
servants from the Judge on a mule, and I left the ship
and went on shore. And when all the people of the
city heard that I had reached the shore, notables came
to me, ChriStians and Marranos, with women and
children, and I rode to that city on a mule, and all the
road was full of men and women, too numerous to
count, and we arrived at the city of Tavira at the
house of a Marrano, and they prepared the house for
us, and beds and tables. The Marrano is an honourable man and his wife very honourable, and the
magiStrate of the city came to me and rejoiced over
us greatly, and said to me, " I am ready and prepared
to do anything thou wisheSt at thy command and for
thy service." He came twice to see me and that
magiStrate wrote to the King to tell him that we had
arrived in Tavira and I wrote a letter to the King of
Portugal and sent it by the hand of David the Rumanian,
and I Stayed in the house of the Marrano to wait for
the King's answer. The Marrano and his wife
showed me much kindness and would not allow us
to spend anything from our pocket, for they wished
to pay all expenses, and we Stayed in their house forty
days until the messenger from the King of Portugal
reached me in Tavira.

In those days a prieSt came from Spain, who spoke
with R. Solomon Cohen Da Porto, and R. Solomon
was angry with him for the prieSt said that there
was no Jewish King and that we had no sons of royal

seed. He was standing before a big window, and I was zealous for God's sake and took hold of him and threw him from the window on to the ground outside before all the Gentiles, and they laughed at the priest and feared to speak against me, and the great magistrate heard of this and was greatly rejoiced. When the messenger returned to me, he brought two letters from the King and in one he wrote that I should come to him in all honour and that he would do my will, and the second he wrote to all the magistrates in his kingdom that they should honour me and advance me from city to city, that they should prepare for me a bed, a table and a light in every place to which we came. The said messenger said that the King had commanded that I should set out to visit him to-morrow, and he gave me five hundred ducats and a scribe of the King's scribes, who should superintend the expenditure. In the morning they gave me horses for me and my servants to ride to the King. We journeyed from Tavira, and the magistrate and all the notables of the city went out with me and returned, but I went on with two notables and the King's scribe and a number of men who came with me from Tavira, and at every place the King's Scribe went to the magistrates so that they should prepare for me a house and a table and a chair and candle according to the King's command. We arrived at a city called Beja and came before the magistrates on horseback, and all the notables of that city, Marranos and Christians, came out three parasangs to meet me, and when we approached the city, men, women and children also came. We arrived at the city and entered the house of a Marrano and stayed there that night and, in the morning, we journeyed on and came to a great city, Evora. On Friday, the eve of Sabbath, the magistrates and many men came to meet me two parasangs outside the city; and I entered the city, and it is very big, and the King's palace is there and also a community of many honoured Marranos. We stayed at the house of a Marrano on the Sabbath and Sunday. And in every city we entered Marranos came, men and women, great and small, and kissed my hand, and the Christians were jealous of me, and said to them, " Show him great honour, but do not kiss his hand but only the hand of the King of Portugal alone." Some were of stout heart, because they believed in me with a perfect faith, as Israel believed in our Master, Moses, on whom be peace! And I said to them in every place we came to that I am the son of King Solomon, and that I have not come to you with a sign or miracle or mystery, but I am a man of war from my youth till now, and I have come to help your King and to help you and to go in the way he shall lead me to the land of Israel. I journeyed from Evora and the magistrates came to escort me, and with them were many honoured nobles and many men, too numerous to count, and they went with me two parasangs and returned. In every road that I passed, Marranos came to me from every side and every corner to accompany me, and they gave me presents, and some righteous Gentiles also, until I arrived two parasangs distance from the King. Now the King was residing in Almeda, for he had fled because of the plague in Lisbon, and I wrote to the King as follows: " Behold I have arrived at this place, and I will stay until thou dost let me know that I may come before thy honour," and I sent an honourable old Gentile to the King and also the King's scribe who had come with me from Tavira and was appointed over the expenses of the journey. They returned to me and said that the King has called his counsellors before him and are taking counsel over this matter. Some say this and some say that; some of them said, " Show him honour and send all the honoured, notables before him to accompany him, for he has come from a distant land to seek thee and serve thee," but Don Miguel, my enemy, because I wished to slay him with a sword in Rome, stood and spoke against me before the King and the notables and the messengers I had sent to the King. They inquired of the scribe if the Marranos showed me more honour than the Christians, and he replied that they honoured me with great honour and kissed my hand, and all the way honoured me and kissed my hand in all the way that I journeyed. Then said Don Miguel to the King, "Did I not say to thee that he is come to destroy thy kingdom and to restore the Marranos to the faith of the Jews? If thou wilt send before him notables to honour him, all the Marranos in thy country will follow him and will take counsel how the Christians are to be made Jews."

All these things said the wicked Don Miguel to the King and to his counsellors and messengers, and the King asked his counsellors what to reply to the Jewish King, and he said to him, "Reply that thy grandmother is dead and that thou art in mourning and canst not show him honour this year as is our custom, and ask pardon of the Ambassador who wishes to come before you with his servants from Tavira."

And when I heard the word of the King and his counsellors I rode with all my servants and the men who had come with me on horses, and we went before the King. We were about fifty men and fifteen horses besides mules which carried my stuff, and we reached Almeda and came to the palace and court of the King. I had been fasting from Sunday to Wednesday when I came to the King and stood before him with all my servants, each one with his sword upon his thigh, and I said to the King and to his wife, the Queen, "I am weary and fatigued from the journey, and have been fasting four days, and cannot speak to thee to-day, but if it seems good in thy eyes I will go to my house to-day and to-morrow we shall speak, I and thou," and I was not willing to kiss his hand either when I came or when I left, because of the anger in my heart which the wicked Don Miguel had caused me. Afterwards I took leave of the King and went to Santarem to the house of a Marrano, which they had prepared for me. It was a big house and the master of the house was quite wicked, but his wife was much honoured. A Marrano came to me who speaks Arabic and had come in the ships of the King, who had sent him once for two years to the land of the blacks (Abyssinia). He told me that he went to an island in the sea a half-day's journey and stayed an hour in that place, and stood near a big mountain from which fire burnt day and night and from which fire and smoke went up to heaven. Near to that mountain the old King of Portugal sent the young children of the Marranos and left them there until this very day. They are near to a tribe in the island who eat men's flesh. That Marrano was learned in astrology. There also came to me one of the captains of the King's ships. He told me that he had journeyed to the capital of our kingdom from Formosa and stayed there one year, in the days of my lord, my father (On whom be peace !), twenty years ago. He had heard that there was a king over the Jews whose name was King Solomon and this ship captain told all this before the King of Portugal. He is an honoured man and the King loves him, and he became my friend in Portugal and I also loved him. He asked me to write my name down as a sign that it should be a memorial between me and him until the hour arrived, and so I did, and it was a secret between me and him. He was a real Christian and loved all the Jews. I fasted continuously six days and nights, and all the Christians and Marranos came to see me by day and by night.

DAVID REUBENI

The King sent to summon me on Wednesday, eight days after I had arrived here, and I went before him, I and old Solomon Cohen and Benzion, my servants, and we came before the King, and the King called a Marrano, an old physician, who was interpreter between me and the King in Hebrew. That old man was somewhat deaf and, when he spoke to the King and to me he was in fear and terrified, and the King said, " I have heard of thee that thou speakeſt Arabic well, and I have an old servant who can speak Arabic well, and he will hear your words from beginning to end and tell them to me." The King called that lord and said, " Speak with that Ambassador in Arabic," and I spoke in Arabic to that lord, and he interpreted my words to the King, and I placed in the King's hand all the letters and I spoke with him on the matter of my mission, and I told him all my journey, which I had travelled from the wilderness, until I came before him, and I also said to the King, " King Joseph, my brother, asks me with reference to the artificers of weapons for his kingdom." The King was greatly pleased with my words and his heart rejoiced within him, and he said, " The matter is of the Lord. I am willing to do so and it shall be my desire." The matter was good in his eyes, and in the eyes of all his lords. Then said the King to me, "Return from Santarem to Almeda, which is near me." The King ordered the old lord to prepare for me a house near to the Palace, and so the old man did, and I sent all that I had in my house, beds and linen and all household furniture, from Santarem to the house which they prepared for me in Almeda, near to the Palace.

Afterwards a great Moslem lord, a Judge of the King of Fez, came to me. He had been sent by this King to the King of Portugal, and is an honourable man, a friend of the Jews. He has ten servants.

This Judge came to my house because the King of
Fez had heard about me and ordered him to go first
to the King of Portugal, and then to come and see
me, and he gave me letters from the Jews of Fez and
from R.Abraham ben Zimori of Asfi-Safi and a third letter
from the Captain of Tangier. Then the Judge asked
me about my country, whether many Jews were there.
And I answered that it is the wilderness of Habor,
and that there are thirty myriad Jews in my country,
and King Joseph, my brother, rules over them and
has seventy counsellors and many lords, and I am a
military lord over ways and war. And the Judge said
to me, " What seekest thou from this kingdom that
thou hast come from the east to the west ? " I answered
that from our youth we are trained in war, and our
war is with the sword and lance and bow, and we
wished to go, with God's help, to Jerusalem to capture
the land of Israel from the Moslems, for the end and
salvation has arrived, and I have come to seek wise
handicraftsmen who know how to make weapons and
firearms that they should come to my land and make
them and teach our soldiers. The Judge was much
amazed at this, and said to me, " We believe that
the kingdom will return to you this time, and if you
return will you do kindness to us ? " I said to him,
" Yes, we will do kindness to you and to all who do
kindness to Israel, which is in captivity under Ishmael
and Edom," and I said to the Judge, " Do you also
believe that the kingdom of the land of Ishmael
will return to us ? " And he replied to me, " In all the
world they believe this." I said to him, " We are
kings, and our fathers were kings from the time of
the destruction of the temple till this day, in the wilderness of Habor. We rule over the tribes of Reuben
and Gad, and half tribe of Manasseh in the wilderness
of Habor, and there are nine and a half tribes in
the land of Ethiopia and other kings. The nearest

to us are the tribe of Simeon and the tribe of Benjamin, and they are on the River Nile, above the kingdom of Sheba, and they reside between the two rivers, the blue river and the black river, which is the Nile. Their country is good and extensive, and they have a king and his name is Baruch, the son of King Japhet, and he has four sons, the eldest Saadiah, and the second Abraham, the third Hoter, and the fourth Moses, and their numbers are as ours in the wilderness of Habor, thirty myriads, and we and they take counsel together." The Judge said to me, " Dost thou wish to write for me a letter to the King of Fez ? " I answered, " I need not write, but you can say all this to him by the word of mouth and give him from me a thousand greetings and say to him that the Jews under his rule should be protected by him, and that he should honour them and this will be the beginning of peace between us and him, between our seed and his seed." The Judge also asked me, " What will you do with the Jews in all the lands of the west, will you come to the west for them and how will you deal with them ? " I replied that we shall first take the Holy Land and its surroundings and that then our captains of the host will go forth to the west and east to gather the dispersed of Israel, and whoever is wise among the Moslem Kings will take the Jews under his rule and bring them to Jerusalem, and he will have much honour, greater than that of all the Moslem Kings, and God will deliver up all the kingdoms to the King of Jerusalem. Further, the Judge asked me, " Is it true that the Jews in Fez and its neighbourhood say, and the Moslems also, that you are a prophet and the Messiah ? " and I answered, " God forbid, I am a sinner before the Lord, greater than any one of you, and I have slain many men, and on one day I killed forty enemies. I am neither a prophet nor the son of a prophet, neither a wise man nor a Kabbalist, but I am a captain of the hoft, the son of Solomon the King, the son of David, the son of Jesse, and my brother, the King, rules over thirty myriads in the wilderness of Habor. Moreover, the Marranos in the Kingdom of Portugal, and all the Jews in Italy and all the places that I passed also thought me to be a prophet, wise man, or Kabbalift, and I said to them, " God forbid, I am a sinner and a man of war from my youth till now." Afterwards the Judge began to write to the Jews of Fez, and to R. Abraham ben Zimori of Asfi-Safi, and I wrote to them and handed the letters to him and he went on his way in peace.

After that there came before the King a great Moslem lord of the royal seed of Formosa, of the country of India, near to the wilderness of Habor. The cause of his coming was that a captain over the King's ship had slain his brother and taken all his money, and this captain was imprisoned because of the accounting for the ship's moneys which he had not brought to the King's treasury. The king honoured the Moslem lord and asked him also about me, and if he had any knowledge of the wilderness of Habor, and he replied to the King, " Yes, and in the wilderness of Habor there are many Jews and rich men who have herds, and they have a king at this time whose name is Joseph, and he has seventy counsellors, and the Jews do great things in the wilderness of Habor." And he told the King in private matters which could not be related in the presence of all his lords. There were then Marranos in the King's presence, and they came and told me all these things. Also Joseph Cordelia came to me and gave me a letter in the Arabic language from the King who rules in the weft, beyond the kingdom of Fez. It is the world's end. There is no kingdom behind it, but only deserts, and they have neighbours, Arabs

and Moslems, who have camps in this desert, and the
King is a Moslem of the sons of the prophet Mahomet,
and his name is Sherif. He is a strong and wise man
and has in his kingdom Jews who reside on the
mountain and the name of the mountain is Asum.
It is at the world's end and those Jews sow and get
in harvest and they are most of them poor but strong,
and one of them came to me who was a Cohen, and
his heart was as a lion's heart. They are not like the
Jews who live under the rule of the Moslems, and
in that letter it was written, " Behold, I have heard
of thee, that thou art come to the King of Portugal
from the tribes. Hast thou heard of this people who
come out of the wilderness separating me from the
blacks, for they have taken from us all the Arabs who
dwell in the wilderness, them and their wives and their
flocks and their young and all that is theirs. Not
one of them returned of those they captured. We
do not know if they have been slain or what has been
done to them, but a fugitive who escaped came and told
me this matter, and I sent the Jews that they should
go and see them, but they did not return and we
wondered about this people and I have written thee
about them that thou, in thy kindness, mayest tell
me and write from thy land all that thou knowest
in fact, and do not hide anything from me, as to thy
place and all the tribes; tell me everything."

After this letter came to me I called the man that
spoke Arabic, the interpreter between me and the
King, and he read this to me and I understood all
that was therein and I replied to him in letters, which
this man that knew Arabic wrote, and said to him,
" I am from the wilderness of Habor and we have
thirty times ten thousand Jews there. (May the Lord
increase them a thousand fold !) They are the sons
of Reuben and Gad and of the half tribe of Manasseh,
and King Joseph, my brother, is their king, and I

am the lord of his host and the other nine and a half tribes are in the land of the blacks in Ethiopia, in four places, and the sons of Moses are in another place and live on the River Sambation, beside the two tribes of Simeon and Benjamin, who reside at the head of the River Nile and the white river behind it. They are between two rivers, beyond the Kingdom of Sheba. These two tribes send men to us and we send men to them, and they tell us what they hear and know of the other tribes in the land of the blacks which are near to them, and our country is far from them, as we are in the east." I wrote all these things and sent the letter to that King, and the messenger went and also R. Abraham Zimori went to King Sherif, who had sent for him. This R. Abraham is a great man and is much honoured by the Christians and their kings, and all the Moslems and their kings; and King Sherif said to R. Abraham all these things, and R. Abraham returned to his country before last New Year, 5286 (1525), and he wrote me, from Asfi-Safi, all that the King told him of the people, who came from the wilderness of Habor, and they said it is a wilderness great as the great sea and they know not the end of the wilderness. The Jews in all the Moslem kingdoms have heard of me, and they sent messengers to me to Portugal from Tlemcen and Mascara and Fez and all their surroundings, and from the hills of Oran and from many places letters came to me to Portugal.

Moreover, Marranos came to me of great importance and said to me that they saw four standards in the heavens, and many men, Christians and priests and Marranos stood by and told this matter to me and to Solomon Cohen, and I found two small boys of the Marranos, who fasted on Mondays and Thursdays with piety and believed in the salvation of the Lord, and I said to them, " trust in the Lord and do good, for the great and fearful day of the Lord is approaching," and I made peace between the Marranos in all places where I went, and they listened to my voice, and among the Marranos are strong and warlike and wise men and artificers in firearms, and I saw that they were stronger and better than all the Jews that I had seen before. And the Signora in Naples had a daughter in Lisbon who fasts every day, and this daughter has a son and daughter who fast on Mondays and Thursdays and she is much esteemed and very charitable and does good deeds like her mother. (May she be blessed of the Lord !) All the Marranos believe in God, except one physician, who was Lazoa, who came to me and spoke against our religion, and I stood up to smite him but Carbalia (? Cordelia), the Marrano from Tavira, held my hand and then he repented.

The man that knew Arabic came to me and said, " The King has a great feast and a joy day and they are preparing his table in the open air, and if the King seest that thou art in his presence his heart will rejoice." I went to the Palace and saw how they prepared the table for him and all the things too numerous to mention; and I saw on the table great and small bowls of silver, and the large vessel from which he drinks water is of gold. The King with his brothers, came out of their house of prayer and stood at the table. In his Palace there were four rooms full of lords and they came out to see how the King was eating, and all the lords stood before the King, each one with his cap in his hand, and the boys of ten years of age and upwards, the sons of the lords, stood before the King round his table each on his knee bowing. The King has four officers, each of whom had a stick in his hand with which they strike and keep off the crowd before the King, for the fear of the King is over all his people. On that

day, during the meal, I sat among the people and the
King beckoned me to come before him, and I went
before him with the man who speaks Arabic and my
servants, and the King called one of the officers and
said to him, "Drive away the men who are in front
of the window," and they were great lords, "and
arrange that the Jewish Ambassador should ſtand
at that window," and I sat in that window, the place
appointed for me by the King, and they were blowing
with trumpets and playing all kinds of musical
inſtruments and the King sat at the head of the table
and his three brothers behind him, and they gave him
a great basin of silver for him to wash his hands,
and the ewer in which the water was was of gold,
and two of his brothers ſtood up and bowed before
the King and they kissed the silver basin before the
King washed his hands in it, and the man who washed
the hands of the King drank some of the water
before the King washed, and the third brother of the
King, who was the Cardinal, bowed before him and
kissed the basin after he had washed, and they ſtood
at the banquet, and on the table there was a lamb killed,
but not by the knife. They removed its ſtomach,
but the lamb was entire from head to feet and had
golden horns. They also placed on the table four
pigs, entire from head to foot, and many birds, and
they removed the former from the table and put on
the latter, and the King and his brothers ate behind
the table and his brothers also drank water and then
ate again, and they cut for the King all kinds of meat
and he ate a little from each kind. And so they did
to his brothers, and each of them had servants by
the table. And they gave the King a second time
water to drink and to his brothers, and they drank
three times water at the table, and afterwards they
gave whole fruits to him by himself and to his brothers
by themselves, and gave them sweets and many

things. Afterwards they removed the cloths from
the table and the King stood up near to the table,
and the priests blessed him and all the people bowed
down. After that the King entered before his wife,
the Queen, and I entered behind him with my servants
and with the man who speaks Arabic, and the great
lords came behind me and stood before the Queen,
and the Captain who had been taken prisoner and had
been in India was brought before the Queen on that
day, and I stood before the King, and in my presence
the King asked the Captain and said to him, " Are
there Jews in India and Calicut ? " and the Captain
replied to the King, " There are very many Jews in
Singoli,² ten days from Calicut." And the King also
asked him, " Have you heard that the Jews have
kings ? " And he replied that they have kings. After
that I went out before the King and the Queen, and
I was in the courtyard and had not yet left when I
saw the King's brother, called Alorsi, and he called me
and the man that speaks Arabic, the interpreter
between us. And we came before him, and he spoke
with me about the journey and other matters, and
I replied to him, " All that thy brother the king desirest
I will do." After that I returned home in life and
peace, and from the day that I saw the King drank
water and his brothers also drinking water, although
they are in their own kingdom, I vowed in my heart to
drink no wine but only water, and the reason is that
I have come from the east to the west for the love
of God and for the love of his people, and the love
of the land of Israel, and I am in Galuth (captivity)
and from the day that I began to drink water I have
eaten at my table at a meal more than I eat before,
and, even after a fast, water is better than wine . . .

After all these things, four Marranos were taken
in custody from my house and placed in prison.
The King's lords did this without his knowledge.

I wrote to the King that they were taken, and when the King heard of it he ordered them to be let out, and those Marranos came to me. After that the King called us before him in the Queen's room and said, " I am glad that thou haſt come to help me, but I hear that thou haſt also come to reſtore the Marranos to the Jewish religion, and the Marranos pray with thee and read in thy books day and night, and thou haſt made for them a Synagogue." I was angry with him and said to him, " I am come from the eaſt to the weſt only to exalt thy kingdom and to help thee. I have not come for the sake of the Marranos, and all that the slanderers have told thee about me is falsehood and not at all true," and the King said to me, " If their words are true, do not so from henceforward if thou wisheſt to do me kindness."

After that the King pacified me with good words, because he saw that I was angry and he spoke with me as to my journey and as to large and small firearms, and promised to give me four mills in ships to take to our country, and I left the King and went home. After this the Emperor sent for his wife, the siſter of the King of Portugal, men and horses and mules in very great numbers, and the ambassador at their head. The Emperor's ambassador came to my house and spoke with me and said that the Emperor had heard about me and was pleased with the matter and wished to see me. I ſtood before the Ambassador for two hours, and Judah, abovementioned, was interpreter between him and me. The Duke also came from his country to Almeda to the King, his kinsman, and the King spoke to him about me and on the second night the Duke came to me in disguise with four servants, and I was sitting at table and eating. He took leave of me and they went away and, after I had retired, Marranos came to me and said he was the Duke and had come to see me in disguise. Next day the Queen departed to go to her espousals with the Emperor, and her brother, the King, accompanied her and the Duke with him, and I also went on horseback to accompany the Queen, and a renegade who had become a Moslem and afterwards a Christian, named Aldeka, from Asfi-Safi, came to see me. After I had accompanied the Queen three parasangs, I took leave of the King and his sister, the Queen, and returned home and arrived at night. The King returned the day after and the Jews told me that Aldeka was a renegade and a wicked man, but, as I saw that he was a strong man and that his face seemed that of a man of dignity, I called him before me that evening and said to him, " I have heard that thou hast become a Moslem and then a Christian, but I believe thee and in thy words that thou desirest to serve me, but it is better that thou shouldest go and leave my house." Aldeka replied, " Be kind to me for the sake of Israel, but not for my sake, for I have sinned and transgressed, and done more evil than the men have told you about me, but I wish to return with thy help and repent, and I swear by the Law of Moses that I wish to repent if thou wilt receive me. God accepts the repentant and I will stand before thee until I die and serve thee, with all thy horses, with all my heart, and will do all that thou biddest me." He placed the Pentateuch on his neck and took oath upon it and stayed in my house. I have a nice horse, better than any of the King's horses, the horse on which I rode. Aldeka was a strong man and every day attended to the horse, fed him and washed him and removed its excrement, and did everything in my house and was efficient. If the Jews went to buy anything in the market, Aldeka went with them and, with the same money bought twice as much. But the Jews quarrelled with him and gave me an ill report of him, and I said,

" I cannot turn him out of my house because he is
efficient and attends to the horse and to the needs of
the house, and you cannot do what he does or the work
he does for me." Those Jews were weak and did
not do work for me. Their only strength was in their
tongue. They were asking of me every day requests
and petitions, and if they came with me before the
King, they shrank back, because they were timid and
weak-hearted and had no manners. The man that
spoke Arabic told me these Jews who come behind
have no manners and are not fit for thy honour,
they are proud and do not remove their hat from their
head, either in my house or in the Palace, and the
Gentiles speak against them and despise them, for
no one of them can wear a sword on his shoulder;
they are a disgrace to us. Those Jews, who came
from Asemur and Asfi-Safi without safe conduct,
were taken into custody on their arrival at Tavira,
and had to give surety in four hundred ducats in case
they did not send their safe conduct to the King,
and the magistrate of Tavira wrote about them to
the King that they had come without a safe conduct.
The King summoned me and I went to him with
Judah and the man who speaks Arabic, and the King
asked me how came the Jews to the country without
safe conduct, and I replied to the King, " I wrote
that they should come to me and they have come to
be my servants. I pray thy Majesty to write to the
magistrate in Tavira to cancel the sureties he had
received from them and for my sake give them a safe
conduct and let no harm come to them in Tavira."
The King ordered his scribe to write thus to the
magistrate. The King summoned me four times in
two days about the Marranos, and wished to know
what I was doing with them and said to me, " I have
heard that thou hast circumcised my Secretary [3] "
and I replied, " God forbid, it is not true, I have not

come to do these things, do not open thy ears to slanderers for I have only come for my business and thy service." The King dropped this subject and spoke with me with regard to the journey and the ships, and I left the King and stayed four days at home. Then the King summoned me and told me in the presence of Judah, and the man who spoke Arabic, "I am pleased with thee that thou hast come to help me, but thou art ruining my kingdom, for all the Christians say that thou hast restored the Marranos to Judaism, and they all kiss thy hand and that when thou sittest at table all the sons of the Marranos bow to thee." I replied to the King in anger and said to him, "I am come from the east to the west to serve thee until thou lettest me go in peace; the door of my house is open to every man, Christian or Marrano, and I do not know whether they are Christians or Marranos; do not listen to the voice of the slanderers, whose every word is falsehood and lies.' Then the King gave me his hand and said to me, "Do me the favour not to allow any man to kiss thy hand," and the King promised to give me in the month of Nisan eight ships with four thousand large and small fire-arms, and I believed him and left and came home and stayed until night. The scribe, who had been secretly circumcised, came and spoke to me that night, and I was angry with him and said, "See what thou hast caused us; go thou to Jerusalem and be not seen here or they will burn or slay thee," and he left me. This secretary had come to me before he was circumcised and told me a dream that he had been circumcised and asked me to circumcise him or to order my servant Solomon to circumcise him, and I was angry with him and said, "Stay in thy duties before the King until the Almighty opens the door. He knows the thoughts of man and that thou hast good intentions, but beware of doing this thing at this time, for thou and I and all the Marranos will be in great danger." He left me after this talk between us about circumcision. He was secretary and honoured by the King, and the matter was known to the King of Portugal and all his lords, and all the Christians and Marranos knew that he had circumcised himself and fled and gone away, and the King and his lords said that I had caused the secretary to circumcise himself, although they knew that I had not done it myself. Afterwards the King sent for me, when I was at home, and next day he sent again his servants to accompany and guard me, and he also sent his officer on horseback to accompany me, and that day I went to the King and he spoke to me saying, " I have many matters to attend to and shall be unable to send the ships with thee to the east either this year or next year ; if thou wilt go to thy country go in peace, for I give thee leave and bless thee for all the days that thou hast come from thy country to serve me and help me. Go to the Emperor, if thou wilt, and tell him all. Or if thou wilt, return to Rome or go to Fez, choose that which thou desirest." I was wrath now unto death about this matter, and replied to the King of Portugal in great anger, and said to him, " Thou didst promise me the ships and to let me go in the month of Nisan, why hast thou changed thy heart ? It is not now my desire to go to the Emperor or to Fez, but to Rome, to the Pope." And the King said to me, " Think the matter over for eight days." I left the King and returned home, and the King afterwards sent for me and said, " What dost thou intend to do, and what way wilt thou go ? " And I replied, " I wish to return to Rome to the Pope. Pray write him letters and let them be a testimony between me and thee, for King Joseph, my brother, that I had reached thy kingdom, and write me a letter of safe conduct for all Christians." The King replied, " I will do what

thou wishest," and he called Antonio Carnieri, his
secretary, and, in my presence, ordered him to write
the two letters, and a third letter he wrote for me to
Tavira that they should give me three hundred
ducats, and said to me, "Follow me to Santarem
and receive the letters and I will send men with thee
to escort thee to Tavira." I left the King and returned
home. That day the King went to Santarem with
the Queen, for they sought there remedy for their
son who was sick. And I stayed three days longer in
Almeda and then journeyed with all my stuff to
Santarem to a fine house near the river, and Aldeka
attended to all my work in the house and outside;
and a report reached me that the Christians had made
an effigy like me and mocked the effigy, and when
the Marranos heard this they rose up against the
Christians and smote them and took the effigy from
them against their will, and the magistrates arrested
two of the Marranos and put them in prison. And they
sent to me to help them, and I at once went to the
King and said to him, "Is it right in thy eyes that
the Christians should make an effigy of me and mock
me, and that, when the Marranos rose up against
them and took the effigy from them, the magistrates
arrested two of the Marranos and put them in
prison?" Now, if I find favour and kindness before
thee, write to the magistrates that they should let
the prisoners go." The same hour the King ordered
that they should write this letter, and he signed the
letter in my presence, and the King laughed and I
said to him, "I beg thy Majesty to give me this
letter and to send one of thy servants to go with me
to let the prisoners free," and it was done accordingly.
And the King asked me about my banners and said,
" I have heard that thou hast beautiful banners, what
dost thou wish to do with them?" I replied that they
are our sign between me and the tribes, and I unfurl

them when I go with the army." The King said,
" Good," and I left the King and stayed two days in
my house. And the Cardinal, the King's brother,
sent for me, and I went to him with the man who
spoke Arabic, and the Cardinal showed me great
honour and asked me about the banners and the
journey. I replied that the banners were my sign
and I was going to Rome, and the Cardinal said, " Wilt
thou join my faith and I will make thee a lord ? "
I replied, " Wouldst thou make me like the raven
that Noah sent from the Ark which never returned ?
This matter would not be good in the eyes of the
kings, my forefathers, for I am the son of a King
of the seed of David, the son of Jesse ; they would
thrust me from my inheritance. I have not come
from the east to the west to do this thing, but I am
come in God's service and to make me a name ever-
lasting for doing the meritorious act I have come to
do. How can thy heart compel thee to ask this matter
of me ? " And I further said, " If I were to tell thee
to join my faith wouldst thou be willing ? " And the
Cardinal answered, " No ". And I said to him, " It
is better that thou remainest in thy faith and I in my
faith : thou sayest that thy faith is true and I that
my faith is true, it is the faith of Moses and Israel."
And I was angry with him. After this he spoke
kind words to me and I left him and returned home.
Next day the Queen sent to me and asked me about
the banners and how I intended to journey, and I
replied that the banners are my sign and that I am
going to Rome, with God's help. And the Queen
rejoined, " Go in peace and return to thy country in
peace. The King has said to me that his heart is
well inclined to thee and I have heard that he has
written letters for thee to the Pope, God bless him ! "
I took leave of her and left her, and all the Marranos
came to my house by day and night, and they were

grieved that I was leaving and their children came
to kiss my hand in the presence of the Christians,
until I left Santarem ; but the Almighty saw to it
that I did no harm to the Marranos in all the kingdom
of Portugal. Thank God ! The King was very good
and was wrath with the slanderers and said to them
that they should say no more about the Ambassador
who should do what he wished. After that the man
that spoke Arabic came to me with the letters written
in beautiful writing on paper by Antonio Carnieri,
and he, in the innocence of his heart, had written good
things with much honour in those letters. And the
man who spoke Arabic said, " Let us go and give
thanks to the King and take leave of him and then
I will hand the letetrs to thee in his presence." And
when I came before him I was angry and said that
the Pope had written letters for me on parchment
and these letters were on paper, and I have come from
east to west for the service of the King, but if the
letters were on parchment they would remain as
a testimony between us and our children's children
after us, and they would know that I had been to
his kingdom. The King replied, " It is not our custom,
like the Pope's, to write on parchment," and I said
to the King, " I ask thee as a favour to·write them
this time on parchment, for I wish the letters to be
a memorial," and he replied that he would do so for
love of me. Then the King told Don Miguel to
write them on parchment and he did so, but they
were without the expressions of honour which Antonio
Corenzi had written. Nevertheless my wrath was
diminished, for the Elders and King Joseph, my
brother, had charged me not to be angry; and when
I was in Pisa in the house of R. Jechiel, his old grandmother Sarah, who was a wealthy and wise woman,
had told me, " I see that thou art angry all thy days ;
if thou wilt avoid this anger thou wilt prosper

in all thy days," and she gave me a great Bible as a gift, and wrote at the beginning of the book, " Anger not and thou shalt prosper." But I have not been able to conquer my spirit from this anger and it had caused me my quarrel with Don Miguel and brought me to this point, and the man that spoke Arabic always went as a spy before Don Miguel and told him everything that I spoke to the King and all that I spoke with him in my house. After that the man who spoke Arabic gave me the letters in parchment but did not tell me that Don Miguel had written them. And I sought for the letter that I have to receive the money in Tavira, for he gave me two sealed letters, one for the Judge in Tavira and one which the man who spoke Arabic said was the writing in which the King had ordered me three hundred ducats ; but this was falsehood and lies, for the true letter Don Miguel had taken and the letter he had sent to me was false and I could not examine the letter because it was sealed, but I took his letters and believed his word. Afterwards I went with the man who spoke Arabic to take leave of the King, and the King said, " I send with thee the man who speaks Arabic to accompany thee to the journey to Tavira, and I have written that they should give thee three hundred ducats, and if thou needest anything write to me."

VII

I left Santarem the next afternoon, I and Solomon Cohen and Judah Perente and Aldeka the renegade and my two servants and the man who spoke Arabic, with four other gentlemen, and all my luggage was on four mules. We went to Almeda the same night ; all the houses were open but nobody inside. We went to one house in which there were residents and stayed in front all that night, and in the morning we journeyed, I on my good horse, from morning until afternoon, until we arrived at Coruche, which is an open city with a few Marranos. We went to the house of a Marrano and they showed us great honour, and all the magistrates of the city came and we spread our banners and they praised their beauty and fine workmanship, one of gold thread and white silk and all round the banner gold embroidery, a finger-breadth wide, and in the centre of the second banner were tablets with two large lions grasping the tablets in their hands, the whole picture in gold, with the ten commandments written on the two tablets, and round the banner on the two sides verses from Deuteronomy from beginning to end and psalms. The second banner was of green silk and all its ornaments of silver, as the other banner was of gold, and five other large banners of white silk. We stayed in Corouche until night, and in the morning we journeyed to Coimbra and reached a wood with streams of water; and the beasts were wearied and they took the packs off them and put them on the ground and eat there. This city is very great, and all the people came to see me, Christians and Marranos, and they went to the house of a Marrano and prepared for me a fine big room with a bed and a table, chair and candlestick; and I ate at the table and slept there all that night, and in the morning I rose, washed and prayed. Afterwards they loaded the stuff on the mules and I rode on my horse with Solomon Cohen and the man who spoke Arabic, and the Marranos rode on their horses, and we left Coimbra on the Evora road and arrived there and went to the house of the Marrano where we had stayed the first time. We stayed there over the Sabbath and the Sunday, and Cublia, the Marrano, who knew Hebrew and had served me from the day that I arrived in Tavira till the day I came before the King of Portugal, came to me. Cublia is an artisan of firearms. On Monday all the people of the city came to see me, and the Marranos were very grieved and wept when we left. We left the city and went to Beja and entered the house of a Marrano and they prepared for us beds and table and everything, and that night many Marranos came to me fearful and weeping, and I said to them, " Trust in the Lord for evermore, for ye shall have the joy of seeing the rebuilding of Jerusalem; be not afraid. I have not come before the King this time to take you away and bring you to Jerusalem, for we have still great wars before ye will come to Jerusalem, but when our country shall be in our hands and I offer sacrifice, we will come to you to bring you to a settled land, but this time I am only come to give you the good tidings that salvation will soon come." On Tuesday we left Beja and arrived at night in a village where there are Marranos, and we stayed the night in a Marrano's house and they prepared for us beds and all that was necessary, and in the morning we came to Almadover, which is a fine place, and many Marranos and the city magistrates came to me and in every place where we were we spread the banners and they praised them. On Thursday we came to Loule, a fine place and a great city, and they wished to see the banners and said to us, " If you want anything command us, for we will serve you with all you desire." We stayed there the whole of Friday and Sabbath and Sunday, and Aldeka returned to attend to some matters and served us, and I was afraid of him; and the Jews from Asemmur came, that is, Solomon Levi and his brother-in-law Isaac, who was from Asfi-Safi; and on Monday we left Loule and many people came with us, and the master of the house, and we arrived at Tavira and entered a fine dwelling with many rooms and slept there until the morning. But we did not receive the money—the three hundred ducats which the King has commanded—for Don

Miguel wrote contrary to what the King had commanded him to write, and the man that spoke Arabic knew all this, because he was the interpreter to the King, and he said to me, " I will tell all this matter to the King," and he asked leave to return to the King. And I bought him a horse in Evora for thirty-five ducats and in Tavira I gave him eight ducats and a golden girdle and two bundles of gold embroidery and sent him to the King. And he promised to bring all my desires before the King and he left me and I stayed in Tavira.

At that time R. Moses Cohen came to me with letters from King Joseph and his Elders, and all day, from morning to evening, my house was full of Marranos and Christians, and I thought it was good to send as a present to the King of Portugal my horse and all its trappings and to send a present to Antonio Corenzi of a burnous which I had bought for seventeen ducats, and I ordered the presents to be sent by a young man called Christopoli who was living in my house and was faithful, and Aldeka came to me and said that none but he could fulfil this mission, for it needed a wise man and strong-minded who should say to him that this was the present from the Jewish Ambassador in order that the matter should seem good to the King. I agreed that he should go with Christopoli to help him on the way, for I feared to send him by himself, and I wrote to the King that I had not found any ship to travel in and was staying in Tavira and did not know what to do, and I sent the gift of my horse and its trappings and asked him to find me some ship of his and told him that I had not received the three hundred ducats he ordered, and that he should write to Tavira to give me them in his name. And I entrusted the horse and burnous to Christopoli and the letter to the King, and I wrote also to Antonio Corenzi; then I said to Aldeka to go

with Chriſtopoli, and I gave them ten ducats for
travelling expenses and ordered them not to ride
upon the horse, and after I sent them to Tavira the
young Ethiopian slave fled from me and only the big
Ethiopian slave was left. He was a bad man and when
he went to the market he used to smite the Chriſtian
slaves, and they came to me and said, "Thy servant
has done us wrong," and he quarrelled with them
because of their women whores, and afterwards
that Ethiopian attacked the artisan who was with
me in the house and wished to kill him, and I ordered
that they should bind his hands and legs with cords,
and I took a great ſtick in my hand and ſtruck him
on the head until I broke the ſtick. And I took another
ſtick and ſtruck him more and I made weals on his
whole body, and then I told the Marrano to give
him one hundred blows, and we put iron chains upon
him and locked him in the house; and he ſtayed thus
for ten days, and after that I let him out and had him
dressed. He was a likely slave, handsome and ſtrong,
and loved me much; and this slave continued to do
all my house matters as before, and I made peace
between him and the artisan, and Solomon Levi was
in my house. He was a fine ſtrong young man,
and knew Arabic, and I gave him my garments of
black velvet and he put them on and went into the
market to the house of the Marranos, his relatives; and
slanderers saw him and slandered him to the wicked
city magiſtrate and said that in all the Kingdom of
Portugal neither Chriſtians nor Jews nor Marranos
might wear garments of silk, and anyone who put on
a garment like this incurred a fine of fifty ducats,
and they put Solomon Levi, who was wearing my
clothes, into prison. When I heard of the matter,
I sent Solomon Cohen to my friend the great lord,
and they let Solomon Levi out with the sureties that
his relatives the Marranos had given for him, and

I sent Solomon Levi to the great good magiſtrate, my friend, to give him a gift of fine clothes, but he would not accept them. He looked after me as the King commanded and treated me as a father his son, and showed me great kindness always. Afterwards I went to his house and took in my hand twenty ducats and said, "Pray for love of me accept this gift, for I have heard that the King will send for thee to go to him, and take these for travelling expenses." And he replied, "I will take nothing from thee," and Solomon Levi was with me and interpreted between us. And I said to him, "I have a large piece of iron armour cap-à-pie for the arms and feet, and helmet for the head and neck through which only the man's eyes can be seen through, and I bought it for thirty ducats and I beg you to accept this gift." He said "If the King hears of this matter he will slay me. All my life I have never accepted a gift." And he further said, "I hear that you have two fine swords," and I said, "If you will accept one of them and the iron armouɪ, I will send them to you and they will be a memorial between you and me of our ſtrong and fearful love," and he said to me, "I will accept them all for thy sake ; send them to me by Solomon Levi and my friend will come to ţhee to-night." At evening I sent him the two swords and the iron armour, and I told Solomon Levi to say that he was to take one of the swords, which he preferred, and return the second; and he took the swords and the armour for which I had paid fifteen ducats, and Solomon Levi returned to me the other sword, and I wrote a letter to the King and gave it to the hand of my friend the magiſtrate who was going to the King. Afterwards there came an old Jew called R. Abraham Ruach of Asfi-Safi, who wished to acquire honour from the King of Portugal by being appointed leader of the Jews. He arrived at Tavira with two friends, and they came to me in the house and he spoke with me. He was the humblest of the Jews in that kingdom, and did not wish to eat at our table but allowed his friends to eat and stayed in Tavira about eight days. Then he went to the King and told him what he had seen and heard, and when the great magistrate, my friend, was away during eight days, another magistrate came in his stead, and he was a thorough bad one, a friend of Don Miguel; and the day he arrived he sent for Carbalia and Solomon Levi and Solomon Cohen and asked them, "Why does the Jewish Ambassador stay here? The King has not given him permission to stay more than two months, and he has stayed more than four months." And Carbalia replied that he stays here until he gets the reply of the King, and he said to Carbalia, "Tell thy friends the Marranos that they shall be wise and not go to the house of the Ambassador." Near us there lived a neighbour, evil and wicked to God and man, who was a friend of Don Miguel, who wrote our doings every week to the King and Don Miguel, how that Marranos were coming to my house. Christopoli returned without a letter from the King but with a letter from the man who spoke Arabic. He told me that Aldeka the renegade had taken from Christopoli the burnous and put it on himself, and taken from him the trappings of the horse and the letters, and Christopoli and the man who spoke Arabic went to search for Aldeka and found him in a wood hiding the horse, for he wanted to bring it to Lisbon to sell it. And they took the horse and the letters from him, and Aldeka fled and went away. They gave the horse to the King, and he was very pleased with it, but did not reply in a letter, but said to the man who spoke Arabic, "I will write and do what he wants." He did nothing and Christopoli came back to me empty-handed. I sent Solomon

Levi with Chriſtopoli to the King with my good
sword, which was worth thirty ducats, as a present,
and I put in their hand two letters, one to the King
and one to Antonio Corenzi, and they went together
to the King. Afterwards that other magiſtrate
wanted to make charges againſt the Marranos every
day, and said to them, " You want to become Jews
again," and he remained angry, but by God's kindness
to them and me, he was not able to do any harm to any
Marranos. (May God be blessed !)

VIII

Afterwards that wicked magiſtrate came to my
house in the morning, he and all his servants. I was
sleeping on the bed, for I had been reading all night
and was sleeping. In the morning Solomon Cohen
came to me and said the cursed magiſtrate is outside
in the big room, and I said to Solomon to say to the
magiſtrate that he should wait and sit in the room
until I am dressed and I will come to him. I washed
with water and the servant helped me on with my
clothes, and I came out to the magiſtrate, and in his
hand was a writing from the King, and he read the
writing and therein was written, " As soon as this
letter reaches you send the Ambassador with a ship
leaving Tavira, and if there is no ship go with him
to Laza and seek a ship for him speedily; do not
delay." I did not believe the magiſtrate and called
Carbalia and took the letter and he read it in Hebrew,
and the wicked magiſtrate said, " Now thou wilt
believe me that I do nothing of my own accord, but
by the King's command, therefore, see that thou
be ready in an hour so that I can go to my house and
I will send thee five mules and a horse for thee to
ride upon."
After that he saw my Ethiopian servant and asked
him if he was a Moslem or a Chriſtian, and the servant

315

replied that he was a Christian; and he took the
Ethiopian and took him away and I spoke nothing to
him. We packed all our things, and what I was not
able to take with me I gave to Carbalia, and I also
gave him the silk robe which R. Jechiel of Pisa
had given me, for he had served me from the day
I came to this country until now. I also called
Berantina and his wife, in whose house I had stayed
and who had shown us great honour, and gave him
a fine sword, and to his wife I gave two golden rings,
and one with diamonds, together worth twenty ducats,
and also a fine and new robe worked with pearls,
worth ten ducats, and I also gave her three dress
lengths of silk, worth ten ducats, for the kindness
and expense they had been put to when first I came
to Tavira and when they asked nothing of me.

After that the magistrate sent the mules to carry
my stuff, and gave me a very bad horse on which
I could not ride, so I went on foot to the city near
to the magistrate's house, and, when he saw this,
he gave me the horse which he had been riding,
and he rode on a mule, and all the Marranos were
troubled and wept, men, women, and children. We
journeyed from Tavira at mid-day, and the cursed
magistrate and his servants came and also the Ethiopian
servant he had taken from me, and with me came
Carbalia with the old Marrano and the Marrano servant who had dressed me and Solomon Cohen, and we
arrived at Faro that night. The magistrate was un-
willing to enter into the house of Marranos, but only
went to Christians, and an honoured Christian prepared
for us a fine house and bed and all that was needed.
We stayed there until the morning, and I prayed the
morning prayer, and the magistrate went to Laza,
to find a ship for us and took the Ethiopian servant
with him. And we stayed in the house of the Christian
about eight days. Many Marranos came to see me

from Tavira and I said to them, " Have no fear about me, be &trong and wise in your a&s. God goes with me and He will lead me in this mission and choose the right way for me." Then the magi&rate returned from Laza and told us to go to Laza, for there was a ship there going to Leghorn and he had ordered the magi&rates to arrange everything for us and he would come after us. And we at once journeyed from Faro, and Carbalia came with me and the Marrano old man and servant. The rain was pouring and we arrived at night in a village on the border of the great city and came to a camp near the gate of the city and they unloaded the &tuff and we &tayed there about half an hour and two honoured magi&rates came before me, and all the men of the village, very honourable, and the magi&rates said to me, " We have prepared for you a nice dwelling, come with us." I went with them and they had prepared for me a nice bed in that dwelling, and Solomon Cohen came and laid the table, and we had a meal and took bread. I slept there until the morning and got up from my bed and washed and dressed and prayed. I was in the inner room and outside in the big room were the magi&rates and all the men of the village, children and women, and they asked me to show them the banners. And Solomon Cohen and Carbalia brought the banners and spread them, and the villagers praised them very much. Then they brought horses and we left the village with all the villagers behind; so we arrived at a great big river, and we paid the muleteers their hire and they put the burdens and the &tuff on the ship and we also embarked on the ship and came to a great city called Villa Nova (di Porto Maio), near the river. They unloaded the &tuff and I also went out to the river bank and all the men of the city, children and women and magi&rates came to see me. The wicked magi&rate had written to them that they were not to let us enter any house of Marranos but only of Christians and they should keep their eyes upon the Marranos so that they should not come to me and should take care that the Marranos should not speak with me, and the city magistrate sent his servant with us and brought us to the house of a Christian outside the city. And all the men came after us, and four Marranos came to me from Villa Nova and I said to them, " Go away in peace because of this wicked man," and we stayed that night, Thursday night, and, when I was asleep, the magistrates came and searched if there were Marranos in the house, and, after they had gone, Carbalia and Solomon Cohen told me this. If I had known that they had come to search I would have given them blows, but I heard nothing, and that was all for the best. In the morning the magistrate brought us mules and gave me a horse, and I rode upon it and we journeyed from Villa Nova to the City of Laza. All the magistrates and men, women, and children of the city came to me and brought us to the house of a Christian, with all our stuff, and the magistrates wanted to see the banners. And I spread them forth before them, and all the great men and nobles of the city came to see them and praised them very much. And the magistrate said, " See this letter from the great magistrate, who orders us not to let any Marranos go before thee." And I replied to them, " I have no wish for Marranos or Christians, there is no difference between the one or the other. If they come of their own accord, let them come, and if they stay away, let them stay away. I will neither call them nor prevent them from coming." The magistrates went on their way and we stayed there eight days. Afterwards the magistrates came before me and said that I was to go in a ship from Cuskini (?) which was leaving the next day, and I said to them, " I will think about the matter until mid-day and reply." Christians and Marranos came to me and said, " Do not go on this ship, for the crew are murderers," and I replied to the magistrates that I did not wish to go on that ship for various reasons, and they said, " Thou must go against thy will and by force," and I said, " I will not go under any consideration." The magistrates left in anger, and that night Christopoli came to me from the King with the King's letter in which was written, " I gave thee permission to stay two months and thou hast stayed four months, and hast mixed with the Marranos in order to bring them back to Judaism, and every week letters come to me from the magistrates of Tavira and all thy dealings with the Marranos are revealed, for I have seen what thou hast done in this regard in my presence and how much the more behind my back. I did not wish to do thee any evil, for thou didst tell me that thou hadst only come for the love of me and my benefit, and therefore I did not believe what the slanderers said against thee, and I told thee to go in peace and return to thy country; therefore, as soon as this letter reaches you go in peace and do not delay."

Christopoli also gave me a letter from the man who spoke Arabic, in which was written that Don Miguel had done all this and the King knows nothing about the matter except to sign the letter, for this was the custom of the King of Portugal, for he trusts Don Miguel, who does everything and he sent the bad magistrate, and spoke with the King day and night against me and he is always in the King's presence. But the man that spoke Arabic could not interfere and, when the King received the horse, he said good things of thee, and afterwards Don Miguel turned him, and therefore I advise thee to go in peace without delay, for there are many slanderers against thee, and they write to the King. I slept till morning and went, I and Carbalia and Solomon Cohen, to the house of the chief magiſtrate and said, " I wish to go, but this ship on which thou desireſt me to travel, its crew are murderers and all the Christians warn me not to go in it, and it would not be pleasing in the King's sight if thou placeſt me in the hands of men of bloodshed and deceit who are our enemies; but, if thou wilt do a great kindness for the love of God and the King of Portugal, find me another better ship in which the crew are of this city, in order that we may be able to travel therein in safety." The magiſtrate summoned the captain of another ship and arranged to hire it for 200 golden ducats to take us to Leghorn. I agreed with them, for the captain of that ship was a good man and upright and of good family, and I could not do anything else and I gave them 200 golden ducats, and the captain of the ship wrote out a bond that he would bring me safely to Leghorn and would return with teſtimony from me that we have arrived in peace at Leghorn, and, if he did not bring a letter from us, he was to pay a fine to the King of ten thousand lire. I went to see the ship, and behold the cabin was in bad ſtate, and I desired that they should make it good. And I gave another ten ducats for cupboards and tables and nails and we ſtayed eight days in order that they should arrange the cabin in the ship, and after they had got the ship in order I entered at mid-day, and before I entered the ship I took leave of the Marranos who served me and they wept, and Carbalia went with me on the ship and arranged all my ſtuff, and he made a big cabin for Solomon and the ſtuff and a bed in it, and he made my cabin very nice. Afterwards Carbalia returned to the city, and the wicked magiſtrate came to the ship with his servants and searched the ship thoroughly to see if there were any Marranos with me, and they opened the boxes and luggage to see if there were any firearms there,

and, thank God, they only found one sword of all the
swords that remained in my hands and they found no
Marranos with me, and the wicked magiſtrate opened
the door of the cabin and begged pardon of me, " I
have only done all this to thee by the written command
of the King," and he showed me another letter
written by Don Miguel. And I said to Carbalia,
" Tell the magiſtrate that as God lives, Who has saved
me from all trouble, if he had been with me and I
had had four servants he would not have come out
of the ship, for I would have taken him with me to
the wilderness of Habor to King Joseph, my brother."
We journeyed that day from Laza and went a diſtance
from the city in the sea, and the ship arrived at Laza,
a place whence Solomon Cohen with the captain had gone
back to Laza that night, and I sent by him the rent of
the house for the old Marrano, and I gave him money
to buy provisions, and Solomon Cohen bought some
things there and returned to me that night. We
journeyed from Laza at midnight and the ship sailed
two days and I faſted three days and three nights
consecutively every forty days, and on the other days
I used to faſt from evening to evening, and I remained
ſtrong and well, thank God ! and my body asked
nothing of me, and I prayed from morning until
evening all the days of the journey I made. The
ship came to within four parasangs of Tavira at the
beginning of the dominions of the Emperor near to
Coſta (Marina) and the ship ſtayed there twelve days,
and we left there with a good wind on the Wednesday,
and for three days we had a good wind until Friday
at midnight, and then a ship came to us of the
Portuguese navy and we thought they were pirates.
And they made a great noise and the ships touched
each other, and the captain came to me and said that
there were Moslems on the other ship, and I said
to them, " I will remain in my cabin until they come

to me and God will choose a good way for me; I trust
in the God of my salvation and I fear no man and no
pirates. If they come to me, I will say that God has
sent them for my good and the good of all Israel."
And they stayed from midnight until the morning
and I stayed in my cabin and prayed the morning
prayer. And the captain saw that it was a ship of
the King of Portugal, and after that we journeyed with
a very bad wind on Friday and were in trouble the
whole of the Sabbath, and the wind brought us back
against our will to Almeda, which is near the sea-
coast and belongs to the Emperor, and we stayed there.
The magistrates of that city came to our ship and said
to us, " I am come to take you in custody, for no Jew
can enter the dominions of the Emperor, without his
permission." Then I produced the Bull and the letter
from the King of Portugal and he read them to me
and said, " These writings are in your hands and you
can come and stay with us and we will write to the
Emperor all about you at length and will do what he
commands." I replied, " The matter is of the Lord,"
and I went with Solomon to the magistrate's house
in Almeda, and I rejoiced and had no fear nor dismay;
and we entered a room of the house and the magistrate
appointed a guard for us by day and by night, and
our ship captain was held in the prison. And the
magistrate sent two men with Solomon Cohen to
bring our stuff from the ship and they saw that the
crew had stolen from it a black silk cap and twenty-
five ducats, and the rest they gave into Solomon
Cohen's hands, and we took the clothes and the banners
and the golden signets and the silver cups and our
money, and the magistrate made a list of them all
in writing and sent a messenger to the Emperor.
On the day after I had been taken into custody and
our stuff remained in our hands and they showed us
honour, and on the third night I thought to send a

messenger of my own to the Emperor, and the magistrate said to me, " Thou canst do this and I will find thee a faithful man as a messenger," and I wrote two letters, one to the Emperor and one to his wife, the Queen, who knew me when I was with the King of Portugal, her brother, and I accompanied her three parasangs, and the magistrate also wrote to the Queen, the wife of the Emperor, in my name, that I had left the dominions of her brother, the King of Portugal, and that it was the wind that had brought me to Almeda and that we were taken into custody, and I gave him all the letters from the King of Portugal and the Pope. The messenger left Almeda on Tuesday and arrived at Granada to the presence of the Emperor and the Queen, and we stayed in the magistrate's house. He was very honourable and of Jewish descent and he revealed this to us; but none of the Christians knew of this, and he showed us great kindness and much honour. And I said to the captain, " I wish thee to take all the money which I have given thee, two hundred ducats, to bring us to Leghorn and thou hast only come with me as far as Almeda," and the captain wanted to give me one hundred ducats back, and I said to him, " Give me my money now." And his servants from the ship, when they heard that the magistrate wished to detain them, journeyed and fled with a good wind and I put manacles of iron upon the feet of the captain and put him into the prison, and I thought to go to the Emperor's presence, and the magistrate honoured me greatly and all the nobles of the city came to see us every day. Also a great Moslem lord came to us and spoke with me at length and asked me, " Why hast thou come from thy country and what seekest thou from the Christians ? " He was a wise man and showed me calculations and figures of apparatus and said to me that the end had come to the rule of the Christians and the rule of the Moslems, and that within three years all the Kingdoms of Edom would be in the hands of the King of Israel in Jerusalem and all the nations would return to one religion. I did not wish to answer him on these matters and the chief of the city sent me a present and afterwards I went to his house to show him honour, and I also sent him a fine present, through Solomon Cohen. He was the most honoured in the city and judge over all the magistrates. That city of Almeda is almost entirely in ruins and only a tenth part remains which had not been destroyed by the great earthquake which occurred five years ago, when the houses fell upon the inhabitants and they died ; and on the day the earthquake occurred there was a great noise in the city, for the noise had come from Jerusalem, and they all heard the sound of words but did not see who was speaking, and we stayed in the city and waited for the reply of the Emperor until our magistrate returned, after twelve days, and brought a letter from the Emperor and a sealed Bull in which the Emperor ordered all his subjects to allow us to go by sea or land and to do us no evil, but to honour us and to give us, for our money, houses to lodge in and all that we needed for the journey in which we might travel in his kingdom. We left Almeda and the city magistrate came to accompany me with his servants for a parasang and a half and returned at nightfall. We stayed that night encamped in a garden, and in the morning we journeyed and arrived at night in a city called Sorbos. It used to be a Moslem city and we went to the Christians and they were all able to talk Arabic; and they were poor, and we slept in camp from night until morning. Monday was Christmas and the muleteers said that they wished to stay in their place because it was their feast, and I gave up my will to theirs and we stayed there. And the magistrate of the city came, an honourable man, and said to me, " If you wish anything, order me for I will do all," and I bought for my muleteers sheep and many fowls, so that they might eat and be satisfied, and the citizens, the Moslems, came to kiss my hands and rejoice much over me. After that I summoned the city magistrate and consulted with him as to the captain, as I was afraid that he would flee away and escape and I had put him in irons. And the magistrate replied, " If you want a man to look after him I will give you a strong man." And I said, "Yes, I will pay his hire." And the magistrate brought him before me and warned him, " If the ship captain escapes thou wilt have to pay 200 ducats, therefore take good care of him."

We journeyed from Sorbos the second morning after Christmas, and the young man was busy all the way looking after the ship captain and even went with him when he wanted to relieve the necessities of nature. We arrived at a city where the citizens had been Moslems but had become Christians, and the name of the city was Purchena. We slept there that night and journeyed in the morning and arrived at Lorca, a big city, where we stayed and journeyed on Friday morning and arrived at Albacete. It is a bath place with hot springs, and we stayed there in camp on the Sabbath and on the Sunday we journeyed to Cartagena, where we stayed in a good lodging. They laid a table and we eat, and many honoured me and came to the house that night to see us, and we stayed until the morning, and the young man who guarded the captain remained on guard. On the Monday I admonished the captain, who had tried to escape, and put him in the prison, and the magistrates came to me and I showed them the Emperor's letter and Bull and also the Bull from the Pope and the King of Portugal and the other writings

I had. When they saw the letter of the Emperor ordering them to do me much and great honour, all the nobles of the province came and showed me honour and kindness and all the citizens, great and small, gathered to see me; none stayed away. After mid-day a magistrate came and said before the other magistrates, " I desire to take these Jews into custody because they cannot come into our country." I produced the letter of the Emperor and showed him everything, and he read the Emperor's letter and wished to take the letter away; and I took the letter and held on to it. After that he produced a writing from the Emperor's great investigator, who lived at Murcia, who had written to him to take us in custody on all accounts. All the magistrates of the city helped me, but that magistrate took no note of their words and said to me and them that he wished to write to the investigator what to do with these Jews and would tell him that I had a letter from the Emperor and a letter from the Pope. And he closed our house and put two guards upon it outside, but I knew this not; and when Solomon Cohen wanted to go to the market to buy something he found that the door was closed and guards outside. And he told me all this, and I was angered unto death and I thought to break the door. And Christopoli said to me, " There is another door by which thou canst go outside, do not break the door," and he showed me the door from which I could go out. And the magistrate came to me, and many men, and I said to them, " Take witness that this magistrate is breaking the command of the Pope and the Emperor, who ordered all the men of his dominions to show me honour on sea and dry land, and he has closed the door and wishes to take me in custody and I hold in my hand the Emperor's letter and I wish to send to-day a messenger to the Emperor and to write to him all the things this magistrate has done, and I will see how the matter falls out in the end." Then the magistrate, who had been sent by the investigator from Murcia, said, " I will on no account shut any of you up, but stay in your house with my two servants until the reply comes to me to-morrow from the investigator, for I can do nothing small or great, except by the investigator's command "; and when I heard this I could do nothing else, and returned to my house and said to the magistrate, " Allow Solomon Cohen to go to the market to buy what is needed and I will stay in the house, and my servants will stay with me "; and so he did, and that night the magistrate was with me and slept on the ground in my house, and so did his servants, in order to guard us ; but I and Solomon Cohen slept on beds and I had no fear and dismay. I was confident and they were in discomfort The messenger whom the magistrate had sent to the investigator at Murcia returned, and the investigator replied in writing that we could stay. . . .

Thus far in the manuscript, which is incomplete, and I know not how many leaves are missing, and so we cannot tell what finally occurred to R. David Reubeni.

These are the expenses which R. Solomon Cohen incurred for our lord R. David, the Commander of the army :—

I, Solomon b. Abraham Cohen of Prato, will write all the expenses I made for David Reubeni from 18th Tebet, 286 (January, 1526), when I took over the money account from Ben Zion of Kurein (?), of the expenses from Tavira till Al Marina, more than 80 ducats spent in Al Marina and Santarem, and the mule hire and in Tavira on our return, and in Lans (?), and in Al Marina until to-day, Mid-Iyyar, 287 (1427), about fourteen and a half months. All the expenses in this time amounted to 2,200 ducats, besides 2,004 ducats taken from us by the lord of Clermont, who took us prisoners on an Island in the Adriatic, and besides the moneys I gave in Portugal to the servants of the King, and besides the horse I sent to the King of Portugal, a gift of the value of 2,004 ducats. . . .

The account ends " 2,173 golden ducats, besides the great expenses which the Jews made to send to Rome to pay the balance of the ransom, for he asked much and beyond estimation, and forced me to make me bounden to pay him nine hundred ducats.

Ended and finished, praise to the Eternal."

SAMUEL JEMSEL THE KARAÏTE
(1641)

I was possessed by a violent and insatiable desire to visit the places of God, to set out for Mount Moriah and the chain of Lebanon, there to render homage to the supreme King of all things, in the bosom of Jerusalem—Jerusalem, for whose speedy rebuilding we pray in the prayers we offer up daily. I was fain, therefore, to depart thither in order to make my prayers and offerings to the most great and good God. As I had learnt that eminent men such as Rabbi Isaac and Rabbi Solomon Levi had also been inflamed with the desire of accomplishing this holy journey, I, being urged on like them by a sort of divine instinct, did not lose sight of the execution of my project ; I would not have suffered myself to be turned aside from it by any reason whatsoever. This desire to set out which had formed itself in my mind was so violent that it was impossible for me to remain in my own home, or to go about my accustomed business. Without any delay I wrote a letter to Rabbi Solomon Levi, asked to be informed of the date of his departure, and proposed to him that, with God's help, he should take me with him as his travelling companion.

After an interval of some little time, Rabbi Solomon Levi arranged to meet me at the town of Koslov (Eupatoria). There we took ship on the fifth day of the week, which fell on the fourteenth day of the month of consolation, the year *Thou shalt be blessed in thy going out and in thy coming in.*[1] Samuel, son of our honoured Rabbi and master, Moses David, blessings on his memory, and Nisan of Lutsk having

329

also joined our company, we started on our voyage the eve of the sixth day of the week, and for five consecutive days sailed on without stopping. God then agitated the sea with a wind so violent that our boat threatened to break in pieces, and we were obliged to make for the port called Gadara,² which with great difficulty we reached. Blessings on the Supreme God who brought us out of our great peril. We remained three days in this place, after which we went on to Constantinople, where we arrived the twenty-fifth day of the said month.³

As we stayed for forty-eight days in this town, we had occasion to celebrate there the feast of the Solemn Day of Expiation. The sixth day, the eleventh of the month of Tischri, in the year *Seek peace and ensue it*.⁴ After leaving Constantinople we arrived at Beshik Tach. There, after we had embarked, we waited two whole days for Muharrem Reis with a chosen band of companions ; at last, on the first day of the Feast of Tabernacles, full of good cheer, we left the city of Constantinople behind us. About fifty ships of large dimensions sailed away at the same time as ourselves, and we took the direction of Alexandria. In our boat there were about a hundred rabbinical Jews of both sexes ; some were intending to go to Jerusalem, others to Safed. There were also about five hundred Mohammedans. We made Afend, whence we reached the town of Gallipoli, sojourning in the latter place for one day only.

Gallipoli is situated by the sea-shore and encircled by a triple wall ; it is a very fine town. There are two Rabbinical Synagogues there ; and there are also twenty-five Mahometan mosques, as well as hostelries for the reception of strangers. Merchandise of different kinds can be procured there, notably various sorts of fruit and spices, There may be seen there a great number of ships, which it is customary to protect by means of a fleet coming from Egypt, when, for fear of the Greeks, it is not considered safe for these ships to sail out to sea without escort.

Our convoy having collected, we sailed out of harbour, and reached Boguz-Hissar in the afternoon. Here was anchored the captain called Bekir Pasha, with a dozen warships : with this naval force he was to accompany the passenger ships and to protect them on their journey against the depredations of the Greeks. For, every year, it was customary to convoy the Egyptian ships to Alexandria, and afterwards to bring them back to Constantinople. So these vessels hoisted signals of mutual friendship and joy in greeting at Boguz-Hissar, and at the same time rendered the honours due to the captain-pasha. There chanced to be in another flotilla of our convoy an important personage named Shaban-Effendi ; he was head of a music guild ; his choir made the air resound with the noise of trumpets all in honour of Bekir-pasha. Every day there was to be heard from this boat the sound of musical instruments, and it was in this gay fashion that we did the voyage to Alexandria. At the end of the day we crossed the strait near Boguz-Hissar and reached the island of Bochsa-Adasi (Tenedos) towards the middle of the night. This strait being excessively narrow, the boats were so crowded together at one spot, that they were all rocking against each other. All night long, therefore, we were much disquieted, fearing lest this thronged overcrowding might end in the destruction of the ships. Thanks be to God for having kept us safe and sound, and for having snatched us from this imminent peril without accident.

The White Sea (Archipelago) is very vast ; with numerous islands, eminences and rocks—like the many hills to be found on land—beautiful to look upon, but very dangerous. We ought to give great praise and glory to God for having permitted us to behold nature in these admirable aspects.

From the city of Constantinople to Rhodes on, we see the continent on both sides of us, as at Stambul Boghuzo (Beikio). For to the east is situated Anatolia and to the west Oros-ili, known everywhere for its vineyards and most pleasant gardens. After that we reached Cabra Istanco, which is situated on a part of Oros-ili. On the coast opposite this place is Natolia Kars-Baglar, which in like fashion rejoices in abundance of vineyards, gardens, and orchards, and of fruit trees and aromatic plants.

Pursuing gradually our course, we crossed the straits of Susam Ada. After this the ships which had made the voyage from Gallipoli and other places in our company separated from us : some taking the direction of Susam Ada, the others that of Izmir (Smyrna). Forthwith we were borne on to the town called Sagis ; none of the ships troubled to enter the harbour there, because they were carried on by a favourable wind. But, as we passed it by, we admired from the distance its ramparts and vineyards, its gardens and magnificent buildings. We kept on our way, and towards the evening of the sixth day we arrived at Rhodes. From Constantinople to Rhodes is seven hundred miles. We remained on our ship because of the Sabbath, which fell on that day. The first day of the week we landed, and to our great content took a bath.

The town of Rhodes is very fine. It is situated on an island, and was founded in the time of the Greeks. It is surrounded by a simple *enceinte* which makes it impregnable. Here we find magnificent palaces, built of squared stones, and like the buildings of the town of Galata. There is not the least admixture of wood in their construction. Lofty towers of

engaging aspeﬅ are placed in regular order along
the ramparts. In the time of the Greeks this town
had another name, and was called Khotsob Malta.
The Rabbanites have two synagogues there, and the
Mohammedans twenty-five mosques. There are
about five hundred baths and hoﬅelries. There are a
great number of merchants to be found, too, trading
in divers wares brought from Egypt in Egyptian
vessels. All the moﬅ delicious kinds of fruits can be
procured : grapes, figs, pomegranates, oranges. In
a word this place is a kind of Paradise. Grapes by
the great pound are to be bought for a single piece
of silver ; figs and pomegranates are within the reach
of all purses ; ten pomegranates can be got for a single
piece ; a measure of wine for three pieces ; and finally
the measure of wheat coﬅs thirty-eight pieces of the
same money. When we were there it was a time of
great scarcity of wheat ; so that one hundred and
sixty drachmas of bread coﬅ eight pieces of money.
This country is so abundantly provided for by imports
of every description that it is impossible to calculate
the riches of its resources. We sojourned there three
days.
On this island there are hoﬅels for mariners
and pilots. The town is surrounded by its fields,
vineyards, and gardens. A tower is built in one of
these gardens.
We departed thence the second day of the week,
leaving there Bekir Pasha, who sent on with our
ships two warships, both as an escort for us, and to
bring him back also, at the same time, news of the
safe arrival of all our ships in port. From the town
of Rhodes to Alexandria not an island is to be any
more seen, nor anything of either continent : nothing
can the eye discern but the sky overhead and the
sea around. After we had voyaged in this wise for
five days upon this dangerous sea, a violent tempeﬅ

arose. We were in great terror and diftress, and on the
point of shipwreck. For a day and a night we were
the prey of moft unhappy fears, and time and again
sent up vows and prayers to God. Then the tempeft
abated, and with joy and tranquility we finished
the remainder of our voyage. At laft, after we had
come safely through all the dangers of the sea, we
reached the town of Alexandria on the sixth day of the
week. Blessed be the supreme God Who brought us
safe and sound to port. Glory to His name, Who has
calmed the tumultuous waves so that we might plough
our path through the ftorm, and ride safe through the
swift moving furrows.

From the isle of Rhodes to Alexandria is five hundred
miles. As for this last named, it is one of the greateft
of cities; but moft of the buildings reared by the care of
Alexander the Great have been laid low and deftroyed.
Some there are, however, which resemble those to be
seen at Rhodes, that is to say, they are conftructed
of squared ftones. There remain ftill ftanding,
moreover, magnificent palaces remarkable for their
columns of marble, and for the variety of their colours.
These it would be difficult to describe, so great is their
beauty. The Rabbanites have here three synagogues
and schools ; the Mahometans thirty mosques. Of
these one ftands out as especially wonderful by reason
of the thousand columns on which it is supported.
We devoted three days here to repose.

Thus far the hiftory of our travels by sea.

On the third day of the week which fell on the third
day of the month of Cheshvan, we mounted camels and
donkeys, and at eventide set forth in the direction
of the ftrait called Mateja. The waves of the sea
at this place move with so rapid and faft travelling a
current, carrying everything swiftly great diftances
away, that it was impossible for us to travel round it,
or to cross it on camels and horses. By great good hap

there were there two ships ready to take men across ; for these boats are appointed to perform this service continuously. On that day there was so great a concourse of persons that, in the interests of all, it was not possible [to permit any] to pass, except by preserving the strictest sequence. It was the duty of little Arab boats to convey every one in the most expeditious order. The camels laden with their burdens were forced to enter into these barques, and in this fashion they crossed the Strait of Mateja. Payment of one single penny, the equivalent of a *para* in Egyptian money, secured for each camel the right to passage. The order was given for us to be taken across towards midnight, and it was at that hour we crossed the strait.

When the number of those who had passed the ferry between evening and daybreak was reckoned up, it was found to be nearly two hundred men and camels. We continued our journey on *terra firma*, and towards evening we arrived at a town called Reshid (Rosetta). From Alexandria to Reshid the roads are bordered with palm trees. The town of Reshid itself is situated on the banks of the river ; it presents a fine appearance, and is distinguished by elegant buildings of diverse ornamentation. Merchandise of different kinds in great quantities is to be found there. A variety of commodities, such as linen and rice, are purchased here by merchants who despatch them to Alexandria, not without difficulty, for the things they trade in have to be conveyed thither by boat. This town contains a great number of inns for the merchants, as well as about forty hostelries for the reception of strangers, and caravanserais also. The Mahometans have mosques here ; I have seen one supported on two hundred and ninety marble columns. Jews of the rabbinical sect possess two synagogues. Fish, both fresh water and sea fish, are very cheap. We tarried in this place for a three days rest.

Towards the afternoon of the sixth day of the week, embarking on a little ship called *Garim*, we left Reshid accompanied by two boats, which were smaller still. For six days we sailed up the river in most tranquil and pleasant fashion, without hindrance from anyone, and without cause to fear the least harm. At night time only we slowed down entirely on account of the Arabian brigands by whom travellers are often attacked. By this time we had arrived at the tenth day of the month of Cheshvan. Now this is a day we celebrate by a solemn fast ; and a second day of expiation was observed by us with all the customs of our religion, for the performance of which we remained on our boat on the river. In this place the river is about a mile in width, elsewhere it is as much as two. Cultivated fields stretch away on both sides; the eye embraces a prospect of leguminous plants, aromatic rushes, precious fruits of all kinds, gardens, orchards. Nowhere else are to be found so many cities and towns set so close together as here. Between Reshid and Misr (Cairo) are nearly a thousand hamlets, covering a distance of one hundred and forty miles. Towards evening we arrived at the town of Bulak, where we again rested.

Here our travels by water, whether by sea or by river, came to an end.

I will now commence my narrative of our journeyings by land. And it is meet that I should begin by rendering praise to the great God Who, when we continued on our way, never ceased to regard us with favour, and ever and always granted us His aid. Having made all our preparations for our journey, we departed from Bulak, and reached Misr on the sixth day of the week, which was the twelfth of the month, a little before mid-day. There we were going to take up our lodging in a public hostelry known by the name of Antioch. But as soon as our Karaïte brethren (may God's blessing light upon them) were informed of our arrival, they sent to us certain personages held in the highest honour and consideration by the whole of their community, who offered their felicitations, welcomed us joyously, and brought us to the home of the honourable master and rabbi Baruch-ha-Nasi. May God the Saviour long preserve him safe and sound and accomplish all his desires. He assigned us for our lodging a magnificent house near the synagogue. There we were able to celebrate at our ease the second festival of Tabernacles, on the fifteenth day of the month of Marcheshvan. It is both a fitting and seemly thing thus to keep the feast days consecrated to the Lord when the fruits of the earth are already producing the harvests of a new season, in the land of Israel—that land that God was wont to look upon as His most holy place.

The city of Misr is situated on the banks of the river. With regard to this river of Egypt, the opinion is commonly held that it is the same as the Pishon ; the Karaïtes, the Rabbanites and the Arabs have always inclined to that view. We, for our part, anxious to arrive at perfect certainty in the matter, did not rest content without making searches in the books of the Egyptian sages, and succeeded in discovering that they speak of the Pishon as flowing through the whole country of Cush (Ethiopia). The inhabitants of Misr showered honours upon us. From the highly respected Rabbi, Baruch-ha-Nasi, we received daily the most hospitable and gratifying attentions, in the shape of the most delicate dishes and exquisite cakes sent by him to us. May he abound in blessings from Almighty God.

The Karaïtes of Misr are endowed with very fine natures : generous, humble of spirit, loving their neighbours, and full of piety towards God and man. They are rigorous in their observance, I would repeat, of God's holy law, they walk in the way which is the way of truth, and they keep the Sabbath punctually. On that day they light no light, they drink no warm drink, but on the eve of the festival they take care to have ready by evening the lights and lamps which burn in the synagogues until the morning. If it should happen that a solemn feast falls on the first day of the week, then it is customary, when the Sabbath is over and the prayer *Beriah* has been recited, to light the lamps. Those who live in the neighbourhood of the Rabbanites are wont to use lights brought by them, unless they prefer to make a light by means of flint and tinder. They observe a special fashion of preparing food during all solemn festivals and at the weekly feast.

Therefore above all they are careful to maintain great strictness in the matter of purity. They receive no meat or drink from the Mahometans, with the exception of vegetables and fruit. They do not partake of the bread of the Rabbanites, and they do not drink the wine, or the wine mixed with honey, prepared by them. For they prefer to keep themselves entirely apart in the matter of feeding from the Rabbanites, whom they know to be by no means scrupulous about refraining from the contact of women in a state of impurity, or from contact with other impure things. To achieve this end, they resort only to their own butchers and bakers, and, by having their own, are entirely independent of bread and meat procured from others. From all this it results that they might with justice be called the only true Jews, veritable children of Israel.

Most of our brethren the Karaïtes of Misr are goldsmiths. They deserve equally to be mentioned with honour and approbation, though they are possessed of but modest means. At the present time no individuals will be found among them in the possession of a considerable private fortune. But for probity of manners they are unequalled. The synagogue of the Karaïtes, our brothers, is built on fourteen columns of marble. It contains five chests for scrolls of the law, and fourteen copies of the divine law. Add to these a great number of books by Karaïte sages, all written in Arabic. There is, moreover, a smaller synagogue here, in the house of a man named Aaron. In it there are two volumes of the divine law, and writings formerly composed by the care of wise men of Egypt.

There still remain in Misr to-day hostels for the poor, formerly consecrated by our first ancestors ; it is claimed that once they numbered as many as seventy, but to-day not more than about fifty are to be seen. There is, in addition, a house particularly consecrated to charity, above which a lofty tower rears itself ; it is the work of the ancients, built by them to enable them to contemplate and observe the moon from its summit. We entered it for a visit, and only reached the top of the tower after climbing up ninety steps. From this place all the land of Egypt can be surveyed. The tower has three floors, passed one after another in the climb to its summit.

It is customary in the community of Misr to bring forth in public a copy of the divine law every Sabbath, on all solemn feast-days, and on the intermediate days, as well as on the second and fifth days of the week. From it is recited, after the daily prayers in the synagogue are over, the section for the week, but on week-days there is no reading out of the prophets. This custom has been continually in existence at Jerusalem (may it please God to grant the speedy rebuilding of this city), as well as among the Karaïtes who live at Damascus (whom may the Great God eternally regard with favour).

The metropolis of Egypt is the greatest of all the cities of this country. Merchandise of all sorts is found there in greater abundance than in any other country. Mahometan mosques abound in great number, and equally numerous are the hostelries, baths, caravanserais, inns, as many as a thousand in all. The Rabbanites have thirty-one synagogues here.

On one of the days following our arrival, we went to visit the old Misr, in the company of Abraham Kodshi, of the house of Levi, and of Rabbi Jacob, who conducted us to the synagogue of this town. It is a very fine synagogue, resting upon a score of marble columns. It has two sacred chests, and owns four volumes of the divine law. In the upper part of the chest is a recess containing a copy of the Mosaic law, written in the very handwriting of Ezra the Scribe himself, of happy memory. We were only able to look upon this chest from below, for it was in vain that we implored the public keeper to grant us permission to see this remarkable volume of the law, and even, to attain our end, offered him money as a reward for doing so. The guardian was not to be moved by our importunity, and he told us that never had it been granted to mortal man to open this volume. He added that fifty years already it had been his task to fill the post of keeper in this synagogue, and that never in all this length of time had he dared to touch this sacred volume. He related to us, moreover, that there had come once upon a time a man celebrated for his learning, who after spending forty days in fast and prayer, and purification by frequent ablutions, had opened this sacred volume and read some passages therein. It had thus never been permitted that any one else should set eyes upon this copy of the divine law ; this learned man alone had enjoyed the privilege. The place for the performance of ablutions is outside the synagogue, and can be seen from the place where the ark stands. It has been reported to us since by a Rabbi who was very much attached to us, that the Rabbanites had severely enjoined upon the public keeper, that in the event of a Jew of the Karaïte sect happening to pay the place a visit, he was not upon any account to allow him to open the sacred book. And that was why the keeper, in obedience to his master's orders, would not show us this book. Our Karaïte brethren tell us that this synagogue had been formerly the meeting place of the Karaïtes, but that later, on account of our great sinfulness, it had become the property of the Rabbanites. And indeed, from the remarkable appearance and the architecture of this edifice, we could see that it had been the work of the Karaïtes. We offered our supplications to God in this temple with prayer and homage, we recited some hymns, and in addition we left a gift of several pieces of money to buy oil for feeding the lamps.

After that we left this place and went next to visit the tombs of the dead. We did not tarry long in ancient Misr. There was an Arab there known to us through his intimate friendship with Rabbi Abraham Kodshi. With him we ate and drank and there we spent the night. In the morning, at our rising up, we recited the accustomed morning prayers ; this duty fulfilled, Abraham, our kindly host, led us to a garden, where we comported and refreshed ourselves amply, and all gave ourselves up to good cheer. For Rabbi Abraham, excellent man, was known to the principal personages of the city and to its men of chief place and dignity. It was his wont to come to the assistance of all his people when misfortune befell them, and he gave quite especial care to the interests of the synagogue. So the community to which he belonged had nominated him its chief, and entrusted to him the keeping of order and care

341

of the sepulchres. May God (praise be to Him) grant him ample recompense in this world and the next.

We went out also to a suburb where the Governor of Misr had his house. There we saw a palace exceedingly well planned and built, made of square stones arranged in diverse fashions; an indication nowadays of great antiquity. From the upper part thereof a considerable number of stones in consequence had fallen away. The common tradition is that Joseph the Just (peace be to him) had built this place for his own use. So to this day in the vulgar tongue of the Ishmaelites it is known as Yusuf Kioski. If anyone will climb to the top of it, there is not a part of the city they can miss seeing, so completely does it dominate the whole neighbourhood, which here lies open to its view, by reason of the great height at which it stands. Nowadays the " ornatus " (brocade vail) is woven year by year in his palace for the Ka'ba of Muhammad.

In the neighbourhood of this magnificent edifice we noticed a well of amazing depth. It had been dug in the earth, and in the popular language was called Yusuf Kuyusu. To reach the bottom of it I went down five hundred and ninety steps. It is a truly admirable and imposing piece of work. Joseph the Just, of happy memory, is said to have had it dug. From the top of the well water can only be got by means of the slope of the wall. It is not possible to bring the water straight up from the bottom. But midway down there is a place where cavities have been dug in the stone. In these, which are very spacious, there are cisterns. Water is drawn from the well by means of the walls, and this water then falls into the cisterns. The place where these reservoirs are is about half-way down the well. By a second operation the water is then drawn up above from these cisterns.

Then by means of aqueducts the water is conveyed
to the baths which are in the suburb where the prefect
of this country has ordinarily his habitation. It is
customary to use this water to assuage thirst, for
drinking purposes. But it has not the sweetness of
running water, of stream or river water. It is a little
more bitter.

We spent forty-eight days at Misr. There is still
to-day a custom in existence among the Ishmaelites as
well as among the Arabs, a custom very strictly enforced,
moreover, by law, which requires that anyone among
them who kills an ox, or lesser cattle, or any other kind
of animal, must pay in tribute to the prefect of the
city the hide, the bones, and all the fat of these beasts.
To this must be added another liability. Neither
Arabs nor Ishmaelites are allowed to go about in the
city after nightfall. If one of their number is surprised
in the act of contravening this prohibition, his goods
are confiscated, and he himself condemned to
ignominious imprisonment, or even to capital punishment. Now some hundreds of years ago there lived
a man called Samuel who was a member of our Karaïte
fraternity, and whose reputation was spread far and
wide in all the universe. Admitted to an audience
with the sovereign Queen of Egypt, and finding
the occasion auspicious, he hazarded the three
following demands, which were graciously granted
to him.

First, that the Jews might be allowed to walk at
night-time on the public highway, on condition,
however, that they should carry in their hand a
lighted torch.

Secondly, that the Jews should not be obliged to
give the magistrates a part of the animals they killed,
except the skin, but that the fat might be retained for
themselves as well as the bones.

Thirdly and lastly, that the Jews might bury their

dead, not as it had been required of them they should do hitherto, either in their own houses or inner courts, but in a special place consecrated by them. This Samuel obtained by official charter a grant of as much land outside the city as he could enclose with the skin of a bull. And this is how, in his wisdom, he put this condition into execution. He cut the skin in question into little slices, and from them he made threads as fine as horsehair. He measured then a plot of ground outside the city, and appointed this spot to serve as cemetery for the Jews.

To this day the custom survives of burying in this place the bodies of the Karaïte dead. No difficulty was made about admitting the Rabbanites to share in this immunity. It is customary among the Jews to go out to bury their dead at night, and even at an advanced hour.

EXTRACTS FROM THE DIARY OF HAIM DAVID AZULAI IN HOLLAND, ENGLAND, AND FRANCE[1]

(1755)

27th Nisan (Parshat Tazria). I thought to journey to England and started to go to some villages in a barque, but because of the strong wind I turned back and arrived in Rotterdam.

6th Iyar. Thursday evening. We journeyed from Rotterdam and slept that night in Elvod, which some people call Hellevoetsluis, a Gentile village at the extremity of Holland.

8th Iyar. On the holy Sabbath, eve and day, we rested in the packet-boat which left at the end of Sabbath.

9th Iyar. (Parshat Emor). At night we reached the port of Harwich, beginning of England, and all luggage and passengers who arrived in the packet were taken to the Custom House and I produced some silver, coins of English currency, to pay to the Customs Officers for my luggage ; I had put my purse in the girdle round my loins, and, when I came to the Office where the goods were and they opened my trunk, they carefully examined very thoroughly all my clothes and between the folds of my turban ; they took all my letters of introduction and took them to their chief, for there was already a rumour of war with France. They were very exact with the sailors and made each take off his shoes and trousers, and when they found that one had a Dutch gulden, they cut it and threw it away. I was sorely troubled and anxious, for I had about a hundred and eighty Dutch guldens in my string purse, but the Officer felt the outside of my garments and heard the rattle of coins, and I was

345

upset, but remembered that the purse with the English coins was in my girdle, so I took it and threw it for him and, when he saw that it contained English money, he was abashed and returned it. I had brought a recommendation to the Postmaster there, and he spoke in my favour, and they returned me my letters, but they did not see the guldens I had. Praise be to God ! How can I thank Him for His goodness unto me. We stayed in the Gentile hospice there two days.

11th Iyar (Parshat Emor). Tuesday at mid-day we left Harwich, and when we had gone out of the gate of the city and the coach was ready, I wished to make water, and got on to a heap of stones ; but as it was a conspicuous place I went on a little further, and seeing on one side of the field a rather deep depression in the ground which I thought was *terra firma*, I jumped over the stone fence between and put one foot to the ground, but my foot and thigh sank right into the mud and dung ; it appears it was a cesspool, so I had one leg in the mud and the other leg in the air and my hand held the fence, and I thought I was in great danger and nearly died there. I called out in a loud voice, but nobody heard, except a woman, who lived some way off, and she also began to cry out, and, in my trouble, I no longer had strength to keep up and I feared that the fence might fall upon me and so, God forbid, I should incur double death by stoning and stifling ; but God helped me and the merit of the Patriarchs. The coach driver and servant saw my trouble and pulled and lifted up Joseph who had been caught in dirty toils. Most of my clothes were in a mess and all spoilt and defiled and stinking, but God in His mercy put it into the mind of a Gentile to come at the sound of the noise, and he took me to his house where there was a water well and I took off my clothes and washed myself and my clothes, in order to remove the mess, and I covered myself with my gown and entered the coach with my clothes beside me. Thank God with all my heart that He punished me, but did not give me to death. I am not worthy of the goodness, thanks be to God, Who delivered me.

On the 12th Iyar (Parshat Emor). On Wednesday evening, at twilight, we arrived in London the great city, and I worried that night about lodging until I found shelter with a Portuguese Jew called Señor Aaron Cohen; and the place was small, but I was glad that it was a clean and respectable lodging. It is the hospice where previous messengers had stayed and, because of my being a messenger, wonders were done to me. Three of the great men of the city sent to me not to come into the city, because I could not do anything ; the messengers from Safed, who had preceded me, had come twice and left empty-handed. I replied that it was my duty to go and nothing could excuse it ; and when I went forth in the daytime God would do as was good in His eyes. When I came to the City all the gentlemen had left town in order to visit their gardens and there was nothing left, so I thought it best to put up with it and said there is no healer like time, and made up my mind not to mention my mission until I had had time to find some friends and some spirit among the gentlemen, for the heart of the gentlemen is smooth inside. I saw also disputes among the learned of the city, one man reviling and cursing his neighbour, each reviling the other, only too much shame for gentlemen, and alas for the poor that see such contempt of the Torah and the learned. I looked at my letters of introduction and found one addressed to the Haham. I at once asked, " Is the Haham the Chief Rabbi of the City, or a Dayan ? " and they answered and said, " There is no great man here. This man is the Haham." But God has not forsaken

His kindness to me. He let me find favour in the eyes of some friends, the chief of whom is the wise and perfect Haham Isaac Del Valle and Señor Phineas Gomez Serra, and there also we found the powerful R. Jacob Kimchi, the son of R. S. Kimchi of Constantinople, and the learned Chaim Alkali, and they are very friendly with one another. They all answered and said that for the purposes of my mission, there must be a great meeting (Mahamad), and it is the custom of the city to make this meeting at the beginning of a winter, and already R. Massud Danon had to wait many months until the time of the meeting. We do not know what you can do, but if you are wise, behold Señor Joseph Salvador, who is one of the Parnassim, is going to the waters; he is very clever and whatever he says is done immediately and, when Joseph returns home, if you find favour in his eyes, he will not rest until he has completed the matter well. So when Señor Joseph Salvador came, I went to him and saw him eye to eye and I spoke as to my mission in a humble and insinuating manner, and he answered, " Do not you know that in these countries no man can do anything except by the assent of the majority, but at any rate go and see Señor Franco and Señor Mendes and they will help you." And so I took my leave of him. The great man took trouble and called a meeting of the Parnassim and I went to the meeting, but the other Parnassim were against me; but he asked for a show of hands and showed that he was in my favour, and I left the Mahamad. He did not cease until he had got a special general meeting summoned. Finally the matter was settled well, and afterwards, through the help of Señor Franco, it was decided that the said Señor Phineas Gomez Serra and Señor Joseph de Abraham Francos should supervise a collection from the Yahidim, and so they did and, when the collection had been made, a letter arrived from the English

Ambassador in Constantinople telling Señor Franco about me. If only this letter had arrived before, it would have been of great use, but anyhow it brought me honour and glory in the eyes of the gentlemen. Praise be to the Almighty !

Among the friends I had, was the Chazan Señor David Castro, who is powerful and renowned and whose words are fruitful and very fruitful among the gentlemen. May the Lord remember it to him for good !

And in the City of London we went to the Fort which is called the Tower, and there I saw lions and an eagle one hundred years old and a great snake from India and another snake and other wild beasts in iron chains, and I also saw a room perhaps fifty cubits long and more, divided into many chambers, the walls between which are guns and weapons most beautifully made, then another wall, with an open door in the middle, the sides and the roof wondrously decorated with thousands and tens of thousands and more weapons. I also saw effigies of all the Kings of England in armour riding on armoured horses and anyone, to look at them, would think that they were alive. I also saw many coats of mail of different kinds arranged in rows, and many kinds of large cannons and weapons of war and shields and lances, which they had captured from their enemies from the time when England first existed and all kinds of strange vessels fearful and big. And in a room, somewhat dark, with an iron rail round inside, was shown the royal crown and sparkling precious stones, full of fire, giving light and flashing, and a golden cup, from which the King drank, and other precious vessels and royal treasure of precious stones and pearls. All this I saw with a sad heart, praying that if He does thus for those who break His commandments, may He do so to those who keep them. May the days come for the glory and grandeur and deliverance of the house of Israel and

may our eyes see it and witness the Saviour shining
forth like the sunlight seven times, crowned with the
crown of crowns and the holy of holies; thus may it
be His will ! I delivered a sermon on Sabbath.

28th Tamuz (Parshat Debarim). On Monday
we left London and arrived at Dover, a city of the
gentiles, after mid-day on Tuesday.

29th Tamus (Parshat Debarim). On Tuesday,
we journeyed from Dover in a ship, and we came to
Calais, a Gentile city in the Kingdom of France,
on the same day near to night, and I was kept in Calais
a few days until there was a coach for Paris.

PARIS

(Arrival in Paris the 22nd Kislev, 5538 (December,
1777))

This city, the capital of France, is of great size,
it is said to be fifteen miles round. Its streets and
squares are wide enough for two coaches to pass
each other with ease, even though foot passengers
are walking along the sides of the roads. The city
is served by its river, the Seine, over which there
is a great bridge, long and wide, called the " Pont
Neuf ", that is to say, the " New Bridge ". All day
long, and all through the night, without ceasing,
pedestrians are wending their way over it. Here
stands the clock "la Samaritaine", which is surrounded
by water. There is a saying that never in the twenty-
four hours is there an instant without a white horse,
a monk and a prostitute at this spot. The city is of
great beauty and everything is to be found in it,
but all at a very high price, except prostitution,
which is very cheap and openly displayed ; there
are said to be thirty thousand public prostitutes
inscribed on the registers, without counting the
thousands who are not public and offered to all

comers. There are academies in great numbers,
and every kind of manufacture is carried on. The
Jews enjoy tranquillity, there are many Germans,
many Portuguese from Bordeaux and Bayonne,
and many who hail from Avignon. People pray
together every Saturday, but there is no fixed
community, birds of passage for the most part
resorting hither for trading purposes. The synagogues
are without " privilege ", and exist only by a miracle.

On Tuesday evening M. Israel Bernal de Valabrègue
came. He enjoys a salary from the King, twelve
hundred livres a year, and the title of the King's
Interpreter, because he pretends to know all the
Oriental languages. He thinks he is a rabbi, a
casuist, a poet, and versed in the sciences : he knows
the (Kabbalistical) names. He boasts that all the
world writes letters to him. He came to see me
three evenings in succession. The first time he sang
his own praises as a scientist, the second time as
having journeyed to Amsterdam ; the third on account
of the ladies who correspond with him, he says,
and the academies which consult him. One evening
his boasting of himself was to the tune of making a
mock of M. Mordecai Ravel ; the latter has roundly
insulted him and lavished praise on him too. But
enough.

In the course of the day M. Fabre came to visit
me, a learned Christian of the Academy of Science.
He plied me with questions about science and
Kabbalist practices, which I answered.

On Friday I paid a visit to him and stayed with
him a couple of hours. He showed me a book in French
in which were written the names of the angels, their
features, and their letters, as well as consultations
in regard to dreams by means of adjurations, all
in the French language. This Christian gave me
a cordial welcome ; I went to him in the company

of M. Mordecai Venture, a grammarian and linguist, who took a great deal of trouble on my behalf. May God reward him!

[Saturday.] The evening before I had gone to dine at the house of the eminent David Naquet. There were present the *parnassim* (administrators) of the synagogue and a certain number of private individuals. It was a great affair. Much honour was paid to me. Then we dined with M. Venture and M. Mordecai Ashkenazi, of the town of Hâvre-de-Grace in France. The master of the house treated me with much distinction, as did also his worthy wife. On that day [Saturday] we went to the synagogue. There was singing in honour of the con-fraternity " Guemilot Hasadim " just founded. My name was placed at the head, and they bought me the honour of opening the ark and of carrying the séfer-torah (Scroll). Much oil was offered to the synagogue in my honour. I took lunch with M. David (Naquet). M. Elie Perpignan, brother of the mistress of the house, and his wife, were fellow guests. Great disputes between this couple had ended in a quarrel, and I had been asked at Bordeaux to make peace. After our meal we went to the synagogue and I preached on morality and the praise of the brotherhood " G. H."., after which they made me an offering without being asked to do so. May God reward them for it !

On Sunday, the 28th Kislev, the first day of " Vayyigash ", came M. Elie Perpignan and his wife. I gave her a " Shema Israel " to swallow, according to the formula of R. Menahem Azariah, because it was feared she contemplated being converted, and I invited them to make peace once and for all.

After that came Mm. Mardochée Ashkenazi and David Naquet, and I visited a rich German

Jew who told me he would come to see me in order
to give me an offering.

On Sunday night Mm. Abraham Vidal and Moses
Perpignan came and gave an offering for Hebron
with many tokens of respect. I thank God that I have
a great name and am held a hundred times higher
in esteem than I deserve. It is useless my telling
them that I am an ignorant man; they think that is
all modesty. My renown has even spread among
Christian savants, who question the Jews about me—
it is extraordinary! When I speak to them they
hold my words more precious than pearls. These,
indeed, are the wonders of Him who "raiseth the
poor out of the dust and lifteth up the beggar from the
dunghill to set them up among princes". But
what rare goodness have I met with from the men of
Avignon! Wherever they are to be found, even if
it is only one, I have reaped honours and profit.
Thus it has been in the seven cities of France where
I have come across them and they have been my
guiding light ; they live in the Four Communities,
Nîmes, Montpellier, Pézénas, Narbonne, Bordeaux,
Paris. To them I owe every care for my comfort
and much honour ; their persons and their money
have been at my service, and they have never ceased
to cherish and respect me—it is extraordinary!
"And David blesses them," them and their houses.
May God repay them, and may their reward be riches
and honour, a long life and worthy posterity ; may
God deliver them from all evil and may the virtue of
the Holy Land protect them and their descendants
so that they may be prosperous and flourishing,
with abundance of all things ! Amen !

That evening there came to me the very wealthy
man M. Peixotto to discuss with me the question
of his wife and induce me to get her to accept the
act of repudiation. He undertook to give a thousand

" crowns " for Hebron if I would move in the matter.
I answered : " If you wish to make peace, I will
interest myself in your affair with a good grace,
for everyone knows that your wife is a virtuous
woman ; lay down what conditions you will, I will
strive to obtain them. But as to a separation, that
would be sacrilege." I added that the Law forbids
him to repudiate his virtuous wife as long as she is
a mother and his first wife. I have told him, moreover,
many other things of this kind. A man even offered
me four " louis d'or " to countersign a decision
written by a celebrated rabbi concerning the marriage
of Israel Vidal to his second wife, and I replied that
though the decision may be just in principle in the
eyes of the people, it was a sacrilege, and that I would
not see the decision and still less would I countersign it. May God help me, for the glory of His
name, and may all our actions be done in the sight
of Heaven, that I may act according to His will !
Amen.

On Rosh-Chodesh Tebet [the Wednesday of
Vayyigash] I went to see Monsieur Fabre, the
Christian savant mentioned before. He showed me
an abridgement of the Kabbalah in French, which
began with the name of seventy-two letters, by whose
help Moses was said to have brought about the
plagues of Egypt and which confounded these
things with the constellations. I told him : " You
must know that that is a branch of the practical
Kabbalah, the ten plagues have not been the work
of this name ; moreover, it has nothing to do with
the constellations." This Christian paid me great
honour, and had us served with chocolate and " pain
d'Espagne ". Snow was falling ; he took us in a
coach to the " Bibliothèque ". But as it was the end
of the civil year, none of the conservators were there,
and we came back again. I went with M. Mordecai

Venture to Elie Perpignan. To his wife I addressed remonstrances of a general nature, and, on her husband's arrival, I got him to concede that he would give her all that was necessary for their expenses, so that she might be the mistress. In short, I strove to do all that was in my power to make peace between them.

On Thursday evening I was speaking in praise of the science (?), when a young Portuguese, Jacob Lopes Laguna, got up to speak in a contrary sense ; he told me he knew he was not orthodox. I was much pained, and afterwards made inquiries about him. I was told extraordinary things, my informants said definitely they had had it from himself, from his own mouth, that he had studied the books of Voltaire and believed in nothing, etc. What is more, a man of standing told me that here in Paris, at the table of the master of the house, he did not drink wine prepared by gentiles, but that he would go forthwith and drink with him in a Christian " auberge " (inn), and had done so many times. In truth, I was much troubled about him for many reasons. If this is all true, may God bring him back to the way of perfection. Amen !

In the daytime, we went to pay a visit to M. Peixotto. It was a considerable distance to go, for, as we wrote above, this is a very large city, said to have nine hundred and fifty streets, five thousand coaches, and more than a million inhabitants ; they say a day is not long enough to go round all the town on foot, if one wants to go everywhere. And at the end of it all he was not at home. In the evening, I went with Hananel de Milhaud and his son in a coach to visit M. Liefmann Calmer. He is a German Jew who in his youth was in the service of the rich Suasso de la Haye in Holland ; then he entered commerce and has elevated himself to the position of Baron of Picquigny, that is to say, lord of the town of Picquigny (which he has bought from the heirs of its lord for the sum of a million and a half francs) and "vidame of Amiens", that is to say, he is a "defender" of the "church", for that is what the lord of Picquigny muſt be. He has a great privilege from the Government. In faĉt, the late King Louis XV had a miſtress whom he had served, and she procured him this elevation. We went to see him ; he gave us a cordial welcome and an offering of two "louis". I recommended to him, and to his son also, M. Benjamin Abraham of Bordeaux, because he is related to him, and grows poorer and poorer. They said they would send him an offering.

On Friday we went with the Chriſtian, M. Fabre, to the "Bibliothéque" of manuscripts, and such is the consideration in which he is held, although it was not the day for it to be open, he received the necessary authority, and it was opened for us. There are thousands of manuscripts there dealing with all the sciences. I saw a Bible on parchment which was written in 1061 of the ordinary reckoning, about seven hundred and seventeen years old now, and which seems quite new, hundreds of our (i.e. Hebrew) books in manuscript, among them David Kimchi on the Psalms, with additions to the edition (on Psalm II, verse 12, we noticed nearly a whole column demi-folio), many works on natural science, on philosophy, on mathematics, on the calendar, the ancient Kabbalah, the works of R. Joseph ibn Caspi, and of R. Isaac Israeli, who composed the "Yesod Olam" for R. Asher ; many copies of "Semak" and of other printed works, the "Shibbole ha-Léket" (1ſt part), and the "Séfer Yereim" complete (it contains 464 precepts and the author says he has followed in his reckoning of the precepts the order of Rab Jehudaï Gaon, the author of the

" Halachot Gedolot ", except that he has sometimes put two precepts together into one), and the notes of R. Isaiah, the Elder, on the Pentateuch (in these he sometimes criticises Rashi).

I took my three Sabbath repasts in the house of the rich David Naquet, where I was a much honoured guest ; on Friday evening and on the day itself M. Abraham Vidal and M. Mordecai Venture partook of these meals.

On Sunday I went to see the decision (about Vidal), but read the question only. I saw that the facts were not correctly stated, so it is possible the decision may differ . . . treats him as a man who has been deceived but with over-abundance of epithets ; probably the copyist's contribution . . . to make a big sum of money out of it . . . I was promised a certain sum if I would countersign, but I avoided " what is ugly and what looks like it ", and may God bring them to penitence ! Enough.

Monday. I took chocolate with Solomon Ravel. Then I went, with David Naquet, to Jacob Goldschmidt, a rich and eminent Ashkenazi. It was a miserable day ; the snow was falling, the distance was great, and we could not find a coach. When we got there he behaved as all the Ashkenazim do, they are full of doubts and arguments ; the end of it was he gave us twelve francs. After that we went to M. Jacob Péreire, who had been twice to see me, he is a notable held in great consideration. I found at his house a letter from my son, written with modesty and respect, etc.

The evening before, Tuesday, the Marquis de Thomé, a Christian savant, came to see me with great demonstrations of respect, as well as another Christian of mark and an " Italian abbé ". They stayed nearly two hours, and I answered their questions. At the end the Marquis asked me to bless him : I

357

blessed him, as well as the other Chriftian—it is ftrange!

Next morning M. Fabre sent a fine coach for us to go to Versailles. We went there with M. Venture . . . I put on a handsome coat, and went to the sign of the "Cheval Rouge" in the "rue du Vieux-Versailles", at Versailles, where M. Fabre was in the house of a relation of his, a lady. We had a cordial reception and drank chocolate.

Then we went to Court. The Chriftian entered and we followed. We came firft into a beautiful room, adorned with numerous gilded columns arranged in two rows and supporting great candle-fticks. This is the gallery, and courtiers were ftanding about. We went through numerous royal apartments to reach the Council Chamber. At the upper end there is a canopy royally gilt and painted. There the king sits on his throne, while the courtiers take their places lower down the room. We next went through into the inner apartments, and ftopped at the further end of the chief room. After a little while some great lords began to pass us, and among them the King's brother, "Monsieur le Comte de Provence," called "Monsieur" and nothing more, and his younger brother, "Monsieur le Comte d'Artois." They ftayed beside me nearly five minutes. Then it was the King who passed, accompanied by great lords, and I pronounced the benediction for the King. He was dressed in red, wearing the "ordre d'azur", on which were arms. Hardly had he passed, when a lord came to say to M. Fabre, who was by my side, that the King was asking from what country I was ambassador. He answered him that I was not an ambassador, but that I came from Egypt out of "curiosity" to see what I could. Then we took our leave, saluted by all the company. Some of the "ladies" who were passing even made a curtsey to us, as their manner is.

We returned to the house of M. Fabre's relation, where great honour was done to me. He gave me a cup with its dish, in " porcelain ", which " Madame la Comtesse d'Artois " had presented to M. Fabre's relation ; the cup bore the arms of King Louis. He gave me also at the same time a little chest for taking papers, such as a newspaper ; this box was made of crystal and in the shape of a coat (?). The mistress of the house asked me what I should like to eat. I replied, some eggs cooked by my servant. They laid the table, we sat down, and I ate some bread with two boiled eggs. I then recited grace and afternoon prayer.

We took our places in the coach again ; everything was covered with snow. The Christian told me there was a collection here of great animals, but that on account of the snow they were shut up under cover, and could not be seen. The " garden " is twenty-one miles round, but in winter, when there is snow, nothing is to be seen. We got back without more ado. The Christian wanted to pay for the coach. It is wonderful to see with what kindly feelings of regard God had filled him for me. I give Him thanks and homage. . . . The relative of this M. Fabre and her daughter asked me to give them my blessing ; I went a little nearer to them and did bless them, but would not place my hand on their heads—it is extraordinary! Praised be God, who has elevated me, unworthy as I am of so many favours, lacking everything, in such wise; it is His mercy which has been granted to me; may He be for ever blessed and exalted !

In the evening, the eve of Thursday, the Marquis de Thomé came, with the Marquise de Croix. She took a seat near me and asked me to pray for her. Then she told me that she was studying the Bible, and that she saw angels and spirits who talked with her, but that, when they were evil, she repulsed them. She made offering of a " louis " for Hebron, and mentioned the *Baal-Shem* of London. She told me that a Jew had given her a book of Kabbalistic lore, and other matters she imparted to me too. How strange it all is ! As for myself, I answered her with such remarks as were suitable to her. Then she informed me that she was a lady held in much consideration and that at Avignon she had saved many Jews from the hands of the Inquisitor, that she was the daughter of a Marquis and her husband was a Marquis—so many tales of this Christian lady. But how many Christians have been led away by the man called *Baal-Shem* who, in his pride and presumption, has revealed the practices of the Kabbalah and the adjurations to so many nobles and ladies out of vanity. I have been plied with many questions about him, which I have answered.

On the morrow I went to the " Bibliothèque " and copied a part of the " Notes " of R. Isaiah on the Pentateuch. I went over the whole building ; it holds many rooms filled with manuscripts in all languages dealing with all the sciences and all the religions. Among the Chinese manuscripts there is a book, long in shape, made out of broad palm leaves, covered with a beautiful, upright clear handwriting. There are said to be nearly fifty-thousand manuscript volumes here. The " Bibliothèque " of printed books I have not, however, seen this time, but I did see all over it twenty-two years ago : it is marvellous and worthy of a king. This " Bibliothèque " of Paris is said to be the largest and most remarkable in the world.

On Friday I went to collect some of the offerings written down below for the Jeshiba " Kenesset Israel " of Hebron.

AZULAI

On the Sabbath—the day itself and the evening of
the day before—I was at the house of M. David
Naquet, where I was received with much honour ;
M. Abraham and M. Venture shared our meals.
May God reward them !

On Sunday we departed in peace from Paris,
accompanied, until we reached the outskirts of Paris,
by M. Solomon Ravel, M. David Naquet and
M. Hananel, who made the start with us in our coach
[they are Portuguese youths. Midday was past
when we arrived at the inn at Louvres]. . . .

July, 1778

On the eve of Wednesday, two hours before
midnight, we set off by " diligence ". We travelled
all night and all day until 7 p.m., at which hour we
came safe and sound to Paris. For about an hour or
thereabouts, however, we had stopped at midday in
the town of Pont-Saint-Maxence. In the evening
we were taken to the " douane " (custom house).
Great confusion prevailed by reason of the many
" diligences " journeying from French towns thither.
The customs officials were very busy, and when the
moment came for inspecting our baggage I was
trembling and agitated. But—thank God!—they
just opened my boxes, glanced through them a
moment, and no more ; praise God ! I took a coach
and we went to the house of M. David Naquet, who
was not at home until night, then we went to the hotel.
Thursday. Abraham had forgotten the " mantle " ;
so in the morning, after prayers, I sent him to fetch
it, and he found it again in the coach. God be praised!]
M. Fabre came, and we went to see his relative,
and he made me stay for four hours in her house.
He and his relative received me with much cordiality
and wanted me to eat with them ; but I told them
I would eat only eggs cooked by ourselves, and they

361

agreed to that. I asked this Christian to tell me in what he believed. He replied : in Adonai, the God of Israel. I examined him on the matter, and it seemed to me that it was so. I said then to him : Since it is thus, you will recite morning and evening the verse " Shema Israel ", you will observe the seven precepts, and you will beware of believing in more than one God in any wise whatever; you will believe only in the unity absolute, in Adonai, the God of Israel. [After this I went to see M. Péreire.]

On Friday I felt worn out and done up with the tribulations of our journey. On Wednesday I had found a letter from my beloved son, Raphael, which filled me with delight, and another came from him on the eve of Friday ; the first was affectionate and respectful to the last degree. We had emerged from the hazards of travel with damage to my great valise and also to the spring of my repeater watch; the former contained a multifarious collection of objects, and a great number of manuscripts and other things got scattered, crumpled, or soiled, the little white inkstand among the rest was broken, stained, and ruined. So I was obliged to purchase another box, and as to the things themselves I gave them away to a workman and was put in a very bad humour. Abraham, into the bargain, stupid lout, elected not to sleep that night and to treat me to a fit of the sulks. To-day again he has been railing against the carriage. What I do have to put up with from his stupidity and insolence !

The Sabbath we have spent with M. David Naquet. Mm. Abraham Vidal and Venture came, too, and dined with us. M. David and his worthy spouse distinguished themselves by the grand repasts they prepared for us, with liveliest demonstrations of respect and affection. Although I have now a synagogue near my hostelry, in the house of M. Hananel de

Milhaud, I have had to put myself to considerable
inconvenience and attend the synagogue of the
Avignon community because I am under obligations
to them, and the amphitroyon, M. David, is praying
there. I have been the recipient of many honours
there, more especially as when I went there for the
firſt time, M. Abraham Vidal asked me to pray that
the Queen might become pregnant, and now for
four months she has been. Whereupon M. Fabre
said to me : You see your prayer has borne fruit.
I answered him : Not by my own merit, but for my
anceſtors' sakes.

Thursday of Balak. When Sabbath was out, after
the evening prayer, Abraham Leon returned with
me from the synagogue. He is a young man
from Bayonne, who waited on me always in that
town, and happened to be now in Paris. I asked him
to buy some coal. Abraham inquired why I asked
him to do my buying, since he (Abraham) spares himself no trouble to serve me and objeċts to anyone
else making purchases for me. I was very much
annoyed and told Abraham Leon to buy me nothing.
So I have gone without "coffee" to see to what
lengths the insolence of Abraham, my servant, who
wants to tyrannize over me, would go. On Sunday
and Monday I have not spoken to him one word;
he has prepared neither food, nor coffee, and I have
lived on bread and cheese only. I was much hurt
because he did not put in an appearance all day until
midnight, but spent the time walking the ſtreets and
squares. Tuesday. I took pity on my servant,
spoke, and made advances to him. Hardly a day
passes but he makes me lose my temper.]

Thursday (14th Tammuz). I went with Monsieur
Fabre to pay a visit to the Comte de Maillebois.
He wrote on my behalf to the curator of the King's
manuscripts at the Bibliothèque, and supplied me

with an order to the same effect for me to have a manuscript given me to copy. We went there, and I took off the Notes of R. Isaiah di Trani on the Pentateuch. It is extraordinary to be allowed to take away a printed book, much more so a manuscript.

After that Monsieur Fabre took us to the house of the lady his relative. We had a meal there of eggs cooked on the fire by M. Ariana and of fruit. The talk turned on the intelligence of animals, and a story was told which is worth setting down. There is in Paris a palace which is the abode of soldiers who are either aged or wounded in the wars and guarded ordinarily by dogs, one of them being particularly large and strong. The custodians do not allow a strange dog to come in ; when the big dog goes out for a run outside, if he wants to, he comes back again and is recognized by the custodian. One day this big dog came back, bringing with him a strange dog of the thinnest and most starving description, which he hid under himself. The custodian was not going to allow the emaciated dog to pass, but the big dog posted himself in front of him, began to bark and hold his ground ; he took charge of the hungry dog and made it come in with him, the custodian turning a blind eye. The big dog then conducted the lean dog to the kitchen and installed him there for a week, during which time it ate and drank till it grew fat. Then the big dog took the dog which had been so lean outside again and told it to go. From that day the guest came at fixed times and waited for the big dog at the gate ; both went for a walk together, but the stranger came in no more.

In the evening my servant came and presented me with the trunk, in which he put his clothes, all torn and cut ; he told me he wanted to buy a bag costing five livres. " Go and buy it," I said, giving him six. He came back and told me he had spent ten. I replied that he was squandering money, and had just got to go and return the bag. He then answered that he had bought it for three, and owed the other three. So many lies are a great trouble to me. The worst of it is that the bag being quite small, he has had to bring along the trunk as well.

The same day brought me more trouble. At Bordeaux, M. Abraham Gradis had inquired of me if a man may repudiate his wife against her will. I had replied that it was forbidden, and he asked me to put this down in writing. In order not to refuse I wrote that it is forbidden to repudiate a first wife if she is virtuous, without fault, and a man has children by her. Now the case in question was that of Samuel Peixotto, at present before the courts here by reason of his desire to repudiate his wife, while she refused the act of repudiation. His avocat has made out a case in which particular reference has been made to my opinion. Concerning this, he said : " This man is an emissary whose business is to receive money for the poor of the Holy Land ; he has been delegated for the purpose because he is honest, not at all because he is learned. What he wrote was for money, or because he does not know these laws. For what he says he gives reference to no authority, and it is not to be found in all the Talmud ; it was simply said in the Hagadah that ' the altar weeps for him who repudiates his first wife ', but laws are not taken by inference from the Hagadah." After writing at great length in that sense he had the whole printed and distributed it to all the " Parlement ". It was all done on the advice of Liefmann Calmer [" Baron of Picquigny, vidame of Amiens ", who " professes " in a church, where he goes and kneels down, and sits in council]. With them is acting Raba of Bordeaux, so we get PoKeR (miscreant), the initials of Peixotto, Calmer, Raba. I have been greatly distressed at

having such a thing written and printed, which will
go to Amsterdam, Bordeaux, London, whose initials
make ABeL (mourning). God grant that it may be
an expiation for my sins and that the wicked may
not torment me any longer !

On Friday I was very much put out, I wanted
to start on Sunday morning, and Hananel de Milhaud
had already paid several visits to the diligence which
goes to Lyons and had arranged a price for the
clothes. He told me the thing would not be settled
till the Friday. But he did not bestir himself in time :
he went on Friday after 4 p.m. and then told me
there were no more places. Now I had everything
tied up and prepared for taking away on Friday
in order to spend the night of Friday to Saturday in
the diligence. I had written letters to that effect
to my dear son Raphael and to Amsterdam. I was
very much distressed.

On the eve of Sabbath I dined with the affectionate
M. David Naquet. I received great honour but was
unhappy and upset because Mordecai Venture had
brought to the synagogue the libel of Peixotto and
read to several persons what had been written about
me. And though he had no intention to humiliate
me, but only to show what a man this Peixotto was,
I felt shamed and said to myself, thinking of my
sins : What have I done to have the measure thus
heaped up. In addition, I was suffering from a change
of humours, because I had spent the whole night of
Thursday to Friday in copying the notes of R. Isaiah.

On the Sabbath morning came Israel Bernal,
his mouth full of his own praises and his tongue
prompt in lying compliments. In the evening came
his companion, Israel Vidal, who has a wife in Avignon.
He had an Ashkenazi servant, called Sara, whom he
suddenly took to wife, sending off at the same time
two children, one aged six the other four. They say

he took them to the " Foundlings ", then had them back again. He, too, was full of boasts about himself, saying that he was powerful and had the support of many noble men: just proud talk and haughtiness.

Sunday in Pinhas. When Sabbath was out, there came Aron Roget, who fell to telling tales of the sinfulness and abominations of Paris, which city is the prey of every form of debauchery. In especial he confessed his own numerous sins, with stories of his own doings and those of others that make your ears tingle at the sound of them. I am extremely grieved at seeing these Israelites so wallowing in the mud with Christians. May God in His mercy fill them with the desire for penitence, and to become good men once more, so that our soul may be redeemed in favour of His name. Amen !

That day I suffered much from the fast, owing to the heat.

On Sunday evening we went to the diligence and came to terms with the proprietor about the clothes.

In the evening, the eve of Tuesday, we went to the hostelry near the " bureau " of the " diligence ", which starts in the morning. We were accompanied by M. David Naquet, M. Mardochée, M. Hananel de Milhaud, M. Silveyra, and several young people. On arrival at the inn, we had a hunt for two pairs of " boots ", which I had handed over to Abraham and which he had forgotten when we got out of the carriage which had brought us thither. While we were talking Abraham went off. I discovered it at once, and went off to find him, but did not succeed. It was a very stupid thing for him to do, for we start early in the morning ; it was already midnight, and he might well have been lost in such a great place as Paris. That was all very, very troublesome for me. Mm. Vidal, father and son (the same Hananel mentioned already) slept at the hostelry in order to accompany us. May God reward them! When day came we started. All that week I suffered much discomfort, for there were only ten places in the diligence, and we were too close packed for the heat of the dog days. At midday we had lunch in the town of Chailly. Certainly the French people are cheerful and polite; they have treated us with respect and cordiality. Thanks be to God, and may He be for ever blessed.

PLATE VI

PASSOVER SUPPER

From an Italian Prayerbook, late XV century

[M^e. Bicart-Sée's collection]

NOTES

p. 6. [1] Romzom (in MS. Rome *Domiom*) is given in the *editio princeps* as one of the seven Kingdoms of Ethiopia.

p. 7. [2] Perhaps the mountains in Kerman, north of the Persian Gulf.

p. 8. [3] Stoning, burning, beheading, and strangling.

[4] *Lectio varia* Khozars.

p. 11. [5] There are two places named Havilah, one in Asia, perhaps near Bahrein, and the other in Africa, South of the Gulf of Suez, the Sinus Avalitis. The latter is here meant. See Gen. x, 29.

[6] These names vary greatly in the MSS. and printed sources and are difficult to identify. See Epstein's edition, p. 38.

p. 15. [7] I.e. is brought up as a student.

p. 16. [8] In Eldad's letter, § 14, the King is named Uzziel.

R. Chisdai

p. 22. [1] This is substantially A. I. K. Davidson's translation, published in the *Miscellany of Hebrew Literature*, vol. i, London, Trubner, 1872. The Hebrew text was first printed at Constantinople in 1577 in the *Kol Mebasser* of Isaac Akrish. Zedner edited most of Chisdai's letter, in Hebrew with a German translation and notes, in his *Answahl historischer Stücke* (Berlin, 1840). Harkavy published a Russian translation from a manuscript

NOTES

in Leningrad. Marquart in his *Osteuropäische und Ostasiatische Streifzäge* (Leipzig, 1903) doubts the authenticity of the King's Answer to Chisdai, but admits that the Khozars were Jews for at least a century. Later information has, however, strikingly confirmed the general accuracy of the story. Schechter published in the *Jewish Quarterly Review* (N.S. iii, 81), a remarkable twelfth century fragment from the Geniza of another letter from a subject of King Joseph. Manuscript material from the works of R. Judah ben Barzilai of Barcelona of the eleventh century gives fresh details about the Khozar Jews. The new material has lately been ably handled by the historian S. Dubnow in a Hebrew article on the Khozars in the *Livre d'Hommage* . . . *à* . . . *Poznanski* (Warsaw), 1927.

p. 25. [2] I.e. the Abbasids.
p. 26. [3] Otto the Great (912–73).
p. 27. [4] I.e. the Slavonians. Ibn Haukal, Mas'udi, etc., give Slavonia a wider extent than the modern Slavonia (see *Ibn Haukal*, ed. Ouseley, p. 10). Murphy in his *History of the Mahometan Empire in Spain* (p. 101) says : " Other embassies (to Abd er-Rahman III) . . . arrived . . . one from the Slavonians, called Ducu."
[5] Constantine VII (905–59).

BENJAMIN OF TUDELA

p. 42. [1] Here follows a description of the way to Jerusalem by way of the Archipelago.

Antioch and Sidon to Jerusalem, in the
account of which Benjamin writes :—

" Jerusalem has four gates—the gate
of Abraham, the gate of David, the gate
of Zion, and the gate of Gushpat, which
is the gate of Jehoshaphat, facing our
ancient Temple now called *Templum
Domini*. Upon the site of the sanctuary,
Omar ben al Khataab erected an edifice
with a very large and magnificent cupola,
into which the Gentiles do not bring any
image or effigy, but they merely come
there to pray. In front of this place is
the Western Wall which is one of the
Walls of the Holy of Holies. This is
called the Gate of Mercy, and thither
come all Jews to pray before the Wall of
the Court of the Temple."

After Jerusalem, Benjamin reached the
River Tigris by way of Bethlehem,
Hebron, Askelon, Tiberias, Damascus,
Baalbek, Hamath, Aleppo, and Nisibis.

p. 50. [2] Imadiya in Kurdistan.

p. 53. [3] This was in the eleventh century the capital
of the Ghaznavids.

[4] Near Meshed.

p. 54. [5] The ancient Rhages or Rages near Teheran.

p. 57. [6] Saadya Gaon translates the word by the
Arabic *lulu*.

p. 59. [7] Ibrig is by some authorities identified as
Ceylon.

p. 60. [8] We may take Benjamin's statement here
to mean that the independent Jews,
who lived in the mountainous country
behind Aden, crossed the Straits of Bab-
el-Mandeb and made war against the
inhabitants of the plains of Abyssinia.

371

Gingaleh, is probably Cangalur, a contraction of Kodungalur = Cranganore. The Cochin Jews call it Singili or Singoli (see p. 299). Gustav Oppert (*Semitic Studies in memory of Rev. Dr. Alexander Kohut,* Berlin, 1897, p. 410) identifies Gingaleh with the *Shinkala* of Abulfeda and *Cyncilum* of Odoric the Franciscan. *Chulan* is perhaps Quilon, like Khulam, on pp. 58–9, one of the MSS., indeed, reads *Khulan.*

RABBI PETACHIA OF RATISBON

p. 64. [1] Little Russia or Ukrainia.
p. 65. [2] The Black Sea.
p. 66. [3] The Crimea.
[4] The Dnieper and its tributaries.
[5] The Putrid Sea.
[6] Armenia.
[7] In the text *Heretics.*
[8] A famous fort on the Tigris.
p. 67. [9] I.e. the Byzantine Emperor.
[10] Mosul called Assur by Benjamin of Tudela.
p. 69. [11] His Jewish title was *Resh Methibta.*
[12] Probably Mostadhi (1170–9).
[13] I.e. the secrets of the Kabbalah.
p. 70. [14] I.e. the Bible.
p. 71. [15] I.e. Armenia.
[16] Literally Ethiopia and perhaps referring to the Falashas, but " Cush " may also include Arabia, as in the first verse of Esther.
p. 72. [17] It is a Persian custom to bury a Jew in his *Tallith.*
[18] A rabbinical metaphor meaning that two dignitaries, with like powers, cannot coexist within the same jurisdiction.

NOTES

p. 73. [19] Seleucia or Izannesopolis (Hit).

p. 74. [20] Benisch suggests that *grona* = the German *grün*.

p. 76. [21] Probably an owl.

[22] The Aboras which joins the Tigris at Carchemish.

p. 77. [23] I.e. "demolished and rebuilt" in allusion to its origin from a ruined building in Palestine.

[24] Perhaps Hillah.

p. 78. [25] The Rabbis of the Talmud (219–478) as distinguished from their predecessors the Tannaim, the Rabbis of the Mishna, who taught between 10 and 220.

p. 80. [26] Struthio-camelis or dromedary.

p. 84. [27] Josephus (Ant. ii, 9) says Ezra was buried in Jerusalem.

p. 85. [28] The Hebrew word for milk = Aleppo.

p. 86. [29] R. Judah the Prince (180) the compiler of the Mishna.

p. 88. [30] Monastery or Church.

p. 89. [31] Probably a crucifix.

p. 90. [32] Zachariah xiv, 4 ; Isaiah lii, 8.

Cairo Geniza

p. 100. [1] This fragment was published with a facsimile in Adler's *Von Ghetto zu Ghetto* (Stuttgart, 1909, pp. 197–200), and is now in the J.T.S. Library, New York.

p. 101. [2] *Baspas* is a medical herb *peganum harmata, ruta.*

Judah-Al-Harizi.

p. 111. [1] See Professor Hirschfeld's article in the *J.W.R.*, xv, 695.

p. 113. [2] This simile is rather frequent in Arabic poetry.

373

NOTES

RABBI JACOB

ISAAC CHELO

ELIJAH OF FERRARA

OBADIAH DA BERTINORO

p. 210. [1] = Monsignor.

p. 213. [2] Meshullam is the writer of the letters translated on pp. 156–208, and must have made a second voyage to the East.

p. 214. [3] This is perhaps Zucco, an island between Palermo and Trapani.

p. 217. [4] Solyman II.

p. 222. [5] By *Tapedi* the low sofas of the East are probably meant.

p. 224. [6] The author regards Prester John's country as Abyssinia.

p. 225. [7] Ibn Ezra also makes this wrong statement. The error probably arose from misreading the Samaritan script.

p. 226. [8] Not by astronomical calculation as the Rabbanites do.

p. 230. [9] The reading of the manuscript is doubtful ; perhaps El-Hamara is meant.

p. 231. [10] About Dimo (Fostat) compare Munk's note in Asher's *Benjamin of Tudela*, vol. ii, p. 198.

p. 233. [11] Hebron is so named in Arabic because the Arabs call Abraham *Kalil Allah*, " the beloved of God."

p. 242. [12] From the Arabic *nafar*, to be frightened.

[13] Perhaps the Arabic *nāib*, which means a magistrate.

p. 249. [14] This letter was probably addressed to Emanuel Chai of Camerino, referred to on pp. 245 and 248.

DAVID REUBENI

p. 270. [1] שור in text, perhaps the משוורתא of Purim, mentioned in the Talmud (Sanhedrin 64B) referring to the ancient custom of kindling a Purim bonfire and jumping across it through a hoop. If so, David associated it with the redemption he hoped for from his approaching visit to the Pope.

p. 299. ² *Singoli* is almoſt certainly Cranganore (see *supra*, note to p. 60). Steinschneider thinks it means Ceylon and Eisenſtein, Senegal, but neither such view is tenable.

p. 302. ³ This was the famous Diogo Pires, after his conversion called Solomon Molcho, author, myſtic, and martyr, burnt by the Inquisition in 1532.

SAMUEL JEMSEL

p. 329. ¹ I.e. 5201 = 21ſt July, 1641.

p. 330. ² Probably Kudros (Cytorus of Paphlagonia).

³ 1ſt Auguſt.

⁴ 17th September, 202 (1641).

AZULAI

p. 345. ¹ From his autograph Diary *Ma 'gal Tob* now in the Jewish Theological Seminary Library, New York, partly published by Freimann in the *Mekize Nirdamim*, Berlin, 1921. See also Marx and Liber in *R.E.J.* lxv, 243–73.

p. 347. ² This refers to the quarrel between Jacob Kimchi and Sahlom Buzaglo, described by Duschinsky in *Jew. Hiſt. Soc. Trans.*, vii, 272–90.

PLATE VII

SCENES FROM THE EXODUS FROM EGYPT

From an Italian Hagadah, XIV century

[British Museum, Add. 27210]

INDEX

INDEX

379

INDEX

INDEX

INDEX

INDEX

INDEX

INDEX

John III, King of Portugal, xviii, 267, 283–91, 297–308, 319–20, 328
John de Brienne, King of Jerusalem, xv, 103
Jonadab b. Rechab, 83
Jonah, the Prophet, 42, 87–8, 92, 97, 145
Jonathan b. Uzziel, his tomb, 94, 107, 123; ha Cohen of Lunel (called Exilarch), xiv, 103
Jordan, 96, 126
Josce b. Yechiel, Archpresbyter of Jews in England, xv
José, R., the Galilean, 109, 123; b. Pedat, 107; b. Yokrat, 123
Joseph, 96, 105, 120; ibn Abulmana, 101; Amarkala the Levite, 54; the astronomer, 42, 52; del Medigo, xxi; Don, Nasi, 16; King of Habor, son of Solomon, 251, 266, 290–1; King of the Khozars, 22–36; of Spain, x; of the Slavonian embassy, 23; R. Haggaris, 25; R. Shir-Guru, 41
Joshua, 13, 16, 86–7, 95
Judah, tribe, 5, 9; b. Bethera, 67, 141; Hadassi, 4; Halevi, xi, 37; Halevi, his grandson Judah, ib.; al Harizi, xiv, xv, 103, 111–14, 373; b. Ilai, 124; b. Korash, 4; b. Meir, 148; b. Nehorai, 86; R., the Prince, 43, 86, 115, notes; b. Tema, 109, 123; the Pious, bar Samuel, 64, 68
Judan, R., his tomb, 110
Judas Maccabaeus, his tomb, 96
Jugglery, 40

Kabbalah, Kabbalists, xvi, 69, 91, 133, 139, 141, 144, 149, 267, 351, 354, 360
Kairouan, 3, 4, 15
Karaïtes, 5, 64, 153, 161, 171, 225–8, 337–9; in Abyssinia, see Falashas, 153
Karkisiya (Carchemish), 43
Katifa = el-Katif, 57
Kedar = Little Russia, 64–5, 67
Kefar (Village), Amuka, 107; Bar'am, 107, 110, 123; Chitim, Chitin, Chitia, 125, 147; Damin Pharuz, 122; Duna, 127; Hanan, 12, 121, 147; Hananiah, 106–7, 147; Hittin, see Chitim; Janak, 125; Manda, 125, 144; Nachum (Capernaum), 147; Nebarta, 107; Raphadia, 122
Kenisat (Synagogue), al-Irakiyyin, 62; al-Shamiyyin, 62
Keshisha, R., his tomb, 128
Khaibar, xviii, xix; see also Habor
al-Khamlij, 3
al-Khan, 179
Khordadhbeh, ibn, x, 2–3
Khorasan, 22, 31, 49
Khozaria (Crimea), 39, 65–7, 83
Khozars, xi, 3, 22–36
Khulam = Quilon, 58
Khuzistan, 57
Kief, 64
Kifl, 74
al-Kifti (al-Qifti), 101
Kimchi, David, 356; Jacob, 348, notes
King of Abyssinia, see Omara; Abuakra of Elgel 255; of Cyprus, see Ferdinand; of Egypt, the Sultan, 170; of Fez, see Sherif; of France, see Louis XV, Louis XVI; of Greece, see Emanuel; of

INDEX

INDEX

INDEX

INDEX

INDEX

INDEX

PLATE VIII

MOSES ADDRESSING THE CHILDREN OF ISRAEL (Deut. xxix. 11). 1296

EGYPTIANS IN THE RED SEA.   XV CENTURY

From illuminated Italian Manuscripts in the Frankfort City Library

A CATALOG OF SELECTED
DOVER BOOKS
IN ALL FIELDS OF INTEREST

A CATALOG OF SELECTED DOVER BOOKS IN ALL FIELDS OF INTEREST

DRAWINGS OF REMBRANDT, edited by Seymour Slive. Updated Lippmann, Hofstede de Groot edition, with definitive scholarly apparatus. All portraits, biblical sketches, landscapes, nudes. Oriental figures, classical studies, together with selection of work by followers. 550 illustrations. Total of 630pp. 9⅛ × 12¼.
21485-0, 21486-9 Pa., Two-vol. set $25.00

GHOST AND HORROR STORIES OF AMBROSE BIERCE, Ambrose Bierce. 24 tales vividly imagined, strangely prophetic, and decades ahead of their time in technical skill: "The Damned Thing," "An Inhabitant of Carcosa," "The Eyes of the Panther," "Moxon's Master," and 20 more. 199pp. 5⅜ × 8½. 20767-6 Pa. $3.95

ETHICAL WRITINGS OF MAIMONIDES, Maimonides. Most significant ethical works of great medieval sage, newly translated for utmost precision, readability. Laws Concerning Character Traits, Eight Chapters, more. 192pp. 5⅜ × 8½.
24522-5 Pa. $4.50

THE EXPLORATION OF THE COLORADO RIVER AND ITS CANYONS, J. W. Powell. Full text of Powell's 1,000-mile expedition down the fabled Colorado in 1869. Superb account of terrain, geology, vegetation, Indians, famine, mutiny, treacherous rapids, mighty canyons, during exploration of last unknown part of continental U.S. 400pp. 5⅜ × 8½. 20094-9 Pa. $6.95

HISTORY OF PHILOSOPHY, Julián Marías. Clearest one-volume history on the market. Every major philosopher and dozens of others, to Existentialism and later. 505pp. 5⅜ × 8½. 21739-6 Pa. $8.50

ALL ABOUT LIGHTNING, Martin A. Uman. Highly readable non-technical survey of nature and causes of lightning, thunderstorms, ball lightning, St. Elmo's Fire, much more. Illustrated. 192pp. 5⅜ × 8½. 25237-X Pa. $5.95

SAILING ALONE AROUND THE WORLD, Captain Joshua Slocum. First man to sail around the world, alone, in small boat. One of great feats of seamanship told in delightful manner. 67 illustrations. 294pp. 5⅜ × 8½. 20326-3 Pa. $4.50

LETTERS AND NOTES ON THE MANNERS, CUSTOMS AND CONDITIONS OF THE NORTH AMERICAN INDIANS, George Catlin. Classic account of life among Plains Indians: ceremonies, hunt, warfare, etc. 312 plates. 572pp. of text. 6⅛ × 9¼. 22118-0, 22119-9 Pa. Two-vol. set $15.90

ALASKA: The Harriman Expedition, 1899, John Burroughs, John Muir, et al. Informative, engrossing accounts of two-month, 9,000-mile expedition. Native peoples, wildlife, forests, geography, salmon industry, glaciers, more. Profusely illustrated. 240 black-and-white line drawings. 124 black-and-white photographs. 3 maps. Index. 576pp. 5⅜ × 8½. 25109-8 Pa. $11.95

CATALOG OF DOVER BOOKS

THE BOOK OF BEASTS: Being a Translation from a Latin Bestiary of the Twelfth Century, T. H. White. Wonderful catalog real and fanciful beasts: manticore, griffin, phoenix, amphivius, jaculus, many more. White's witty erudite commentary on scientific, historical aspects. Fascinating glimpse of medieval mind. Illustrated. 296pp. 5⅜ × 8¼. (Available in U.S. only)   24609-4 Pa. $5.95

FRANK LLOYD WRIGHT: ARCHITECTURE AND NATURE With 160 Illustrations, Donald Hoffmann. Profusely illustrated study of influence of nature—especially prairie—on Wright's designs for Fallingwater, Robie House, Guggenheim Museum, other masterpieces. 96pp. 9¼ × 10¾.   25098-9 Pa. $7.95

FRANK LLOYD WRIGHT'S FALLINGWATER, Donald Hoffmann. Wright's famous waterfall house: planning and construction of organic idea. History of site, owners, Wright's personal involvement. Photographs of various stages of building. Preface by Edgar Kaufmann, Jr. 100 illustrations. 112pp. 9¼ × 10.
23671-4 Pa. $7.95

YEARS WITH FRANK LLOYD WRIGHT: Apprentice to Genius, Edgar Tafel. Insightful memoir by a former apprentice presents a revealing portrait of Wright the man, the inspired teacher, the greatest American architect. 372 black-and-white illustrations. Preface. Index. vi + 228pp. 8¼ × 11.   24801-1 Pa. $9.95

THE STORY OF KING ARTHUR AND HIS KNIGHTS, Howard Pyle. Enchanting version of King Arthur fable has delighted generations with imaginative narratives of exciting adventures and unforgettable illustrations by the author. 41 illustrations. xviii + 313pp. 6⅛ × 9¼.   21445-1 Pa. $5.95

THE GODS OF THE EGYPTIANS, E. A. Wallis Budge. Thorough coverage of numerous gods of ancient Egypt by foremost Egyptologist. Information on evolution of cults, rites and gods; the cult of Osiris; the Book of the Dead and its rites; the sacred animals and birds; Heaven and Hell; and more. 956pp. 6⅛ × 9¼.
22055-9, 22056-7 Pa., Two-vol. set $20.00

A THEOLOGICO-POLITICAL TREATISE, Benedict Spinoza. Also contains unfinished *Political Treatise*. Great classic on religious liberty, theory of government on common consent. R. Elwes translation. Total of 421pp. 5⅜ × 8½.
20249-6 Pa. $6.95

INCIDENTS OF TRAVEL IN CENTRAL AMERICA, CHIAPAS, AND YUCATAN, John L. Stephens. Almost single-handed discovery of Maya culture; exploration of ruined cities, monuments, temples; customs of Indians. 115 drawings. 892pp. 5⅜ × 8½.   22404-X, 22405-8 Pa., Two-vol. set $15.90

LOS CAPRICHOS, Francisco Goya. 80 plates of wild, grotesque monsters and caricatures. Prado manuscript included. 183pp. 6⅞ × 9⅜.   22384-1 Pa. $4.95

AUTOBIOGRAPHY: The Story of My Experiments with Truth, Mohandas K. Gandhi. Not hagiography, but Gandhi in his own words. Boyhood, legal studies, purification, the growth of the Satyagraha (nonviolent protest) movement. Critical, inspiring work of the man who freed India. 480pp. 5⅜ × 8½. (Available in U.S. only)
24593-4 Pa. $6.95

ILLUSTRATED DICTIONARY OF HISTORIC ARCHITECTURE, edited by Cyril M. Harris. Extraordinary compendium of clear, concise definitions for over 5,000 important architectural terms complemented by over 2,000 line drawings. Covers full spectrum of architecture from ancient ruins to 20th-century Modernism. Preface. 592pp. 7½ × 9⅜. 24444-X Pa. $14.95

THE NIGHT BEFORE CHRISTMAS, Clement Moore. Full text, and woodcuts from original 1848 book. Also critical, historical material. 19 illustrations. 40pp. 4⅝ × 6. 22797-9 Pa. $2.25

THE LESSON OF JAPANESE ARCHITECTURE: 165 Photographs, Jiro Harada. Memorable gallery of 165 photographs taken in the 1930's of exquisite Japanese homes of the well-to-do and historic buildings. 13 line diagrams. 192pp. 8⅜ × 11¼. 24778-3 Pa. $8.95

THE AUTOBIOGRAPHY OF CHARLES DARWIN AND SELECTED LET-TERS, edited by Francis Darwin. The fascinating life of eccentric genius composed of an intimate memoir by Darwin (intended for his children); commentary by his son, Francis; hundreds of fragments from notebooks, journals, papers; and letters to and from Lyell, Hooker, Huxley, Wallace and Henslow. xi + 365pp. 5⅜ × 8. 20479-0 Pa. $5.95

WONDERS OF THE SKY: Observing Rainbows, Comets, Eclipses, the Stars and Other Phenomena, Fred Schaaf. Charming, easy-to-read poetic guide to all manner of celestial events visible to the naked eye. Mock suns, glories, Belt of Venus, more. Illustrated. 299pp. 5¼ × 8¼. 24402-4 Pa. $7.95

BURNHAM'S CELESTIAL HANDBOOK, Robert Burnham, Jr. Thorough guide to the stars beyond our solar system. Exhaustive treatment. Alphabetical by constellation: Andromeda to Cetus in Vol. 1; Chamaeleon to Orion in Vol. 2; and Pavo to Vulpecula in Vol. 3. Hundreds of illustrations. Index in Vol. 3. 2,000pp. 6⅛ × 9¼. 23567-X, 23568-8, 23673-0 Pa., Three-vol. set $36.85

STAR NAMES: Their Lore and Meaning, Richard Hinckley Allen. Fascinating history of names various cultures have given to constellations and literary and folkloristic uses that have been made of stars. Indexes to subjects. Arabic and Greek names. Biblical references. Bibliography. 563pp. 5⅜ × 8½. 21079-0 Pa. $7.95

THIRTY YEARS THAT SHOOK PHYSICS: The Story of Quantum Theory, George Gamow. Lucid, accessible introduction to influential theory of energy and matter. Careful explanations of Dirac's anti-particles, Bohr's model of the atom, much more. 12 plates. Numerous drawings. 240pp. 5⅜ × 8½. 24895-X Pa. $4.95

CHINESE DOMESTIC FURNITURE IN PHOTOGRAPHS AND MEASURED DRAWINGS, Gustav Ecke. A rare volume, now affordably priced for antique collectors, furniture buffs and art historians. Detailed review of styles ranging from early Shang to late Ming. Unabridged republication. 161 black-and-white drawings, photos. Total of 224pp. 8⅜ × 11¼. (Available in U.S. only) 25171-3 Pa. $12.95

VINCENT VAN GOGH: A Biography, Julius Meier-Graefe. Dynamic, penetrating study of artist's life, relationship with brother, Theo, painting techniques, travels, more. Readable, engrossing. 160pp. 5⅜ × 8½. (Available in U.S. only) 25253-1 Pa. $3.95

HOW TO WRITE, Gertrude Stein. Gertrude Stein claimed anyone could understand her unconventional writing—here are clues to help. Fascinating improvisations, language experiments, explanations illuminate Stein's craft and the art of writing. Total of 414pp. 4⅝ × 6⅜. 23144-5 Pa. $5.95

ADVENTURES AT SEA IN THE GREAT AGE OF SAIL: Five Firsthand Narratives, edited by Elliot Snow. Rare true accounts of exploration, whaling, shipwreck, fierce natives, trade, shipboard life, more. 33 illustrations. Introduction. 353pp. 5⅜ × 8½. 25177-2 Pa. $7.95

THE HERBAL OR GENERAL HISTORY OF PLANTS, John Gerard. Classic descriptions of about 2,850 plants—with over 2,700 illustrations—includes Latin and English names, physical descriptions, varieties, time and place of growth, more. 2,706 illustrations. xlv + 1,678pp. 8½ × 12¼. 23147-X Cloth. $75.00

DOROTHY AND THE WIZARD IN OZ, L. Frank Baum. Dorothy and the Wizard visit the center of the Earth, where people are vegetables, glass houses grow and Oz characters reappear. Classic sequel to Wizard of Oz. 256pp. 5⅜ × 8. 24714-7 Pa. $4.95

SONGS OF EXPERIENCE: Facsimile Reproduction with 26 Plates in Full Color, William Blake. This facsimile of Blake's original "Illuminated Book" reproduces 26 full-color plates from a rare 1826 edition. Includes "The Tyger," "London," "Holy Thursday," and other immortal poems. 26 color plates. Printed text of poems. 48pp. 5¼ × 7. 24636-1 Pa. $3.50

SONGS OF INNOCENCE, William Blake. The first and most popular of Blake's famous "Illuminated Books," in a facsimile edition reproducing all 31 brightly colored plates. Additional printed text of each poem. 64pp. 5¼ × 7. 22764-2 Pa. $3.50

PRECIOUS STONES, Max Bauer. Classic, thorough study of diamonds, rubies, emeralds, garnets, etc.: physical character, occurrence, properties, use, similar topics. 20 plates, 8 in color. 94 figures. 659pp. 6⅛ × 9¼. 21910-0, 21911-9 Pa., Two-vol. set $14.90

ENCYCLOPEDIA OF VICTORIAN NEEDLEWORK, S. F. A. Caulfeild and Blanche Saward. Full, precise descriptions of stitches, techniques for dozens of needlecrafts—most exhaustive reference of its kind. Over 800 figures. Total of 679pp. 8⅛ × 11. Two volumes. Vol. 1 22800-2 Pa. $10.95 Vol. 2 22801-0 Pa. $10.95

THE MARVELOUS LAND OF OZ, L. Frank Baum. Second Oz book, the Scarecrow and Tin Woodman are back with hero named Tip, Oz magic. 136 illustrations. 287pp. 5⅜ × 8½. 20692-0 Pa. $5.95

WILD FOWL DECOYS, Joel Barber. Basic book on the subject, by foremost authority and collector. Reveals history of decoy making and rigging, place in American culture, different kinds of decoys, how to make them, and how to use them. 140 plates. 156pp. 7⅞ × 10¾. 20011-6 Pa. $7.95

HISTORY OF LACE, Mrs. Bury Palliser. Definitive, profusely illustrated chronicle of lace from earliest times to late 19th century. Laces of Italy, Greece, England, France, Belgium, etc. Landmark of needlework scholarship. 266 illustrations. 672pp. 6⅛ × 9¼. 24742-2 Pa. $14.95

ILLUSTRATED GUIDE TO SHAKER FURNITURE, Robert Meader. All furniture and appurtenances, with much on unknown local styles. 235 photos. 146pp. 9 × 12. 22819-3 Pa. $7.95

WHALE SHIPS AND WHALING: A Pictorial Survey, George Francis Dow. Over 200 vintage engravings, drawings, photographs of barks, brigs, cutters, other vessels. Also harpoons, lances, whaling guns, many other artifacts. Comprehensive text by foremost authority. 207 black-and-white illustrations. 288pp. 6 × 9. 24808-9 Pa. $8.95

THE BERTRAMS, Anthony Trollope. Powerful portrayal of blind self-will and thwarted ambition includes one of Trollope's most heartrending love stories. 497pp. 5⅜ × 8½. 25119-5 Pa. $8.95

ADVENTURES WITH A HAND LENS, Richard Headstrom. Clearly written guide to observing and studying flowers and grasses, fish scales, moth and insect wings, egg cases, buds, feathers, seeds, leaf scars, moss, molds, ferns, common crystals, etc.—all with an ordinary, inexpensive magnifying glass. 209 exact line drawings aid in your discoveries. 220pp. 5⅜ × 8½. 23330-8 Pa. $3.95

RODIN ON ART AND ARTISTS, Auguste Rodin. Great sculptor's candid, wide-ranging comments on meaning of art; great artists; relation of sculpture to poetry, painting, music; philosophy of life, more. 76 superb black-and-white illustrations of Rodin's sculpture, drawings and prints. 119pp. 8⅜ × 11¼. 24487-3 Pa. $6.95

FIFTY CLASSIC FRENCH FILMS, 1912–1982: A Pictorial Record, Anthony Slide. Memorable stills from Grand Illusion, Beauty and the Beast, Hiroshima, Mon Amour, many more. Credits, plot synopses, reviews, etc. 160pp. 8¼ × 11. 25256-6 Pa. $11.95

THE PRINCIPLES OF PSYCHOLOGY, William James. Famous long course complete, unabridged. Stream of thought, time perception, memory, experimental methods; great work decades ahead of its time. 94 figures. 1,391pp. 5⅜ × 8½. 20381-6, 20382-4 Pa., Two-vol. set $19.90

BODIES IN A BOOKSHOP, R. T. Campbell. Challenging mystery of blackmail and murder with ingenious plot and superbly drawn characters. In the best tradition of British suspense fiction. 192pp. 5⅜ × 8½. 24720-1 Pa. $3.95

CALLAS: PORTRAIT OF A PRIMA DONNA, George Jellinek. Renowned commentator on the musical scene chronicles incredible career and life of the most controversial, fascinating, influential operatic personality of our time. 64 black-and-white photographs. 416pp. 5⅜ × 8¼. 25047-4 Pa. $7.95

GEOMETRY, RELATIVITY AND THE FOURTH DIMENSION, Rudolph Rucker. Exposition of fourth dimension, concepts of relativity as Flatland characters continue adventures. Popular, easily followed yet accurate, profound. 141 illustrations. 133pp. 5⅜ × 8½. 23400-2 Pa. $3.50

HOUSEHOLD STORIES BY THE BROTHERS GRIMM, with pictures by Walter Crane. 53 classic stories—Rumpelstiltskin, Rapunzel, Hansel and Gretel, the Fisherman and his Wife, Snow White, Tom Thumb, Sleeping Beauty, Cinderella, and so much more—lavishly illustrated with original 19th century drawings. 114 illustrations. x + 269pp. 5⅜ × 8½. 21080-4 Pa. $4.50

SUNDIALS, Albert Waugh. Far and away the best, most thorough coverage of ideas, mathematics concerned, types, construction, adjusting anywhere. Over 100 illustrations. 230pp. 5⅜ × 8½. 22947-5 Pa. $4.00

PICTURE HISTORY OF THE NORMANDIE: With 190 Illustrations, Frank O. Braynard. Full story of legendary French ocean liner: Art Deco interiors, design innovations, furnishings, celebrities, maiden voyage, tragic fire, much more. Extensive text. 144pp. 8⅞ × 11¾. 25257-4 Pa. $9.95

THE FIRST AMERICAN COOKBOOK: A Facsimile of "American Cookery," 1796, Amelia Simmons. Facsimile of the first American-written cookbook published in the United States contains authentic recipes for colonial favorites—pumpkin pudding, winter squash pudding, spruce beer, Indian slapjacks, and more. Introductory Essay and Glossary of colonial cooking terms. 80pp. 5⅜ × 8½. 24710-4 Pa. $3.50

101 PUZZLES IN THOUGHT AND LOGIC, C. R. Wylie, Jr. Solve murders and robberies, find out which fishermen are liars, how a blind man could possibly identify a color—purely by your own reasoning! 107pp. 5⅜ × 8½. 20367-0 Pa. $2.00

THE BOOK OF WORLD-FAMOUS MUSIC—CLASSICAL, POPULAR AND FOLK, James J. Fuld. Revised and enlarged republication of landmark work in musico-bibliography. Full information about nearly 1,000 songs and compositions including first lines of music and lyrics. New supplement. Index. 800pp. 5⅜ × 8¼. 24857-7 Pa. $14.95

ANTHROPOLOGY AND MODERN LIFE, Franz Boas. Great anthropologist's classic treatise on race and culture. Introduction by Ruth Bunzel. Only inexpensive paperback edition. 255pp. 5⅜ × 8½. 25245-0 Pa. $5.95

THE TALE OF PETER RABBIT, Beatrix Potter. The inimitable Peter's terrifying adventure in Mr. McGregor's garden, with all 27 wonderful, full-color Potter illustrations. 55pp. 4¼ × 5½. (Available in U.S. only) 22827-4 Pa. $1.75

THREE PROPHETIC SCIENCE FICTION NOVELS, H. G. Wells. *When the Sleeper Wakes, A Story of the Days to Come* and *The Time Machine* (full version). 335pp. 5⅜ × 8½. (Available in U.S. only) 20605-X Pa. $5.95

APICIUS COOKERY AND DINING IN IMPERIAL ROME, edited and translated by Joseph Dommers Vehling. Oldest known cookbook in existence offers readers a clear picture of what foods Romans ate, how they prepared them, etc. 49 illustrations. 301pp. 6⅛ × 9¼. 23563-7 Pa. $6.00

SHAKESPEARE LEXICON AND QUOTATION DICTIONARY, Alexander Schmidt. Full definitions, locations, shades of meaning of every word in plays and poems. More than 50,000 exact quotations. 1,485pp. 6½ × 9¼. 22726-X, 22727-8 Pa., Two-vol. set $27.90

THE WORLD'S GREAT SPEECHES, edited by Lewis Copeland and Lawrence W. Lamm. Vast collection of 278 speeches from Greeks to 1970. Powerful and effective models; unique look at history. 842pp. 5⅜ × 8½. 20468-5 Pa. $10.95

THE BLUE FAIRY BOOK, Andrew Lang. The first, most famous collection, with many familiar tales: Little Red Riding Hood, Aladdin and the Wonderful Lamp, Puss in Boots, Sleeping Beauty, Hansel and Gretel, Rumpelstiltskin; 37 in all. 138 illustrations. 390pp. 5⅜ × 8½.   21437-0 Pa. $5.95

THE STORY OF THE CHAMPIONS OF THE ROUND TABLE, Howard Pyle. Sir Launcelot, Sir Tristram and Sir Percival in spirited adventures of love and triumph retold in Pyle's inimitable style. 50 drawings, 31 full-page. xviii + 329pp. 6½ × 9¼.   21883-X Pa. $6.95

AUDUBON AND HIS JOURNALS, Maria Audubon. Unmatched two-volume portrait of the great artist, naturalist and author contains his journals, an excellent biography by his granddaughter, expert annotations by the noted ornithologist, Dr. Elliott Coues, and 37 superb illustrations. Total of 1,200pp. 5⅜ × 8.
Vol. I 25143-8 Pa. $8.95
Vol. II 25144-6 Pa. $8.95

GREAT DINOSAUR HUNTERS AND THEIR DISCOVERIES, Edwin H. Colbert. Fascinating, lavishly illustrated chronicle of dinosaur research, 1820's to 1960. Achievements of Cope, Marsh, Brown, Buckland, Mantell, Huxley, many others. 384pp. 5¼ × 8¼.   24701-5 Pa. $6.95

THE TASTEMAKERS, Russell Lynes. Informal, illustrated social history of American taste 1850's–1950's. First popularized categories Highbrow, Lowbrow, Middlebrow. 129 illustrations. New (1979) afterword. 384pp. 6 × 9.
23993-4 Pa. $6.95

DOUBLE CROSS PURPOSES, Ronald A. Knox. A treasure hunt in the Scottish Highlands, an old map, unidentified corpse, surprise discoveries keep reader guessing in this cleverly intricate tale of financial skullduggery. 2 black-and-white maps. 320pp. 5⅜ × 8½. (Available in U.S. only)   25032-6 Pa. $5.95

AUTHENTIC VICTORIAN DECORATION AND ORNAMENTATION IN FULL COLOR: 46 Plates from "Studies in Design," Christopher Dresser. Superb full-color lithographs reproduced from rare original portfolio of a major Victorian designer. 48pp. 9¼ × 12¼.   25083-0 Pa. $7.95

PRIMITIVE ART, Franz Boas. Remains the best text ever prepared on subject, thoroughly discussing Indian, African, Asian, Australian, and, especially, Northern American primitive art. Over 950 illustrations show ceramics, masks, totem poles, weapons, textiles, paintings, much more. 376pp. 5⅜ × 8.   20025-6 Pa. $6.95

SIDELIGHTS ON RELATIVITY, Albert Einstein. Unabridged republication of two lectures delivered by the great physicist in 1920–21. *Ether and Relativity* and *Geometry and Experience*. Elegant ideas in non-mathematical form, accessible to intelligent layman. vi + 56pp. 5⅜ × 8½.   24511-X Pa. $2.95

THE WIT AND HUMOR OF OSCAR WILDE, edited by Alvin Redman. More than 1,000 ripostes, paradoxes, wisecracks: Work is the curse of the drinking classes, I can resist everything except temptation, etc. 258pp. 5⅜ × 8½.   20602-5 Pa. $3.95

ADVENTURES WITH A MICROSCOPE, Richard Headstrom. 59 adventures with clothing fibers, protozoa, ferns and lichens, roots and leaves, much more. 142 illustrations. 232pp. 5⅜ × 8½.   23471-1 Pa. $3.95

PLANTS OF THE BIBLE, Harold N. Moldenke and Alma L. Moldenke. Standard reference to all 230 plants mentioned in Scriptures. Latin name, biblical reference, uses, modern identity, much more. Unsurpassed encyclopedic resource for scholars, botanists, nature lovers, students of Bible. Bibliography. Indexes. 123 black-and-white illustrations. 384pp. 6 × 9. 25069-5 Pa. $8.95

FAMOUS AMERICAN WOMEN: A Biographical Dictionary from Colonial Times to the Present, Robert McHenry, ed. From Pocahontas to Rosa Parks, 1,035 distinguished American women documented in separate biographical entries. Accurate, up-to-date data, numerous categories, spans 400 years. Indices. 493pp. 6½ × 9¼. 24523-3 Pa. $9.95

THE FABULOUS INTERIORS OF THE GREAT OCEAN LINERS IN HISTORIC PHOTOGRAPHS, William H. Miller, Jr. Some 200 superb photographs capture exquisite interiors of world's great "floating palaces"—1890's to 1980's: *Titanic, Ile de France, Queen Elizabeth, United States, Europa,* more. Approx. 200 black-and-white photographs. Captions. Text. Introduction. 160pp. 8⅞ × 11¾. 24756-2 Pa. $9.95

THE GREAT LUXURY LINERS, 1927–1954: A Photographic Record, William H. Miller, Jr. Nostalgic tribute to heyday of ocean liners. 186 photos of Ile de France, Normandie, Leviathan, Queen Elizabeth, United States, many others. Interior and exterior views. Introduction. Captions. 160pp. 9 × 12. 24056-8 Pa. $9.95

A NATURAL HISTORY OF THE DUCKS, John Charles Phillips. Great landmark of ornithology offers complete detailed coverage of nearly 200 species and subspecies of ducks: gadwall, sheldrake, merganser, pintail, many more. 74 full-color plates, 102 black-and-white. Bibliography. Total of 1,920pp. 8⅜ × 11¼. 25141-1, 25142-X Cloth. Two-vol. set $100.00

THE SEAWEED HANDBOOK: An Illustrated Guide to Seaweeds from North Carolina to Canada, Thomas F. Lee. Concise reference covers 78 species. Scientific and common names, habitat, distribution, more. Finding keys for easy identification. 224pp. 5⅜ × 8½. 25215-9 Pa. $5.95

THE TEN BOOKS OF ARCHITECTURE: The 1755 Leoni Edition, Leon Battista Alberti. Rare classic helped introduce the glories of ancient architecture to the Renaissance. 68 black-and-white plates. 336pp. 8⅜ × 11¼. 25239-6 Pa. $14.95

MISS MACKENZIE, Anthony Trollope. Minor masterpieces by Victorian master unmasks many truths about life in 19th-century England. First inexpensive edition in years. 392pp. 5⅜ × 8½. 25201-9 Pa. $7.95

THE RIME OF THE ANCIENT MARINER, Gustave Doré, Samuel Taylor Coleridge. Dramatic engravings considered by many to be his greatest work. The terrifying space of the open sea, the storms and whirlpools of an unknown ocean, the ice of Antarctica, more—all rendered in a powerful, chilling manner. Full text. 38 plates. 77pp. 9¼ × 12. 22305-1 Pa. $4.95

THE EXPEDITIONS OF ZEBULON MONTGOMERY PIKE, Zebulon Montgomery Pike. Fascinating first-hand accounts (1805–6) of exploration of Mississippi River, Indian wars, capture by Spanish dragoons, much more. 1,088pp. 5⅜ × 8½. 25254-X, 25255-8 Pa. Two-vol. set $23.90

A CONCISE HISTORY OF PHOTOGRAPHY: Third Revised Edition, Helmut Gernsheim. Best one-volume history—camera obscura, photochemistry, daguerreotypes, evolution of cameras, film, more. Also artistic aspects—landscape, portraits, fine art, etc. 281 black-and-white photographs. 26 in color. 176pp. 8⅜ × 11¼. 25128-4 Pa. $12.95

THE DORÉ BIBLE ILLUSTRATIONS, Gustave Doré. 241 detailed plates from the Bible: the Creation scenes, Adam and Eve, Flood, Babylon, battle sequences, life of Jesus, etc. Each plate is accompanied by the verses from the King James version of the Bible. 241pp. 9 × 12. 23004-X Pa. $8.95

HUGGER-MUGGER IN THE LOUVRE, Elliot Paul. Second Homer Evans mystery-comedy. Theft at the Louvre involves sleuth in hilarious, madcap caper. "A knockout."—Books. 336pp. 5⅜ × 8½. 25185-3 Pa. $5.95

FLATLAND, E. A. Abbott. Intriguing and enormously popular science-fiction classic explores the complexities of trying to survive as a two-dimensional being in a three-dimensional world. Amusingly illustrated by the author. 16 illustrations. 103pp. 5⅜ × 8½. 20001-9 Pa. $2.00

THE HISTORY OF THE LEWIS AND CLARK EXPEDITION, Meriwether Lewis and William Clark, edited by Elliott Coues. Classic edition of Lewis and Clark's day-by-day journals that later became the basis for U.S. claims to Oregon and the West. Accurate and invaluable geographical, botanical, biological, meteorological and anthropological material. Total of 1,508pp. 5⅜ × 8½.
21268-8, 21269-6, 21270-X Pa. Three-vol. set $25.50

LANGUAGE, TRUTH AND LOGIC, Alfred J. Ayer. Famous, clear introduction to Vienna, Cambridge schools of Logical Positivism. Role of philosophy, elimination of metaphysics, nature of analysis, etc. 160pp. 5⅜ × 8½. (Available in U.S. and Canada only) 20010-8 Pa. $2.95

MATHEMATICS FOR THE NONMATHEMATICIAN, Morris Kline. Detailed, college-level treatment of mathematics in cultural and historical context, with numerous exercises. For liberal arts students. Preface. Recommended Reading Lists. Tables. Index. Numerous black-and-white figures. xvi + 641pp. 5⅜ × 8½.
24823-2 Pa. $11.95

28 SCIENCE FICTION STORIES, H. G. Wells. Novels, *Star Begotten* and *Men Like Gods,* plus 26 short stories: "Empire of the Ants," "A Story of the Stone Age," "The Stolen Bacillus," "In the Abyss," etc. 915pp. 5⅜ × 8½. (Available in U.S. only)
20265-8 Cloth. $10.95

HANDBOOK OF PICTORIAL SYMBOLS, Rudolph Modley. 3,250 signs and symbols, many systems in full; official or heavy commercial use. Arranged by subject. Most in Pictorial Archive series. 143pp. 8⅛ × 11. 23357-X Pa. $5.95

INCIDENTS OF TRAVEL IN YUCATAN, John L. Stephens. Classic (1843) exploration of jungles of Yucatan, looking for evidences of Maya civilization. Travel adventures, Mexican and Indian culture, etc. Total of 669pp. 5⅜ × 8½.
20926-1, 20927-X Pa., Two-vol. set $9.90

DEGAS: An Intimate Portrait, Ambroise Vollard. Charming, anecdotal memoir by famous art dealer of one of the greatest 19th-century French painters. 14 black-and-white illustrations. Introduction by Harold L. Van Doren. 96pp. 5⅜ × 8½.
25131-4 Pa. $3.95

PERSONAL NARRATIVE OF A PILGRIMAGE TO ALMANDINAH AND MECCAH, Richard Burton. Great travel classic by remarkably colorful personality. Burton, disguised as a Moroccan, visited sacred shrines of Islam, narrowly escaping death. 47 illustrations. 959pp. 5⅜ × 8½.   21217-3, 21218-1 Pa., Two-vol. set $17.90

PHRASE AND WORD ORIGINS, A. H. Holt. Entertaining, reliable, modern study of more than 1,200 colorful words, phrases, origins and histories. Much unexpected information. 254pp. 5⅜ × 8½.   20758-7 Pa. $4.95

THE RED THUMB MARK, R. Austin Freeman. In this first Dr. Thorndyke case, the great scientific detective draws fascinating conclusions from the nature of a single fingerprint. Exciting story, authentic science. 320pp. 5⅜ × 8½. (Available in U.S. only)   25210-8 Pa. $5.95

AN EGYPTIAN HIEROGLYPHIC DICTIONARY, E. A. Wallis Budge. Monumental work containing about 25,000 words or terms that occur in texts ranging from 3000 B.C. to 600 A.D. Each entry consists of a transliteration of the word, the word in hieroglyphs, and the meaning in English. 1,314pp. 6⅜ × 10.
23615-3, 23616-1 Pa., Two-vol. set $27.90

THE COMPLEAT STRATEGYST: Being a Primer on the Theory of Games of Strategy, J. D. Williams. Highly entertaining classic describes, with many illustrated examples, how to select best strategies in conflict situations. Prefaces. Appendices. xvi + 268pp. 5⅜ × 8½.   25101-2 Pa. $5.95

THE ROAD TO OZ, L. Frank Baum. Dorothy meets the Shaggy Man, little Button-Bright and the Rainbow's beautiful daughter in this delightful trip to the magical Land of Oz. 272pp. 5⅜ × 8.   25208-6 Pa. $4.95

POINT AND LINE TO PLANE, Wassily Kandinsky. Seminal exposition of role of point, line, other elements in non-objective painting. Essential to understanding 20th-century art. 127 illustrations. 192pp. 6½ × 9¼.   23808-3 Pa. $4.50

LADY ANNA, Anthony Trollope. Moving chronicle of Countess Lovel's bitter struggle to win for herself and daughter Anna their rightful rank and fortune—perhaps at cost of sanity itself. 384pp. 5⅜ × 8½.   24669-8 Pa. $6.95

EGYPTIAN MAGIC, E. A. Wallis Budge. Sums up all that is known about magic in Ancient Egypt: the role of magic in controlling the gods, powerful amulets that warded off evil spirits, scarabs of immortality, use of wax images, formulas and spells, the secret name, much more. 253pp. 5⅜ × 8½.   22681-6 Pa. $4.00

THE DANCE OF SIVA, Ananda Coomaraswamy. Preeminent authority unfolds the vast metaphysic of India: the revelation of her art, conception of the universe, social organization, etc. 27 reproductions of art masterpieces. 192pp. 5⅜ × 8½.
24817-8 Pa. $5.95

CHRISTMAS CUSTOMS AND TRADITIONS, Clement A. Miles. Origin, evolution, significance of religious, secular practices. Caroling, gifts, yule logs, much more. Full, scholarly yet fascinating; non-sectarian. 400pp. 5⅜ × 8½.
23354-5 Pa. $6.50

THE HUMAN FIGURE IN MOTION, Eadweard Muybridge. More than 4,500 stopped-action photos, in action series, showing undraped men, women, children jumping, lying down, throwing, sitting, wrestling, carrying, etc. 390pp. 7⅞ × 10⅝.
20204-6 Cloth. $19.95

THE MAN WHO WAS THURSDAY, Gilbert Keith Chesterton. Witty, fast-paced novel about a club of anarchists in turn-of-the-century London. Brilliant social, religious, philosophical speculations. 128pp. 5⅜ × 8½.   25121-7 Pa. $3.95

A CEZANNE SKETCHBOOK: Figures, Portraits, Landscapes and Still Lifes, Paul Cezanne. Great artist experiments with tonal effects, light, mass, other qualities in over 100 drawings. A revealing view of developing master painter, precursor of Cubism. 102 black-and-white illustrations. 144pp. 8¾ × 6⅝.   24790-2 Pa. $5.95

AN ENCYCLOPEDIA OF BATTLES: Accounts of Over 1,560 Battles from 1479 B.C. to the Present, David Eggenberger. Presents essential details of every major battle in recorded history, from the first battle of Megiddo in 1479 B.C. to Grenada in 1984. List of Battle Maps. New Appendix covering the years 1967–1984. Index. 99 illustrations. 544pp. 6½ × 9¼.   24913-1 Pa. $14.95

AN ETYMOLOGICAL DICTIONARY OF MODERN ENGLISH, Ernest Weekley. Richest, fullest work, by foremost British lexicographer. Detailed word histories. Inexhaustible. Total of 856pp. 6½ × 9¼.
21873-2, 21874-0 Pa., Two-vol. set $17.00

WEBSTER'S AMERICAN MILITARY BIOGRAPHIES, edited by Robert McHenry. Over 1,000 figures who shaped 3 centuries of American military history. Detailed biographies of Nathan Hale, Douglas MacArthur, Mary Hallaren, others. Chronologies of engagements, more. Introduction. Addenda. 1,033 entries in alphabetical order. xi + 548pp. 6½ × 9¼. (Available in U.S. only)
24758-9 Pa. $11.95

LIFE IN ANCIENT EGYPT, Adolf Erman. Detailed older account, with much not in more recent books: domestic life, religion, magic, medicine, commerce, and whatever else needed for complete picture. Many illustrations. 597pp. 5⅜ × 8½.
22632-8 Pa. $8.50

HISTORIC COSTUME IN PICTURES, Braun & Schneider. Over 1,450 costumed figures shown, covering a wide variety of peoples: kings, emperors, nobles, priests, servants, soldiers, scholars, townsfolk, peasants, merchants, courtiers, cavaliers, and more. 256pp. 8⅜ × 11¼.   23150-X Pa. $7.95

THE NOTEBOOKS OF LEONARDO DA VINCI, edited by J. P. Richter. Extracts from manuscripts reveal great genius; on painting, sculpture, anatomy, sciences, geography, etc. Both Italian and English. 186 ms. pages reproduced, plus 500 additional drawings, including studies for *Last Supper, Sforza* monument, etc. 860pp. 7⅞ × 10¾. (Available in U.S. only) 22572-0, 22573-9 Pa., Two-vol. set $25.90

THE ART NOUVEAU STYLE BOOK OF ALPHONSE MUCHA: All 72 Plates from "Documents Decoratifs" in Original Color, Alphonse Mucha. Rare copyright-free design portfolio by high priest of Art Nouveau. Jewelry, wallpaper, stained glass, furniture, figure studies, plant and animal motifs, etc. Only complete one-volume edition. 80pp. 9⅜ × 12¼. 24044-4 Pa. $8.95

ANIMALS: 1,419 COPYRIGHT-FREE ILLUSTRATIONS OF MAMMALS, BIRDS, FISH, INSECTS, ETC., edited by Jim Harter. Clear wood engravings present, in extremely lifelike poses, over 1,000 species of animals. One of the most extensive pictorial sourcebooks of its kind. Captions. Index. 284pp. 9 × 12.
23766-4 Pa. $9.95

OBELISTS FLY HIGH, C. Daly King. Masterpiece of American detective fiction, long out of print, involves murder on a 1935 transcontinental flight—"a very thrilling story"—NY Times. Unabridged and unaltered republication of the edition published by William Collins Sons & Co. Ltd., London, 1935. 288pp. 5⅜ × 8½. (Available in U.S. only) 25036-9 Pa. $4.95

VICTORIAN AND EDWARDIAN FASHION: A Photographic Survey, Alison Gernsheim. First fashion history completely illustrated by contemporary photographs. Full text plus 235 photos, 1840–1914, in which many celebrities appear. 240pp. 6½ × 9¼. 24205-6 Pa. $6.00

THE ART OF THE FRENCH ILLUSTRATED BOOK, 1700–1914, Gordon N. Ray. Over 630 superb book illustrations by Fragonard, Delacroix, Daumier, Doré, Grandville, Manet, Mucha, Steinlen, Toulouse-Lautrec and many others. Preface. Introduction. 633 halftones. Indices of artists, authors & titles, binders and provenances. Appendices. Bibliography. 608pp. 8⅜ × 11¼. 25086-5 Pa. $24.95

THE WONDERFUL WIZARD OF OZ, L. Frank Baum. Facsimile in full color of America's finest children's classic. 143 illustrations by W. W. Denslow. 267pp. 5⅜ × 8½. 20691-2 Pa. $5.95

FRONTIERS OF MODERN PHYSICS: New Perspectives on Cosmology, Relativity, Black Holes and Extraterrestrial Intelligence, Tony Rothman, et al. For the intelligent layman. Subjects include: cosmological models of the universe; black holes; the neutrino; the search for extraterrestrial intelligence. Introduction. 46 black-and-white illustrations. 192pp. 5⅜ × 8½. 24587-X Pa. $6.95

THE FRIENDLY STARS, Martha Evans Martin & Donald Howard Menzel. Classic text marshalls the stars together in an engaging, non-technical survey, presenting them as sources of beauty in night sky. 23 illustrations. Foreword. 2 star charts. Index. 147pp. 5⅜ × 8½. 21099-5 Pa. $3.50

FADS AND FALLACIES IN THE NAME OF SCIENCE, Martin Gardner. Fair, witty appraisal of cranks, quacks, and quackeries of science and pseudoscience: hollow earth, Velikovsky, orgone energy, Dianetics, flying saucers, Bridey Murphy, food and medical fads, etc. Revised, expanded In the Name of Science. "A very able and even-tempered presentation."—The New Yorker. 363pp. 5⅜ × 8.
20394-8 Pa. $5.95

ANCIENT EGYPT: ITS CULTURE AND HISTORY, J. E Manchip White. From pre-dynastics through Ptolemies: society, history, political structure, religion, daily life, literature, cultural heritage. 48 plates. 217pp. 5⅜ × 8½. 22548-8 Pa. $4.95

CATALOG OF DOVER BOOKS

SIR HARRY HOTSPUR OF HUMBLETHWAITE, Anthony Trollope. Incisive, unconventional psychological study of a conflict between a wealthy baronet, his idealistic daughter, and their scapegrace cousin. The 1870 novel in its first inexpensive edition in years. 250pp. 5⅜ × 8½.   24953-0 Pa. $4.95

LASERS AND HOLOGRAPHY, Winston E. Kock. Sound introduction to burgeoning field, expanded (1981) for second edition. Wave patterns, coherence, lasers, diffraction, zone plates, properties of holograms, recent advances. 84 illustrations. 160pp. 5⅜ × 8¼. (Except in United Kingdom)   24041-X Pa. $3.50

INTRODUCTION TO ARTIFICIAL INTELLIGENCE: SECOND, EN-LARGED EDITION, Philip C. Jackson, Jr. Comprehensive survey of artificial intelligence—the study of how machines (computers) can be made to act intelligently. Includes introductory and advanced material. Extensive notes updating the main text. 132 black-and-white illustrations. 512pp. 5⅜ × 8½.   24864-X Pa. $8.95

HISTORY OF INDIAN AND INDONESIAN ART, Ananda K. Coomaraswamy. Over 400 illustrations illuminate classic study of Indian art from earliest Harappa finds to early 20th century. Provides philosophical, religious and social insights. 304pp. 6⅜ × 9⅜.   25005-9 Pa. $8.95

THE GOLEM, Gustav Meyrink. Most famous supernatural novel in modern European literature, set in Ghetto of Old Prague around 1890. Compelling story of mystical experiences, strange transformations, profound terror. 13 black-and-white illustrations. 224pp. 5⅜ × 8½. (Available in U.S. only)   25025-3 Pa. $5.95

ARMADALE, Wilkie Collins. Third great mystery novel by the author of *The Woman in White* and *The Moonstone*. Original magazine version with 40 illustrations. 597pp. 5⅜ × 8½.   23429-0 Pa. $7.95

PICTORIAL ENCYCLOPEDIA OF HISTORIC ARCHITECTURAL PLANS, DETAILS AND ELEMENTS: With 1,880 Line Drawings of Arches, Domes, Doorways, Facades, Gables, Windows, etc., John Theodore Haneman. Sourcebook of inspiration for architects, designers, others. Bibliography. Captions. 141pp. 9 × 12.   24605-1 Pa. $6.95

BENCHLEY LOST AND FOUND, Robert Benchley. Finest humor from early 30's, about pet peeves, child psychologists, post office and others. Mostly unavailable elsewhere. 73 illustrations by Peter Arno and others. 183pp. 5⅜ × 8½.   22410-4 Pa. $3.95

ERTÉ GRAPHICS, Erté. Collection of striking color graphics: *Seasons, Alphabet, Numerals, Aces* and *Precious Stones*. 50 plates, including 4 on covers. 48pp. 9⅜ × 12¼.   23580-7 Pa. $6.95

THE JOURNAL OF HENRY D. THOREAU, edited by Bradford Torrey, F. H. Allen. Complete reprinting of 14 volumes, 1837-61, over two million words; the sourcebooks for *Walden*, etc. Definitive. All original sketches, plus 75 photographs. 1,804pp. 8½ × 12¼.   20312-3, 20313-1 Cloth., Two-vol. set $80.00

CASTLES: THEIR CONSTRUCTION AND HISTORY, Sidney Toy. Traces castle development from ancient roots. Nearly 200 photographs and drawings illustrate moats, keeps, baileys, many other features. Caernarvon, Dover Castles, Hadrian's Wall, Tower of London, dozens more. 256pp. 5⅜ × 8¼.
24898-4 Pa. $5.95